CRITICAL
INSIGHTS

The Aeneid

by Vergil

CRITICAL
INSIGHTS

The Aeneid

by Vergil

Editor
Robert J. Forman
St. John's University

Salem Press
Pasadena, California   Hackensack, New Jersey

In memory of my parents
Henry and Helen Forman
to whom I owe so much.

Cover photo: ©Duncan Walker/iStockphoto.com

Library of Congress Cataloging-in-Publication Data
The Aeneid, by Vergil / editor, Robert J. Forman.
    p. cm. — (Critical insights)
Includes bibliographical references and index.
    ISBN 978-1-58765-835-8 (alk. paper) — ISBN 978-1-58765-821-1 (set for Critical insights : alk. paper)
    1. Virgil. Aeneis. 2. Aeneas (Legendary character) in literature. 3. Epic poetry, Latin—History and criticism. 4. Rome—In literature. I. Forman, Robert J.
    PA6825.A683 2012
    873'.01—dc23
                                                            2011019113

PRINTED IN CANADA

Contents_____

Resources

About This Volume

Robert J. Forman

Vergil's *Aeneid* has long remained a staple of the Western literary canon. At certain times it yields in its popularity to Homer's poems, particularly to the *Odyssey*. At others, it takes center stage as the classical epic read in traditional school and college curricula. One reason for its staying power is its careful composition. It is, quite simply, a model of syntax, concinnity, and style. It has, therefore, proved a challenge for translators. W. F. Jackson Knight published an English prose translation in 1944 that renders elegantly the idiom of Vergil's poem, while Robert Fagles has come very close to perfection in his verse translation of 2008. The names of both appear frequently in this volume.

Vergil began the *Aeneid* after receiving a subvention from the emperor Augustus in about 30 B.C.E. and was still at work on the poem at the time of his death in 19 B.C.E. This would mean that he composed, on average, slightly more than one line per day. An old joke runs that Vergil was the first person to perfect the art of extending a government grant. Even so, despite the long labor, Maurus Servius Honoratus, the late-fourth-century commentator on Vergil's works more simply known as Servius, reports that Vergil had made a deathbed request to destroy the unfinished *Aeneid*. Only the direct intervention of the emperor himself managed to save it. This story, so dramatic in its telling, probably became more so as each ancient biographer and literary commentator retold it. In itself, it is an excellent reason to include here a short essay on Vergil's life; Walter Petrovitz supplies this.

Often, knowing biographical details makes little difference to the reading of an author's fictive work, but this is not so in the case of the poet of the *Aeneid*, given that production of the poem depended to such a great degree on what Vergil had written and on his personal relationship with the emperor, not to mention the extraordinary political events that surrounded the poem's composition. Vergil's undoubtedly close relationship with Augustus also allowed judiciously placed cautions concerning a leader's relationship to his people to play an important part in the poem. Augustus is not Aeneas, but he is the leader of a new Rome, the first emperor operating in a new political construct, one that he himself devised. Petrovitz's biographical essay also allows the reader to see many such connections between Vergil's life and that of his poem.

In essence, the *Aeneid* has just about everything a reader might desire: a journey that parallels that of Odysseus, a thrillingly dramatic story of the wooden horse and the fall of Troy (which the Homeric poems completely lack), the sexual tension inherent in the Dido and Aeneas narrative, a second Trojan War in *Aeneid* 7-12 for a second Helen named Lavinia. Added to this is the historical awareness of Rome's future greatness as well as significant psychological and ethical questions on fate and free will and on personal glory versus the responsibilities of those who lead. The essays in this volume examine all of these areas as well as the profound influence the *Aeneid* has had on Christian authors such as Saint Augustine and Dante Alighieri. Readers should find it accessible, even without knowledge of the poem in its original Latin.

The editor's essay titled "On the *Aeneid*: Biography and Allegory" locates Vergil's epic within the tradition of Homer and Apollonius of Rhodes but identifies the characteristics that allow it to be read as a foreshadowing of formal allegory. It also considers the peculiar historical circumstances that permit the *Aeneid* to serve as a seminal document of Roman prehistory. The *Aeneid* demonstrates that Vergil prefers a cyclical view of history, and this essay notes how key episodes in the poem not only have a connection with Augustus's city but also have universal application to human behavior, authority, and the use of power.

Saint Augustine, a Father of the Christian Church, had virtually memorized the *Aeneid* for declamation when he was a child. At the beginning of his *Confessions* he notes the early praise his rhetorical skills had won him; nevertheless, after his conversion to Christianity, he denounces Vergil's poem in *Confessions* 1.13 as *dulcissimum spectaculum vanitatis* (the sweetest show of vanity). There never was a Dido or an Aeneas, he claims, yet the false words that describe them make human beings weep. Words, all of them, need to refer to the source of all language, the Word itself, the Creator. Having made his point, Augustine proceeds to describe the particulars of his own life in terms that recall the life of Aeneas. Augustine understood, though he does not acknowledge, that Aeneas metaphorically can be nearly anyone. Fiorentina Russo makes a parallel point in her essay in this volume offering comparative examination of Dante's *Divine Comedy* and the *Aeneid*. She demonstrates that the written word, with its multiple significations, is inherently metaphorical, and metaphor, because of its symbolism, produces allegory.

Every work of art struggles for independence, though none achieves it in an absolute sense. It is true that each episode in the *Aeneid* bears some narrative or verbal similarity to Homeric epic. In the case of Vergil's portrait of Dido, there are possible comparisons to Apollonius's Medea or even to that of Euripides. Even so, it is just as clear that the *Aeneid* invariably makes some narrative swerve that allows Vergilian originality to shine through. In fact, Vergilian narrative is so distinctive as to be unlike that of any other ancient Roman poet. A second essay by the editor, titled "Independent Imitation: The *Aeneid* and Greek Epic," focuses on the distinctive ways in which Vergil achieves originality, even as he recalls Greek literary tradition. Such echoes would have been an indicator of sophistication and thus a positive aspect of Vergilian composition. It is undoubtedly true that Vergil directed the Latin language along paths it had never traversed previously. The poem thus became as much an ornament to the Augustan Pax Romana as did the emperor's Ara Pacis, the great "Altar of Peace" that commemorated an idealized Augustan balance of civic and religious life in a prosperous imperial Roman state.

The *Aeneid* appeared in the wake of civil war and subsequent land seizures. Vergil's own family farm was seized in 41 B.C.E., like those of others, for land redistribution to war veterans. Restoration of the farm to Vergil's family, through the intervention of Octavian (Augustus), inspired Vergil's first *Eclogue*. The Vergilian chronology that concludes this volume indicates how deeply the events that attended Vergil's times influenced what he composed and how he approached his themes.

Bernard J. Cassidy considers the historical background against which Vergil wrote the *Aeneid* in a new essay written for this volume. History was as much an influence on Vergil's work as the historical era was on the poet's life, and the essay by Patrick Loughran synthesizes historical fact with insightful observations on the content and motivations behind Vergil's poem.

That many Romans shared the strains of upheaval and governmental transition accounted for the wide popularity the *Aeneid* enjoyed from its first appearance. In her new essay here, Kathleen Marks examines the immediate popularity the *Aeneid* enjoyed and the combination of circumstances that accounted for that popularity. Vergil's death combined with the clever political application to the Pax Romana that Augustus engineered, and the confluence of these made the *Aeneid* part of the school curriculum that grammarians taught the sons of those families able to afford a primary education. The numbers of such families were increasing even in the early years of imperial Rome, and this circumstance ensured close study of the *Aeneid* by successive generations of schoolboys, not just in the city itself but in every area of the Empire.

The reprinted essays in this volume range from classic works such as that of Viktor Pöschl on the poetry of Vergil to the feminist psychoanalytic approach of Robin N. Mitchell-Boyask. The essays are intentionally dovetailed to create synthetic response. The Mitchell-Boyask essay, for example, intriguing in itself, complements more traditional examinations, such as that of Francis A. Sullivan on the role of suffering, which is seen as pathos in Greek tragedy yet as a positive concomitant of establishing a society in Vergil. Pöschl, known for his study of exponential motifs in the *Aeneid*, appears in this volume in "The Poetic Achievement of Virgil," an essay that examines the reasons for the exceptional place the work has held from its first appearance in early imperial Rome.

Clifford Weber's essay "The Dionysus in Aeneas" discusses the Dionysiac element in Vergil's depiction of Aeneas at Dido's court. The violence that Aeneas introduces by his fated presence in the idealized landscape of Italy is the theme of Richard F. Moorton's "The Innocence of Italy in Vergil's *Aeneid*."

The Sibyl of Cumae was in the Roman mind equivalent to the Pythia of Delphi. One indication of her importance to Romans was the serious way in which they accepted the Sibylline Books. These codified the prophecies, and codification creates history. History is just what Augustus wished to create for the imperial city. J. H. Waszink examines the role of the Sibyl in *Aeneid* 6 and her importance to Rome as a cultural and religious phenomenon.

The Golden Bough, which allows the living Aeneas to enter the Underworld, has become a symbol of permission and sensible balance. Mary Randall Stark considers the Golden Bough and its metaphorical value for those who read Vergil. This is an old essay, dating from 1930, yet it is so filled with a teacher's earnest enthusiasm for the *Aeneid* that it deserves reprinting. What it lacks in fashionable critical idiom it supplies in idealism. When readers familiar with Vergilian criticism think of the Golden Bough, they may find it difficult not to think also of the Golden Mean, the mathematical proportion of perfection. George E. Duckworth was known for his study of accentual symmetry and mathematical proportions in Vergilian poetry. His book-length study on the mathematical constant that recurs in the lines of the *Aeneid* as surely as a musical motif appears in shorter, more accessible essay form in this volume.

In another reprinted essay, Michael C. J. Putnam analyzes the Daedalus relief that appears on the doors of Apollo's temple at Cumae. This relief did indeed exist on the doors of the temple that stood on the site during Vergil's lifetime. The temple's foundations are much older, dating from the Greek emigrations and possibly as early as the seventh century B.C.E. The Daedalus excursus that describes the doors implies that inventor's escape from Crete, where Minos had kept him in order to build the labyrinth that housed the Minotaur. Daedalus's escape cost him his son Icarus, who flew too close to the sun. Aeneas is himself a fugitive. Augustus is inventor of a new political construct. Sons are essential for carrying on the cycles of history, whether Pallas, Lausus, Ascanius/Iulus, or Octavian Augustus, the adopted son of Julius Caesar.

Just how much of Vergil's poetry is actually Vergil in any translation? John Dryden produced a completed English translation of Vergil's works in 1684 and a second edition in 1698. Dryden's love for the Vergilian poetry is obvious. His translation is elegant, yet read one of Dryden's own poems, then read his *Aeneid* and consider whether the translation is more a product of Dryden than of Vergil. This is the kind of question that begs asking whenever one reads translated literature. Because the majority of modern-day readers will come to the *Aeneid* through translations, the essay on Vergil's most celebrated (yet un-Vergilian) translator by William Frost appears among the reprinted works presented here.

The volume closes with a chronology of Vergil's life and times as well as an annotated bibliography listing works that represent some classic as well as some unusual approaches in aeneidic scholarship.

THE BOOK
AND
AUTHOR

On the *Aeneid*:
Biography and Allegory _____

Robert J. Forman

Vergil's *Aeneid* clearly is about Aeneas, but it is also the story of every human being's stages of life through violent upheaval, love, uncertainty, self-examination, loss, and ultimately accommodation with surroundings not unlike those of one's starting point. This cyclical epic remains consistently personal and subjective for any careful reader even as its personalities, locations, and details appear to range far from the experiences of most people and to be directed toward the great national construct that came to be known as the Roman Empire.

Though the *Aeneid* employs elements of Homer's *Odyssey* and *Iliad*, it entirely avoids the supernatural elements of these poems. There are no lotus flowers that make a warrior forget his home, no Sirens with seven rows of teeth to devour mariners, no witches like Circe who turn men into swine. Aeneas sails past the island of the Cyclopes, but they do not influence the narrative of the poem. The gorgon fury Allecto incites Lavinia's mother, Amata, and Lavinia's fiancé, Turnus, to a second Trojan War in *Aeneid* 7, but she is more a metaphor for uncontrolled jealousy than a monster. Aeneas makes a journey to the Underworld, but the entrance to Aeneas's realm of the dead is through a cave at Cumae, a place as real to the average Roman as the Luray Caverns would be to any Virginian, and the spirits he sees are shadows of his past and intimations of the community that would incorporate his own people. In essence, all that happens in the *Aeneid* can be seen in purely natural terms. Even the council of deities, when it meets on Olympus, is like a board of governors with extraordinary human failings rather than extraordinary power, and like many such human arrangements is prone to either inaction or mismanagement. Even Jupiter recognizes the primacy of Fate and bows to it of necessity.

All this is not to imply that the *Aeneid* is without Homeric influence—far from it. Indeed, the first six books of Vergil's poem parallel the experiences of Odysseus, while the final six portray a war in Italy fought for possession of a woman. This woman, Lavinia, is, however, a prototypical Roman maiden rather than a copy of the seductive Helen. The Trojans invade a region of the Italian peninsula so heavily settled by Greek emigrants that the Romans called it *Magna Graecia*, but they fight native Italic tribes and have Etruscans as their allies, thereby localizing for imperial Roman readers the war's sites and participants. This emphasis on the course of life and human emotions is a primary differentiating feature of Vergil's poem.

Homer's warriors rarely act in the way the humane Aeneas does. Even Hector (who comes closest to the kind of personality Vergil's Aeneas displays), after he leaves Andromache and Astyanax in *Iliad* 6, reverts to the warrior's role, as does Achilles when he returns to battle in *Iliad* 20 following his violent mourning following the death of Patroclus. This emphasis on the commonality of human experience and the cyclical nature of history has made the *Aeneid* a template upon which many other masterpieces have been written. Saint Augustine (354-430), a Father of the Christian Church who held that all words must reflect truth and through this the Word (that is, the Creator), damns the *Aeneid* as mere fiction that redirects vulnerable moral sensibility (*Confessions* 1.13). While practicing his profession as rhetor, Augustine had taught the *Aeneid* and had, in fact, virtually memorized its text for rhetorical presentation.

Perhaps it is because Augustine recognizes that Vergil's poem so easily translates itself into common human experience that he then proceeds to write the narrative part of his *Confessions* (397-98) in terms that implicitly relate his own life and journey to those of Aeneas. Indeed, the first nine books of Augustine's *Confessions* selectively present a young man entering Carthage, being seduced by its sensuality and secular culture, leaving Monica, his mother, weeping on the shore as he sails for Italy, then undergoing a conversion in Milan through a spiritual alliance with Saint Ambrose, the city's bishop. He ultimately returns to North Africa to establish his diocese at Hippo in

Roman Numidia, and of course to write *The City of God* (410) even as Rome was being sacked by the Visigoths. In short, Augustine becomes a historical Aeneas. Augustine's words thus serve the Word and recognize the cyclical nature of history. The cycles of history, for Augustine, will culminate in the return of the Redeemer.

La Divina Commedia (c. 1308-21; *The Divine Comedy*, 1802) of Dante Alighieri (1265-1321) recasts *Aeneid* 6 in a Christian mode in the *Inferno* and makes the poet of the *Aeneid* the Pilgrim's Sibyl. This is only one of the obvious aeneidic acknowledgments in Dante's poem. More telling, given the cyclical nature and historical awareness of the *Divina Commedia*, is the poem's conception of the life of the individual in relation to the community that surrounds it. Passing beyond those persons bound by sin or in need of repentance to the pure love of the Celestial Rose is an Augustinian-like conversion to the purity of the Word and the ineffable signification of language that *Paradiso*, the poem's third canticle, represents.

Aeneas undergoes a conversion to an awareness that his importance relates directly to the advancement of his community rather than to a glorification of self. His recurring Vergilian epithets are *Pius Aeneas* and *Pater Aeneas*, and these epithets imply humble reverence and patriarchal responsibility. His life and well-being mirror those of his people. The Neoplatonist Plotinus (205-270) saw the adventures of Homer's Odysseus as a journey of the soul. This represents an attempt common among Neoplatonist allegorists to retain classical literature during a period of history potentially hostile to it, during the ascendancy of the Christian Church.

Though Odysseus is a leader of warriors, there is no doubt that they serve him and receive little in return. One telling argument for this point of view is the near anonymity of Homer's Ithacans. Odysseus exists for himself and his own glorification, not that of his almost nameless men. In contrast, Aeneas repeatedly receives reminders of his responsibilities to his people, from the ghost of his wife, Creusa, as Troy burns (*Aeneid* 2); from Mercury when he remains too long at Carthage with Dido (*Aeneid* 4); from his father, Anchises, in the Underworld (*Aeneid* 6); from the sight of a brooding white sow on the banks of the Tiber (*Aeneid* 7); from Evander at Pallanteum (the future site of Rome), who sees the fated nature of Aeneas's mission, as well as from his mother, Venus, who presents him with a shield that glorifies the city of Romulus and its first emperor, Augustus, as victor over Pompey at Actium (*Aeneid* 8).

From even these particulars, it is possible to discern allegory that is political (concerned with the management and life of a city-state), moral (treating the ethical responsibilities an individual has to the community), and metaphysical (relating to the spiritual obligations of the individual beyond the natural order). These levels sometimes complement one another and sometimes conflict. They offer a way to explain the conflicting decisions that repeatedly plague Aeneas and account for their recurrence in the poem. Should Aeneas fight to the death or flee from Troy (*Aeneid* 2)? Should Aeneas reveal himself to Dido (*Aeneid* 1)? Should he stay at Carthage or go (*Aeneid* 4)? Where should he go (*Aeneid* 5)? Will he be able to enter the Underworld while still alive (*Aeneid* 6)? Who are the unborn heroes he sees there, and what is their relationship to him (*Aeneid* 6)? Will he be able to negotiate a treaty with Latinus (*Aeneid* 7)? Since this fails, will he be able to convince Evander's Etruscans to support him (*Aeneid* 8)? Should he attack the apprentice warrior Lausus in order to reach Lausus's father, the wicked Mezentius (*Aeneid* 10)? Should he refuse the suppliant Turnus or grant him his life (*Aeneid* 12)?

These existential questions, which arise in every book of the *Aeneid*, relate not only to the fate of Aeneas but also to his civic enterprise. They are comparable to the personal doubts of most human beings at important junctures of their lives. Beyond this, they reflect the uneasiness of many Romans living in the early Empire. In the *Aeneid*, Rome is always in the shadow of Lavinium, the already existing city at whose site Aeneas founds his own new version of Troy. *Aeneid* 8 places Aeneas at Evander's city Pallanteum, the site at which Romulus would found his city. Such associations allow gentle but persistent Vergilian admonitions on the new political construct of the Empire and specifically to its first emperor. They allow the *Aeneid* to move beyond being a mere ornament of the Augustan Pax Romana and idealized patriotism to a primer on human behavior and the responsibilities of a leader toward his community.

Augustus was fond of saying that he had found Rome a city of mud brick and turned it into a city of marble. His continual emphasis on this achievement made him actually as well as figuratively the builder of his city, just as his creation of the role of *imperator* (implying a combined military and political leader) redefined the political construct of the Roman state. In the first two books of the *Aeneid*, Aeneas sees both the fallen civic order of Troy and the new as typified by Dido's Carthage, just as Romans living during the reign of Augustus had known both the Republic and the Empire.

The violence of the fallen city of Troy is the narrative Aeneas relates to Dido in *Aeneid* 2. It balances Aeneas's tear-filled recollection of the Trojan War as depicted on Carthage's rising walls in *Aeneid* 1. The scenes as portrayed recall the event for Aeneas; they pair Troy and Carthage even as Augustan marble was replacing the mud brick of the Republic. This is not to say that Augustus's entire city was marble, only the most frequented public buildings. The lives of Rome's average plebeians changed relatively little. Still, Aeneas's perception of idealized heroism complements Augustus's conception of the Roman state following its civil wars both in its art and in its new imperial construct.

It is worth noting that the Ara Pacis Augustae (Augustus's Altar of Peace) was commissioned in 13 B.C.E. It idealizes in brilliant marble relief both the imperial family and the members of the Senate. Its side panels portray *Mater Roma* and a goddess with twins upon her lap, possibly *Mater Italia*. By extension, they also reflect the prosperous Augustan city at peace because of Augustus's victories. Accessibility to the altar was clearly wider than accessibility to the *Aeneid*, given that its images required no degree of literacy and were so obviously allegorical. For literate Romans, the *Aeneid* offered a parallel view of Rome through the mythos of its origins. For all Romans, the Ara Pacis conveyed a comparable message.

Consecrated in 9 B.C.E., even as the *Aeneid* was swiftly becoming the national epic, the altar tangibly linked Rome to the idealized history of Troy as portrayed on the new walls of Dido's Carthage in *Aeneid* 1. By the time of the altar's consecration, Vergil had become the Roman Homer and his *Aeneid* was already the primary literary text of the *grammatici*, the "grammarians" who privately taught the sons of more prosperous Romans. The Ara Pacis also allowed Augustus to claim the title of *Pontifex Maximus* (Chief Priest), and this allowed him to bring the powers of dynastic ruler, primary leader of the military, and head of the Roman priestly orders within his purview.

Finally, the altar and the *Aeneid* share a cyclical view of history. The Roman past as well as its present and future complement each other on its panels. The same is true of the *Aeneid*. Vergil appears to arrange certain scenes consciously and then freeze them emblematically, much as would a sculptor or painter. For example, at the conclusion of *Aeneid* 2, even as Troy burns, Vergil resets the farewell of Homer's Hector and Andromache as Aeneas first considers fighting to the death and then, swayed by his wife, Creusa, determines to escape from the fallen city with Creusa, their son, Ascanius, and his father, Anchises.

Anchises asks for a heavenly sign that this is what Fate has decreed. A tongue of fire appears over the head of Ascanius, and then a great thunderclap and shooting star illuminate the forests of Mount Ida. Mount Ida was the location of the judgment of Paris, the place in which Priam's son had selected Venus as the most beautiful goddess and in return received Helen. The war among the goddesses Juno, Venus, and Minerva began on Mount Ida when Paris chose Venus as most beautiful, bribed by her offer of the most beautiful woman in the world, Helen. It continued at Troy, then at Lavinium, and would ultimately find resolution in Romulus's murder of his brother Remus.

The tongue of fire and falling star convince Aeneas that his fate is to leave his burning city. He does so with the aged Anchises on his shoulders; Ascanius clings to Aeneas's arm, and Creusa trails behind. This tableau is a careful arrangement. Fire, a falling star, and a fleeing family are emblems of existential disasters that all human beings have witnessed, even if never firsthand. Even so, one can mimetically empathize with such victims, whose situation is common to every historical era. Vergil himself was forced to leave his farm during the land confiscations of 41 B.C.E. that followed the civil wars. The emperor Augustus restored Vergil's farm sometime toward the end of 40 B.C.E., and Vergil praises him obliquely in his first *Eclogue*. It was, indeed, Vergil's pastoral poems, the *Eclogues* (37 B.C.E.) and *Georgics* (30 B.C.E.), that brought him to the attention of the emperor and ultimately secured for him an imperial subvention to write the *Aeneid*.

Vergil thus clearly knew firsthand the tenuous nature of the human condition. He could not help but recognize how the historical cycles of the Great Roman Civil War (49-45 B.C.E.) had nearly forced him to leave his ancestral home. He also would have seen how easily a just ruler could set things aright. This is not to say that Vergil saw an absolute identity between the shepherd Tityrus of his *Eclogue* 1 and himself, nor is Aeneas a masque for Augustus. What Vergil did see is the comparability of historical cycles and the ways in which significant historical events influence individual lives.

The *Aeneid* is, after all, poetry, and poetry loves metaphor. Fire consumes Aeneas's present as Troy burns. He carries the burden of his past, as does every human being, though in *Aeneid* 2 the past is particularized in the form of his father, Anchises. Aeneas likewise clings to his future, as embodied in the form of his son, Ascanius, yet he must leave a part of his past behind. This emerges in the ghost of Creusa, killed in the chaos of their departure when separated from Aeneas. Creusa then serves as the emissary of Fate through her exhortation to Aeneas to continue his flight with his father and son. She is as much a pawn of fate as Dido, though less dramatically in that she realizes that destiny is inexorable.

As readers of the *Aeneid* can easily see, Creusa is the first of a trinity of women who mark significant stages of Aeneas's life. Without the injunction of Creusa's ghost to continue his flight, Aeneas would have died at Troy. Without Dido's sanctuary at Carthage, he might have perished at sea or would not have had the strength to resume his search for a new homeland. Without Lavinia, there would have been no second Troy and consequently no city of Romulus. The irony, which thematically suits the emphasis on community that characterizes the *Aeneid*, is that Lavinia, the woman Aeneas knows least (and possibly loves least), is the one Fate has determined as essential to the survival of the Trojan people and to the grand design of historical destiny.

Gian Lorenzo Bernini captures the tableau of the flight from Troy in his famous statue of Aeneas, Anchises, and Ascanius, completed in 1619. He weaves the three figures into a near spiral or helix. Son Ascanius wraps his arm around Aeneas's leg and holds the Penates, the household gods associated with the goddess Vesta. Anchises is perched on Aeneas's left shoulder. Aeneas holds *his* leg, and Anchises holds the Lares, Roman protective deities and guardians of the household. Their mutual dependence links past, present, and future. Centuries of art historians have criticized this statue for its precarious instability. Even so, this is precisely the quality Bernini desires. Just as the parallel scene in Vergil's poem links past, present, and future as tenuous, precarious, and unknown, so does the Bernini statue. The family and community deities held by Ascanius and Anchises link the individual to the community, precisely as the *Aeneid* itself repeatedly does through the fictive lives it creates for Aeneas and those whose lives touch his.

Just as Augustus's Ara Pacis served as a constant projection of the Rome he had created, so do the temple, altar, and sacrifice as well as what they represent become exponential symbols in the *Aeneid*. The serpents that kill Apollo's priest Laocoön and his sons disappear under the shield of Minerva's cult statue after they have done their deed (*Aeneid* 2). Apollo's Sibyl of Cumae emerges crazed from her sacrifice to greet the Trojans and inquire what their reasons for visiting this Greek site may be (*Aeneid* 6). Vergil revisits this connection of the altar and the city in *Aeneid* 8 when Aeneas journeys north against the Tiber's current to Pallanteum, the site of the city Romulus would found, the seat of Augustus's Empire.

Pallanteum, the name Vergil gives to the Etruscan city that preceded the establishment of Rome, is the home of Evander and his son Pallas. When Aeneas first sees them, they are celebrating the annual sacrifice to Hercules at the temple that stands in the Forum Boarium (Cattle Market). Evander will be Aeneas's ally against the Latin tribes, and the ritual Evander and Pallas are celebrating, the feast of the Ara Maxima (the altar sacred to the deified Hercules), was held in precisely the same location throughout the cycles of Rome's history. Here again, Vergil's epic links with daily life, familiar location, and long-standing religious ritual. The Temple of Hercules remains standing in the contemporary city of Rome, and the Ara Maxima is in the crypt of Santa Maria in Cosmedin, an Orthodox Christian church built over the site of the altar.

During the years of Augustus's reign (27 B.C.E.-14 C.E.), Carthage was the most important Roman port of the southern Mediterranean. It was the principal city of Numidia, the proconsular province, but it was earlier Hannibal's city and the staging point of the Punic Wars (264-146 B.C.E.), which saw the invasion of Italy and the near destruction of Rome itself. Here as well, the implications of Aeneas's abandonment of Dido in *Aeneid* 4 to establish a new Troy and Dido's consequent anger go far beyond the immediate narrative. They conjure up a part of Roman history that looks backward at near disaster and ahead at the unknown construct of the Empire. Aeneas's awareness of his obligation reflects Augustan awareness of Roman destiny as well as the dangers inherent in pursuing this inexorable course.

Three deaths directly relatable to Aeneas's personal life mark this phase of the *Aeneid*: Dido's by suicide at the conclusion of *Aeneid* 4; that of Aeneas's father, Anchises (*Aeneid* 5); and that of Aeneas's nurse, Caieta (*Aeneid* 7). Caieta serves as an emblem of Aeneas's remote past, Anchises of his Trojan past, and Dido of his immediate past at Carthage. These three bracket the deaths of Aeneas's helmsman Palinurus, of whose death Aeneas remained entirely unaware until meeting the young man's ghost in the Underworld (*Aeneid* 6.384-423), and that of Aeneas's trumpeter and herald Misenus, of which he learns from the Sibyl. Misenus had challenged the gods to match him blast for blast on his shell trumpet, and Triton, representing the unforgiving forces of the sea, had drowned him in response. This death relates directly to Aeneas's obligations to his community, and he obeys the Sibyl's command to perform the required funeral rites immediately. The Sibyl is quick to absolve Aeneas of any implication of responsibility through neglect of duty. As valuable as Misenus had been as herald, his own pride had caused his death.

The death of Palinurus also directly relates to Aeneas's obligations toward his community, to what one might consider his life as leader and founder of the new city. The spirit of Palinurus begs Aeneas for burial just after Aeneas has entered the Underworld in the company of the Sibyl. He makes clear that Aeneas is not to blame for his death, nor was Apollo false in assuring Aeneas that Palinurus would reach Italy. This passage, then, is a double absolution of Aeneas, yet it makes the deaths of Palinurus and Misenus stand as contrasts. Whereas the Sibyl relates details of Misenus's death, it is the ghost of Palinurus himself that tells his former master a strong headwind had pulled the rudder from his hands and had washed him overboard.

Aeneas assures Palinurus that he will perform the rituals that guarantee the helmsman's soul passage across the Styx. (The burial site on the western coast of Lucania received the name of Cape Palinurus in antiquity and remains Capo Palinuro in modern Italy.) Both Misenus and Palinurus receive the burial rites a civilized community requires. While both deaths are tragic, that of Misenus is the less sympathetic of the two because of Misenus's hubris (a variety of selfishness that arises through excessive pride in personal skill). Palinurus, in contrast, steers the Trojans safely through dangerous waters and allows the Trojans to reach Italy. That Vergil allows him to tell his own story makes the selfless nature of the death more affecting. With the deaths of Dido, Anchises, Caieta, Misenus, and Palinurus, Aeneas and the surviving Trojans can separate themselves from the past even as they remember it.

This kind of interface between the personal and the collective appears dramatically at the conclusion of *Aeneid* 6 when the spirit of Anchises introduces Aeneas to the unborn heroes of the city that will one day be called Rome. They appear as an *ekphrasis*, merely a silent procession, before an uncomprehending Aeneas, who nevertheless realizes that he is a witness to something historically significant. The figures he sees range through all three political incarnations of the city, from Rome as monarchy to Rome as Republic, to Rome as Empire. They begin with the semilegendary king Numa Pompilius and conclude with Augustus himself. They include the Republican general Marcus Claudius Marcellus, who defeated the Gauls in the Gallic War (225 B.C.E.) and the Second Punic War against Hannibal (218-201 B.C.E.). Though Aeneas does not fully understand what he sees, he does appear to realize that his life touches on other lives and influences generations of civic life.

The final six books of Vergil's poem describe what amounts to a second Trojan War with Lavinia in the role of Helen, Aeneas as Achilles, and Pallas, Aeneas's protégé, as Patroclus. These parallels, however, are merely superficial resemblances to the heroes of the *Iliad*. More important are the ways Vergil juxtaposes young and old, apprentice and veteran, and good and evil. The realism he employs in this iliadic half of the *Aeneid* blurs obvious distinctions. For example, Evander, father of Pallas and king of Etruscan Pallanteum, is wholly good. In this sense, he is easiest to contrast with Mezentius, father of Lausus and ostracized king of Etruscan Cumae. Even so, their love for their sons is equally strong, and it is on this personal level that we pity both men when Turnus kills Pallas and Aeneas kills Lausus. Aeneas's unequal fight with Lausus finds justification in his attempt to reach

Mezentius, whom Lausus defends. The son's defense of his father and Mezentius's brave death in *Aeneid* 10 mitigate what might otherwise be a simple portrait of a villain.

There are three pairs of fathers and sons in the *Aeneid*: Aeneas and Ascanius (renamed Iulus after arrival in Italy to identify him with the Julio-Claudian line of emperors), Evander and Pallas, and Mezentius and Lausus. Their relationships, viewed as personal history, are completely congruent. All three fathers love their sons; all are concerned with their training and education. On the civic level, however, they are different. The good king Evander and the wicked king Mezentius are mirror opposites. Evander rules well, observes ritual, and understands the larger historical importance of Aeneas's petition for an alliance and a guest-host relationship. Mezentius, whose people despise him, wages war with his own Etruscan race. Evander recognizes the larger destiny toward which an individual life contributes. Mezentius, however, never correctly understands his relationship to the larger community, though he accepts his own fate of death at the hands of Aeneas with remarkable courage. His death is thus personally heroic but historically insignificant.

Vergil could have matched Pallas and Lausus. This would have been an even combat, but it would not have served the larger purpose of the poem. The fact that Lausus stands before his father and separates him from the attacking Aeneas illustrates the filial piety that Romans considered so much a part of their national character. That a son would do this, especially for a father whose own community considers wicked, gives the action an even greater moral validity as well as a special poignancy. The individual battles of *Aeneid* 10 and 11 serve to illustrate the increasing *violentia* of the war. As this increases, the civic fabric itself deteriorates. Fate rules, and the primary actors in these combats come to accept this, yet the war continues albeit with increasing irrationality.

Turnus also comes to recognize his destiny, but Vergil presents him as initially passive and orchestrates his *violentia* over the whole of the iliadic section of the text, from *Aeneid* 7 through 12. When the fury Allecto first incites Turnus to oppose Aeneas's claim to Lavinia, he is indifferent. Even so, Allecto's incitement of Amata before this seems almost immediate. Indeed, Amata's desire for *violentia* exceeds that of Turnus. At the beginning of *Aeneid* 12, however, the situation is just the reverse. Turnus, consumed with *violentia* so complete as to be self-destructive, has determined to meet Aeneas in combat. When he tells this to Latinus, who knows that Fate will not allow Turnus to escape alive from this meeting, Latinus begs the young man to submit to what is inevitable. Amata, Lavinia's mother, tries to control Turnus's violence and uses the approach of reason, but to no avail.

Turnus certainly recognizes the inexorable nature of Fate, but he is willing to face self-destruction. He has become as willing to die as Dido, though not for loss of his beloved Lavinia. His *violentia* springs more from hatred of his having been displaced; in essence, his determination to continue the war, his civic defect, springs from his own hubris. He seems willing to accept the fact of his likely death. He appears to know that his meeting in combat with Aeneas will end unfavorably, yet *violentia* has so consumed him that he cannot make a decision that would redound to the collective good and to his own as well, namely, to end the war and acquiesce to the *fatum* he knows is inexorable.

Aeneas kills Lausus. Turnus kills Pallas. One might argue that each of the victors is guilty of accepting an opponent much less proficient than he. Nevertheless, because Aeneas has learned to make every decision with the benefit of his community in mind, his vacillations become fewer as the poem reaches its final books. His warnings have no effect on Lausus because Lausus is as faithful to Mezentius as Aeneas had been to Anchises. Neither man can decline the combat that each knows will end with Aeneas's victory.

Turnus has a different calculus, however, when he faces Pallas. He wishes to pursue his own *aristeia* (moment of glory) and to thwart that of the younger man. This is a consequence of his *violentia* as it plays out in its final self-destructive phase. The unfairness of the fight is clear, but Turnus's claim of a *tropaeum*, a tangible "reward" to commemorate the event, is what makes Aeneas administer the coup de grâce, the stroke of grace or final blow that kills Turnus, despite his suppliant plea. This scene, with which the *Aeneid* ends, is noteworthy for its pause just before Aeneas's thrust. The only thing that forces Aeneas to deny what ordinarily would never be denied, the plea of a suppliant, is the *tropaeum*, the belt Turnus had claimed from Pallas's corpse and that he himself wears to celebrate that victory. Vergil thus leaves his readers with two rulers, one wise because he has tempered his *violentia*, the other whose *violentia* has produced the hubris that can destroy cities—or empires.

Works Cited

Homer. *The Iliad*. Trans. Robert Fagles. New York: Penguin, 1998.
_____. *The Odyssey*. Trans. Robert Fagles. New York: Penguin, 1999.
Virgil. *The Aeneid*. Trans. Robert Fagles. New York: Penguin, 2008.

Biography of Vergil_____

The traditional date of Vergil's birth is October 15, 70 B.C.E. Vergil was born to a moderately prosperous family with a farm and land-holdings at Andes, a village near the city of Mantua in northern Italy. Little is known about Vergil's early life. His father's name is not known. According to the earliest surviving full biography, that written by the second-century historian Suetonius, Vergil's father was from a poor family but found employment with a civil servant named Magus, whose daughter he eventually married (Vergil's mother's name would thus be Magia), and increased his wealth through the purchase of land and beekeeping. This may explain Vergil's easy familiarity with things agrarian in his *Georgics*. Although scholars are uncertain of the reliability of this account, it is clear that the family had enough means to provide Vergil with a good education in the northern Italian cities of Cremona and Milan and then in Rome.

Vergil would have received an education typical for his time. Although science and mathematics were part of the curriculum in Roman schools, the emphasis was always on what modern education designates as the humanities or liberal arts. Central to this was the study of literature, especially that of Greece, studied in Greek. Vergil went to Naples sometime after 40 B.C.E. to study philosophy. The fourth-century literary critic Servius, who wrote an extensive commentary on Vergil's works, claims that the young Vergil was very shy, which earned him the Greek nickname *parthenias* (virgin). It is perhaps then natural that this unsocial young man would be drawn to the solitary craft of writing. It is believed that it was while he was in Naples that Vergil began to write poetry.

Life's Work

A collection of poems in various styles and metrical patterns, the *Appendix Vergiliana*, assembled after the poet's death, was believed in

Biography of Vergil   **17** ancient times to contain compositions by the young Vergil. Its topics include various aspects of the lives of shepherds and farmers, scenes from nature and country life, mythological themes, praise or attacks aimed at various individuals, love, politics, and even a recipe for an herb paste similar to the modern Italian pesto. Modern scholars, however, by analyzing the styles of the collection's poems in comparison with works known to be Vergil's, regard all or nearly all of them to be those of other authors.

Vergil's first major work is the *Eclogues* (Latin *Eclogae*), meaning "selections" in Greek, originally (and more descriptively) called the *Bucolics* (Latin *Bucolica*), from the Greek word meaning "rustic" or "pastoral." It is a collection of ten short poems, most under one hundred lines, focusing on rural life and the pursuits of simple shepherds. It is closely modeled on the poetry of the third-century B.C.E. Greek poet Theocritus in both style and content. It appeared at a time of some turmoil in Italy, with the land confiscations following a conflict between Octavian, who later became Caesar Augustus, and Marc Antony, and there is a suggestion in the first *Eclogue* that Vergil's family's properties may have been among those taken. The overall tone of the *Eclogues*, however, is one of peace and serenity. Direct narratives by the poet and exchanges of songs among the shepherds interweave mythological themes with idyllic depictions of countryside.

The fourth poem of the *Eclogues* in particular has gained lasting notoriety. It describes the birth of a miraculous child, an oblique reference to Octavian himself, whose appearance will mark the beginning of a golden age in which wars will cease and the earth of its own accord will provide for all the needs of human beings. The language is so reminiscent of that used by the prophet Isaiah in the Hebrew scriptures that influence from that source has been suggested, although this is not a widely held view. It was, of course, only natural that in late antiquity and the Middle Ages Christians would see in this poem a prediction of the birth of Jesus.

After the publication of the *Eclogues* in 37 B.C.E., Vergil's fame began to spread. It was at this time that he made the acquaintance of Maecenas, a wealthy and influential patron of the arts who was also an adviser to Octavian. He also came into contact with other great poets of the Augustan age, most notably Horace, in whose verse Vergil occasionally appears. Vergil was thus able to enter into the very highest echelons of Roman society. It was also the time of the composition of his second major work, dedicated to Maecenas, the *Georgics* (Latin *Georgica*), from the Greek word meaning "agricultural." Vergil's style in this poem is didactic, as though intended to instruct the reader on the methods of managing a farm. Clearly, however, its artistry idealizes the farmer's life and tasks and was never intended as a farmer's manual. Vergil's most immediate model was the *Res rusticae* (rural matters) by the encyclopedic first-century B.C.E. scholar Varro, which had been published in 37 B.C.E. Vergil's *Georgics* also displays familiarity with the seventh-century B.C.E. Greek poem of Hesiod, *Works and Days*.

The *Georgics* consists of four books. The first and second deal with raising crops, the third with caring for livestock, and the fourth with tending bees. It is common in didactic literary works for the author to intersperse the instruction with more abstract or imaginative material in one way or another connected to the concrete theme at hand. Thus book 2 contains an extended "praise of Italy," book 3 includes the description of a plague, and book 4 provides a mythological explanation of the origins of beekeeping. If the *Eclogues* allowed Vergil to enter the literary world, it was the *Georgics*, portions of which he recited to Octavian, that cemented his reputation.

The Battle of Actium, in 31 B.C.E., ended Octavian's rivalry with Marc Antony, who committed suicide after his defeat. While restoring the outward form of a republic, Octavian transformed Rome permanently into an authoritarian state with himself as the sole and absolute ruler. A period followed known as the Pax Romana, in which Rome expanded its borders and became the unopposed regional power. It is against this backdrop that Vergil composed his most famous work, the

Aeneid (Latin *Aeneis*), named for its protagonist, Aeneas, a Trojan prince who flees Troy after its defeat and destruction at the hands of the Greeks. The work is a ten thousand-line poem in twelve books. It was to become the Roman national epic and one of the most famous and influential works in all literature. If, as generally held, Vergil began its composition sometime after 25 B.C.E. and had not completed it at his death in 19 B.C.E., he would have written at the rate of less than two lines per day.

Many versions of Aeneas's story were in circulation before Vergil began. His account, however, became the standard one. The obvious models for the *Aeneid* are the *Iliad* and the *Odyssey* of Homer. Like those epics, the *Aeneid* has no prologue—Vergil takes the reader directly into the action.

Aeneas is the son of Venus and Anchises, the king of Dardania, a region adjacent to Troy. The first part of the poem gives an account of Aeneas's attempts to found a new kingdom after leaving Troy with Anchises and a small group of Trojans. He is repeatedly frustrated by Juno, the wife of the Jupiter, who held a deep hatred of the Trojans after Paris, the son of Priam, the king of Troy, did not judge her to be the fairest of the goddesses. Juno causes a storm to force Aeneas to land in North Africa, where he meets Dido, the queen of Carthage. He recounts for Dido the story of the defeat of Troy and his flight. They become lovers, and Aeneas seems content to remain with her. At the behest of Jupiter, Mercury appears to Aeneas to warn him to leave. He does so, and the distraught Dido commits suicide. Another storm drives Aeneas to Sicily, where Anchises dies. After funeral games are held in his honor, Anchises appears to his son and instructs him to visit the Sibyl of Cumae in southern Italy. With the Sibyl, Aeneas journeys to the Underworld, where he encounters his father and learns of his own destiny and the future glory of Rome.

In the second part of the epic, Aeneas journeys to Latium in Italy. The king of Latium is Latinus, with whom Aeneas attempts to have peaceful relations. Juno, however, again intervenes and causes Turnus, king of the Rutulians, a neighboring people, and Latinus's wife, Amata, to urge war against the Trojan visitors. This occurs after a pet stag is unknowingly killed by Aeneas's son, Iulus. After a visit to the king, Evander, who rules the territory where Rome is to be founded, Aeneas gains the support of the king's son, Pallas, who joins the Trojan forces. Terrible fighting ensues in which Pallas is killed. In the final book, Aeneas and Turnus meet in battle. Aeneas is tempted to spare his rival, but after seeing that Turnus is wearing the belt he had taken from the dead Pallas, he kills Turnus.

One cannot overestimate the importance and influence of Vergil's *Aeneid*. It is easily the most important work of the Augustan period. Echoes of it can found in the works of many subsequent Roman writers, such as Ovid and Lucan. The work remained influential throughout the Middle Ages and the Renaissance, and its translation into vernacular languages has given it a worldwide audience. Although it has been widely regarded since antiquity to be a work fostering patriotic pride in the glories of the Roman Empire and Augustus's worldview, more recent scholarship has suggested that the horrors of war it depicts perhaps mask a dissenting view. Whatever the case, the *Aeneid* must be considered as one of the founding texts of Western civilization and among the most important works in world literature.

Final Days

In the late summer of 19 B.C.E., Vergil began a strenuous trip to the Greek Peloponnesus and Asia Minor. A fever, perhaps malaria or cholera, overcame him at Athens. Ironically, he would never see Troy, the city of Aeneas. Augustus himself accompanied the dying poet back to Italy, where he died on September 21 just after having reached Brundisium, the modern Brindisi, on the southeast coast of the Italian peninsula. Tradition holds that Vergil, knowing he was dying, made a deathbed request to burn the manuscript of the *Aeneid*. Augustus himself intervened to preserve it and entrusted its editing to two poets who were friends of Vergil and who knew his painstaking methods of composition, Lucius Varius Rufus and Plotius Tucca. The degree to which Varius and Tucca made any significant changes in the manuscript is moot. One suspects the changes were minimal. Half lines remain in the final text, and many critics contend this is one sign of the poem's unfinished state. One might just as easily argue that these half lines provide dramatic syncopation that enhances the narrative.

Vergil's death and the times in which he lived were so dramatic that they have inspired allegorical interpretations and narrative retellings in every subsequent era. Almost immediately after his death, even as the *Aeneid* was becoming a cornerstone of the Roman school curriculum, the poem assumed bibliomantic status, and some viewed it as a tool for interpreting the future. The name of Vergil's mother, Magia Pollia, also conferred on the dead poet the status of *Magus* (soothsayer or magician). This made it logical that commentators and scribes altered the spelling of Vergil's name during the Middle Ages to identify it with a *virga*, or magician's "wand." The magic wand then became associated with the Golden Bough that Vergil's hero Aeneas requires as passport to the realm of the dead.

Following World War II, the Austrian writer Hermann Broch published *Der Tod des Vergil* (*The Death of Virgil*, 1945). This novel, begun after Germany's annexation of Austria in 1938, followed upon Broch's arrest and detention in the infamous Altaussee, the prison the Nazis designated for political dissidents. It is in effect a political allegory in which the dying Vergil feels profound misgivings at the ability of a writer to distort history. Broch was, of course, thinking of Nazi propaganda, though he sees this through the prism of Augustus's Pax Romana. The dying poet corresponds to the tortured and dying artists in Altaussee, while the stream-of-consciousness style of the novel resembles that of Broch's acquaintance James Joyce.

Works Consulted

Duff, J. Wight. "Virgil." *A Literary History of Rome from the Origins to the Close of the Golden Age*. 3d ed. Ed. A. M. Duff. New York: Barnes & Noble, 1960. 316-52.

Frank, Tenney. *Vergil: A Biography*. 1922. Ithaca, NY: Cornell Digital Editions, 2010.

the PARIS REVIEW

The *Paris Review* Perspective _____

Patrick Loughran for *The Paris Review*

October 23, 42 B.C.E. A forty-two-year-old Roman commander flees into the hills near the city of Philippi (in modern-day Greece). He is accompanied by a small detachment of soldiers, all that is left of an army that just three weeks earlier was large enough to threaten a takeover of Rome. The commander, defeated and close to capture, is about to take his own life. His name is Marcus Junius Brutus, and he is one of the assassins of Julius Caesar, last ruler of the Roman Republic.

From these events, the publication of the *Aeneid*, great patriotic epic of Ancient Rome, will result. But it will take another two decades; the poet himself, Vergil, will be driven to declare the composition of the work, his own idea, an insane task; and ultimately, only his death will make its publication possible. Yet the *Aeneid* will go on to become one of the most important works of Western literature.

Publius Vergilius Maro, or Vergil, lived during one of Rome's most precarious periods. After the disruption of several civil wars, Caesar was installed as dictator of the Republic. His assassination by Brutus and Cassius on the Ides of March, 44 B.C.E., sparked a new conflict that ended when Brutus committed suicide in the hills near Philippi. The army that Brutus and Cassius had amassed in Greece had been defeated by the forces of Caesar's great-nephew and adopted son, Octavian—later Augustus, first Roman emperor—and his ally Marc Antony. The veterans of the victorious army were rewarded with land seized from Italians in the region of Mantua, Vergil's home. These land seizures partly inspired Vergil's *Eclogues*, gaining him the patronage of Octavian, which would in turn lead to the composition of the *Aeneid*.

It was not long before Octavian and Antony's alliance descended into another civil war, which concluded in Octavian's favor at Actium. The suicides of Antony and his lover, Cleopatra, followed. After the unrest of these further disputes, Octavian wanted an epic about himself that would help seal his claim to power. Vergil agreed to write it. He toiled away for more than a decade, but by his death in 19 B.C.E., the poem was still not published because Vergil had forbidden it, asking that it be destroyed. Only Octavian's disregard for the dead poet's wishes ensured that the *Aeneid* survived.

Vergil struggled with the *Aeneid*. Six years before his death, he wrote a letter to Octavian expressing his frustration: "What I have undertaken is of such magnitude I think I must have been almost out of my mind to embark upon so great a task." It remains unclear what Vergil meant. It seems unlikely that he was referring to the daunting scale of the work, since by the time he wrote the letter, he had completed most of what was eventually published. Perhaps the task of "such magnitude" referred instead to Vergil's underlying concept for the *Aeneid*—Vergil had set out to write nothing less than the dramatic history of Rome.

At its simplest, the *Aeneid* is the story of a man trying to find a home for himself. Aeneas, a pious warrior, survives the Greek sack of Troy and leads the few remaining Trojans on a seven-year voyage in search of safety. He finds love with Dido, queen of Carthage, but leaves her to her death in order to obey the gods, who call on Aeneas to start a new city. He passes through the Underworld and ends up in Italy, where his war, and eventual peace, with the Italians leads to the founding of Lavinium, forerunner of Rome.

Vergil had burdened himself with a grand undertaking, to write the creation myth for an empire that would stretch over what Edward Gibbon called "the fairest part of the earth." The complexity of Vergil's writing project required him to try to balance his narrative between the demands of historical foreshadowing, an argument for the destiny of Rome and its ruler Augustus, and a faithful reaching back to the mythical past of the Greek Homeric myths of the Trojan War, the *Iliad* and the *Odyssey*. This alone would likely have been enough to justify his lament in his letter to Octavian.

But Vergil was no mere propagandist. He had also set himself another task in writing the poem—a task more in step with the timeless concerns of poetry, and one that was again complex enough to justify his complaint to Octavian. It was a question about the concept of human free will. It first appears explicitly in the text when Aeneas describes to the Carthaginians his horror at watching the gods help the Greeks sack his city:

> "Even Father himself, he's filling the Greek hearts
> with courage, stamina—Jove in person spurring the gods
> to fight the Trojan armies!"

Yet Aeneas goes on to follow the call to duty of this same Jove (Jupiter), king of the gods, to found a new city in a distant land. But if it was the will of the gods that Troy be destroyed, why should Aeneas still love these same gods and show them his devotion? One answer is that Aeneas survived, so it was equally the will of the gods that he be spared. But Aeneas has suffered greatly. He has lost his wife, his home, his comrades, his city, and his country, although his life has been, we know from Vergil, an example of piety. Plus, many other Trojans who have suffered, even died, at the hands of the Greeks were also pious.

It seems the will of the gods is random and unpredictable, cruel even. The *Aeneid* asks: What is the role of human free will, and faith, in this light? It does not offer easy answers to these questions; instead, it makes them matters of expansive poetic discourse, pools of language in which our own suffering can be reflected. It shares much here with one of the most mysterious, and heartbreaking, sections of the Bible— the book of Job. The central question of the book of Job is also about the meaning of human free will in a world where God lets good people suffer. There are no easy answers in Job either. Both books are still relevant to secular readers. They are as much about why we should choose hope and morality over despair as they are about God. These are questions that have troubled many of the greatest thinkers of the post-Enlightenment age, from Søren Kierkegaard to Arthur Schopenhauer, to Albert Camus in *The Myth of Sisyphus*. But two thousand years before these conundrums vexed modern thinkers, Vergil, poet of Rome, asked these questions and proceeded to present the full panoply of human life—both bleak and joyous—as the answer.

Works Consulted

Cary, M., and H. H. Scullard. *A History of Rome*. London: Macmillan, 1975.

Everitt, Anthony. *The First Emperor: Caesar Augustus and the Triumph of Rome*. London: John Murray/Hachette, 2006.

Gibbon, Edward. *The History of the Decline and Fall of the Roman Empire*. 1776-89. New York: Penguin Classics, 2005.

Quinn, Kenneth. *Virgil's "Aeneid": A Critical Description*. Ann Arbor: U of Michigan P, 1968.

Virgil. *The Aeneid*. Trans. C. Day Lewis. New York: Oxford UP, 1986.

_____. *The Aeneid*. Trans. Robert Fagles. New York: Penguin Classics, 2006.

_____. *The Aeneid*. Trans. David West. New York: Penguin Classics, 1990.

Williams, R. D. *The Aeneid*. Boston: Allen & Unwin, 1987.

CRITICAL
CONTEXTS

Independent Imitation:
The *Aeneid* and Greek Epic _____

Robert J. Forman

I

One may read Vergil's *Aeneid* with complete indifference to its structure or its indebtedness to its predecessors yet easily appreciate its elegance, taut narrative, and profound emotional appeal. The poem presents the essence of a Roman Italy in which the emperor Augustus wanted Romans to believe in an ancient legacy mapped by destiny itself that would evolve into the emperor's own city of marble. The origins of that mythic imperial Rome lay in Troy, in Aeneas's Lavinium, in Iulus's Alba Longa, and by decree of Fate in little Etruscan Pallanteum, which Romulus would ultimately name after himself. Vergil deals with all this mythic history, which Romans knew only through oral tradition, in a mere ten lines, the first of his *Aeneid*. The power of his words is undeniable, and their appeal to patriotism is so clear that even a cynical contemporary reader cannot help but feel it. This is a perfect example of Vergilian independence, a first codification of Roman prehistory.

Augustus wanted a pedigree for his city, and he offered the pastoral poet Vergil an imperial subvention if only he would create one. Vergil did this using the oral tradition familiar to many though never written. He explicitly establishes a connection to the Julian line of emperors through Aeneas's son Ascanius, significantly renamed Iulus for this reason once the Trojans reach Italy. By extension, he connects the imperial family to Aeneas's mother, Venus, and through her union with Mars provides a link to the patron deity of the Roman army. Carthage, the Roman North African port strategically placed to ensure dominance of the Mediterranean, was Dido's city, and it might have been Aeneas's had Fate permitted. It was also Hannibal's, and Aeneas's desertion of Dido was nearly repaid in the Carthaginian invasion of Italy during the Punic Wars, fought between 264 and 146 B.C.E. Vergil directly connects this mythic desertion and the historical event in Jupiter's words at the beginning of *Aeneid* 10.

In melding myth and history, Vergil was also directing the Latin language into uncharted territory. It is true that both Gnaeus Naevius (c. 270-201 B.C.E.) and Quintus Ennius (239-169 B.C.E.) had written epic, but they had done so in the tradition of annalist historians. Their works remain only in fragments. Ennius's *Annals* dealt with events in series from the fall of Troy to the censorship of Cato the Elder in 184 B.C.E. It was a primary school text of the Republic, but Augustus believed that imperial Rome needed a new poem to complement its new political construct. The task facing Vergil was to create a poem that extended the Trojan War to Italy; hence, in choosing what to call his poem Vergil looked to Homer. He settled upon a Greek title, *Aeneis* (the genitive being *Aeneidos*), preferring this formulation to the Latin for its linguistic association to Homeric epic, and this is only the first of many nods Vergil gives to his Greek predecessors.

II

Classical epic traditionally begins in the middle of an event (in medias res), and in the *Aeneid* Vergil upholds tradition. In fact, if one recalls the narrative Odysseus provides for the Phaeacians in *Odyssey* 9.110, the very storm that carries him off course at Cape Malea to the land of the lotus-eaters would have to have been the storm that brought Aeneas to Dido's Carthage (*Aeneid* 1.88). The storm descriptions are parallel, and both locations would be North African, since Odysseus passes Cythera, his ship blown to the southwest. Just as striking is the pleasant but ultimately destructive indolence that having landed among the lotus-eaters and at Dido's Carthage connotes.

Even so, for every one of these similarities there is difference apposite to Vergil's larger plan. Eating the lotus causes one to forget one's homeland. Odysseus watches without interference as some of his men eat the flower, though he himself does not. The implication is that while Odysseus wishes to return to Ithaca, he remains indifferent to whatever the wishes of the Ithacans who sail with him may be. Aeneas, though tempted by the ease of living at Carthage (the city that Dido founded after fleeing from her own city of Tyre in Phoenicia), ultimately recalls that his primary obligation is to his community. Driven by the injunctions of the ghost of his wife, Creusa, and by the message of Mercury, Aeneas ultimately remains true to establishing a new Troy at Lavinium.

It is significant, therefore, that in the two instances at which Mercury's Greek counterpart, Hermes, appears to redirect Odysseus (the Circe episode of *Odyssey* 10 and the Calypso episode of *Odyssey* 5), primary focus remains with the well-being and future of the hero, not those of his men. Hermes offers the antidote to the potion with which Circe turns Odysseus's men into swine to Odysseus alone. Odysseus then secures his men's return to human form only after he himself has overcome Circe's magic. In contrast, when Mercury appears to remind Aeneas that he must be mindful of his mission to establish a new Troy in Italy (*Aeneid* 4.334), he accuses Aeneas of laying the foundations of someone else's city and, by doting on a personal love, of being blind to his proper dominion. The priority of responsibility for community over self is clear in this episode and increasingly so from this point onward in the *Aeneid*.

III

One could say that Dido is Vergil's Penelope, Circe, Calypso, and Medea all in a single persona. Vergil knew the *Argonautica* of Apollonius of Rhodes as well as he did Homer's poems, and it is likely that he drew elements of his Dido's personality from that of Apollonius's Medea. The result is that in Dido he creates a complex woman who can be a pathetic pawn, sexually driven and magnetic, yet anger-filled and wishing revenge. Dido exhibits all of these qualities within two of the twelve books (*Aeneid* 1 and 4) of Vergil's poem.

Her background, which Vergil presents in a few lines of Venus's words to Aeneas (1.343ff.), directly parallels Dido's experience to that of Aeneas. Dido's wicked brother Pygmalion, king of Tyre in Phoenicia, killed her husband, Sychaeus, from envy of his wealth, and she herself is thus an exile like Aeneas, forced to build a new city. By emphasizing the parallelism, Vergil underscores the all-too-true fact that in the *Aeneid* personal concerns remain secondary. Both Dido and Aeneas had had perfect spouses, Sychaeus and Creusa. The ghosts of each warn them to flee their cities. Dido and Aeneas both face the task of building new cities for their people. Still, Fate will not allow Dido to become Aeneas's destined bride, since an Italian Troy and ultimately Rome can never eventuate unless Aeneas leaves Dido and Carthage.

IV

One might reasonably call *Aeneid* 1-6 the work's "odyssean" half, as it retraces Aeneas's journey to his new home in episodic details suggestive of the *Odyssey*. Even so, it is clear how different Aeneas's journey is from that of Odysseus. In addition to the community emphasis that increases throughout the *Aeneid*, Vergil provides five ascending motifs, with Fate (*fatum*) the motif that overrides the other four. The most obvious of these is love (*amor*), then work (*labor*), sorrow (*dolor*), and dutiful humility (*pietas*). There is the love of Dido and Aeneas, but there is also their love for their cities and their people. The work that builds these cities depends upon the achievements of warriors and their rulers. Sorrow finds its connection in death, whether of Aeneas's father, Anchises, of Dido's husband, Sychaeus, or of Dido herself. *Dolor* is also found in the deaths of cities and ways of life, whether of Tyre, Troy, or Dido's Carthage. *Pietas* appears in acceptance of Fate, the motif so overriding in the *Aeneid* as to be almost a personification.

Fate decrees that there will be a Rome, but for that to happen Tyre,

Troy, Carthage, Lavinium, and Alba Longa must achieve their foundation and, in the cases of Tyre and Troy, their usurpation and destruction. To support the development of these motifs in *Aeneid* 1-6, Vergil provides two key images: the flame, to describe the fall of Troy, the flames of Dido's passion, and the ignited pyre on which she commits suicide; and the serpent, to portray Juno's vengeance upon Laocoön and his two sons, to describe the cunning Trojans who dress in Greek armor to surprise their enemies, and to describe the suicidal anger that lurks in Dido's breast following Aeneas's desertion.

It is beyond question that Vergil is aware of these elements, for they are what differentiate his poem from those of his predecessors. This is why he orchestrates his poem through variations in mood supported by internal metrical patterns that balance Aeneas's journey to the Underworld in *Aeneid* 6 with the death and funeral games for Anchises in *Aeneid* 5. The Underworld visit to Anchises ostensibly provides the direction Aeneas needs in order to assure himself that he is correctly pursuing what *fatum* has decreed. On one hand, the journey parallels that of Odysseus in *Odyssey* 11, though the prophet Teiresias tells Odysseus what lies ahead and his dead mother, Anticleia, actually impedes her son's discovery. Emphasis in the *Aeneid* is, however, predictably with the well-being of the community, the Roman more so than the Trojan.

At the conclusion of his Underworld journey, Aeneas sees what amounts to an imperial triumphal procession of great Romans yet unborn, including the emperor Augustus himself. Aeneas is no more able to make contact with the leaders and generals he sees than he had been able to make Dido respond at the beginning of *Aeneid* 6. What is significant is that the spirits of Dido and his ship's pilot, Palinurus, appear at the beginning of the journey, recalling Aeneas's personal failings and obligations. At the book's conclusion, however, Aeneas can recognize the importance of the leaders he sees even though he cannot appreciate his own part in allowing these individuals to come into existence as a consequence of his leadership of the community.

V

Aeneid 6 is the pivotal book of the entire poem. The Golden Bough, which Aeneas plucks from a tree located at the Cumaean entrance to the Underworld, allows him, though still living, to enter the realm of the dead. The notion of a living person among the dead is rooted in mythic tradition, and parallels to Odysseus's experience are clear. Even so, Vergil makes important modifications. The prophet whom Aeneas seeks is his father, Anchises, not Teiresias. The woman who leads him is not Medea (who leads Jason to the Golden Fleece) but Apollo's Sibyl, and she is from the Italian, Greek-settled town of Cumae.

Cumae had always been the Italian Delphi. The earliest foundations of its temple of Apollo predate the founding of Rome. This fact allows Vergil to set the rationale for the eventual founding of Rome in the context of unification of Trojan, Greek, Etruscan, and native Italic ethnicities. By directing Aeneas to the spirit of his dead father, a Greek priestess facilitates the founding of a new Trojan city at Lavinium, alliance with an Etruscan king, Evander, and what amounts to a second Trojan War with the Trojans in the role of the invaders fighting for the marriage of Aeneas and Lavinia. This mythic history, built upon mutual suffering (*dolor*), a good deal of work (*labor*), assimilation through marriage (*amor*), and humble fidelity (*pietas*), creates an idealized amalgam of the Roman people, a thing destined by Fate (*fatum*). This explanation of Roman genealogy clearly suited Augustus's purpose, for it made a virtue of the imperial city's increasingly complicated ethnicity.

The memorable conclusion of *Aeneid* 6 corresponds to Homer's description of the Cave of the Nymphs in *Odyssey* 13. Homer's cave is the site on Ithaca at which the Phaeacians deposit a sleeping Odysseus. He is home, though he does not recognize it. There are two entrances to this cave, one for the gods and the other for mortals. Vergil's cave is an exit from the Underworld. It is in Italy, Aeneas's new home, and it also has two entrances, one for true dreams (dead spirits communicating with the upper world), called the Gate of Ivory, the other called the Gate of Horn for false dreams (the living who leave the realm of the dead). Aeneas and the Sibyl leave through the Gate of Horn. This is significant, for their return signals metaphorical rebirth.

VI

The final six books of the *Aeneid*, its iliadic section, reconfigure the Trojan War in terms appropriate to the Augustan scenario. Though individual episodes correspond to those of the *Iliad*, what is most striking is how brilliantly Vergil recasts them. In doing this, he follows a pattern he had established in the first six books. The odd-numbered books (1, 3, 5, 7, 9, and 11) provide background, while the even-numbered books (2, 4, 6, 8, 10, and 12) advance the narrative. This allows sustained description and less episodic narrative than one finds in the Homeric poems. It is true that Vergilian narrative would logically be more sustained, given that it was written, whereas rhapsodes recited Homeric poetry, but Vergil never forgets his Greek predecessors.

In *Iliad* 3, Hector rouses Paris from his bedroom so that he can fight Menelaus and Helen can watch. In *Aeneid* 7, Vergil invokes the Muse Erato, to direct the reader's attention to the assembled populace of Lavinium at sacrifice, to its prophet who foresees the coming of Aeneas, and, more significant, toward Lavinia, daughter of Latinus and Aeneas's destined bride. Lavinia's hair catches fire as she is about to offer sacrifice, and this flame imagery directly relates her to Dido, the flame that consumes her with love and her burning funeral pyre. The flame imagery also anticipates the second Trojan War, which the Trojans will fight for the right to establish their city and for Aeneas's right to marry Lavinia.

Ilioneus, one of Aeneas's men, offers Latinus a short catalog of gifts if he will agree to Trojan settlement and the marriage of Aeneas and Lavinia. The compact is all but assured with mutual gifts from Latinus when the gorgon fury Allecto flings a snake from her black hair at

Amata, Lavinia's mother, and thrusts it down the woman's breast. She flings a torch at Turnus, Lavinia's fiancé. Serpent and flame imagery is also identifiable with the consumed Laocoön, and Dido returns and signals war and anger. Such imagery has a cumulative, exponential value in Vergil's poem. Laocoön and his sons died because he foresaw the consequences of accepting the wooden horse. Dido died as a pawn of Juno and Venus for having accepted Aeneas within her walls. Turnus, Lavinia's fiancé, dies at the poem's conclusion, another victim of Juno and afflicted by Allecto's fiery poison, at the hands of Aeneas.

Furor thus juxtaposes itself to *amor,* the anger of Juno and the love of Venus for her son, recasting the anger of Hera and Thetis's demand for glorification of her son Achilles in *Iliad* 1. Significantly, Juno refers to Aeneas as "Paris reborn" in *Aeneid* 7.377 and notes that a funeral torch will consume a second Troy. Vergil thus combines the personae of the two Homeric heroes, Achilles and Paris, the man who killed him, in his Aeneas. The *Iliad* also makes use of ambiguous identities when Hector kills Patroclus thinking that he is Achilles since he is wearing Achilles' armor and subsequently when Achilles kills Hector, who wears the armor he had stripped from the body of Patroclus. One could argue that in killing Hector, Achilles is in effect killing himself, for he hastens the prophecy that he will have a short but glorious life if he remains to fight at Troy or a long but obscure life if he returns to Phthia.

VII

The iliadic *Aeneid* retains a comparable series of encounters leading to Aeneas's final meeting with Turnus, but their method of arrangement is entirely unlike those of the *Iliad*. The bloody battlefield combats emphasize the local origins and onomatology rather than the vaunts of victorious warriors. These meetings intensify to underscore the pathos shared by Aeneas's Etruscan ally Evander and Mezentius, the ostracized king of Etruscan Caere, at the deaths of their sons Pallas and Lausus. The grief (*dolor*) they experience goes beyond the personal. It affects the entire community and recalls not only Aeneas's grief upon learning of Dido's death but Carthaginian reaction to it. Aeneas deserts Dido, and Hannibal nearly conquers Rome. The two events appear entirely unconnected until one adds the mythic ingredient that the *Aeneid* supplies.

Symbolism is likewise particularly important in the final six books of the *Aeneid*, and this appears with different emphasis as well. All of these elements focus on Italy and the new ethnic amalgam from which Rome will one day draw its strength. What is more, they connect to lend coherence to the poem. One example of this is the hunt of *Aeneid* 4.195, during which the young Ascanius, still untried as a warrior, wishes for the appearance of a frothing wild boar or lion upon which he could try his mettle. Before he can face any challenge, a thunderstorm drives Dido and Aeneas into a cave, in which they consummate their love. Since Fate overrides all, Ascanius cannot find his quarry until the affair of Dido and Aeneas has reached its conclusion. Even so, what breaks the alliance of Aeneas and Latinus is Ascanius's killing of the stag that belonged to the family of Tyrrhus (*Aeneid* 7.583). The sons of Tyrrhus had raised the animal as a pet; their sister Silvia taught it to accept food from the hand. Ascanius is unaware of this when the fury Allecto directs the arrow he shoots to mortally wound the stag. The Latins close on Ascanius, the Trojans defend him, and Almo, the eldest of Tyrrhus's sons, is first to fall. This assures the fated second Trojan War.

As important are the onomatological connections no ancient reader of the *Aeneid* could miss. Tyrrhus's name etymologically relates to Tyre, Dido's city of origin. Silvia's name recalls Rhea Silvia, the mother of Romulus and Remus, the twins raised by a she-wolf. Vergil continually employs such suggestive elements. The most significant, serpents and flames, appear throughout the poem. In *Aeneid* 7, they appear in association with Allecto, the gorgon fury who serves Juno and starts the war.

Once the war begins, it is plain how dire the position of the Trojans is. Their resources, both human and material, are seriously depleted. The poor gifts Aeneas had been able to offer Latinus in the hope of an alliance, when compared with the opulence of Latinus's offerings (*Aeneid* 7.280ff.; 320ff.), underscore this state of affairs. The situation also allows Vergil to move his narrative directly to what would become Rome itself, the Etruscan city called Pallanteum. In *Aeneid* 8, Aeneas prays to Father Tiber, chooses two ships, and sets off against the current.

What assures him that he is on the destined course is his sight of a brooding white sow stretched out on the river's banks with her young (*Aeneid* 8.90). This token of recognition, provided by his surrogate father, the Tiber, complements the Golden Bough his mother, Venus, had had her doves identify. The bough was the token that allowed Aeneas to make the Underworld journey to his father Anchises. The sow, a token that Father Tiber has accepted the petition, allows the cycles of history to continue without another impediment. Aeneas offers the sow and her young to his divine nemesis Juno in the hope of propitiating her. From this point, it is clear that Juno's direct opposition becomes less active. She becomes reconciled only at the Olympian council in *Aeneid* 10, when Jupiter assures her that Rome will suffer at the hands of the Carthaginians.

VIII

The current of the Tiber would not have allowed any ancient ship to pass beyond Tiber Island, and modern archaeology has demonstrated that the most ancient part of Rome is the Forum Boarium, the cattle market just at the Tiber's bend. It is here that Aeneas stands at *Aeneid* 8.112. All the details of this scene would hold meaning for an imperial Roman. Evander, king of Pallanteum, is offering a sacrifice to Hercules assisted by his son Pallas, the young man whose death compares to that of Patroclus in the *Iliad*. The Temple of Hercules and the Ara Maxima, the altar upon which Romans offered an annual sacrifice to Heracles, both appear assigned to the Etruscan who would be Aeneas's first ally in Italy. Evander's wisdom corresponds to that of Homer's Nestor, the senior warrior of the *Iliad* to whom the Greeks invariably turn for sage advice. The temple and altar are so much a part of Roman tradition that they have survived even to the contemporary city.

Evander and Aeneas walk the extent of Pallanteum. They see the cave of Cacus, and Vergil retells a tale familiar to every Roman, the monster's theft of Heracles' cattle. Any visitor to the Roman Forum can see the cave, just as one can see the Capitoline Hill and the Tarpeian Rock, which are also on the itinerary of Evander and Aeneas. These details and others, even Vergil's description of Evander in priestly dress for sacrifice, resemble what every imperial Roman would recognize in daily religion and ritual.

Description of the shield that Venus secures from Vulcan closes *Aeneid* 8. The scene parallels Thetis's request for Achilles' shield from Hephaestus, but Vergil's shield has seven scenes on its periphery and a scene in its center portraying Augustus's victory over Marc Antony at Actium. The peripheral scenes include Romulus, Remus, and the she-wolf; the rape of the Sabine women (through which the first Romans populate the fledgling city); the haughty king Tarquin; the Roman priesthoods; the traitor Catiline; and the patriot Cato. Each, therefore, focuses on some aspect of Roman history or its mythic underpinning, with the triumph that established unquestioned *imperium* as the shield's central feature.

Evander's entrusting of his son Pallas to Aeneas for tutelage in the art of war indicates the depth of his commitment and, by extension, the antiquity of the Etruscan-Trojan alliance. That Rome did all it could to extirpate Etruscan influence on the Italian peninsula is a historical detail that needs the revision this mythic alliance supplies if the Augustan perspective is to prevail. On a superficial level, the relationship between Aeneas and Pallas resembles that of Achilles and Patroclus in the *Iliad*. Both Patroclus and Pallas are apprentice warriors. Their deaths impel their teachers, Achilles and Aeneas, to the rages that terminate in the deaths of Hector and Turnus, the warriors who killed the young men. The major difference, however, is the position of their teachers in regard to these deaths.

The death of Patroclus elicits a purely personal response from Achilles. He is aware that he has lost a student whom he loves. He is simultaneously aware that he must reenter battle and await his own fated glory and early death. Aeneas, while he feels the love of a surrogate father for Pallas, recognizes that the Trojan-Etruscan treaty connects directly with Evander's having entrusted his son to Aeneas. War with the Latin tribes began with Ascanius's accidental killing of a pet. Pallas's death is much more serious, yet the Trojan-Etruscan alliance holds. Neither Juno nor Allecto intervenes, though the way destiny plays out continues to surprise. This follows from the warrior pairings that fill the poem's final three books.

The council of Olympian deities with which *Aeneid* 10 begins is on its face as unproductive as the council of *Iliad* 1. As in that meeting, the goddesses concerned, Thetis and Hera in the *Iliad* and Venus and Juno in the *Aeneid*, plead their cases for Achilles and Aeneas. Vergil's Jupiter is as thundering and almost as ineffectual as Homer's Zeus in most instances. In these Olympian councils, however, both Jupiter and Zeus demand obedience to Fate. Achilles will be glorified, but he will also die young. The question before Vergil's Olympians, however, is whether there will be a new Troy in Italy, not Aeneas's glorification. He is merely the instrument through which the important founding of this city will flow. Juno needs to be satisfied with the dangers Rome, the city that Romulus can found only if Aeneas establishes his city at Lavinium, will face after its establishment. Though Jupiter alludes only to the Carthaginian invasion, Romans may well have thought of Actium and the civil wars that brought Augustus to power. These events were immediate and nearly contemporary to the new political dispensation that the Empire represented.

IX

Vergil's warriors are strikingly different. They share degrees of prowess that are proper to them. Turnus and Aeneas are contemporaries and apparently of comparable ability. Mezentius, the ostracized king of Etruscan Caere, is closest in description to a villain, though he loves his son Lausus just as fiercely as Evander does Pallas, or Aeneas does Iulus (Ascanius). They differ in their relationships to their people and in their *pietas*, the degree to which they have a humble awareness of their functions in the working out of history. One might expect a meeting of Aeneas's son Iulus and Mezentius's son Lausus. This does not occur. In view of the fact that Turnus entered the war only through the incitement of Allecto, one might expect he would refuse combat with a warrior as relatively inexperienced as Pallas. He does not. One might expect that the unmitigated villain Mezentius would die without the sympathy of the reader. On the contrary, he dies bravely and his son Lausus defends him until Aeneas, of all warriors, kills both the young man and his father at the conclusion of *Aeneid* 10. One might suspect that Aeneas, who has seen so much suffering and who has himself killed Lausus, a young man with as fine instincts as Pallas, would yield to Turnus's pleas for life at the end of *Aeneid* 12. He hesitates, but then kills the Rutulian king immediately upon seeing that Turnus wears the belt he had taken from the body of Pallas.

There is, without doubt, an element of narrative surprise in the way Vergil chooses to present this series of deaths. Though wounded and bereft of his son, Mezentius holds on until Aeneas kills him. He is brave in a way that the suppliant Turnus does not appear to be. What is inescapable in these narratives, however, is that personal pain remains secondary to the social dislocation these deaths cause. The citizens of Caere, the modern Cerveteri so known for its tombs, cannot tolerate the tyranny Mezentius represents, so they depose him. Pallanteum, Vergil's Etruscan Rome, loses its heir when Turnus kills Pallas just as surely as Caere when Aeneas kills Lausus, a young man with what appears a comparable degree of filial piety.

X

The chaos of the war seems to invert all social norms. Camilla, an Amazon warrior comparable to Penthesilea, enters battle on the side of the Latin allies and exults in war for the sake of war. Juturna, the sister of Turnus, does likewise to defend her brother; even so, her name, as well as *Aeneid* 12.160ff., implies a strong allegiance to Juno, the enemy of the Trojans. This begs a question concerning Vergil's intentions. The *Aeneid* was doubtless a symbolic embodiment of the Augustan Pax Romana, peace by force of arms that brought what Romans saw as the entire civilized world under Roman sway.

Romans saw this phenomenon in the way that empires invariably do. Rome's rule was benevolent; it offered protection, efficient uncorrupted government, and local rule. All this was true, and nothing in the *Aeneid* gainsays it. Indeed, it has been traditional critical practice to read the *Aeneid* as a literary statement of patriotism as clear as the great Altar of Peace (Ara Pacis) that Augustus had erected to celebrate Rome, Roman government, and the imperial office itself. Even as one observes the remarkable ways in which Vergil praises his patron Augustus, it is hard not to notice the admonitions against concentration of power that accompany these encomia. Rome will achieve glory without end, but suffering will accompany it. Augustus will defeat Antony, but there will always be another Catiline to plot against legitimate rule. Aeneas is a great leader, but only when he realizes that he rules for his people, not for his own glorification.

Works Cited

Homer. *The Iliad*. Trans. Robert Fagles. New York: Penguin, 1998.
_____. *The Odyssey*. Trans. Robert Fagles. New York: Penguin, 1999.
Virgil. *The Aeneid*. Trans. Robert Fagles. New York: Penguin, 2008.

History, Culture, and the *Aeneid*_____

Bernard J. Cassidy

The years following the assassination of Julius Caesar (44 B.C.E.), culminating in the ascendancy of Octavian to the principate and his assumption of the title of Augustus (27 B.C.E.), left most Romans with the realization that a restoration of the Republic was a lost dream. Actually, there were few still living who had experienced a period free of the internal strife that had torn the fabric of the city since the last years of the previous century. The civil wars waged by Marius and Sulla, with their bloody proscriptions, had purged Rome of many of its leaders and had paved the way for the conflicts to follow, first between Julius Caesar and Gnaeus Pompey, then between Marc Antony with Gaius Octavian against Marcus Brutus and the other assassins of Caesar, and finally between Marc Antony and Octavian themselves.

Vergil's readers knew the history of their city, even from its legendary beginnings. Aeneas, the Trojan hero, was already acknowledged as having brought to Italy the household gods of Troy. The story of Romulus and Remus and the she-wolf was familiar to all. Both legends had more or less been integrated into the founding story of Rome by the time of the poet Ennius (239-169 B.C.E.). Camillus was recognized as the "second founder of Rome" for his success in fighting off the Gauls in 390 B.C.E. Rome's historical enmity with Carthage resulted in three devastating Punic Wars, beginning in 264 and ending in 149 B.C.E. Indeed, Vergil's success depended on the fact that his audience would be very familiar with the people and events that are foretold to Aeneas in various ways throughout the poem, but that he cannot comprehend.

Much has been written even from ancient times about how the *Aeneid* is modeled on the *Iliad* and *Odyssey* of Homer. One could make a mistake, however, in judging the *Aeneid* by how faithful it is to Homer's works. A twenty-first-century reader must remember that one of Vergil's contemporaries would have read the *Aeneid* with a much deeper involvement than an Athenian of the age of Pericles would have read the *Iliad* or the *Odyssey*. After all, to an Athenian of the fifth century B.C.E. the Homeric poems recounted great legends and recalled the great legendary heroes of Bronze-Age Greece. However (and this is a big "however"), no Athenian or any other Greek of that time (except perhaps an inhabitant of Ithaca, Odysseus's home island) saw any connection whatever between daily life and the events portrayed in the poems. Fifth-century Greece would have been the same whether or not the Greeks had successfully vanquished the Trojans or Odysseus had successfully reached his homeland to reclaim his rightful authority and avenge the wrongs done to his wife, Penelope, and his son, Telemachus.

A Roman of the early Augustan period, however, would read the story of Aeneas as the birth of the Roman race—"Such a great task it was to found the Roman race" (1.33). If Aeneas had failed to escape the fires of Troy (after being encouraged to escape by an apparition from Hector) or had failed to establish himself in Italy, whether by deciding to remain with Dido in Carthage or by some other happenstance, Rome would not have come into existence, and there would have been no such celebratory epic to read.

The date of the Trojan War, and hence Aeneas's escape from that burning city, was traditionally believed to have been a few years after 1200 B.C.E., about four and a half centuries before the traditional date for the founding of Rome (753 B.C.E.). By the time of the historian Livy (59 B.C.E.-17 C.E.), the gap had been filled by the tradition that Aeneas founded Lavinium, not Rome, and his son Ascanius founded the city of Alba Longa, long known as a famous religious center. After generations of kings that fill the chronological gap, Romulus and Remus set out from Alba Longa and settled on the Palatine Hill, thereby setting the stage for the famous confrontation between the brothers.

One of Vergil's most amazing accomplishments in the *Aeneid* is his interweaving of various layers of time into his story without the reader's even realizing that he is doing so. Throughout the poem he manages to provide allusions to events that fall into the legendary or historical past of the reader of Augustus's day but are in contrast, either past, present, or future, to Aeneas, as he moves from one setting to another. Philip Hardie points out that this trait presents a "thoroughly Alexandrian cast" (88). I note below a few more instances of the influence of Hellenistic literature on the *Aeneid*.

Even before Vergil indicates to us the theme of his tale on line 33 of book 1, he has provided the reasons Juno is angry with Aeneas and his expatriate Trojan companions—those "left over by the Greeks" (1.30). Vergil asks, "How can such anger exist in divine minds?" (1.11). He goes to explain first and foremost, "There was an ancient city" (1.12). Here he introduces Carthage and notes how dear the city was to Juno—how she held it dearer even than Samos, where there was an ancient temple to her, and how she planned worldwide dominion for Carthage "if in any way the fates would allow it" (1.12-19). Vergil thus introduces the thought that Juno is jealous because Aeneas will found a race in Italy that is destined to destroy her beloved Carthage. Already Vergil has introduced the historic Carthage, presented as existing before the fall of Troy, and he has thrown in a glimpse of the future (as far as the characters of the story are concerned). This future is 150 years in the past to the Roman reader. Every Augustan reader of the *Aeneid* knew that this destruction of Carthage had taken place a century and a half earlier. Juno is upset because it will happen; at this point Aeneas has no clue about it at all.

However, Juno was already upset with the Trojans, even before the war began. This animosity accounts for her siding with the Greeks in the war itself. She hated the Trojan race, sprung from Dardanus, a child of Elektra, with whom Juno's husband, Jupiter, had had an affair. She also complained that it was Paris who had judged Venus to be more beautiful than she and that a Trojan youth had replaced Hebe, her daughter, as cup-bearer of the gods.

Each of these citations sends the reader back into Rome's mythological and legendary past. Later in book 1, when Aeneas first enters

Carthage, he views the great temple that Dido is constructing in honor of her protector, Juno. Interestingly, as Aeneas views the images on the great temple, Vergil mentions nothing about Aeneas's seeing any images of Carthage's Phoenician history. However, the images of the downfall of Troy bring him to tears as he realizes that the story of the destruction of his homeland has traveled across the seas to this distant shore. He cries: "O Achates, what place, what region on earth is not full of our suffering?" (1.459-60).

When Aeneas descends to the Underworld in book 6 to visit his father, Anchises, who will reinforce his foretold destiny, he approaches Anchises as by chance "he was reviewing the whole number of his descendants, his own dear grandsons, and their destinies and fortunes, their character and exploits" (6.680-81). In book 8 Aeneas meets Evander at Pallanteum, the site at which Rome will be founded. Vergil tells us: "Aeneas marvels, and turns his eyes quickly around, and is happily charmed by the place, and he asks and learns about the stories of the earlier men" (8.310-11). The revelation that the site is indeed the site of the future city of Rome is presented in Vergil's narrative as Aeneas and Evander walk from Rome's ancient cattle market, the Forum Boarium, to the Tarpeian Rock on the Capitoline Hill. Only those knowing Rome's topography are privy to this information. Evander and Aeneas, while aware of the sacred history of the site, do not share our knowledge that this is the site where Aeneas's descendants will found a city.

Later in the same book, Venus gives Aeneas his armor, including a shield on which Vulcan had fashioned "Italy's story and Rome's triumphs, since he was hardly unversed in prophecy and unaware of the things destined to come" (8.626-28). As Wendell Clausen notes, "Only a few scenes are described," and Aeneas does not comprehend the events described on the shield: "The fiction of Aeneas as spectator, bewilderedly studying the various scenes on the shield, allows Vergil to present, subtly and without embarrassment, the Augustan conception of Roman history. Attention is concentrated almost equally on early

Rome . . . and on the Battle of Actium" (80). Clausen cites the sack of the city by the Gauls in 390 B.C.E. as the first great crisis of the Republic and the Battle of Actium in 32 B.C.E. as the second.

Cultural Background

In the first few lines of the *Aeneid*, Vergil reports that Aeneas is bringing the gods of Troy to Rome: "suffering much in war too, until he should found a city and bring his gods [i.e., the gods of Troy] to Latium" (1.5-6). It emerges in the second book that these gods (at least Vesta, goddess of the hearth) had been given to Aeneas by the spirit of Hector, as he appeared to Aeneas during Troy's final battle and gave him the responsibility to save these gods from the destruction that threatened them. In some ways the portable figures (Virgil does not describe their form) seem to be understood as being the gods themselves. "Troy entrusts to you her holy rites and her Penates; take them as companion of your destinies; seek walls for them" (2.293-95).

Again, later in Aeneas's description of the destruction, he recounts that Pantheus, a priest of Apollo, came to his house with "the holy things and conquered gods" (2.320). What exactly is one to make of these two occurrences? Each household had its Penates, those deities that protected the family. The state, which the Romans understood as a large family, also had its protective deities. Although the belief in the Penates probably originated in Italy, Vergil here attributes their origin to Troy and establishes a religious connection between Troy and Rome.

The Romans were extremely conservative both in religion and in their cultural and legal traditions. The basis of their legal system (what we call the Roman constitution) was not a written constitution as we know it but a combination of written laws, edicts of magistrates, and custom, among other things. Tradition was an extremely important factor in the determination of right and wrong, legality and illegality. The phrase *mores maiorum* (traditions of the ancestors) appears repeatedly in ancient Roman writings. Cicero (106-43 B.C.E.) sums up in

Topica the components of law; in explaining the type of definition made by enumeration, he says, "One should define the civil law as made up of statutes, decrees of the Senate, judicial decisions, opinions of those learned in the law, edicts of magistrates, custom and equity" (5.28). It is interesting to note that more than five and a half centuries later, the emperor Justinian in his *Institutes* comments, "Daily customs sanctioned by those who use them are like law." He calls it "unwritten law" (I.ii.9).

One aspect of the study of the cultural background of the *Aeneid* has to be the occupations and leisure activities that were typical of the Roman citizen of the last two and a half centuries of the Republic, since it is from this period the first surviving examples of literary activity originated. The aristocratic Romans of the last centuries of the Republic were very concerned about their public image, whether that image rested in their lineage or in the number of clients that came to their doors each morning to declare their dependence. Even Augustus proclaimed his family line from Iulus, another name for Ascanius, Aeneas's son. Having been adopted by Julius Caesar in his will, Octavian (Augustus) inherited the noble lineage claimed by that ancient family. We have to remember that adoption in ancient Rome served a totally different purpose from that it serves in twenty-first-century America. In modern-day society adoption serves largely to protect minors. In Rome, adoption of adults was not uncommon and often served to protect families without children from oblivion after the death of the last male. In the case of Octavius, adoption served to make him not just an heir named in Caesar's will but the legal son of Julius Caesar. The adopted individual (usually male) took on the name of the adoptive father, often changing his own name to an adjective. Hence, after 44 B.C.E. Gaius Octavius became Gaius Julius Caesar Octavianus. That is why historically accurate sources refer to him as Octavius before his adoption and Octavian afterward.

Exposure to the Greek language and literature had an unnatural effect on the development of Roman literature. On one hand, this expo-

sure gave the Romans firsthand experience with the full body of literature of all styles, from epic to drama to history and philosophy, and it
was relatively easy for them to incorporate the developed Greek style
into their own. On the other hand, the Romans distrusted the Greeks.
Many Romans saw Greek culture as extravagant and foreign to the
principles of frugality and moral virtue characteristic of early Rome.
Cato the Elder in the early second century decried the influence of
Greek culture on Roman literature.

Literary Patronage

The primary occupation suitable for a respectable Roman aristocrat was farming; hence the widespread existence of estates (villas)
throughout Italy. A Roman aristocrat would be expected to enhance his
reputation through his exploits in war and in the forum. He could read
literature in his leisure time, but writing as a career (particularly the
composition of poetry) was not suitable. By the first century B.C.E. Roman aristocrats were well-educated in both Greek and Latin. We do not
know, however, how far down the social ladder literacy extended (even
in Latin). The theaters were well frequented, but, of course, attendance
at dramas does not involve the ability to read. Romans normally read
out loud; therefore, an illiterate populace could still have become
familiar with literature through public recitals.

Roman poets (writing genres other than drama) did not receive
monetary compensation for their work. If they were not financially
self-sufficient they depended on the support of aristocratic *patrones*,
who provided them with the necessities to live and sometimes much
more than that. In addition, these patrons often introduced their client
poets to the elite of Rome who were the intended audience. This arrangement fit neatly into the Roman practice of the patron-client relationship. Patrons would support and defend clients, who in turn would
show up daily on the patrons' doorsteps (often before dawn) to pay
daily homage and to receive the daily dole.

The literary circle that developed around Gaius Maecenas and included, among others, the great poets Horace and Vergil was not a new phenomenon in Rome. Livius Andronicus had probably been brought to Rome by a Roman aristocrat as a slave and freed. The same is probably true of the comedian Terence. In all likelihood Naevius had the assistance of the Claudii Marcelli in producing his plays, and Ennius celebrated the exploits of G. Fulvius Nobilior, his patron, after having been brought to Rome by Marcus Porcius Cato. Literary clients had an advantage over other clients—they could pay public homage to their patrons through dedications or by singing their praises in their poems. Horace addressed his first *Epode* to Maecenas, and his ninth *Epode* was a celebration of Octavian's victory at Actium. Vergil praised Augustus in the *Aeneid* (6.791): "Here is the man, here is the one whom you hear promised rather often, Augustus Caesar, offspring of a god, who will found a golden age in Latium's fields once ruled by Saturn." Horace and Vergil had already benefited from the munificence of Gaius Asinius Pollio, and Vergil extols Pollio's consulship of 40 B.C.E. in the fourth *Eclogue*.

Much has been written concerning how much Vergil intended to make Augustus the model for his Aeneas. Maecenas, the influential adviser of Augustus, was indeed supporting Vergil, and the poet must have felt at least a certain degree of indebtedness to Augustus, since ultimately the *princeps* (literally "prince," used as an honorific of the emperor) was his patron. Study of the effects that the system of patronage had on Vergil's character makes it is clear that Aeneas was a far from perfect model. His character develops as the epic progresses. Although Vergil echoes a similar passage in the *Odyssey*, he must have surprised many in his audience with the first lines Aeneas speaks in the middle of the introductory storm: "O three and four times happy those whose lot it was to die before the faces of their fathers under the lofty walls of Troy!" (1.94-95). Did Vergil really intend to identify with Augustus a hero whose first lines are the equivalent of "I wish I were dead"?

Aeneas is human, the founder of the Roman race. He has his faults, even at the end of the poem when he succumbs to emotion and slays Turnus because he sees that Turnus now wears the belt of Pallas, the youth Turnus has slain. But, after all, Augustus, in his attempts to initiate an era of peace, the Pax Augusta, had to face the fact—a fact of which his people were fully aware—that he had contributed as much as anyone else to the bloody decade that preceded his rule.

Literary Background

The term "Hellenistic," meaning "like Greek," is commonly used to describe the Greek culture and literature flourishing between the death of Alexander the Great (323 B.C.E.) and the end of the first century, when Rome had completely conquered the Mediterranean basin. After the death of Alexander many cities of the area "Hellenized"—that is, they adopted Greek culture. The center of this movement (but not the only great hub of activity) was the city of Alexandria in Egypt, where Ptolemy had built a great library and scholarship and literary criticism flourished.

Some critics have argued that the Hellenistic age marked a decline in the quality of Greek literary production. Although it is true that there were no successors who equaled the output of the great tragedians Aeschylus, Sophocles, and Euripides or the historians Herodotus and Thucydides, Hellenistic writers went off in other directions. Greek culture around the Mediterranean had become much more cosmopolitan, and the writers of the period reflected that view. Tragedies indeed were still written and performed frequently, but poets returned to the lyric genre, which had not flourished for several centuries. Theocritus perfected bucolic poetry that provided the model for Vergil's *Eclogues*. A passion for scholarship and literary analysis provided new areas of exploration. Apollonius of Rhodes even composed an epic *Argonautica*, although it was not the equal of the Homeric poems and seemed more of a scholarly composition.

The influence of Hellenistic literature on Vergil's *Aeneid* can be seen in such elements as the interrelating of past and present; the descriptions of the origins of cities, particularly Rome itself; the bucolic nature of the city of Evander (book 8) and the elegiac nonepic hints in Aeneas's romance with Dido in Carthage (see Hardie 88). Regarding the idea of the *Aeneid*'s presentation of Rome's origins, Hardie notes: "In the most general terms the *Aeneid* is not so much an epic about the hero Aeneas, as about the 'origins' or 'causes' (*aitia*) of a city and its institutions." He refers to the clause noted above: "Until he might found a city."

In the late second century and during the first century B.C.E. Romans who could afford the expense sent their sons to study in one of the centers of literary or scholarly activity, whether it be Athens or Asia Minor or Alexandria. As Sander M. Goldberg notes, "The fascination with Greek culture that comes to dominate second-century Rome brings with it a refusal to be intimidated by its example" (20).

Primary and Secondary Epic

C. S. Lewis, in his wonderful little book titled *A Preface to "Paradise Lost,"* devotes several chapters to the topic of Primary and Secondary Epic. Since his subject will eventually be Milton's great *Paradise Lost*, he discusses epic in both the Greco-Roman and English traditions, including Homer's *Iliad* and *Odyssey* as well as *Beowulf* as primary epic as opposed to Vergil's *Aeneid* and Milton's *Paradise Lost*, which are representative of secondary epic. Lewis states: "I prefer to divide it into Primary Epic and Secondary Epic—the adjectives being purely chronological and implying no judgments of value. The *secondary* here means not 'the second rate', but what comes after, and grows out of, the *primary*" (13).

Essentially, primary epic develops in an oral tradition (whether Homer actually wrote down his epic is irrelevant here—the poems are oral in style). Oral poetry depends on features such as repetition to be comprehended by an audience listening to these poems being sung. The oral poet cannot afford to have listeners "read between the lines" because, as they pause to reflect on some profound statement, they lose the next line as the singer moves on. Secondary epic, in contrast, develops in a literate culture. The writer of secondary epic can weave multiple meanings into the poem, letting the audience "come back for more," since the poem will be available in exactly the same form for future recitations or readings. Vergil capitalizes on this ability by intertwining the various aspects of time—past, present, and future—in his story. Certainly Homer would never have been able to develop a story that carried multiple layers of meaning. As Hardie notes: "Homer is a pan-Hellenic poet and his supreme god Zeus is not tied to any one Greek state. Zeus' Latin equivalent, Jupiter, is the state god of Rome, and the Latin epic tradition became a national epic in a way impossible in Greece" (84).

Epic Poets Before Vergil

Livius Andronicus, a major literary figure in the middle of the third century B.C.E., gained his reputation as a teacher and a playwright (of both tragedies and comedies). Ancient authorities claim that Livius was born in Tarentum in southern Italy and brought to Rome as a slave when Tarentum was conquered by the Romans in about 270 B.C.E. His dramas, the first of which appeared about 240 B.C.E., seem to have been original compositions of Italian character. Livius is credited with essentially being the first writer of Latin literature. Goldberg, however, persuasively argues that Livius could not have produced his dramas in a vacuum, noting that in the fragments of his tragedies that still exist, Livius shows "considerable skill in adapting the quantitative metres of Greek drama to Latin requirements." Goldberg goes on to note that "successful performance required actors sufficiently skilled to speak and sing complex Latin from the stage" (16).

Livius's translation of the *Odyssey*, however, deserves attention as the first recorded attempt to take a major work in the Greek canon and adapt it to Rome. Livius kept the Greek title of the work, calling it *Odussia*, but changed the hero's name from Odysseus to Ulixes. He refrained from attempting to force his Latin into the Greek dactylic hexameter (a quantitative meter, as all Greek meters were) and instead employed the Latin Saturnian meter, usually reserved for invocations and based on an accentual rhythm (that is, using the accents of the words for the beat). It is important to note here that the Latin language (much like English) relies on accented stress for its beat, whereas the Greek language uses the "quantity" of the syllables—whether they are long or short—for more of a musical determination of accent. This incongruity of the Latin language and Greek meters serves to highlight the accomplishment of later writers in the Latin tongue who mastered the weaving of an accented language with quantitative meters, as did the Roman writers after the middle of the second century B.C.E.

Another epic poet who preceded Vergil was Gnaeus Naevius, who was born in Campania (west central Italy) in about 270 B.C.E. and became a playwright, composing tragedies (probably on both Greek and Italian models) and comedies (on the Italian model). He also wrote the first Latin epic, a poem in Saturnian meter on the First Punic War, *Carmen belli Poenici*. Selections of this work were quoted by Romans for more than a century. Naevius was famous for his criticism of certain aristocratic families of his day and was probably imprisoned at some point for libel. He died in exile in the Phoenician city of Utica on the North African coast. Unfortunately, most of Naevius's *Punic Wars* has been lost; only fragments have survived. Naevius seems to have introduced his account of the First Punic War with an account that traced the legendary beginnings of both Rome and Carthage.

Vergil owed a great debt to Naevius, and some ancient commentators accused Vergil of a lack of originality. We can see for ourselves an example of Vergil's adaptation of Naevius by comparing a line of the older poet about Quintus Fabius Maximus Cunctator, the famous opponent of Hannibal, with Vergil's use of almost a direct quote. Naevius wrote: "unus homo nobis cunctando restituit rem" (One man by delaying restored the state to us). Vergil's account is "unus qui nobis cunctando restituis rem." However, the context is totally different. In the Underworld, Aeneas is viewing from afar with his father the long line of famous Romans who are waiting to ascend to the upper world to begin their lives, and when Anchises sees the famous general he exclaims, "Tu Maximus es." When that address is added, Vergil's statement becomes: "You are Maximus, who alone restore the state to us." It is unnecessary to discuss Vergil's use of the present tense here, except to note that the events being described in this scene—namely, the military exploits of Quintus Fabius Maximus—are, from the perspective of Aeneas and Anchises, a millennium in the future. Accordingly, the past tense used by Naevius would have been inappropriate.

Quintus Ennius was born in Rudiae, a town in southern Italy, in 239 B.C.E. Cato took him to Rome in the early second century. We have fragments of his tragedies, but his most important work for the purposes of this discussion is his *Annales*, an epic in hexameters portraying the story of Rome from the time of Aeneas down to his own day. Ennius omitted the First Punic War because Naevius had treated that subject. If we credit Naevius with writing the first original epic in Latin, then we must single out Ennius for presenting the Roman epic in dactylic hexameter, the meter of Homer. Once Ennius adapted the Latin language to hexameter verse, Saturnian verse would never again be considered a fit vehicle for Latin epic.

Goldberg presents an interesting argument that if Ennius had not made the conscious decision to use hexameters, Roman epic might very well "have taken a different path." In making the point that the evolution from Saturnians to hexameters was not inevitable, he praises "the success still discernible in the fragments of Naevius' poem" (20). As it happened, Ennius did employ hexameters, and Roman epic was forever changed. Ennius's *Annales* was considered the literary masterpiece for almost two centuries until Vergil took on the challenge of writing the definitive epic of Rome. Some of Ennius's lines were quoted as the summary of what the spirit of Rome was all about, such as "Moribus antiquis res stat Romana virisque." Ennius's balance in putting key words at both ends of the sentence was a model of style. The line loses much of its effect in translation: "The Roman state stands on its tradition and its men."

From the title *Annales*, it seems that Ennius followed the model of the records kept by the *Pontifex Maximus*, which followed a strict chronological order in yearly divisions. It also seems that in their accounts of the early history of Rome's founding, both Naevius and Ennius ignore the four and a half centuries between the traditional dates of the fall of Troy and the founding of Rome. They both declare that Romulus is the grandson of Aeneas, dropping out the series of kings of Alba Longa, already in the Roman tradition, to fill that chronological gap. Servius Honoratus, in his *Commentary on the "Aeneid" of Vergil*, says, referring to line 273 of book 1: "Naevius and Ennius relate that Romulus, the founder of the city, is the grandson of Aeneas by his daughter."

Clearly the environment that surrounded Vergil influenced the development of his poetic output. No writer composes in a vacuum; all writers are affected to some extent by their times and by those who came before them—it is the great writers who can synthesize the best of the past and the present and produce something new and better.

Works Cited

Clausen, Wendell. *Vergil's "Aeneid" and the Tradition of Hellenistic Poetry.* Berkeley: U of California P, 1987.

Goldberg, Sander M. "The Early Republic: The Beginnings to 90 B.C." *A Companion to Latin Literature.* Ed. Stephen Harrison. Malden, MA: Blackwell, 2005.

Hardie, Philip. "Narrative Epic." *A Companion to Latin Literature.* Ed. Stephen Harrison. Malden, MA: Blackwell, 2005.

Lewis, C. S. *A Preface to "Paradise Lost."* New York: Oxford UP, 1942.

Dante's Vergil in Limbo

Fiorentina Russo

As Dante's first guide through Hell and Purgatory, Vergil plays a major role in the pilgrim's journey to salvation. His presence in *La Divina Commedia* (*The Divine Comedy*) is indeed essential not only for the salutary effects that he has on Dante and his journey but also for what he represents. Vergil was the poet whom Dante admired and imitated most. He represented the noblest of qualities that a human being could attain without the intervention of Christian revelation. Dante also saw in Vergil an embodiment of the Roman Empire, created by God as one of the two institutions—along with the Church—whose duty was to guide humankind to live a happy life on earth. Dante saw Vergil as an emblem of human philosophy and reason. As poet, Vergil describes in book 6 of his *Aeneid* Aeneas's descent into Hades, the most direct precedent for Dante's *katabasis*, or descent to the underworld. While the concept of a journey to the netherworld is an archaic motif, Dante's *katabasis* is closely connected to Vergil's model. These are some of the reasons Dante chose Vergil as a guide for his own descent into hell. There is, however, at least one other reason that has received little critical attention, if any; this reason will emerge from a recounting of the first exchange between Dante and Vergil in *Inferno* 1 of the *Comedy*.

As Dante wanders up the mountain of Purgatory, three beasts bar his way. The most pernicious is the She-Wolf. As the frightened poet is about to flee, the ghostly figure of Vergil appears. He explains what the nature of the She-Wolf is—the reader will learn that she represents avarice—and how she is responsible for a corrupt society. One day, Vergil announces, a Greyhound will come to chase the She-Wolf back to hell. The Greyhound, of course, is an allegorical figure for a savior who would save an unhappy Italian peninsula and restore happiness on earth. Vergil then tells Dante that he needs to follow a route other than the one he has thus far undertaken and that he, Vergil, will be his guide on such a journey, with a more powerful guide taking over where Vergil cannot go. The Roman poet's words are basically a revisitation of his famous *Eclogue* 4, in which he prophesies the arrival of a child of Justice who will reestablish the Golden Age, that fabled happy time enjoyed by humankind at the onset of time. Christians identify it as the Earthly Paradise, but classical antiquity knew it as the Golden Age in which the god Saturn reigned along with Astraea, the goddess of justice. As avarice entered into the minds of men, Astraea fled, leaving behind a society of corruption.

Thus Vergil's first utterances in the *Comedy* establish a link with the poem that was most responsible for establishing his reputation as *vates* (poet-seer), and even sorcerer, that was commonly held in the Middle Ages. His announcement of the arrival of the savior-child, despite his own original authorial intentionality, was interpreted during Dante's times as a prophecy of the arrival of Christ, yet another reason for Dante's selection of Vergil as guide. In a more general sense, however, Dante chose Vergil for the fact that he had become known as the poet of the Golden Age. Although the topic of the Golden Age had been treated by a number of poets, including Hesiod, Ovid, and Aratus, they dealt with it as a *laus temporis actii*, a praise of a time forever lost. Vergil offered a more hopeful scenario, of a recapture of such a time, shifting the focus from the past to the future. Vergil's poem claims that the happiness that reigned in the Golden Age was not lost forever, but would return thanks to the intervention of an unnamed child (*puer*). This window of hope for the future motivated Dante, who felt Vergil's understanding most suitable for his *Comedy*, as he intended not solely to condemn societal disarray but to offer a corrective for a more solid society based on justice, thus offering a blueprint for the salvation of humankind. Dante delineates such a plan in his famous letter to Can Grande della Scala, where he maps out his agenda for the narrative.

This is the same hope that Vergil expresses in his first appearance in Dante's drama of salvation. Thus Dante immediately associates Vergil with the idea of a *restauratio*, or restoration of humankind to its prelapsarian origins of happiness. Vergil in short is the poet of the pagan Golden Age, and this is one of the additional important reasons Dante chose him as guide. Dante, as will be shown, intended to take up the baton as poet of a Christian Golden Age. His vision, illuminated by revelation, will tread where Vergil was unable to because of the limitations inherent in his paganism. In essence, then, the relationship between Vergil and Dante will be one of tension, akin to that between a father and a son or a teacher and a disciple—a relationship between a leader whose guiding powers eventually will wane and the one to whom he must surrender leadership. As in all such relationships, sons replace their fathers, disciples expand on their teachers' work, and new leaders emerge with more informed visions of the world.

In the following pages, this tension between teacher and disciple will be explored, exposing the positive and negative polarities that eventually result in a shift of Dante's initial position regarding Vergil. The process necessarily will include subtle changes designed to show the natural limitations of the Roman poet and the expansion of the Christian poet's understanding. Dante, the all-knowing poet, casts himself in the role of *scriba Dei* (God's scribe) while demonstrating the superiority of Christian knowledge, based on Revelation, undermining the pagan poet's understanding. This is a balancing act that only a poet such as Dante could handle, for such undermining occurs despite his great admiration and affection for Vergil.

The parameters of the relationship are clearly marked from the beginning, for both the positive and the negative elements that characterize it. When Vergil tells the pilgrim that he is the poet who sang of Aeneas, Dante immediately recognizes him and, unable to contain his astonishment, seeks confirmation, asking if Vergil is indeed that fountain of knowledge that spread so far and wide. As will happen elsewhere, Dante formulates his question echoing the *Aeneid*. When Dante asks, Are you that Vergil?, he practically repeats Dido's first words to Aeneas: "Tune ille Aeneas quem" (Are you not that Aeneas whom . . .). The *Aeneid* as subtext demonstrates that Dante knew the poem and had devoted a great deal of time to studying it—indeed, he knew it by heart, as emerges in the course of the narrative. Dante openly manifests his admiration and indebtedness to his master, who was for him the teacher and author from whom he learned the beautiful style that brought him honor and fame.

Dante recognizes the debt owed to his poetic father and acknowledges him as an *auctoritas*, or textual "authority." This tribute to Vergil is rivaled in the poem perhaps only by the episode in Limbo in *Inferno* 4, where the inhabitants of Limbo welcome back Vergil as *altissimo poeta* (the loftiest poet), and in *Purgatorio* 21, where the Roman poet Statius, who considered Vergil his teacher and who often in the *Comedy* serves as an alter ego for Dante, upon learning that he is in the presence of his great master, refers to the *Aeneid* as his "mother" (*mamma*) and "nursemaid" (*nutrice*), whose sparks inflamed him and a sea of readers with great love.

When Dante realizes that he is standing before his poetic father he is awestruck. His affection for Vergil never wavers in the course of the journey even though his initial confidence in his guide's abilities is shaken at times. At the beginning Vergil is the all-knowing sage, but as the journey proceeds Dante cannot help but notice the limitations in Vergil's knowledge and power. The parameters of Dante's perspective on Vergil are evident from their first conversation. When Vergil begins to speak, his words seem to betray Dante's bias, a hidden agenda of sorts. Thus the Roman tells Dante that he was born *sub Iulio* (under Caesar's rule), adding, "at the time of false and lying gods." Vergil's repudiation of his pagan beliefs seems somewhat gratuitous, more likely dictated by Dante's requirement to balance the positive and negative in his relationship with the poet of the *Aeneid*. Dante's effusive praise of his master is here undermined by Vergil's admission of his shortcoming. Thus praise is granted only to be later retracted. Stated differently, the two voices belong to Dante, the all-knowing poet, and Dante, the pilgrim who is experiencing the journey for the first time. Dante, for all intents and purposes, knows exactly that Vergil must give up his role as guide and teacher. He is bound to lose his influence over his charge, and his power will eventually have to wane. Dante, the *scriba Dei*, must therefore program Vergil's decline. In Dante's *Comedy*, Vergil is therefore a paradoxical figure who makes it possible for the pilgrim to attain salvation while remaining outside that sphere of privilege. Naturally this does not occur suddenly, as Teodolinda Barolini notes in *Dante's Poets*, observing that Vergil

> does not lose his authority all at once, but in a more subtle fashion, step by step from the moment he enters the poem. When Vergil arrives, an hourglass is set, and the grains of sand fall one by one until, in *Purgatorio* XXX, the glass is empty. (202)

As the journey unfolds, Vergil's powers prove to be sufficient, with few exceptions, to shield Dante from the dangers encountered of Hell's nine circles. Vergil stands between Dante and those who would harm him as a protecting father, chastising Dante's antagonists into submission to God's will. Vergil's authority comes straight from Heaven (through Beatrice's intercession) as he reminds the recalcitrant guardians of Hell with a refrain bearing the power of an incantation: "vuolsi così colà dove si puote/ciò che si vuole, e più non dimandare" (Thus it is willed there where Will and Might are one and ask no more!). Vergil uses this formulaic mantra in *Inferno* 3 when Charon, the infernal ferryman, challenges Dante's presence in Hell, and again in canto 5 when Minos, who sentences the sinners to their rightful circles, objects to Dante's passage and tries to undermine Vergil's authority.

The poet of the *Aeneid*, who in book 6 wrote of the descent of Aeneas into Hades to seek his father's shade, knows all the characters of the classical underworld and deals with them authoritatively and effectively, in most cases. In more than a dozen encounters, he paraphrases the aforementioned magic formula. He does so with Cerberus, the three-headed hound of hell, and with the Minotaur, Pluto, and Phlegias, and other infernal figures. It is interesting to point out that

Dante, in structuring these infernal confrontations, and in many other cases, used the *Aeneid* as a model. In this case, the confrontations are modeled on the episode when Aeneas descends to the underworld and must show the Golden Bough to the Sibyl in order to be admitted. Vergil's mantra is basically a substitute for the Golden Bough. The Vergilian episode is also used to provide the actual structure of the encounters. Thus Vergil's intervention successfully guards Dante from harm and guarantees the continuation of his journey.

In the Inferno, Vergil's limitations emerge when he encounters realities that are unknown to him because of his pre-Christian birth. Two episodes provide sufficient examples. The first is when the devils refuse to let Dante and his guide enter the City of Dis in *Inferno* 9. Vergil does not know what devils are and is unable to conquer their stubbornness with the usual refrain. His failure causes him moments of self-doubt and apprehension that shake Dante's confidence in him. A higher authority, in the form of an angel, must come to solve the impasse and scatter the devils. The potentially disastrous consequences of becoming petrified by the glance of the lurking Medusa are avoided, but the character Dante notes down in memory that Vergil's power is limited and will remind him later of it.

The second episode that underscores Vergil's lack of savvy has to do with his knowledge of the topography of Hell. In the *bolgia* of barratry in *Inferno* 21, Vergil is easily fooled by the devil Malacoda, who tells him that there is a bridge leading out of the area. Vergil is confident that the bridge is there, having seen it during his previous descent into Hell, but when he and Dante approach the place where the bridge should be they see it as *ruine*, a heap of rubble. Malacoda lied—the bridge was destroyed by the earthquake that accompanied Christ's crucifixion. Vergil's reliance on his own memory and his lack of knowledge of that momentous event—Christ's Passion—have caused him to fail.

In Purgatory, however, Vergil's lack of knowledge becomes more noticeable. He does not know the way up the mountain and is forced to ask some of the souls. He seems to lose sight of the goal at hand and is chastised by Cato for dallying at the foot of the mountain instead of leading Dante to purge his sins. Vergil fails to alert Dante about the dangers of the Hag-Siren in *Purgatorio* 19. Again, as in *Inferno* 9, a higher power must come to Dante's rescue: a Holy Woman (*donna santa e presta*) alerts the dreaming poet to the real nature of the stinking Hag while simultaneously chastising Vergil for his laxity.

Perhaps the most poignant admission of Vergil's limitations comes when he finally manages to bring his pilgrim to the river that separates them from the Earthly Paradise. There, having completed his task, he crowns and miters Dante master of his own destiny and admits his limitations: "se' venuto in parte/dov'io per me più oltre non discerno" (You have reached a place where on my own I can no longer see further). Vergil acknowledges that his vision is not sufficient to see beyond the river that separates the lower part of Purgatory and the Earthly Paradise. This is the point of separation between Dante and Vergil, between the Christian and the pagan sage.

The poet of the pagan Golden Age is not allowed to enter the Christian equivalent of that primal time and must return to his place in Limbo. And in fact before Dante realizes it, Vergil vanishes, leaving the poet distraught. As Rachel Jacoff notes, the poet expresses his grief for the loss of Vergil in a manner reminiscent of Orpheus's cry for Eurydice, repeated three times as she returned to Hades. Here Vergil's name is repeated three times in the span of a *terzina* that is charged with the subtext of a creature that, like Persephone and other mythical characters, escaped for a time from its confines to return to its predestined, infernal abode. Vergil, too, like Euridice, must exit the narrative in the backdrop of the echo of his name to return to his eternal place in Limbo (135).

Vergil's disappearance from the scene and his return to Limbo confirm once again that he is a figure of paradox. His character is conditioned by tragic fragilities and shortcomings that Dante goes to great pains to underscore throughout his poem from the beginning. The most consequential of Vergil's shortcomings, from the Christian poet's point of view, is his pagan status, which determines his collocation in Limbo. Through no fault of his own, Vergil is incomplete; his lack of Christianity renders his vision cloudy and thus in need of a corrective.

Vergil's gradual inadequacy to fulfill his role as guide, which reveals itself along the journey through Purgatory, becomes even more evident with the appearance of the poet Statius, who fills the gap in knowledge displayed by Vergil and essentially assumes authority. This is clearly demonstrated when Vergil is unsure as to what road to take to proceed up the mountain and Statius nods to confirm that he has guessed correctly. From this point forward Statius is the soul who has the right knowledge. As many critics have realized, Dante's choice of Statius was in function of the Vergilian character. Paul Renucci asserts that Dante included Statius for the greater glory of Vergil, on account of the wonderful tribute he paid to the Roman poet (333). Barolini, however, believes that "whatever works to Vergil's advantage in Dante's poem also works simultaneously to his detriment . . . Statius' presence both glorifies Vergil and undercuts him" (262).

Dante's introduction of Statius prepares the reader for Vergil's eventual disappearance. Statius is in fact an intermediary figure whose presentation in *Purgatorio* 21 parallels the first appearance of Vergil in *Inferno* 1, perhaps to underscore the two poets' importance as Dante's guides. But, whereas Vergil introduces himself as having lived under Julius "at the time of false and lying gods," Statius volunteers that he lived when good Titus avenged the wounds from which the blood sold by Judas was spilled. The difference between Vergil and Statius emerges from these two statements. Vergil was a pagan and Statius is a Christian in the poem, and this endows the latter poet with greater knowledge. From the moment he appears, he assumes the role of guide, explaining the significance of the *tremoto* (earthquake) that shook the mountain of Purgatory that had puzzled Vergil and Dante. The fact that Statius calls himself a famous poet who was once without faith, which parallels the *famoso poeta* addressed to Vergil in *Inferno* 1, is also of importance, as the term until this point has been almost exclusively reserved for Vergil and because Dante is creating a kind of hierarchy here that goes from the older pagan master, Vergil, to the Silver Latin poet, Statius, and finally to the new poet of the Christian world, Dante himself. It is not the first time in the *Comedy* when Dante views himself in a relationship within such a hierarchy of poets. In Limbo, he asserts proudly that he occupied sixth place in the procession that formed when Vergil introduced him to the great men of antiquity. There Dante says that he was sixth among such wisdom (*tra cotanto senno*). In Purgatory, he is third in succession to Vergil and Statius. But in both cases, he is a forerunner among his contemporaries as the new Christian poet who possesses the poetic gifts of his master Vergil and the faith of Statius.

This hierarchical descent among Vergil, Statius, and Dante has a distinct familial feel to it. Statius addresses the *Aeneid* in terms of endearment as mother and nursemaid, and when he realizes that he is facing Vergil himself, bows to embrace his feet. Vergil in turn humbly reciprocates Statius's love by calling him brother, *frate*. We have already seen that Vergil is frequently addressed by Dante as father, thus it is not surprising that Statius too would refer to Dante as son in *Purgatorio* 25. Hence the triad of poets represents in a symbolic way three generations closely linked as father and son.

The kinship among the three poets is underscored by the debt of gratitude each generation owes to the previous one. Statius owes a tripartite debt to Vergil: he chose to end his prodigality, punished in the same terrace as avarice, after reading the Roman poet's condemnation of avarice in the *Aeneid*, "Quid non mortalia pectora cogis, auri sacra fames?" which Dante conveniently changes to "Why cannot you, o holy hunger for gold, restrain the appetite of mortals?"—he became a poet because of his love for the *Aeneid*, and finally he became a Christian when Vergil in the Fourth *Eclogue* prophesied the arrival of a new Golden Age through the action of a new progeny descended from heaven.

The three poets are bound even more by the nature of their poetic goals. Dante regards Vergil as the quintessential poet of the Golden Age, not only for his Fourth *Eclogue* but also for the reference to Augustus as emperor under whose rule Rome would experience a period of peace and tranquillity. Augustus would bring back the goddess Astraea, who had fled from earth because of the avarice guiding men's actions. Justice, closely intertwined with the concept of the Golden Age in Vergil's mind, would return. In his *Thebaid*, Statius ascribes a role similar to that of the Roman emperor for his hero, Theseus: to restore order and peace in the corrupt society of Thebes. In both cases, the intent is the restoration of a lawless society through the reestablishment of Justice. This is also the goal for which Dante strives in writing the *Comedy*.

The analogous roles played by Vergil, Statius, and Dante in regard to the corrupt state of society are underscored by Christopher Kleinhenz:

> All are concerned with the ordering of the temporal sphere: Virgil with the establishment of Empire; Statius with the restoration of justice in the earthly city and Dante with renovatio imperii. . . . The sort of allegorization to which the Thebaid was subjected in the Middle Ages points to order and peace as being the desired goals of earthly society, and these can only be achieved through the advent of the peacemaker, the bringer of justice, figured by Theseus. (45)

Dante's self-assigned role is analogous to that of his two father figures: he will be the prophet of a Christian Golden Age. The new Christian poet, whose superior vision, sustained by the grace of God and illuminated by Revelation, will write a new chapter in humankind's quest for a happy life. The contents of Vergil's Messianic poetry will be glossed and corrected by Dante, whose vision continues to penetrate deeper into the mysteries of God as he approaches the *Paradiso*. Dante embraced his role as the poet of a Christian Golden Age, and, like his precursors, he saw himself as a promoter of justice, and the reestablishment of that justice on earth was the centerpiece of his political thought. Dante believed that the only way to eradicate avarice, the main source of injustice on earth, was through the restoration of the two institutions that God himself set up for the guidance of humankind, the Empire and the Church. In the *Monarchia* Dante clearly states that Providence proposes two goals for man:

> The first is the happiness in this life, which consists in the exercise of his own powers and is typified by the earthly paradise; the second is the happiness of eternal life, which consists in the enjoyment of the divine countenance (which man cannot attain to of his own power but only by the aid of divine illumination) and is typified by the heavenly paradise. We attain to the first by means of philosophical teaching. . . . We arrive at the second by means of spiritual teaching (which transcends human reason). (3.16.7-8)

This makes it clear why Vergil must disappear once the role assigned to him is accomplished. He has led Dante to the Earthly Paradise, as far as human reason can go. Statius, an inferior poet who, being Christian, possesses superior knowledge, replaces Vergil and makes the transition between the ancient pagan world and the Christian world smoother. In the end the former too will disappear, leaving Dante alone as the new poet of the Christian Golden Age. For Vergil and the other ancient poets the ultimate goal was to reach the garden of delights imagined through the Golden Age, but for Dante the Earthly Paradise was but a necessary stop on the way to that unknown realm that only a Christian poet could imagine: Paradise.

Readers of the *Comedy* and in particular those new to Dante's cosmology rarely react passively to the collocation of Vergil in Limbo. The absence of Vergil from the third canticle does all but heal the wound for those who question Dante's choice to situate Vergil in an infernal realm. Despite the medieval lore that hailed Vergil as a prophet who in some medieval traditions was granted salvation, Dante denies his guide the eternal solace of paradise. While one may question whether or not such lore was available to Dante, the fact that Vergil is not saved is important. Dante uses his authorial discretion to grant salvation to other characters who were not Christians—the examples of Cato, Statius, Ripheus, and even the emperor Trajan are marked as exceptions to the rule. These choices make readers more puzzled regarding the age-old Vergil equation.

The paradox is made even more astonishing by the fact that the cases of Statius and Ripheus are connected with Vergil in Dante's work. Statius, by virtue of Dante's pen, converted to Christianity after reading Vergil's announcement of the arrival of a child who would bring forth a new Golden Age on earth. Ripheus, a rather minor character of the *Aeneid*, was a comrade of Aeneas who joined him in the defense of Troy before the city fell to the Greeks. Vergil immortalized him as an emblem of justice and as a hero unrewarded by the gods for his virtue: "cadit et Ripheus, iustissimus unus/ qui fuit in Teucris et servantissimus aequi/ dis aliter visum" (Ripheus also fell, one of the most just of all Trojans, the most faithful preserver of equity; but the gods decided otherwise). Dante, the pilgrim, cannot contain his disbelief on seeing Ripheus occupying a place as the fifth light forming the eye of the eagle in the heaven of Jupiter with the souls of the just. But Dante, the *scriba Dei*, chose Ripheus because of Vergil's encomium of the Trojan hero. Indeed, Dante repaired the injustice of Ripheus's actions that went unrewarded. For the *scriba Dei*, Ripheus's presence there is meant to underscore the seeming randomness of divine election. Vergil's words are credited for saving others, but not himself. The fact that Statius's conversion may be a figment of Dante's imagination only drives home Dante's authorial discretion in both cases.

Dante also elected the pagan Cato, who loved justice more than life, to be a sort of guardian of Purgatory and included among those virtuous pagans who are saved the emperor Trajan, who in medieval tradition was often granted a felicitous Christian reward, despite his pre-Christian birth. Here Dante bends to medieval tradition, whereas he does not do so in favor of Vergil. The question of God's mysterious criteria for salvation, which surfaces as early as *Inferno* 2, surpasses virtually any human prophecy, yet the pagan seer Vergil was able to foresee the lot of Ripheus. Hence Vergil's poetic vision crosses paths with divine foreknowledge, and this fact serves to salt the wounds of his own tragedy, as Dante, through his representation of such ironies of salvation history, defies the Christian theology that makes clear that faith in Christ alone can gain a man entry into Paradise. Once again Dante leans on Vergil's textual authority in the *Aeneid* to coin something as novel as Ripheus's salvation.

If ardor for justice is indeed the fundamental key to Ripheus's salvation, it is important to note that Dante himself attributes that very quality to Vergil's epic protagonist, Aeneas, who is from the very onset of the *Comedy* and in Vergil's own words, "quel giusto figliuol d'Anchise" (that just offspring of Anchises). Dante's corrective on his master Vergil extends itself to Vergil's hero, Aeneas, who despite his *pietas* and ardor for justice in Vergil's epic, shares a place in limbo with his bard. What is perhaps even more surprising is the great absence from the *Comedy* of Augustus, the emperor to whom the *Aeneid* is dedicated and the emblem of the Pax Romana, which Vergil credited for the return of the Golden Age, one harmonious world. Apart from the encomiastic references to *Ottavian* within Dante's narrative, Augustus does not occupy a physical place in Dante's *Comedy*. He instead is conjured in Dante's encomium to his own political hero, Henry VII of Luxembourg, in whom Dante had placed his hopes for the fate of the troubled Italian peninsula. Henry could not fulfill Dante's aspirations, owing to Florentine and papal opposition and his untimely death in 1313, but the emperor will be hailed in the *Paradiso* as the *alma agosta* (the Augustan soul) who, in the fullness of time, along with Dante, will take his rightful place among the coveted seats of the Empyrean along with the other blessed souls.

Thus Vergil, along with the two figures, literary and historical, through which he defines himself in the narrative, his epic hero, Aeneas, and his political Golden Age hero, Augustus, are all destined for a place, at best, among the elect souls of Limbo. Instead Dante, simultaneously poet and protagonist of his own epic, and his monarch, Henry VII, whom he hails in his *Epistles* as a new Augustus of a new Golden Age, will both reside in the Empyrean in the fullness of eternity. Readers may wonder why Dante reserved such harsh treatment for Vergil. Scholars such as Barolini have glossed the curious treatment of Vergil in light of the poet's aforementioned role as a figure for paradox in the *Comedy* as well as the dynamics of the Dante-Vergil-Statius triad, noting Dante's pitting of his two poetic precursors, Vergil and Statius, in a way that diminishes and undermines Vergil throughout the narrative (200). I posit that this undermining emerges from Dante's own agenda in the *Comedy*, springing from his self-proclaimed role as *scriba Dei*, who sets out to show the way through the poetry of his *Comedy* a Christian Golden Age, as a political and social restoration after the death of Henry VII was no longer possible. If Italy could not be brought into a new era of justice by the action of a monarch, at least the way to it could be shown through poetry. The *Comedy* could serve as a blueprint for the establishment of Dante's new Christian Golden Age.

Works Cited

Barolini, Teodolinda. *Dante's Poets: Textuality and Truth in the Comedy*. Princeton, NJ: Princeton UP, 1984.

Jacoff, Rachel. "Intertextualities in Arcadia: *Purgatorio* 30.49-51." *The Poetry of Allusion: Virgil and Ovid in Dante's "Commedia."* Ed. Rachel Jacoff and Jeffrey T. Schnapp. Stanford, CA: Stanford UP, 1991. 131-44.

Kleinhenz, Christopher. "Virgil, Statius, and Dante: An Unusual Trinity." *Lectura Dantis Newberryana*. Vol. 1. Ed. Paolo Cherchi and Antonio C. Mastrobuono. Evanston, IL: Northwestern UP, 1988. 37-55.

Renucci, Paul. *Dante disciple et juge du monde gréco-latin*. Paris: Les Belles Lettres, 1954.

Critical Reception of the *Aeneid*_____
Kathleen Marks

The *Aeneid* had enormous advantages for enthusiastic critical acceptance even before its publication. After all, the emperor Augustus himself had commissioned it. Augustus wished to create a pseudo founding document of the Roman state that he was in the process of transforming from a republican to an imperial model. He wanted a literary adjunct to his marble city, the Urbs whose public buildings he had caused to metamorphose from mud brick to precious stone. To this architectural mythology, Augustus also wished to supply ancient origins that connected Rome and its population with Mycenaean culture as Romans knew it through the prism of the Homeric epics. Vergil, by using the familiar mythology that had currency even before Homer and his world of the eighth century B.C.E., made this possible. Vergil gave mongrel Rome, a state whose ethnic backgrounds included Etruscan, Oscan, Umbrian, tribal Italic, and Greek, a pedigree traceable to Venus and Mars, and Romans were grateful for this.

The *Aeneid* obviously meant much to the Roman Empire. It served the purposes of the Augustan Pax Romana. As Rome was on the ascendant through the imperial model Augustus had designed, so was the *Aeneid*. It instantly became the primary text of the *grammatici*, the "grammarians" whose primary schools instructed the boys of families that could afford the tuition. It quickly became a model for rhetoricians, who admired its elegance and who educated the young men about to enter public life.

The appearance of the *Aeneid* signaled an important shift in emphasis from the *controversiae* and *suasoriae*, the historical and theoretical exercises that prepared one for the legal arguments of the courts, to Latinate literary elegance even native speakers had never dreamed the language could achieve. One can hardly appreciate the daunting task Vergil faced in attempting to adapt the relatively rustic Latin language to a Homeric template. He succeeded brilliantly after nearly fourteen years of composition, in everyone's estimation but his own. Vergil's deathbed wish was to destroy the *Aeneid*. Only the personal intervention of Augustus saved it, and it was Augustus who selected Lucius Varius Rufus and Plotius Tucca, friends of Vergil sympathetic to the poet's wishes, to edit the poem.

The *Aeneid* has continued to influence Western civilization's understanding of political and communal life, its notions of public versus private responsibility, and even the supposedly modern perception that a nation's strength arises from diversity. Contemporary notions such as nation building, manifest destiny, and justice were also influenced by this most important work. The *Aeneid* is thus not merely an important text for the ancient world; it has remained significant for almost every era, and one of its hallmark themes, most readers would agree, is the meaning, possibility, value, and costs of *civilization* itself.

The *Aeneid* had an immediate, positive, and enduring reception in the Roman world. It remained a pillar of the school curriculum from the first century B.C.E. right through the fifth century, more than a century after Alaric had plundered the city and Constantine had divided the Empire, making Constantinople the real locus of power. Rome by then had become a sad shadow of its former self, but the idea of Rome survived and did so primarily through the *Aeneid*.

Vergil was already a well-known author when Augustus entrusted him with the important task of writing imperial Latin epic. The emperor's only reservation would have been that Vergil's fame, such as it was in approximately 25 B.C.E., was limited to pastoral lyric. His *Eclogues* were ten relatively short poems in the mode of the Greek poet Theocritus (c. 308-260 B.C.E.), while his *Georgics* resembles the seventh-century B.C.E. didactic farmer's almanac *Erga kai Hemerai* (*Works and Days*) of Hesiod. As impressive as these early efforts were, they were no guarantee that their author would be successful as a Latinate Homer. One wonders whether Vergil himself had doubts about his ability to bring the vernacular language of Rome into the most exalted of verse genres. It could well be that he undertook the task out of profound gratitude for the emperor's restoration of his family's farm at Andes, a village near Mantua.

The earliest readers read the *Aeneid* largely as a patriotic genealogical history of the Roman people. It was published as the Republic embarked on the Augustan political order that would become the Empire. It thus has an overtly political origin. Read in the way audiences often come to a new work of art, it appears to present an entirely positive portrait of the particulars that would shape the political construct of Rome that was then gradually emerging. As contemporary politicians create favorable political environments through their biographies, so did Vergil create a grand foundation for Rome's humble actuality. More careful reading of what Vergil writes concerning Aeneas as he moves from self-centered needs to those of his community, however, shows that Vergil's praise of Augustan Rome is invariably tempered by admonition.

The *Aeneid* has thus always reached beyond propaganda. It reflects Vergil's own conflicting thoughts about the Roman Empire and considers the nature of a civilization, how it coalesces and how those who form it themselves become civilized. Even the first lines of the *Aeneid* imply that civilizations are continually in the process of reformulation. Aeneas has fled from Troy to Latium, but much has happened in between, including an abortive attempt to graft Troy to Carthage. This might seem to work, but it does so only for Dido, Carthage's queen. It does not, however, satisfy *fatum*, the "fate" even the deities cannot change. Put another way, the opening of the epic has Aeneas finding himself at a crucial point in history. He vacates the known and comfortable past for the unknown but destined future. Romans thus continued to see in the *Aeneid* a narrative of the Empire's own evolution from monarchy and through Republic. They could appreciate it as a document outlining their political community, their social relations, and their ultimate destiny.

Nowhere is this drive more evident than in book 6. Aeneas has traveled to the underworld, and his father reminds him of his task: "But

Romans, don't forget that world dominion/ Is your great craft: peace, and then peaceful customs;/ Sparing the conquered, striking down the haughty" (851-53). One can imagine an imperial Roman (though perhaps not a republican Roman) reading these verses approvingly. Imperial Romans were meant to bring peace and a measure of justice to others; that was their self-identity. One sees this in the Empire's increasingly generous granting of citizenship to its subject peoples.

Because the *Aeneid* summarized the destiny of all Romans, its influence was far-reaching. It was not "popular" in the sense that it had widespread plebeian currency—most of the plebs could not read. It was meant for an educated audience, but Romans of all social strata venerated it for its cultural worth as Christians and Jews privilege the Bible though they may never have read it. And yet it found its way into the popular imagination. Some of its lines appear scratched on walls in Rome and Pompeii, and on everyday objects such as spoons (Horsfall 253ff.)

Even as the Empire weakened, the *Aeneid* remained a constant presence. Unlike many classical texts that were forgotten until their rediscovery during the Renaissance, most of Europe had access to some manuscript version of it. It became allegorized and interpreted through bibliomancy in the Middle Ages, parallel to and perhaps exceeding that of the moralized Ovid. Considering the complexity of the poem's language and literary allusions, it is understandable that early criticism of the *Aeneid* sought to interpret the text's literary, religious, mythological, and historical references. Much of what survives are commentaries, the most important of which is that by Servius, written in the fourth century. Servius's commentary does not offer a general "theory" of the *Aeneid* but rather gives a running series of comments on words, lines, allusions, and rhetorical patterns. For example, one of the comments traces out a description of the goddess Juno and compares it to how other writers have described her. These comments give a good, if limited, indication of a scholarly reading of the text. Another measure of just how influential the *Aeneid* and its author were is the Roman practice of *sortes Vergilianae*, or "Vergilian lots": one would flip through a Vergilian text and find a random quotation to meditate on or act upon.

The *Aeneid*, then, was a source of national pride, literary beauty, and even personal fortune-telling for the ancient Roman world. Its mixture of the personal and the imperial, its embedding of private moments in a meaningful cosmic realm, made it Rome's most important work of literature. Even Saint Augustine, the early Christian writer and bishop of Hippo, reveals in his *Confessions* (c. 398 C.E.) that as a youth he was an avid reader of the *Aeneid* and was especially taken by the romance between Dido and Aeneas, though he quickly damns the falsity of the *Aeneid* as "dulcissimum spectaculum vanitatis" (the sweetest spectacle of vanity). This reflects Augustine's determination to establish a new Christian literature befitting the immanent second coming of Jesus Christ. It is odd but appropriate that the narrative portion of Augustine's *Confessions* describes Augustine's journey from Carthage to Italy and his abandonment of his mother, Monica, with specifics that parallel Aeneas's abandonment of Dido and his journey to Italy. One suspects that even Augustine could not despise the *Aeneid* on a personal level. It had been the primary text he had used as a rhetor, a teacher of rhetoric to Roman adolescents.

One might think that Christianity would exclude such a "pagan" text as the *Aeneid*, but Vergil and his epic very much survived this cultural shift. The *Aeneid* became a schoolbook freely allegorized in accord with the critical preferences of the Middle Ages. Bernardus Silvestris, a twelfth-century Neoplatonist, sees each book of the *Aeneid* as representing a stage of human life, book 1 representing infancy and books 2-4, youth. This is not far from the civilizing theme many modern critics prefer. Readers of the Middle Ages then, so steeped in the Christian religion, often appropriated classical "pagan" texts for their own purposes. Domenico Comparetti rightly notes that

Vergil occupied in literature the same position among the Christians as he had done among the pagans, but also . . . there was a keen desire among the former to assimilate the words of the poet they admired to the ideas imposed upon them by the new faith, and to purify him from what was in their eyes his only fault, the pagan spirit. (97-98)

Medieval readers and writers were interested in the *Aeneid* not as a description of Rome's global destiny but as a foreshadowing of the Christian vision of the world. The universal rule of the Church and Christ's message of salvation would replace the secular domination of Rome. Augustine's *De civitate Dei* (c. 410; *The City of God*) represents the first codification of this idea.

For the medieval world, Vergil is not quite Christian and not quite pagan. Like Aeneas, he occupies a transitional place conceptualized through allegorisis. The late medieval Italian poet Dante Alighieri (1265-1321) transformed Vergil and his epic when he incorporated this pagan into his Christian masterpiece *La Divina Commedia* (c. 1308-21), or, as it was later known, *The Divine Comedy*. Dante used Vergil as his mentor and guide for his own great epic poem. Dante's *Comedy* is an allegory of the conversion of the sinner. It is accomplished over three days as its pilgrim (who is the poet) journeys from a "dark wood" to a vision of Hell, Purgatory, and Heaven. This story of conversion is *the* Christian plot, allegorized. Vergil's role is that of pious guide through the first two realms, Hell and Purgatory; since he is an unbaptized pagan, he cannot enter the realm of Heaven. Here is Dante's reverent description of the master poet when he first sees him:

> O light and honor of all other poets,
> may my long study and intense love
> that made me search your volume serve me now.
> You are my master and my author, you—
> the only one from whom my writing drew
> the noble style for which I have been honored.
>
> (82-87)

In Dante's allegory, Vergil represents the best that a human may attain without the added grace of knowing the one true God. As J. H. Whitfield writes, "During the Middle Ages Vergil had come to be regarded as the highest representation of that pagan culture destined by Heaven as a preparation for the Christian age" (97). Granted, this important work treats Vergil more than it treats the text of the *Aeneid*, but the approach is typical of the time. Many texts were read "backward" as giving hints and guesses about the coming of Christ. Another work of Vergil, *Eclogue* 4, receives special attention for speaking of a *puer*, a boy who would usher in a reign of peace; medieval readers were eager to interpret this as a prophecy of the coming of Christ. It is actually a reference to Vergil's patron, Augustus.

Dante's recasting of the *Aeneid*'s political founding to spiritual conversion, with Vergil as mentor, marks a height few could reach. The *Aeneid* continued to exert its influence through the European Renaissance, and imitators show their various debts, with scattered results. As Colin Burrow points out, Vergil's global reach and Dante's cosmic reshaping were difficult performances to follow: "Poets such as Ariosto and Tasso . . . confronted the central problem with Renaissance epic: that in comparison with the example of Vergil their state was provincial, and their celebrations . . . could in no way match the imperial authority which underwrote the poem of Virgil" (85).

Their failure was perhaps a lesson for John Milton (1608-74), who though he wrote the Christian epic *Paradise Lost*, shows a different attitude toward the *Aeneid*. Milton's relationship with Vergil is double; he is obviously heavily indebted to the *Aeneid* and the Greek epics before him for the structure of his poem, but unlike Dante, Milton cannot take Vergil, the author of a poem that has as its mission human "dominion," as his mentor. Christian humility contrasts too sharply with Roman Empire.

As Milton's epic shows, the *Aeneid*'s influence was not limited to Europe, but extended to the English-speaking world. Geoffrey Chaucer (c. 1343-1400), poet of *The Canterbury Tales*, knew at least parts of the text, though his primary source for the Trojan War is Publius Papinius Statius (c. 46-96 C.E.). An early complete translation of the *Aeneid* from Latin to Middle Scots was made by Gavin Douglas, the *Eneados* (1513), but the most influential translation is that of John Dryden (1631-1700). Dryden was a poet and essayist of the so-called Augustan Age of English literature; the name harkens back to the great Roman writers of the time of Augustus. In this period interest shifted to the moral lessons that might be drawn from literature. Dryden's translation of the *Aeneid* (1697) is done in what he calls in his introduction "heroic verse"—that is, rhymed couplets. The emphasis in this translation is not on Christian allegory, or on reawakening classical myths, or on the emotional trials of Aeneas, but on the story of a heroic life complete in virtue. As the first lines of Dryden's introduction declare, "A heroic poem, truly such, is undoubtedly the greatest work which the soul of man is capable to perform. The design of it is to form the mind to heroic virtue by example" (ix).

Dryden's translation was immensely popular, not only because it was definitely an *English* rendering of the poem that takes liberties with the Latin text ("I thought fit to steer betwixt the two extremes of paraphrase and literal translation" [lx]), but also because it showed the self-sacrificing, virtuous behavior appropriate to a leader. After all, Dryden dedicates the translation to "John, Lord Marquis of Normanby, Earl of Mulgrave, &c, and Knight of the Most Noble Order of the Garter." Dryden makes it clear that literature is meant to "delight, while it instructs" (ix), so the text's moral instruction are underlined. His sixty-page introduction therefore had a strong influence on the way the poem was approached, at least by its English-speaking audience of the time.

The Augustan Age of Dryden, as R. D. Williams notes, "wanted to keep clear of the jungle in which lurked the terrifying creatures of the imagination, to avoid the peculiar, the eccentric, the excessive, the abnormal" (123); it was rather Vergil's "moral content and excellence of artistic control" that were valued (127). But the English romantic poets such as Samuel Taylor Coleridge and William Wordsworth who came after thought quite differently. Very broadly, the English romantics, active in the second half of the eighteenth century, built their aesthetics around key concepts such as the *sublime* (an experience at once powerful and indeterminate) and the emotional engagement with *nature*; Wordsworth's poem "Daffodils" (also known as "I Wandered Lonely as a Cloud"; written in 1804) is typical of a romantic depiction of a sudden, emotional response to the ordinary in nature. The romantics' devotion to direct, unmediated experience coincided with an appreciation of the innocent eye, a sort of "childish" vision. They also expressed a love of darkly imaginative realms; Coleridge's visionary poem "Kubla Khan" begins with the strange, transporting lines, "In Xanadu did Kubla Khan/ A stately pleasure-dome decree." Considering this worldview, it is understandable that the romantics would find little to love in the *Aeneid:* it is too goal-oriented in content, and too stately and ordered in form. One damning quotation from Coleridge might give an indication of their general rejection of Vergil: "If you take from Virgil his diction and metre, what do you leave him?" Granted, Coleridge was likely referring somewhat to the difficulty in translating Vergil's Latin, but still, it is hardly a ringing endorsement. So focused on exploring the human capacity for intense feeling and emotional depth, the romantics, as Williams notes, "did not respond to the Roman values of the poem, . . . and in particular they were unable to appreciate the 'unheroic' heroism of Aeneas" (132).

But perhaps one should avoid blanket statements about the *Aeneid*'s reception during this time. Certainly book 4, which covers the emotional turmoil of Aeneas and Dido, received critical approval; in addition, Wordsworth actually spent two years (1822-24) translating the first three books of the *Aeneid* (Doherty 214), and a Victorian writer such as Matthew Arnold could speak of a "sweet, a touching sadness" he found in Vergil (qtd. in Williams 134).

The *Aeneid* understood as a tale of westward expansion toward a "fated" destiny would find a more consistently positive reception in America. "Virgil occupied," Theodore Ziolkowski writes, "a place of honor in the minds of our Founding Fathers" (147). That is, the epic's politics—the refounding of a political order in a "new world"—matched the American understanding of America as (to use John Winthrop's image) "a city upon a hill," destined for greatness, and a model for others. The American mission during the colonial and republican periods and straight through the nineteenth century was westward from Europe and then again toward the Pacific coast. On a telling note, Ziolkowski points out that "the three mottoes of the Great Seal of the Republic [*novus ordo seclorum, annuit coeptis,* and *e pluribus unum*—also found on the U.S. dollar bill] were adopted in 1782 from Virgil's poems" (147). Ziolkowski goes on to list the many American writers who were influenced: Willa Cather, Robert Frost, and most especially the Fugitive Group, the poets associated with Vanderbilt University—Allen Tate, John Crowe Ransom, Robert Penn Warren, and others—during the early 1920s. Readers of the twentieth century, then, in the English-speaking and non-English-speaking worlds, continued to see in the *Aeneid* both a brilliant work of literature in itself and a mirror for their own concerns.

Historical, feminist, reader-response, and other interpretations have all had their say on the poem, and all are worth exploring, but two main, if very broad, directions appear in the twentieth-century reception of the *Aeneid*. During the first half of the century, readers tended to see in the *Aeneid* the problems that faced the age—the rise of modernity, industrialism, the growth of independent nations, and the instability caused by an immensely destructive conflict justifiably called a "world" war. Most histories of the modern era point to a crisis of values, an intellectual instability that haunted the twentieth century, but the roots of which can be found in the nineteenth century. Karl Marx argued for a worldwide revolution against an exploitative status quo, Charles Darwin's studies implied that humans are not the apex of creation but one part of a complex process of nature, Friedrich Nietzsche sought to unmask the deceptions of accepted tradition, and Sigmund Freud described the dark inner workings of the human mind. Twentieth-century critics of the *Aeneid* tended to fall under the spell of one of these giants.

One commentator on the modern condition, Louis Dupre, sums up the situation: under such intellectual and spiritual conditions, "the modern self has become severed from those sources that once provided its content" (119). That is, modern humans are rootless and isolated, cut off from God, others, and even themselves. Here is where Vergil's *Aeneid* fits in; the *Aeneid* was originally crafted to try to recall the Roman people to their ultimate purpose. There exists, therefore, something of an analogy or parallel between the Roman condition and the modern condition; according to Ziolkowski, "The Roman analogy and, ultimately, the powerful appeal of Vergil to the modern thinkers can be seen as another manifestation of this same urgent attempt to find meaning in history" (12). England, France, Italy, and the United States all had different "readings" of Vergil and his texts in the first half of the twentieth century, but they appropriated them in response to the crisis of values whose seeds were sown in the previous century and came to a head in the murderous trenches of World War I.

But again, responses to the *Aeneid* varied; perhaps the most well-known poet in English of the twentieth century, T. S. Eliot, praises Vergil for what he sees as his piety and adaptability to Christian culture, while later, in a famous reply, the writer Robert Graves savages Vergil for being a dull imitator of Homer, and Aeneas for being a "cad." Another important critical response formed over the second half of the twentieth century is less sympathetic to Vergil's epic—it is an overtly political reading that cannot come to terms with the *Aeneid*'s implicit imperial design. An important context to this reading of the *Aeneid* is the move toward the independence of colonized nations from European control. The independence of India from Britain in 1947, Indonesia from the Netherlands in 1949, and Algeria from France in 1962 are just a few examples of peoples' attempts to establish themselves as separate nations. Of course, one could argue that the movement of the *Aeneid* is precisely the opposite; its plot, after all, shows Aeneas and his men landing on the coast of Latium and doing battle with the natives, Aeneas marrying Latinus's daughter Lavinia, and the resulting establishment of a new political system. In other words, these exiled Trojans "colonize" a native country and destabilize the inhabitants' lives and culture.

In the context of such "postcolonial" thought, one can imagine that the *Aeneid* would come under criticism and its imperial mission would be rejected. In his discussion of European colonization of the Americas, Richard Waswo describes what he sees as the *Aeneid*'s role in supporting such invasive projects; he argues that "Virgil's epic is our founding legend. . . . What gets founded is an empire and its colonial outposts, which entails the bringing of culture to the indigenous inhabitants of the place where the empire builders will plant their fields and their metropolis" (743). Waswo argues that the *Aeneid* offers a "master narrative," an overarching picture of an expansion into foreign lands and, ultimately, the European and American exploitation of native peoples—an aggressive, morally objectionable stance.

These readers show the complexities of the West's colonizing tendencies and the interplay of the powerful and the colonized. These back-and-forth struggles for power occur not just in fact, in history, but in the literatures that grow out of the various cultures involved. Thus Craig Kallendorf, in his book *The Other Virgil*, argues that Milton's appropriation of the *Aeneid* contains an implicit criticism of the master poet and his beloved epic. Milton emphasizes not the valorous side of ancient heroism; rather, he emphasizes the moral dubiousness of Aeneas's goals. One can infer that Milton might recognize that colonization is, as he might have it, sinful. Aeneas's weaknesses become appropriated as Adam's sinfulness: "grasping," whether it be an apple or another's land, is a flaw (161ff.). Here, then, is Kallendorf, an early twenty-first century critic, discussing an early modern author (Milton) as he reads and transforms an ancient writer, Vergil. As one can see, how a text is received and read at any one time is a complicated affair.

The *Aeneid*'s critical reception in the twentieth century shows the tensions that are present in any set of thoughtful interpretations of a literary text. The point is not that Eliot is merely imposing his conservative faith on his reading, or that Graves is interpreting through his own secular/modernist eyes. Nor is the point that those who admire the *Aeneid* must inevitably advocate the colonial project contained therein, and advocate the exploitation of native peoples. Neither is it that those who point out the text's limitations are unfairly holding Vergil up to too-rigorous moral standards. Rather, it is that all interpretations depend on unique historical circumstances, such as what translations are available, what the reader brings to the text, and everything else that makes up the *con*-text. Even interpretations by expert scholars of Latin and historians of Rome will inevitably take place at certain times, in certain places; there is no perfectly "accurate" interpretation. But more important, one must see that works such as the *Aeneid* have enough "thickness" or "density" to support many different interpretations and still leave room for as-yet-to-be-accomplished readings.

Works Cited

Burrow, Colin. "Virgils, from Dante to Milton." *The Cambridge Companion to Virgil*. Ed. Charles Martindale. New York: Cambridge UP, 1997.

Comparetti, Domenico. *Vergil in the Middle Ages*. Trans. E. F. M. Benecke. 1895. Princeton, NJ: Princeton UP, 1997.

Doherty, Kevin F. "On Wordsworth's *Aeneid*." *The Classical World* 54.7 (April 1961): 213-17.

Dryden, John. "Introduction." *Vergil: The Aeneid*. Trans. John Dryden. New York: Heritage Press, 1944. ix-lxi.

Dupre, Louis. *Passage to Modernity: An Essay on the Hermeneutics of Nature and Culture*. New Haven, CT: Yale UP, 1993.

Horsfall, Nicholas. "Virgil's Impact at Rome: The Non-literary Evidence." *A Companion to the Study of Virgil*. 2d rev. ed. Ed. Nicholas Horsfall. Leiden, Netherlands: Brill, 2001.

Kallendorf, Craig. *The Other Virgil: "Pessimistic" Readings of the "Aeneid" in Early Modern Culture*. New York: Oxford UP, 2007.

Waswo, Richard. "The Formation of Natural Law to Justify Colonialism." *New Literary History* 27.4 (Autumn 1996): 743-59.

Whitfield, J. H. "Virgil into Dante." *Virgil*. Ed. D. R. Dudley. London: Routledge & Kegan Paul, 1969. 94-118.

Williams, R. D. "Changing Attitudes to Virgil." *Virgil*. Ed. D. R. Dudley. London: Routledge & Kegan Paul, 1969. 119-38.

Ziolkowski, Theodore. *Virgil and the Moderns*. Princeton, NJ: Princeton UP, 1993.

CRITICAL
READINGS

The Poetic Achievement of Virgil _____

Viktor Pöschl

At the end of antiquity the poems of Virgil were regarded as the sum of all wisdom and all knowledge. Donatus conceives the three main works of the poet, the *Eclogues*, the *Georgics* and the *Aeneid*, as the expression of three steps in the evolution of civilization: that of shepherds, of farmers and of warriors. Servius understands the three manners of style in Virgil not as stages but as forms of existence. In the Neoplatonic outlook of Macrobius there is a "great similarity" between the divine creation and the poetic work of Virgil. The work of the poet is for him an image and mirror of the universe. These are exaggerations of right perceptions, but Virgil's works are indeed comprehensive syntheses. He is the classic of the Occident because his poetry achieves a synthesis of ancient civilization.

The *Aeneid* leads us to the most important places of the Roman Empire. Aeneas comes from Troy to Italy and visits famous places: Delos; Crete; the coast of Epirus, where Actium will be later; Sicily; Carthage; Velia, the famous Elea in southern Italy, the town of Parmenides; Cumae; Latium; Roman Palatine; Etruria and the main lands of Italy. The Homeric wanderings of Odysseus, the travels through far and fabulous countries, wonderlands of fairy tale, turn into travels which lead the hero through countries of historical significance: the mountains, Olympus, Athos, Aetna, Atlas, Eryx, Ida, the Apennines and the Alps, are drawn in impressive verses; the rivers: the Rhine, Euphrates, Ganges, legendary Eridanus, and the Italian Tiber, Atesis and Po. The epic gives an image of the world of that time. This image is, as Herder pointed out, a characteristic feature of the epic genre in general.

Greek and Roman gods, Greek and Roman rites, are present in the *Aeneid*. But there is no distinction between Greek and Roman elements. Virgil as a Roman has the proud feeling: all that belongs to us. These are our gods, this is our world, immense and various in its riches and full of history. Thus Greek and Roman religion and history have found their place in the *Aeneid*.

But the works of Virgil are still more the summary of an inner civilization. They are the quintessence of the moral ideals that Greeks and Romans laid down. We are faced with the ideal of Homeric heroism in Turnus, the enemy of Aeneas. He is a second Hector, struggling heroically against foreign invaders, but at the same time he is Achilles in his readiness for death. This readiness is hinted at by the simile of the wounded lion, which stands like an emblem on the first leaf of the book of Turnus, the last book of the *Aeneid*, suggesting the greatness of the hero in his fall. In his talk with King Latinus he declares himself ready to die for glory's sake (12.49: *letumque sinas pro laude pacisci*). This is an echo of the decision of Achilles, *Iliad* 18. 114-16 (Lattimore's translation):

> Now I shall go, to overtake that killer of a dear life,
> Hektor; then I will accept my own death, at whatever
> time Zeus wishes to bring it about, and the other immortals.

But the marvelous composure with which the Homeric hero looks forward to his end is blended with a strained strength and sullen readiness to fulfill his fate which another Greek hero shows as he goes to the duel with his brother: Eteocles in Aeschylus' tragedy *The Seven against Thebes*.

Loneliness, too, Turnus has in common with Achilles. "Hector is the defender of Troy, but also son, husband, father, brother, brother-in-law. On him rests the fortune of many. This makes his struggle so hard, his figure so human" (W. Schadewaldt, *Iliasstudien*, p. 108). Turnus, on the contrary, is alone like Achilles. His relations with Lavinia, his bride, remain dim. His father and his divine mother do not appear at all. Only his sister Juturna gives a human dimension to his fate as Thetis does for Achilles. Turnus in his loneliness contrasts with Aeneas who appears among his family and his people, like

Hector. It is one of the most outstanding features in the figure of Aeneas.

Moreover, Turnus is connected with Achilles by his loyalty to his followers and by the fact that he is compelled to betray them. Deceived by the gods, he follows a phantom and goes on board a ship, while Aeneas advances victoriously. And when he becomes aware of the delusion, he is torn by despair and tortured by the feeling of having lost his honor through his flight and the sacrifice of his followers to the enemy. These are feelings that the Homeric Achilles knows, too (*Iliad* 18.98-100):

> I must die soon, then; since I was not to stand by my companion
> when he was killed. And now, far away from the land of his fathers,
> he has perished, and lacked my fighting strength to defend him.

But again with the Homeric reminiscences are combined others from tragedy. In his bitter loneliness and abandonment, Turnus, like Ajax in Sophocles' tragedy, turns to the forces of nature, to which alone he can address his longing for death (10. 676).

Dido, too, in many respects is a mirror of Greek heroines. She has in her something of the Medea and the Phaedra of Euripides. Like Antigone she turns in her distress to her sister: Dido's address, *unanima soror*, is a reflection of *ô koinòn autádelphon Ismé·ne·s kára*, the first words of Sophocles' *Antigone*. The death of Lausus, who sacrifices his life for his father, is a reflection of the death of Antilochus, who dies for his father Nestor in the epic called *Aethiopis*; this epic has not been preserved, but Virgil probably knew it. Hellenistic poetry contributes essential elements, too, especially the epic of Apollonius Rhodius. We find traces of Roman tragedy, and would notice them more clearly, if there were more of it extant. Above all, Ennius, the creator of Roman hexameter epic, is merged into the *Aeneid*. Beyond Ennius, Virgil goes back to Naevius, who first introduced Dido in Roman poetry and to the pre-literary Roman epic, whose existence can hardly be doubted. It is proved by the archaic form of the epic language of the oldest epic poet, Livius Andronicus, who uses forms certainly not current in his own time; Rome had an oral epic tradition which conserved these archaic forms.

Lucretius, too, contributed a good deal to the *Aeneid* and the *Georgics*. Without the ardor of his philosophy and his design of investigating the system and the nature of the universe, the sixth book of the *Aeneid* would not have been possible.

The Neoterics, known to us only by the most famous of them, Catullus, must not be forgotten, either. They contributed much toward the refinement of the poetical language and the art of composition of the Romans. Dido is akin to the Ariadne of Catullus, in whom the passion of frustrated love struck a new note in Latin and Occidental poetry. Some of his poems anticipate the most moving strains of Virgilian language and style. Virgil himself began as a Neoteric poet: the *Eclogues*, which follow the *Idylls* of Theocritus, are inventions in the playful manner of the Neoteric poetry.

The poems of Virgil are the sum of ancient poetry and of ancient *humanitas*. The *Aeneid* represents, in impressive scenes and gestures, a cosmos of human relationships: relationships of father and son, of sister and brother, of friends with friends, of enemy with enemy, man and wife. The moral cosmos of the *Aeneid* is the result of a long permeation of Roman civilization with Greek ethics. The famous words of Dido, "Not ignorant of evil,/ I know one thing, at least,—to help the wretched" (*non ignara mali miseris succurrere disco*; Humphries' translation), are linked with Hellenistic philosophy, with Menander and Terence: I am a human being, nothing human is alien to me (*Homo sum: humani nihil a me alienum puto*). The statement of Hellenistic philosophy, that it is a property of virtue to win men's hearts (Cic. *Off.* 2.17), is Virgil's conviction. Without Panaetius and Cicero the *Aeneid* could not be imagined, and still less without Plato and Platonism. The view of the world that underlies the whole poem is based on Platonic ideas; thus the idea of the transcendent origin of the soul and of the home to which it is longing to escape from the fetters of the body (6.314); their hands, in longing, reach out for the farther shore: *tendebantque manus ripae ulterioris amore.* Aeneas is so filled with the brightness of the Elysian fields, so depressed by the painful experiences of this earthly life, that he cannot conceive the soul's wanting to come back from the place of bliss to the earth. And no less Platonic is the idea that the cosmos of the state realizing itself in Roman history rests on the greater cosmos of the universe. Both ideas had been naturalized in Rome by Cicero.

But the *Aeneid* is more than an inspired selective synthesis. It contains new modes of human behavior and new poetic forms.

One important feature I should mention is the extreme tenderness and discretion with which Virgilian characters communicate with one another. It has always struck me, with what perfect tact Anchises speaks with his son about the Dido affair. He does not mention Dido, of course, nor the word "love." He only says: *Quam metui ne quid Libyae tibi regna nocerent!* In the *Georgics* Aristaeus, son of a god and a nymph, has lost his bees. The reason for his loss, as it turns out, was that the nymphs were angry with him because he had pursued their sister Eurydice and that, while she was fleeing from him, she had been bitten by a snake and had died. Orpheus went to the underworld to win her freedom and succeeded by the power of his song. But when he was returning, Eurydice was lost for ever. Then the nymphs make Aristaeus' bees die. He comes to his mother, the nymph Cyrene, to complain and ask her help. She advises him to go to Proteus, who knows all things, to ask why he has lost the bees and to seek his help. Proteus reveals why he lost them, but says nothing about how to get them back, although this might have been expected from the words of Cyrene. With perfect feeling for what is appropriate, Virgil attributes the part of helping to the loving mother who will do everything for her son. Why then—so it has been asked—did Virgil need Proteus? Could not Cyrene know the reason for the death of the bees? Certainly she could. But Virgil spared her the awkward role of telling her son that he had behaved badly to Eurydice, and of explaining to him what had been the result of it. That was one of the reasons why he introduced Proteus. The same feeling for the fitting, the sense of tact, the striving not to jar upon the sensibilities of others, is to be noticed in the shepherds of the *Eclogues*, who differ in this respect from those of Theocritus. Even in the passage where some have thought that Aeneas lacks tact—in the famous episode where he withstands Dido's entreaties not to go away—he is not to be judged so severely. It has been well pointed out that here he is cruel not only to Dido but to himself. And I suppose one feature at least shows the subtle sensibility of the poet: to make his situation understandable to his beloved, Aeneas speaks of another renunciation fate had forced upon him, the renunciation of return to Troy and of rebuilding the destroyed city. The departure from Dido revives this deep wound in his heart. He tries to make Dido realize that he is condemned to give up all he loves best.

Turnus, as we said, mirrors the Homeric form of heroism. But it is new, that he is the mythological symbol of Italic heroism, of those peoples who for centuries struggled against Rome and bled to death. Virgil, of Italic origin himself, admires and loves them as does Livy. And it is new, that he lends expression to the irrational principle in history and in the political world, the working of demonic forces that delay the empire of justice and peace willed by the gods. Homer was not aware of the irrationality of power as Virgil was. The Romans had an instinct for the irrational forces in politics long before Tacitus.

The figure of Aeneas is determined not only by Greek ethics and the Roman *mos maiorum*, but by a new, very personal note, in which we feel the coming of Christianity. When Aeneas hears that he is chosen to be the leader of all the Italians, he is seized by sorrow and sadness, not because he has been given too few soldiers, as ancient and modern commentators believe—how can he be disappointed, when the mighty nation of the Etruscans comes under his command?—but because of the burden which descends upon his soul, the thought of the calamities which the command of the gods will bring upon Italy. At this moment lightning is seen accompanied by thunder, the sound of trumpets is heard, weapons gleam in a red light. He recognizes in the heavenly prodigy the sign of Venus and the weapons promised by his divine mother, but he does not speak of triumph and victory and the fulfillment of his mission, now granted by the help of the gods. He gives expression to the pain that takes possession of him. The grave losses that the Italians and Trojans will suffer appear before his eyes, the terrible slaughter that is to come, the Tiber, which will carry away the corpses, like the Trojan stream whose image haunted his mind during the storm at sea (8. 539). The terrible image of war, that has lived in his memory since Troy, will become real again. This idea of war coming again echoes the feeling of the age of Virgil, the bitter experience of the succession of wars, the experience that history repeats itself during a lifetime in its most horrible aspects. This shudder sounds from the prophecy of the Sibyl in the sixth book (6. 86) and the prophecy of the Fourth Eclogue (Loeb):

A second Tiphys shall then arise, and a second Argo to carry chosen heroes; a second warfare, too, shall there be and again shall a great Achilles be sent to Troy.

And in all these passages there is something of the horror of the verses of the *Georgics* (1. 505-506; Loeb):

For here are right and wrong inverted; so many wars overrun the world, so many are the shapes of sin. . . .

And the experience of the horrors of the war is accompanied by an almost painful yearning for peace: Virgil is really, as Gino Funaioli called him, the poet of peace.

But the greatness of Aeneas lies in the fact that, in spite of the yearning for peace, in spite of the deep sympathy with the sufferings to come, he is ready to fulfil the command of fate. Characteristic is the way in which he gives expression to his readiness: "Now let them call for battle, and break treaties." He is ready for struggle, but not for aggression. The others have to take the first step. In battle, too, he never takes the initiative, and when he sees the face of his young enemy Lausus pale in death, he sighs deeply and gives his hand to the dying. He eases his death, promising to leave him his weapons and to bury him with honors. With his own hand he raises the dead from the soil: *terra sublevat ipsum.* . . . So in the *Iliad* Menelaos lifts up his young friend Patroklos, a gesture seen in the sculpture in the Loggia dei Lanzi (B. Schweitzer, *Die Antike*, 1938); and on a sarcophagus Achilles raises his enemy Penthesilea (Maréchal, *Mélanges offerts à Ernout*, 1940), atoning for his cruelty by this gesture of love. But in the *Aeneid* it is not the friend who does this service of love to the friend, and not the hero in whom the feeling of passionate love awakes, but the man who considers the enemy a human being; some of this is to be found in the encounter between Achilles and Priam in the *Iliad*. Of a friend dying for his friend the poet says (9. 430): *infelicem nimium dilexit amicum*. It is not by chance that this recalls the *quoniam dilexit multum* of the *Gospel of Luke* (7. 47). It is the guilt of all the characters of the *Aeneid* that they love too much.

The figure of the hesitating, suffering, sympathizing Aeneas who is full of pain and charity might not seem a splendid one, and the romantic poet Leopardi called him the opposite of a hero. But if we try to understand his true nature, his steadfast consciousness of law, his feeling of responsibility, his humility before god and his mission, then even today his figure will radiate. Virgil in the impressionable years of his youth had seen times of boundless infringement of law and boundless suffering. From this he conceived his hero as an ideal that was needed. He created new patterns of being a hero, patterns going beyond Homer and preparing the arrival of the Christian world. The *Aeneid* is not only a synthesis of antiquity but a preparation and foretaste of a new system of values, a bridge, a turning-point.

This is true also of the achievement of Virgil in the history of poetry, which cannot be separated from his significance in the history of the mind. We must ask: what part does Virgil play in Western poetry? What new, artistic, poetic devices did he give to Western poetry? I believe it can be shown that Virgil brought something new indeed. He made even a revolutionary artistic discovery. I should like to show this by the *Aeneid*.

It is customary to call the *Aeneid* an epic, but it is certain that in comparison with Homer it represents a quite new form of epic. Here one might see confirmed the view of Benedetto Croce, who maintained that there never was such a thing as a genre. That, of course, is exaggerated. But it is true that each great poet changes the genre. It is equally true that it is extremely hard to find a pure genre and an example that really conforms to the rules stated by the critic. (For my part, I cannot see that the epic of Homer really conforms to the rules given by Emil Staiger in his excellent book, *Grundbegriffe der Poetik* [2nd ed., Zürich, 1951].) This is particularly true of the epic.

The *Aeneid* contains epic, dramatic and lyric elements. First, it is an epic, of course, representing past events in narrative form. It is an epic also because the parts of the poem show a certain independence. From the biography of Donatus we know that Virgil read the second, the fourth and the sixth books of the *Aeneid* to Augustus, each on one day. These songs could be enjoyed independently. But on the whole this principle does not hold. On the contrary, it is not the principle of the independence of the parts that rules, but of their function. The *Aeneid* is ruled by the law of rigid unity. This principle in its essence is more dramatic than epic. The dramatic law of suspense dominates the whole narrative. The victory of Aeneas and behind it the *pax Augusta* is the goal of the poem and the goal of Roman history.

In the composition of the *Aeneid* a unity is attained that differs from the Homeric poems. The *Aeneid* is divided in the following ways. *First*, 6 times 2 books: the odd books—1, 3, 5, etc.—are the less tragic ones; the even books, the tragic ones, the books in which Aeneas, the suffering hero, proves himself. *Second*, 2 times 6: 1-6, wanderings; 7-12, war (the *Odyssey* and the *Iliad*). *Third*, 3 times 4: books 1-4, 5-8 and 9-12 form three units complete in themselves. In the first third, the scene is Carthage, although books 2 and 3 carry the narrative of Aeneas back to the end of Troy and the wanderings of the Trojans. Books 5-8 bring the contact with Sicily, the temple of Apollo in Cumae, Latium, the site of Rome, Etruria: the contact with Italy in various places. Books 9-12 deal with the struggles in Italy. Books 1-4 have a homogeneous setting, and so have books 9-12; in 5-8 the setting changes.

The first third contains the Odyssean trials of Aeneas, the wanderings and the great temptation by Dido as the culmination, the most perilous of his errors. The last third, 9-12, contains the Iliadic trials, the struggles and the duel with the most dangerous enemy, Turnus, again as the culminating end. These two sets of books which form the framework are the books whose model is Homer in many scenes and images. But the middle third, 5-8, the heart of the poem, brings before us the splendor of Rome and the splendor of Italy: book 5, the contests in which the unbroken strength of Trojan youth proves itself and—in the middle of the book—the *ludus Troiae*; 6, the glorious pageantry of Roman heroes; 7, the bright catalogue of the Italian nations which are to fight against Aeneas, but partake in the glory of Rome in the Augustan view of history; 8, the triumph of Augustus, represented on the shield of Aeneas. In the central books, the development of events, in spite of all the dramatic episodes, is more calm than in the books forming the framework. Here in the center the Roman subject-matter, the unhomeric, is revealed. From this center the framework—the fortune of Aeneas and of those who are involved in his fate—receives splendor and meaning.

These three principles of division permeate one other, creating the marvelous architecture of the epic, a harmonic unity, which cannot be compared with the structure of the Homeric epic. Here we are concerned with Roman-Italic composition. The art of composition which permeates Virgil's poem is akin to the composition of Roman architecture as it appears first and very impressively in the age of Sulla in the Temple of Fortuna at Praeneste. This temple became known as the result of bombardment during the last war. With the multiplicity of its buildings and terraces and with its manifest and hidden relationships, with its surprisals, this temple presents something new in the history of Western architecture.

In Virgil the principles of classic composition and of classic form appear for the first time in poetry. These aesthetic principles are the same as those described by Heinrich Wölfflin for the classic art of the Renaissance. In the *Aeneid* the bright center of the poem is framed by units ruled by the dark colors of the tragic, containing in changing settings the sufferings of war and sea. The First Eclogue is determined by the same rhythm: dark-bright-dark. The unhappy fortune of the shepherd, doomed to leave his native country, dominates the beginning and the end. With his fate contrasts the happiness of the other shepherd, who under the shadow of the beech plays a tune in praise of his beloved. The middle of the eclogue is occupied by his trip to Rome and by praise of the divine youth who gave him this happiness. The Second Eclogue shows the same principle of composition. The despair of Corydon is the framework for the courting of his beloved, which soars to paradisaic images. In both eclogues the end is enveloped in darkness, but this darkness is softened by the peace of evening, the human kindness of Tityrus receiving Meliboeus in his cottage for the night, by the sympathetic words of the poet to the unhappy Corydon.

The Tityrus Eclogue as well as the *Aeneid* or the *Georgics* is a model for a composition by contrasts: the values of the eclogue fall into symmetrical and contrasting patterns, like happiness and calamity, the calm of the shepherd world and the troubles of politics, the seclusion of a universe illuminated by music and poetry and the expulsion to unknown countries, the small world of the shepherds and the city of Rome and the immense scope of far nations included in the Roman Empire during Virgil's age, home and homelessness, departure and return; all these are contrasts that we feel to be complementary contrasts. Such an arrangement in contrasts is not only dictated by a musical need, by aesthetic principles, but conceals a view of the world. Brightness and darkness, happiness and calamity, spirit and passion join in a higher harmony, an order, resting on the adjustment of the opposites. The poet knows about cosmic and historical connections in which the opposites join in a higher whole, a balance, which loses and reestablishes itself time and again.

No less we find in Virgil the relaxed tension typical of classical art. Tityrus lies *lentus in umbra*. This classical art which appears in Virgil cannot be separated from Italian *humanitas*, holding at its command the human art of softening all the dreadful and the dark, of subduing it, of transfiguring it. The conception of art as a healing power, a consolation, is determined by the deep impulse to make life happier by art. The music of Tityrus and his hospitality spring from the same deep feeling of humanity. They show in a pure and intense symbol what poetry can mean to those who suffer.

Another classic principle in Virgil is the tendency to the Universal and Typical. Underlying the Tityrus Eclogue there is a general fate: the distribution of land for the veterans of Philippi and the expulsion of thousands of farmers, peasants and lords from their possessions. A poet could have described an individual fate. But Virgil represents his personal fate and that of his countrymen not as an individual one but as a typical one. He removes it into the pastoral world, as in the *Aeneid* he removes the fate and the greatness of Rome and the Augustan age into the world of mythology. We might speak about idealization, but that term does not fit the Virgilian and the Italian feeling for form. Virgil is convinced of finding in the pastoral world—as in the rural sphere of the *Georgics* and in the mythical universe of the Homeric age—a universe more simple, more natural, purer and more human, than the universe of his time.

In Virgil the Italian feeling for form has taken hold of poetry. But earlier it had appeared in Roman architecture and in the prose of

Cicero. In later times we have this Italic classic form in the Italian architecture and painting of the Renaissance and in the classic Viennese music of Haydn and Mozart, owing so much to the Italian feeling of form and bearing witness at the same time to a deep humanity. The analogy of music matters even more for Virgil than the analogy of the visual arts. For by its essence music is nearer to the art of words than are painting and architecture: like poetry, it displays its power in time. And it is especially near to the eminently musical art of Virgil, to his musical form of composition, to the lyric element in his poetry. With this we have touched upon one of the most important features of the poetry of Virgil. His poetry realized for the first time in antiquity a lyric style in a modern sense, if we leave out of consideration Sappho, who seems to come near to the lyricism of Virgil, and Catullus, who is the forerunner of Virgil in this respect too. But Catullus' epyllion of Peleus and Thetis shows that he is far from reaching the musical perfection of Virgil. A modern lyric poem is characterized by unity of image, music and feeling. The poetic images and the music of the verse express above all a certain mood. This lyric mood is closely linked with the phenomena of memory and hope. Memory and hope give things mood, color intensity.

The attitude of Aeneas is determined by the fact that he is a man filled with memory; the memory of Troy, above all, and the hope to find a new home. Hope, on the other hand, is the deepest impulse of the existence of Anchises: he waits for the coming of his son Aeneas, counting the time, *tempora dinumerans*—what a touching expression, very simple, very human, and yet never expressed before in Greek or Latin poetry, as far as I know. The moment when memory reaches a climax of intensity is the moment of departure. Some of the most moving scenes in the *Aeneid* are scenes of departure, and they are sometimes linked together. So the departure of Aeneas and Dido in the middle of book 4 and the other final departure in the center of book 6. The First Eclogue is a poem of departures, too. It receives its beauty and its fascinating intensity from the shepherd, who has to leave his country, and his pain is reflected in the animal world by the she-goat which has to leave her two kids born during the flight—another departure. The world of the animals reflects on a lower level the world of man; man and nature are linked together by a deep sympathy. This deep sympathy is the root of Virgil's lyricism; and this is not merely a human quality of Virgil but also his Stoic belief in the Sympathy of the world.

A poem of Virgil is a sequence of lyric moods, a perpetual movement, gradually changing, gradually increasing and diminishing its intensity. The movement of mood, of feeling in Virgil, as in each lyric poem or lyric passage, can be described as a movement of waves, a going up and down, an alternation of crescendos and decrescendos, of light darkening to deep shadow and shadow clearing up to brightness. The whole poem is a big flowing movement, and everything told fits this inner movement.

The solid factual coherence between the things of the world and human existence, on which rests the universe of Homer and still that of Greek tragedy, has been replaced in Virgil by a coherence of feelings. For the first time we find this lyricism in the pastoral poetry of Virgil, in a perfection not reached before and not surpassed in the frame of Roman poetry. Nothing is more miraculous in the history of poetry. The achievement of Virgil can be compared to the achievement in painting ascribed by the Spanish critic Ortega y Gasset to the discovery of chiaroscuro, especially in Velázquez. The old painters, so he argues, including those of the Renaissance, painted pictures seen from nearby. They are fond of the solid body, painted with a "tactile look." But with the painters of chiaroscuro, a new matter intrudes into the elements of the pictures. This magic matter is light, which dominates the whole composition. What light has been since then for painting—feeling, mood, inner musical movement have been since Virgil for poetry. As light changes and transfigures the objects of painting, feeling changes and transfigures the objects of the poetic representation. Homer and most of the Greek poets are associated, as it were, with the older painters painting their subject matter with the "hand," the "tactile tightness of look."

How could Virgil make this discovery? As with all manifestations of genius, we are faced here with a question not to be answered clearly. The great poets are, like all great artists, discoverers of provinces in the realm of the human soul. Each artistic discovery is a liberation of slumbering forces. Of course, there was an extreme sensitiveness in Virgil. The discovery of the atmospheric element, the mood element, in poetry may be connected with a phenomenon appearing in Pompeian painting: the joy in atmosphere, in the "painterly" element, clearly separated from the achievement of Greek painting.

But above all this entrance of the lyric into poetry gives voice to a deep change in man. It announces the intense introspection leading to Christianity. The change of form—the immense step made by Virgil from the plastic-tactile to the painterly-musical, from factualism to symbolism, from epic to lyric, is only another aspect of the change in man. So the poet Virgil, formed by the experience of civil war, which as a "trauma" determined his inner life, discovered a new realm of soul, from which a healing force can radiate in our time, too. That Virgil can play a part in our culture results from the fact that he embodies an important moment in Western history, the moment when man by the contact with Hellenic thought passed beyond it. The work of Virgil— still factual and yet transparent, still devoted to the ideals of honor and glory and yet subject to the values of love and pain, still praising and transfiguring the order of Roman law and Roman custom, Roman religion, the Roman Empire, and yet in the service of a transcendent task—the work of Virgil is a symbol of the great moment between the ages, between the ancient and the modern order. Originated at the great turning-point—*tanto cardine rerum*—it is achievement and promise at the same time. As long as our civilization exists, it will be a model, in the sense that great works can be models. It is not to be imitated in mere repetition, but to be assimilated and to be transferred into our existence in a very different age, when our best minds long to go back to the great moments of our history, to the sublime images in which we recognize our souls, souls that we must and shall preserve in spite of the increasing menace.

Virgil and the Mystery of Suffering_____

Francis A. Sullivan

All the works of Virgil, from the *Bucolics* to the *Aeneid*, make it clear that he was preoccupied with the problem of pain in the world.[1] And, as he pondered the question, searching for some meaning to the awful suffering of his own days, it was often Greek literature that haunted his imagination and nurtured his mind. For Homer and Hesiod, the Greek dramatists and Plato had, each in his own way, explored the dark continent of evil and suffering in human life. Behind the many happy scenes in Greek literature there lurk dark, sinister forces (*moira* and *daimones*) which may strike suddenly and bring final frustration.

What has Homer to say of suffering? Towards the end of the *Iliad* (XXIV, 527ff.), Achilles, now chastened by his sufferings, speaks thus to Priam, a man of sorrow: "On the floor of the house of Zeus there are two jars, full of the gifts he gives; the one jar is full of bad gifts, the other of blessings. . . . To my father Peleus the gods gave glorious gifts but later they gave evil. And you, sir, once were happy, but now. . . ." His final word is "endure, bear up."[2] In the *Iliad* and the *Odyssey* the action often takes place on two planes: an event is seen as the issue of divine action, then as the result of human effort. "The divine perspective dramatizes the passing moment against the background of events in their totality."[3]

But it is especially in Greek tragedy that the problem of reconciling human suffering and divine justice is presented in all its stark realism. Broadly speaking, there are two types of Greek tragic drama: the Sophoclean and the Euripidean. Sophoclean tragedy is based on the sense of man's responsibility for his acts. Through some error (sinful or not), the hero fails and falls, and his fall illustrates the inexorable workings of divine justice in the world. In this type of drama, the divine background shows symbolically that a universal law is at work in this particular case; even in the imbalance between man's acts and the (at times) catastrophic results, "even in this was Heaven ordinant." This is true also of Aeschylean drama, with some notable differences of tonality. In the *Oresteia*, we see the world painfully emerging from moral chaos into an intelligible world ruled by law; we see all the evil and the suffering shaping slowly towards the fulfilment of Zeus' will. By the dramatic form he imposes on the old, terrible stories, Aeschylus traces man's spiritual history, his search for the will of Zeus, the god "who moves amid a dark thicket" in ways mysterious to man.[4] But at least one precious insight has been granted man as a grace from the gods: by suffering, man can learn wisdom.

Euripides also makes use of the two planes, but for a different purpose. In some of his greatest plays (the *Hippolytus*, the *Heracles*, the *Bacchae*), we seem to be moving in an "absurd" world where the gods kill men for their sport. But it is important to grasp clearly what these Euripidean gods mean in their poetic context. They are *theoi*, that is, symbols of those dark, demonic forces which are active in men's lives, often to their bane. As Kitto says, "a *theos* may typify what does happen rather than what 'ought' to happen."[5] In such plays Euripides is showing us the pitiable and terrifying spectacle of man torn by contrary passions or by a passion which collides with his better judgment.

After the great dramatists came Plato with his eschatological myths and other-worldly views; the old Stoic Cleanthes with his *Hymn to Zeus*, where Zeus is described both in Stoic and in poetic terms; neo-Stoics like Posidonius with their modified views of Fate and Providence. They softened the rigid ideas of old Stoicism by blending them with the Roman religious view of *fata* as divine communications which man may come to know through oracles and other means. Such, briefly sketched, was the rich heritage of ideas about suffering and the divine which fell to Virgil. He absorbed them all and, by a kind of poetic alchemy, transformed them into something new and marvelous, the *Aeneid*. And now we turn to this, to try and discover there what meaning he found in human suffering.

What is our precise task? It is to inquire into Virgil's basic allegiances, his over-all views of the world and man's destiny, as these are set forth in the *Aeneid*. A great poem is an imaginative vision, not a philosophical solution to a metaphysical problem. And this vision is generally presented in a "myth" and in concrete symbols which serve an age-old purpose of peering into the meanings at the heart of things. The theme of the *Aeneid* is Rome's predestined mission in the world, set forth in the mythical tale of Aeneas and accompanied by a network of symbols. All the past history of Rome, as Virgil read it, was "an immense parturition," the vision of a world laboring to bring forth in the fullness of time, if not a new heaven, at least a new and better earth, the reign of peace and justice under Augustus, Jupiter's vicegerent on earth. And, implied in this theme, and ever accompanying it like a *basso ostinato*, is the theme of the pain and suffering inseparably involved in this herculean task: *tantae molis erat Romanam condere gentem*. Homer's epic world, says Whitman, "is a visionary structure whose chief pillar is the heroic aspiration." Virgil's epic world too is a visionary structure (an ideal Rome), but a structure whose every stone is laid at the price of heroic sacrifice.

Whence comes suffering in the *Aeneid*? Virgil sets forth the problem at the very start of his poem (1-296), making use of the two planes discussed above. The hero is a man with a mission: *Romanam condere gentem*. An exile from his Trojan homeland "by Heaven's declared will" (*fato*), he yet suffers much from the gods, and especially from the abiding wrath of Juno. Then the theme (great achievement by great suffering) is restated in the appeal to the Muse (8-11): what reasons moved Juno to persecute a man so marked by his sense of duty (*insignem pietate virum*)? Does wrath so dire find a home in heavenly hearts? Long ago Servius noted the problem posed here: "if Aeneas is a just man, why does he suffer from the hatred of the gods?" Now this theme is briefly developed (12-28) and Juno's motives are given: her love for Carthage and her old, implacable hatred of the Trojans. Then once more (29-33) the problem returns: driven ever onwards towards their destined goal (*acti fatis*), Aeneas and his men are kept for years from reaching it by Juno's contriving. Thus the hero is caught between two powerful forces, the *fata* and the queen of Heaven, and we wonder how this can be. There follow (34-222) the demonic storm aroused by Aeolus at the bidding of Juno, the landing of the survivors on the African coast, and a short speech of Aeneas, reminding his men of their destiny.

Thus far, clearly outlined, we have the *mythos* of the *Aeneid*, viewed from the human plane and enveloped in mystery. It will be a tale of wars and wanderings like the Homeric epics (hence the wealth of Homeric reminiscence in the early books); yet in spirit and intention it will differ radically from the old poems. For upon the broad shoulders of its hero rests the future of Rome and a great shift in the world-order. Up to now the poet has been spinning a web of symbols whose inner significance still eludes us. Who or what are these *fata* which drive Aeneas on to Latium and a new home? Who is this Juno who thwarts him at every turn? Now (222-96), to set us inside the story and to help us read its symbolic meaning, Virgil shifts to the divine perspective. Venus, saddened at the woes of her son, restates the enigma of the sufferings visited upon a good man: why, she asks Jupiter, despite your promises that from these Trojans would come in time Romans to rule the world, why are they at the mercy of a wrathful goddess? As Servius notes here, the whole intent of her speech is to show "that the Trojans are unjustly hounded by Juno." Is this the way Jupiter rewards goodness: *hic pietatis honos*?

Jupiter's reply, in the form of a prophecy, gives us the key by which to unlock some aspects of the mystery and to discern its final outcome. The *fata* of which we have heard so much thus far are the expression of Jupiter's will (I, 260); *neque me sententia vertit*. Scholars have often discussed the relations between the *fata* and Jupiter, making Jupiter now subservient to them, now their mouthpiece or executor.[6] More recently they have come to the conclusion—surely the right one—that the *fata* which dominate the story of Aeneas are the *fata Iovis*, the expression of Jupiter's will. No small part of the difficulty comes from translating the words *fatum* and *fata* as "fate" and "fates," with all the sinister overtones of these words, suggesting a chain of events brought about by some blind necessity, independent alike of man's and God's will.[7] Long ago St. Augustine, in his *City of God* (V, 1), warned Christians against using the word *fatum*, even for the expression of God's will, because of its deterministic connotations. In the *Aeneid*, *fata* means first of all "divine utterances," *quae dii loquuntur* (Servius *ad* II, 54). They are conveyed to man by the voice of prophets, in dreams or waking visions, or even by the voice of conscience. Secondly, they mean the content of these utterances, "destiny." Now these *fata* do not reveal what will inexorably come to pass, despite men's actions, but what will and *ought* to result, *if* men actively cooperate with them. In other words (and this is most important for the right understanding of the *Aeneid*), the *fata* do not override rational calculation and free will; they count on these and work through them. A man may forget them (cf. V, 703: *oblitus fatorum*), or fail to heed them, or try to go beyond them. Book II, the fall of Troy, is on first reading the most "fatalistic" of all the poem. The gods, including Jupiter, have decreed the fall of Troy (II, 54, 601ff.; III, 1-2). But this decree is worked out by men. The Trojans are blind and over-credulous (54); they are duped by Sinon (*credita res*); they fail to heed the warnings of Laocoön and Cassandra, and they do not interpret aright the portent of the snakes from Tenedos. Thus one tragic error after another brings about the fall of Troy.[8] In all this, of course, Jupiter had his own beneficent designs: Troy must disappear that something greater may arise in the west. There is mystery here, hidden in the counsels of the divine, but it is not blind fatalism.

Again, in Book VI, the Underworld scenes make it clear that a man is responsible for his acts; he is, to a large degree, the maker of his fate. Bad luck (*fortuna*) may dog his steps but, as the Sibyl tells Aeneas (VI, 95-6), "do not give way to misfortune but go to meet it more boldly than your luck will allow." In VI, 756ff., Anchises unfolds before the eyes of Aeneas the glorious future: *te tua fata docebo*. But this bright future will come true only if Aeneas and his descendants do their heroic best to achieve it. Thus he and the Romans to come are not mere puppets of the *fata*; they are their human instruments who freely work with them—or against them. As another telling illustration of this truth, let us take the scene where Jupiter lifts the scales during the duel between Aeneas and Turnus (XII, 725-7). He puts on the scales the different lots of the two, to see which weight sinks down, spelling death and doom:

> Iuppiter ipse duas aequato examine lances
> sustinet et fata imponit diversa duorum
> quem damnet labor et quo vergat pondere letum.

This is modelled on two scenes in the *Iliad* (VIII, 69ff.; XXII, 208ff.), in the latter of which Zeus weighs the *Keres* of Hector and Achilles. Whitman explains the meaning of this symbolic gesture as follows: "Never are the roles of the gods or the meaning of fate more clear than in the scene of Hector's death. Zeus lifts the scales—always a sign of what is true—and Hector's *Ker* or fatality descends towards Hades. . . . In single combat Hector must fall to Achilles. Homer's method is the most subtle imaginable mode of revealing both the freedom and the inevitability of action."[9] In Virgil too we have a symbolic gesture: Jupiter lifts the scales with the *fata* of Aeneas and Turnus, not to decide the issue beforehand but, as it were, to consult the facts and show us what will inevitably but freely result from this meeting. Turnus will and must fall before Aeneas because, when weighed in the balance, he is physically, morally, and spiritually inferior to Aeneas.

This is also the import, as I believe, of the rather mysterious words of Jupiter in X, 104ff. Since Juno and Venus will not compose their feuds and stop the fighting on earth, Jupiter declares his will: the actions of each side will bring them suffering or success; he himself need not intervene personally, for the *fata* (his will) will find a way to decide the issue: *fata viam invenient*. Presently Aeneas will arrive on the scene and his superior prowess will prevail. Despite some occasional obscurities in Virgil's use of the word *fatum* (or *fata*), it is clearly his over-all view that the *fata Iovis* which companion and guide Aeneas on his way express what *ought* to happen, what ought to emerge from man's work, from the freedom of the human spirit, so that the world may come to be what Jupiter intended. And in the great prophecy of Jupiter (I, 257-96) the poet gives us the long view of events on earth. Despite the human weaknesses of Aeneas, despite the human and demonic forces arrayed against him and his mission, he will win his way by his *pietas* and *virtus* through sufferings and frustrations to final victory. The *Aeneid* is anything but a story of blind fatalism.

But who is this Jupiter whose will means so much for the future of Rome? Virgil is a poet, and it is one important function of the poetic imagination to give life and personality to those mysterious but very real powers which are active in nature and in human lives. So Homer had done, so too the Greek dramatists. Following their example, Virgil gives his Jupiter some anthropomorphic traits: he is a god who personally intervenes in the action—but only at critical moments in the story (cf. IV, 219ff.; V, 687ff.; XII, 843ff.). But he is not the Jupiter of the Roman pantheon nor, despite some resemblances, is he the Zeus of Homer. He is the highest Power in the universe, *pater omnipotens, rerum cui prima potestas* (X, 100), the symbol of god-willed order in the world of physical nature and in the history of mankind. Over against the other gods in the poem Jupiter represents not merely a higher power but, as Pöschl says, "a higher quality of being" (*ein höheres Sein*). Properly speaking, we should call him "Jupiter" and recall what Heraclitus said of Zeus: "One thing, the only truly wise, does not and does consent to be called by the name Zeus."[10]

Now what is the will of this august deity? In the *Georgics* (I, 121ff.), he wills that men work hard and thus achieve self-perfection and happiness: *pater ipse colendi/ haud facilem esse viam voluit*. In the *Aeneid*, his will is predominantly for peace, and for war only when war is the inescapable path to peace. Anchises expresses this ideal in the well known words (VI, 851-3):

Remember always, Romans, that to govern is your task!
Be these your arts: to accustom men to peace,
To be generous to the conquered, and war down the proud.

Through most of the poem "Jupiter" as symbol stands opposed to Juno as symbol: as light against darkness, reason against passion, order against chaos. With the defeat and submission of Juno and the death of Turnus, the great issue of the *Aeneid* is finally decided on both planes: the *fata* of Jupiter triumph in the person of Aeneas. And Jupiter saw that it was good. For this Aeneas is not a mere individual fighting for personal glory but a Rome-bearer. When he raises his great shield at the end of Book VIII and makes ready for the war forced on him, he shoulders at the same time a great symbolic burden: *attollens umero famamque et fata nepotum.*

Over against Jupiter and forever trying a fall with his *fata* is Juno, the arch-villain of the poem.[11] In the *Iliad*, Juno (that is, Hera) had been the implacable foe of the Trojans; in the *Annals* of Ennius (Servius *ad Aen.*, I, 281), she had opposed the Romans until the Second Punic War. So it was natural for Virgil to cast her for this same role in his epic. Her enmity sets the mythological story in motion. But he converts the mythological goddess into a powerful symbol. In so doing, he was influenced by the Greek dramatists, but especially by Euripides. In the *Helen*, Aphrodite and Hera gradually reveal themselves "as mythological embodiments of the incalculable and unmanageable forces which preside over all man's strivings."[12] In the *Heracles*, Hera brings madness upon Heracles at the peak of his triumphs. Euripides first dramatizes the legendary story in all its grim realism; but then he converts the mythological Hera into a symbol of those dark, inscrutable forces which bring suffering on men without apparent reason. Thus "the Heracles is a play which imposes suffering upon men as their tragic condition, but it also discovers a courage equal to that necessity, a courage founded on love."[13] Early in the *Aeneid* (as we have seen above) Juno's hatred of Aeneas and his mission is motivated: the judgment of Paris still rankles in her. But, as the tale progresses, her opposition to him and his *fata* becomes more and more maniacal and senseless, until Jupiter calls a halt to her wildness (XII, 806): *ulterius temptare veto*. The parallel between the work of Aeneas and the labors of Heracles is suggested early in the poem (I, 9-10) in the words: *tot adire labores impulerit*. Aeneas, like Heracles, is engaged in a great civilizing mission and, like him, is made to suffer by Juno. Thus Virgil, like Euripides, takes over an old story and infuses into it a new, symbolic meaning: Aeneas, like Heracles, wins his way through suffering to a new courage and a new nobility of character.

But, as I believe, Roman history also helped Virgil to shape this symbolic figure of Juno. Often, as he pondered over his poem, a crowd of ghosts pressed about him, the troubled spirits of Pompey and Caesar, Brutus and Cassius, Antony and Cleopatra. What fearfully real, obsessive forces had bedeviled them, driving them on to their doom and the near-doom of Rome! Recall the scene in the Underworld (VI, 826ff.) when Anchises sees the spirits of the future Pompey and Julius drawing near. Foreseeing the havoc they will bring on Rome if they reach the light of life, he pleads with them: "Do not, my sons, make a home in your hearts for terrible warfare. Turn not against your country's heart her own mighty strength." Horace too had been appalled at what he saw happen time after time: Roman against Roman fighting and falling. "Quo, quo scelesti ruitis?" he cries (*Epode* 8); what awful force is behind this madness? These words were written some years before Actium. In 30 B.C. the Gates of War were closed, the first time since 235 B.C., and peace dawned at last over a war-weary world. All this helps us to understand better why, at the climax of Jupiter's prophecy (I, 294-6), Virgil shows us in a vivid symbol the meaning of the *pax Augusta*:

> claudentur Belli portae; Furor impius intus
> saeva sedens super arma et centum vinctus aenis
> post tergum nodis fremet horridus ore cruento.

The demon of civil strife will range the Roman world no more; bound fast with bronzen chains and sitting upon his cruel arms, he will howl horribly (and helplessly) with blood-stained lips.

In the *Aeneid*, Juno has a multiple symbolic role: she symbolizes those various forces in Roman history which opposed and retarded the realization of Rome's imperial mission in the world as willed by Jupiter.[14] All through the poem we see her at work arousing *furor* in her human agents. It is an evil thing, a distraction of mind, the fire in the blood which drives its victims to compass their ends at any cost. It is a contagious plague, spreading from Queen Amata to the women about her, from Turnus to his followers until all Latium is ablaze with the *scelerata insania belli*.

Now what does the presence of this goddess, as inspirer of *furor*, add to the effectiveness of the poem? Virgil is generally careful to motivate naturally the actions of his characters. The Trojan women, tired of seafaring and yearning for a settled home, decide to end it all by burning the ships (V, 615ff.): *urbem orant, taedet pelagi perferre laborem*. Turnus is young and impulsive. How natural it was for him, seeing his affianced bride being taken from him and given to a stranger, to react with violence. Yet in both these cases, as in many others in the poem, Juno is called in to inspire their sudden, mad resolves. Of course, what we are really asking here is why great poets like Homer and Euripides, Dante and Shakespeare, employ such symbolic figures. First of all, they enrich the dramatic effectiveness of a scene by showing us what evil looks like at work. So, in *Macbeth*, "the Weird Sisters are the incarnation of evil in the universe. . . . They set the play moving because they bring with them 'the filthy air' of ineffable evil which is its atmosphere."[15] How does it happen that a group of people like the Latins, leading quiet, normal lives, are suddenly filled with war-madness and, *contra fata deum* (VII, 584), rush to arms against those who have come to them as friends? To make us see that war, when unjust and unnecessary, is an unnatural and irrational thing, Virgil shows us Juno summoning to her aid Allecto, a fiend from hell. After rousing the queen to open opposition against her husband, Allecto turns her baneful arts against Turnus as he lies sleeping (VII, 413ff.), that is, "when the conscious, rational, and moral self is dormant."[16] Like a sleeping volcano, Turnus awakes and erupts into madness; *furor* in the shape of uncontrolled violence dominates him from now on and, in the end, brings him and many others to destruction. Distracted in mind, he dupes himself into thinking that he has on his side *fata* stronger than those of Aeneas (IX, 136-7). Like a victim of schizophrenia, he is never quite clear as to what he is doing and why. Too late he awakens to the awful truth (XII, 895) that the gods and especially Jupiter are against him. Surely symbolism is here justified by its work. For how else could Virgil bring home to us so vividly the workings of those obsessive powers and passions, those irrational forces which so often upheave human life?

In sum then we may say that Virgil, like Sophocles and Euripides, used divine figures like Juno (and Venus) first, because they were an integral part of the myth he was following; secondly, because these traditional figures offered him wide artistic possibilities of making visible to us the stern realities which condition human life. A discerning reader of the *Aeneid*, by following the interplay of human and divine agents in the poem, comes gradually to perceive in the symbolism a coherent and meaningful interpretation of reality as Virgil saw it. And how did he see it as he looked about him? Ideally, as Heraclitus had said, "man's character is his daimon"; his personal destiny is determined largely by his character, not by outward circumstances. Or, as Shakespeare put it in *Hamlet* (III, 2, 66ff.):

> blest are those
> Whose blood and judgement are so well commingled
> That they are not a pipe for Fortune's finger
> To sound what stop she please: give me that man
> That is not passion's slave. . . .

But actually, as life is lived, there are powerful forces active in the world which can limit a man's striving. Within man himself—and in his fellow men—there are dark, irrational instincts and feelings (love and hatred and vaulting ambition) which often lure a man to go his own reckless way against conscience and the will of Jupiter. Moreover, man is battered from without by forces beyond his control: a sudden storm may ruin a harvest or wreck a fleet, a plague may decimate a herd or lay waste an army. It is forces like these that are embodied and made visible to us in the gods of Homer and Euripides and Virgil.

Virgil's Aeneas is no impassive Stoic hero. He felt the hot breath of these forces on his back, tempting him to despair in the storm, to self-indulgence at Carthage, to forgetfulness of his mission in Sicily. He had often to struggle against his human feelings to gain the mastery. But struggle he did and gained a crown. How often we read of Dido and Turnus that their fault lay, not in themselves but in their stars or in the unfeeling gods. But, despite the pity the poet lavishes on them and the lovely music which accompanies them on their tragic way, his judgment, though unspoken, is clear enough. In Dido's words (IV, 552), "I have not kept faith which I promised to the ashes of Sychaeus," and in the words of Turnus (XII, 931), "I know, I have deserved it, I beg not life," there is much for tears, but the tears should not blind us to the truth.

So far we have been trying to answer the question: whence comes suffering to Aeneas and the others in the *Aeneid*. We have seen that it may come from the will of Jupiter, or from Juno and her agents, or from within man himself, from a sensitive heart or a splintered will. And this suffering may be a chastisement for wrongdoing, or a test and trial, or a teaching.[17] All through the poem Aeneas suffers greatly in body and soul from all these agencies. He suffers the fall of Troy, the loss of wife and friends, and exile to a dimly known new home. As he wanders over the seas, he endures gnawing discouragement and frustration and finally, close to his goal, near-despair in the storm. All of these trials were closely linked to his mission and so willed (or permitted) by the *fata* for the spiritual progress of Aeneas and the great good of the world. At Carthage and in Sicily his sorrows were, in part at least, of his own making. He yielded to the advances of Dido and to the comforts of an oriental city. When the summons comes from on high, he obeys, but at what a price to himself and to Dido! In Sicily, he is plunged into deep depression by the defection of the Trojan women. In this crucial test of his moral courage his *pietas* to his father and his prayers to Jupiter (V, 687-92) bring their reward. In sum, up to his landing at Cumae most of his sufferings subserve the high purpose of the *fata* to test and teach their chosen instrument: he must learn to die to the past (Troy and its bitter-sweet memories), mortify his human affections (Dido and a home at Carthage), steel himself against reverses (the burning of the ships), and begin to live for the future. The loss of Palinurus and the death of Misenus serve this same purpose. For up to now Aeneas has had no deep spiritual understanding of his vocation.[18] Now at Cumae begins for him a mysterious journey of life into death. In the darkness of the Underworld he meets his past in the symbolic figures of Palinurus, Dido, and Deiphobus, and tearfully comes to terms with it; in Elysium he meets his future and looks deep into the mysterious meaning of his sufferings. Finally, on the soil of Rome to be (Book VIII), he is reborn into an unshakable depth of purpose by vital contact with *pauper* Evander and the heroism of Hercules. From this experience he comes forth a *Roman* hero, endued with a new-found courage. Trials still await him in the wars stirred up by Juno and in the violence of Turnus. But now he is a fit instrument of the *fata*, well tempered in the crucible of suffering. With their aid his *pietas* and *virtus* prove equal to the human and demonic forces arrayed against him. For, as Lear tells his much tried daughter, "upon such sacrifices, my Cordelia, the gods themselves throw incense."

But what meaning did Virgil find in the sufferings and deaths of those attractive lads who wore the rose of youth upon them? Virgil does not disown the horror and heartbreak of war, but he transcends it and redeems it by themes of heroic sacrifice and courage which make us feel that "the nobleness of life is to do thus." And always the muted music of the poetry which accompanies their passing soothes the pain we feel. The boy Euryalus dies (IX, 435-7), "as when a bright flower is clipped by the plow and droops dying." His friend Nisus avenges his death, then falls dying over the dead lad, and there, at long last, we hear the words "Fortunati ambo!" Inseparable in life and ever restless for action, they are together in death and at peace. Again, when Mezentius is wounded and retiring from the battle, his young son Lausus gives his own life to save his father. Aeneas, his slayer, is stricken with pity at the dying boy's look (X, 821ff.) and sighing deeply says (in Dryden's translation):

> Poor hapless youth! what praises can be paid
> To love so great, to such transcendant store
> Of early worth and sure presage of more?
> Accept whate'er Aeneas can afford;
> Untouch'd thy arms, untaken be thy sword;
> And all that pleas'd thee living, still remain
> Inviolate and sacred to the slain.

But nowhere does Virgil effect a catharsis of pity so wonderfully as in the scene where young Pallas meets Turnus (X, 460ff.). Conscious of his weakness but unafraid, the lad prays to Hercules (now in Heaven) for aid. Hercules weeps at his inability to save him. Then Jupiter consoles him—and us—in words winged with solemn music, words which link the fate of Pallas with the common lot of man on earth:

> Every man's day is appointed. Short and unrenewable
> For all is the span of life; but to make fame live on by deeds,
> That is the brave man's task.

"So beneath Troy's walls fell my own son Sarpedon; so Turnus will soon meet his fated end." In all these deaths there is a sense of triumph over death which is more than reconciliation, the same feeling as that which pervades many epigrams of Simonides: "dying, they have not died." Among the *beati* in Elysium Virgil sets those who fell fighting for their fatherland (VI, 660): *hic manus ob patriam pugnando vulnera passi.*

Returning now to Dido and Turnus, can we find in their sufferings any redeeming insights? Both of them seem, in some mysterious way, victims of the gods. As we gaze at them, we see feelingly "the giant shades of fate, silently flitting,/ Pile the dim outline of the coming doom." And yet, as their tragic careers unfold, it is the human drama that absorbs us, the age-old drama of temptation, fall, and calamitous consequences that seem to reach far beyond their deserts. Of the two, Dido is in every way the more pitiable. Virgil compares her (IV, 69-73) to a wounded deer, a poor creature taken off its guard, while Turnus is often compared to a wild beast of prey, a wolf, a lion, a tiger. As Dido lies dying on the pyre, the poet says of her (IV, 696-7):

> Nam quia nec fato, merita nec morte peribat,
> sed misera ante diem subitoque accensa furore . . .

"Nor by a death that was her desert." But from Turnus, soon to die, we hear the revealing words (XII, 931-2): "I know; I have deserved it. I'll not beg life." Here we have the stuff of tragedy, the tragedy of Lear and Othello, and the tragic stuff that is woven into the heart of life on earth. Like Sophocles and Shakespeare, Virgil gives us the whole picture, the dark side and the bright. In the very fact of human existence there is a risk and a provocation: one sudden twist of the net, one wrong decision, and the trap is sprung. Is it not this that Virgil is showing us here, that, if we are not careful to bridle our impulsive sensibilities, we may sow the wind and reap the whirlwind?

And Juno, what part has she in this sad story? Let us recall the symbolic role of the gods in Homer, Sophocles, and Euripides: at times they represent what *ought* to happen in the world, at other times what *does* happen. The key to Juno's symbolic role in the *Aeneid* is, I believe, to be found in the word *furor*. Jupiter "stands for" order in the world, for right reason, for what ought to happen; Juno appears from the outset of the poem as inspirer of *furor* and *insania*. In Book I, through Aeolus, she stirs up a furious hurricane which all but ruins the fleet of Aeneas. But most of the time she upheaves the souls of men, clouding their judgments and splintering their wills: in Dido and Turnus, in the Trojan women and the Latins. In all these cases there comes in the end a revulsion of feeling, a return to sanity—when it is too late. In other terms, we may say that Juno is (in most cases) a poetic symbol of those irrational forces in life which tempt and all but compel us to make a morally wrong and disastrous decision. They were there all the while, deep buried within us, needing only some stimulus or pressure from without to erupt suddenly. But in retrospect they seem to have come upon us like some demon, suddenly invading us and overturning our normal selves. "O the mind, mind has mountains, cliffs of fall/ Frightful, no-man-fathomed." Macbeth dallied with ambitious thoughts, but suddenly come murderous thoughts when he realizes that "the devil can speak true." So Dido feels a new love stirring within her; she resists and takes a solemn oath to remain true to her first love. But suddenly, after Anna's words (IV, 31ff.), she gives way—and the flood-gates are opened wide. Virgil does not moralize her story or that of Turnus. Indeed, he tells it with such a depth of human understanding that, until we recollect our emotions in tranquillity, we wonder at times where his sympathies lay, with them or with the *fata Iovis*. His Dido dies, like Cleopatra, every inch a queen, with a noble epitaph framed by her own lips (IV, 655-8). And, as though that were not enough, he composes a lovely coda to her tragic symphony (VI, 450ff.). We meet her again in the "Mourning Fields" of the Underworld, reunited with her first love.

The mystery of suffering has been the theme of many noble works of literature. Perhaps nowhere is the problem set forth with such intensity of feeling as in the Book of Job. After a long and heated debate between Job and his friends, out of the whirlwind comes the voice of the Lord—but not to give reasons for His dealings with men. Only humble faith in the goodness and wisdom of God can be man's response to the bewildering ways of the Creator with His creatures. Aeschylus and Sophocles, Euripides and Shakespeare dramatized the problem, each in his own way. At the end of *King Lear,* after we have witnessed suffering that is appalling in its intensity, we catch a glimpse of a new and brighter order of things to come. "The sombre tone at the end is due to a pressing awareness in the author at the price; but the price has not been in vain."[19] Virgil has not tried to dissipate wholly the dark cloud that encircles the mystery of suffering. But he has tried—and surely not in vain—to show that suffering *has a meaning*, a meaning partly discoverable in this life but wholly unveiled only in the life to come. That great achievement comes only with great suffering, that nobility of character needs testing in the furnace of affliction, and that love inevitably spells sacrifice, these are some of the insights he has left us. We are not left darkling.[20]

From *The American Journal of Philology* 90.2 (April 1969): 161-177. Copyright © 1969 by The Johns Hopkins University Press. Reprinted with permission of The Johns Hopkins University Press.

Notes

1. Virgil was no naive optimist. The peaceful world of the *Bucolics* is darkened at times by the clouds of war; the farmer's world is visited by sudden storms which wreck his hopes; the *Aeneid* is a story of wars and wanderings.

2. Cf. also *Odyssey*, XVIII, 130ff. For Hesiod's views on suffering, see F. Solmsen, *Hesiod and Aeschylus* (Ithaca, 1949), pp. 27ff.

3. C. H. Whitman, *Homer and the Heroic Tradition* (Cambridge, Mass., 1958), pp. 275ff.

4. Cf. E. T. Owen, *The Harmony of Aeschylus* (Toronto, 1952), p. 126.

5. H. D. Kitto, *Form and Meaning in Drama* (London, 1956), p. 74.

6. For some recent discussions of the relation between fate and free will, see K. Büchner, *P. Vergilius Maro: Der Dichter der Römer* (Stuttgart, 1956), cols. 433-40; G. E. Duckworth, "Fate and Free Will in Vergil's *Aeneid*," *C.J.*, LI (1955-6), pp. 361ff.;

and most recently Brooks Otis, *Virgil, A Study in Civilized Poetry* (Oxford, 1963), pp. 220, 353-4 and *passim*.

7. Tchaikovsky's Fourth Symphony begins with a dramatic, hammering figure in the horns. "This," wrote the composer to a friend, "is Fate, the inexorable force that prevents our hopes of happiness from being realized."

8. Cf. R. G. Austin, *P. Vergili Maronis Aeneidos Liber Secundus* (Oxford, 1964), notes to lines 228 and 244.

9. *Op. cit.* (note 3), p. 229.

10. For this fragment, see G. S. Kirk and J. E. Raven, *The Presocratic Philosophers* (Cambridge, 1957), p. 204.

11. See C. M. Amerasinghe, "Saturnia Iuno—Its Significance in the *Aeneid*," *G.R.*, LXV (1953), pp. 61ff.

12. Cf. G. Zuntz, "On Euripides' Helena," in *Euripides* (Entretiens Hardt, Geneva, 1958), p. 217.

13. Cf. W. Arrowsmith's Introduction to the *Heracles*, in *The Complete Greek Tragedies: Euripides*, II (ed. D. Grene and R. Lattimore, Chicago, 1956), p. 53.

14. These obstructive forces were of three kinds: 1. historical antagonisms between nations and peoples, such as the rivalry between Carthage and Rome and the struggles between Romans and Latins; 2. personal feuds between Roman leaders culminating in the civil wars; 3. natural catastrophes such as storms at sea. As late as 38 B.C., Octavian was reduced to near despair by the wrecking of his fleet.

15. Cf. *Macbeth* (ed. J. Dover Wilson, Cambridge, 1951), p. xxi.

16. See S. G. P. Small, "The Arms of Turnus: *Aeneid* 7.783-92," *T.A.P.A.*, XC (1959), p. 246, n. 10. Cf. also G. E. Duckworth, "Turnus and Duryodhana," *ibid.*, XCII (1961), pp. 81ff.

17. So too in Livy "the whole of early Roman history is depicted as a period of trial, in which the military and civic virtues of the Roman people are thoroughly tested so that they may become physically and morally capable of world-leadership." Cf. P. G. Walsh, *Livy, his Historical Aims and Methods* (Cambridge, 1961), p. 51.

18. Cf. M. C. J. Putnam, "Unity and Design in *Aeneid V*," *H.S.C.P.*, LXVI (1962), pp. 205ff.

19. Cf. *King Lear* (ed. G. I. Duthie and J. D. Wilson, Cambridge, 1960), p. liv.

20. To call Jupiter and Juno poetic symbols is not to deny that Virgil believed in them *qua* gods. That however is a separate question. One thing above all should be kept in view in reading the *Aeneid*: the actions of the gods do not displace or deny human freedom and human responsibility. On this important point there are some excellent observations in the recent book of J. P. Brisson, *Virgile, son temps et le nôtre* (Paris, 1966), pp. 288ff.

Sine Fine:
Vergil's Masterplot

Robin N. Mitchell-Boyask

> KENT: Is this the promised end?
> EDGAR: Or image of that horror?
>
> —*King Lear*, Act 5 scene 3

> . . . the raging and incredulous recounting (which enables man to bear with living) . . .
>
> —Faulkner, *Absalom, Absalom!* 161

Psychoanalysis has not been brought to bear on the study of Roman culture as thoroughly as it has engaged Hellenic studies, and to date most work has consisted of the psychoanalytic literary study of symbolism or character, as witnessed recently by the Vergilian studies of Gillis (*Eros*), Putnam ("Possessiveness"), and Mitchell ("Violence").[1] These studies have often yielded important insights into the *Aeneid*, and while they provide a foundation for the present examination, I believe that we can now further develop this line of thought by engaging such approaches as the psychoanalytic dynamics of reading, or the function of language in the unconscious, areas outlined in the important collection edited by Felman (*Literature and Psychoanalysis*) which presents Peter Brooks' preliminary version of a Freudian practice of reading narrative.[2] In this paper I shall investigate Vergil's narrative project in the light of the model proposed more completely by Brooks in *Reading for the Plot*, whose focus on issues central to reading the *Aeneid*, such as the desire for the end and the function of repetition, could further our understanding of how the *Aeneid* works and why, in particular, its ending is so disturbing.[3] I intend this study as a contribution to the larger discussion of closure in classical texts that Don Fowler initiated recently in a more general survey of the prospects for such endeavors.[4] The *Aeneid*, I submit, problematizes the idea of an

---

end through its deployment of the word *finis*, and then frustrates the reader's desire for diegetic closure by merely stopping, not ending, the narrative, despite clear signals of its completion.[5] This inquiry thus engages the techniques of traditional literary formalism in the service of a text-centered psychoanalytic theory of narrative in the belief that the older forms of literary formalism and psychoanalysis are occasionally deficient in their rigidity, their seductiveness, their lack of concern with the relationship between text and reader, and simply because the older forms of psychoanalytic literary theory have been at times, in Brooks' words (*Psychoanalysis and Storytelling* 20), "something of an embarrassment."

Far from the idea that a plot is a static self-sufficient entity, Brooks sees narrative emplotment as "a form of desire that carries us forward, onward through the text" (*Reading for the Plot* 37) in pursuit of meaning, a pursuit that gives pleasure. Stemming from the Freudian Eros of *Beyond the Pleasure Principle*, this desire seeks, as Brooks quotes Freud (37), "to combine organic substances into ever greater unities." Our need for coherence, for knowledge, drives us continually toward discovering the "Masterplot" of the origins, unfoldings and ends of the plots of our lives and our stories. A plot's beginning arouses certain desires and expectations that carry the reader to the end. "The sense of a beginning" is "determined by the sense of an ending," and present moments have "narrative meaning only because we read them in anticipation of the structuring power of those endings that will retrospectively give them the order and significance of plot" (94). Repetition, one of the most powerful narrative tools for the pleasurable ordering of the plot, can also be a disruptive, painful force; Brooks recalls Freud's account of the child's game of throwing and returning a toy, an activity designed to master the unpleasant, regular disappearance of the mother. Similarly, neurotic patients, in narrating dreams, repeat distressing trauma, attempting to move from passivity to mastery. The pleasure principle thus conflicts with, and often yields to, the repetition compulsion. Narrative repetition both advances the plot and returns it to its origins, or it is a return of some repressed material. Repetition functions as a "binding of textual energies that allows them to be mastered by putting them into serviceable form" (94). Plot, like organic life, striving to "restore an earlier state of things" (Brooks quoting Freud, 102), thus aims at quiescence—the plot's end, death: "What operates in the text through repetition is the death instinct, the drive toward the end" (102). Brooks' Freudian model of narrative thus offers a dynamic economy that necessitates the end, through desire, and the detour, through repetition. Finally, Brooks suggests textual repetition itself subverts the notion of beginning and end because "the idea of beginning presupposes the end, that the end is a time before the beginning, and hence the interminable never can be finally bound in a plot" (109).

Although Brooks finds his initial impetus in "the great nineteenth-century narrative tradition," which also encompasses Freud's work, Brooks locates this thought in the larger tradition of theorizing about plot that began with Aristotle.[6] These ideas promise much for an epic whose end has no formal closure, returns earlier repressed material, and opens to the endlessness of history. The *Aeneid* does show a self-consciousness about its form and about the active relationship between narrative and reader. David Quint, who has recently brought Brooks' ideas to bear on the problem of repetition in the *Aeneid*, argues that the Trojans only overcome their repetition compulsion, their reiterated attempts to resurrect Troy, when they achieve mastery over their situation in Books 7-12, but that their assumption of the Achaeans' Iliadic role undercuts any sense of progress. However, despite the many virtues of this important work, Quint's focus falls on character analysis (Aeneas' repetition compulsion), and thus Quint negates Brooks' desire to shift from the psychoanalysis of character to the dynamic relationship between plot and reader, which is where I center my reading of Vergil's "Masterplot." Quint places surprisingly little emphasis on endings and concentrates on the repetition of actions and themes, while I shall focus on the interplay among the epic's verbal texture, the function of generic expectations, and the role of narrative desire. My

---

main concerns are the *Aeneid*'s literal inconclusiveness, its deployment at crucial moments of *finis*, and the role of repetition in its diegetic economy. Generic practice, what Conte calls "the epic code," involving structural features such as a traditional epic proem, leads us to expect closure, just as Aeneas repeatedly is told, or he himself promises, that there will be a *finis*, an end. Philip Hardie, in an important study on closure in Latin epic, argues the "openness of closure" in classical epic stands out all the more due to the obvious clarity and strength of proemial devices in early Greek epic and may in fact be characteristic of the genre as it developed in Rome.[7] Given the frequent discussion of and anxiety over endings in the *Aeneid*, the epic's form, I shall contend, is thematized.

The text's insistence on *finis* to signify finality is crucial, since Vergil does have other choices for the hexameter: *modus, supremus, meta, terminus*. And while *meta*, for example, cannot occupy in all cases the same metrical position as *finis*, Vergil can remind us of his options by clustering them together, as is the case for the most famous instance of *finis* in the *Aeneid* (1.278-79):[8]

> his ego nec metas rerum nec tempora pono:
> imperium sine *fine* dedi

> To these I place neither boundaries of things nor time:
> I have given empire without end

Jupiter could proclaim, *imperium sine meta dedi*.[9] This variant would lack the assonance of Vergil's choice, *sine fine*, but it is interesting to note that *meta* does appear in the immediately preceding line, and with this alternative present the preference in the next line seems all the more marked. Thus his word choice and the implications of its multiple uses are motivated.

Like the English "end," the Latin *finis* has several overlapping senses, all of which Vergilian usage suggests: death, territorial borders, the conclusion of speech, the end of struggle, or just a plain end. These usages are inseparable and Vergil subtly ties them together by reserving their deployment to key moments that highlight them and to key characters; *finis* is not a word typically spoken by or about minor figures. Vergil, however, strangely front-loads the first six books, especially Book 1, with references to the end, and his characters there continually talk about endings in a way that suggests this will be a problematic concept. After Juno has arranged for the storm that washes the fugitive Trojans up on the shores of Libya, Aeneas, in attempting to raise the spirits of his men, promises them, *dabit deus his quoque finem* (199), which, indeed, quickly occurs: *Et iam finis erat* (223). However, we are not told that Jupiter himself is responsible for this ending, which in turn suggests a disjunction between the ending of an episode, however provisional it may be, on the human plane, and the far more wide-reaching interest in endings on the divine plane. The identical repetition, though, intimates the god is taking Aeneas a bit too literally and narrowly, which Venus indicates when she next asks Jupiter: *Quem das finem, rex magne, laborum* (241)? It is as if Venus questions the cessation of suffering so that she suspects all endings are merely temporary. Shortly after this sequence, Jupiter's famous reply, *imperium sine fine dedi* (279), invoking the sense of the absence of physical borders and limits to authority, appears to end affliction by promising power, and yet this promise is undermined both in the poem and the lived history of its audience by the knowledge that with *imperium* comes *labor*.[10] The text's repetition of *finis* suggests that Jupiter somewhat facilely and evasively changes the subject to assuage the worries of Venus; to promise an empire without end is to promise toil without end.[11] Territory is defined by *fines*, and the next five instances in Book 1 describe the borders of Dido's land. To end his wandering and struggle Aeneas must himself establish a land with secure borders (ends), but his rule will lack such limitations. Thus, we come to the paradox that to end *labor* is to renew it. Book 1 foregrounds the dissonances created by these semantic ambiguities because here Vergil lays out his own "Masterplot,"—

Aeneas' destiny as founder of Rome. Aeneas promises, and narrative practice requires, a conclusion to this plot, but Jupiter has already cast doubts on that promise, and consequently a sense of anxiety surrounds the word's occurrences. The reader's desire for an end, for fixity, matches Aeneas', and hence this anxiety about the circulation of requests and promises increases due to the slippage among the various meanings of *finis*. Jupiter's pronouncement of empire without end evokes temporal and territorial borders, and thus further supplements Aeneas' hope that god will give an end with the latent sense that god will give a bordered territory. Jupiter is playing a verbal trick on Aeneas: he receives one kind of end and he loses another.

For both the main character/narrator and the divine guarantor of the plot's completion *finis* marks narrative ending. In Aeneas' two-book narration it denotes death, the end of suffering and the conclusion of narration, and the three usages shade into one another. Venus advises her son (2.619), *Eripe, nate, fugam, finemque impone labori*, while Aeneas similarly describes Anchises advising the Trojan men (3.145): *quam fessis finem rebus ferat*. Note the concern with authority figures placing limitations, a concern that typifies the tendency among the divine characters towards ends while humans orient themselves around delays.[12] And given the association between *fuga* and *labores* in the proem, there is some irony in Venus' suggestion that flight will bring an end to *labor*. For the human Aeneas, however, his divine mother's warning disappears in the anarchy of the situation around him, as he describes himself as losing such limits (2.771-73):[13]

> quaerenti et tectis urbis sine *fine* ruenti
> infelix simulacrum atque ipsius umbra Creüsae
> visa mihi ante oculos et nota maior imago.

> To me seeking and rushing without end on the city's roofs
> the unhappy image and shade of Creusa herself
> and her great known image appeared before my eyes.

The unique repetition of *sine fine* so soon after Book 1 must give us pause and suggests reconsideration of Jupiter's pronouncement. Jupiter promises power without end, but Aeneas finds a maddened rush without end. Now, an objection might be raised that Jupiter in Book 1 is declaring a scheme that puts an end (eventually) to experiences such as the Fall of Troy, and thus *imperium sine fine* takes precedence over *sine fine ruenti*. Here we must distinguish between narrative and historical sequence. In the historical time articulated by the narrative, Jupiter's promise comes second, but the narrative representation of these two instances of delimitation places Aeneas' sense of endlessness second, thus making it seem like a gloss on the first. For the immortal Jupiter endlessness seems a cheerful prospect; for the mortal Aeneas, it is a different matter entirely. That these are the only instances of *sine fine* in the *Aeneid* marks them even more. The sole *finis* in the chaos of Book 2 is death–*Haec finis Priami fatorum* (554)—which thus also highlights the end of the narrative about this death. Vergil then closes Aeneas' story about Troy and his wanderings in a similar language of death and narration (3.716-18):

> sic pater Aeneas intentis omnibus unus
> fata renarrabat divum, cursusque docebat.
> conticuit tandem, factoque hic *fine* quievit.

Thus father Aeneas alone with all intent
was narrating the fates of the gods, and was explaining his voyages.
Then he fell silent, and with the end made he became quiet.

Because this clearly articulated end is accompanied by a description of the scene that adds to the sense of completion, its absence will be all the more marked in Book 12.[14] However, like the end of Book 12, this sense of quiescence is undermined, here by the beginning of Book 4, which opens with *at* ("But"), to indicate the tension between the closure of Aeneas' narrative and its arousing effect on its auditor, Dido, whose own curse on Aeneas, after all, extends beyond the end of the *Aeneid*'s narrative and generates the Punic wars, despite the reconciliation of Juno in Book 12. This will typify a pattern in the *Aeneid* whereby even complete stories are destabilized by the implied or stated continuation of the events they represent, and Vergil thus provides a model for the active relationship between narrative and reader that is strikingly evocative of Brooks' theory.

These patterns of destabilized closure and verbal plays on *finis* continue in Aeneas' *katabasis*. The same word also signifies the close of Aeneas' request to the Sibyl that she sing the prophecies herself: *finem dedit ore loquendi* (6.76). However, Apollo's immediately subsequent assault on her renews the dark undercurrent around this word and the anxiety surrounding the ends of narrations. Vergil then in the same book plays on the established ambiguity when Aeneas addresses Palinurus' ghost in a stressed enjambment (6.343-46):

> dic age. namque mihi, fallax baud ante repertus,
> hoc uno responso animum delusit Apollo,
> qui fore te ponto incolumem, *finis*que canebat
> venturum Ausonios. en haec promissa fides est?

> Come on and say. For did Apollo, having hardly been found
>   false before,
> with this one answer did he trick my mind,
> who was singing that you unharmed by the sea
> would reach the Ausonian borders? Was this the promised faith?

The enjambment plays on the expectation that the prophecy of an end to suffering would be achieved through acquiring secure borders.[15] Apollo sings endings; Apollo sings Palinurus will reach the Italian border. But the brief semantic suspension in the enjambment also registers the third meaning, death. Aeneas, however, lacks the necessary interpretive acumen, and misses the fact that Apollo spoke truthfully all along: Apollo was singing death. Further, Aeneas' meeting with Palinurus occurs shortly before he learns that death does not bring an ending to the toils of corporeal existence after all because of the *dira cupido* of the soul to be returned (*reverti*) to the flesh (6.719-21). While Aeneas realizes that our belief that the Masterplot of our lives has closure rests on a great misunderstanding of the true natures of desire and repetition, still the soul's trip to the river Lethe saves the newly re-embodied spirit from the painful memory of this recurrence.[16] And while the souls desire to return to life again because they become *immemores* (6.750) of all that occurred before, Aeneas and the readers of this narrative lack such therapy and remain mindful of the endless repetitiveness of existence. Thus, twice in Book 6 Aeneas learns how difficult it is to achieve and to understand endings.

The *Aeneid*'s last quarter engages in further word play on *finis* as the end of speaking, the border of territory, and the end of the war. Jupiter, after castigating Juno because *nec vestra capit discordia finem* (10.106), has a *finis fandi* (116); discord does not end, but narratives do. Moreover, the persistence of *finis* becomes even more problematical in the context of a speech whose meaning is so difficult to pin down, even devious, as Lyne (*Further Voices*) and O'Hara (*Death and Optimistic Prophecy*) argue. The end of the war—*belli finis* (10.582)— then becomes paramount. After Pallas' death, Aeneas worries about Turnus' desire to *bellum finire manu* (11.116); we shall return to this passage later. Throughout these episodes, a steady use of *finis* denotes borders, so all meanings are kept in play.

Finally, the end of Book 12 features two instances that, coming at moments of high drama and intensity, are heavily marked, point back to the similarly stressed cases in Book 1, and problematize its ending. This is appropriate since Vergil toward the close returns to themes and language important to the epic's opening. Through Jupiter's exasperation with his wife's continuing hostility, the narrative recapitulates a major theme of the proem and raises the issue of the epic's end (12.793):

quae iam finis erit, coniunx? quid denique restat?

What now will be the end, wife? What finally remains?

And then, a few lines later, Jupiter adds: *ventum ad supremum est* (803). These remarks, I submit, have a strong "metanarratological" element, betraying a self-consciousness about the work's literal length and its size as a metaphor for the scale of the suffering. The proem establishes that Juno's wrath is the plot's driving force: once it ends, the narrative should as well. And even then the matter is not fully settled, for, as Feeney observes of the narrative function of the later conflicts between Carthage and Rome, "the final reconciliation of Juno which Jupiter prophesies is not represented in the narrative, but lies beyond the poem's close" ("Reconciliations" 181). This discussion between gods merely delays in the narrative the human resolution.

This postponement typifies the closural difficulties late in this epic that conflict with other structures more indicative of a simpler teleology. At line 793, Book 12 is already longer than four other books, one third of the *Aeneid*'s total, and the final three books are its longest in sequentially increasing length, both of which show that Vergil the narrator is having as much difficulty "finishing" the *Aeneid* as did Vergil the poet. Every student of the *Aeneid* knows the story of how Vergil supposedly claimed his epic remained unfinished and requested that it be burned at his death, and Philip Hardie, appropriately for my purposes, even suggests that this final request "may reflect . . . a more general anxiety about the possibility of setting a *finis* to such a poem" (*Epic Successors* 2).[17] We see this anxiety in the basically overextended physical state of the last few books as well as in their thematic concerns. Following Walter Benjamin's lead, Brooks argues that narrative arises as one of the categories of understanding that enables us to negotiate with and around our consciousness of mortality. Thus "plot is the internal logic of the discourse of mortality" (*Reading for the Plot* 22). Vergil's characters, both divine and human, definitely are aware of the meaning of mortality, so when one figure who has become immortal expresses a concern with endings and with the "plot" of her life, and especially so soon after Jupiter has asked about the end, we should pay close attention.

At line 880, as Juturna ponders the horror of watching her brother's imminent death, Book 12 already surpasses in length all but three books of the *Aeneid*, and, after realizing the true cost of her immortalization, she laments her own inability to finish her life (12.880-81):[18]

> possem tantos finire dolores
> nunc certe et misero fratri comes ire per umbras!

> If only I could end such suffering
> now certainly and accompany my wretched brother through the
> shadows!

The phrase *tantos dolores* epitomizes and describes an epic that is, in Putnam's words, "the poetry of *dolor*" ("Daedalus" 184). Because Juturna serves as the vehicle for expressing the epic's anguish over Turnus' death and as our eyes for the final events, she symbolizes also the narrator's struggles with the plot. In Homer the lamentation of women begins the tradition of commemorating the deeds of the hero; the *Iliad* closes with the women of Troy singing dirges to Hector's corpse, and, similarly, late in the *Odyssey* we are told of the symphony of mourning at Achilles' burial. Thus epic attributes its origins in part to female voices. Moreover, Achilles' mourners in the *Odyssey* are the Muses themselves. Interestingly, though, epic mourning, unlike lament in tragic drama, commemorates not the individual work's hero, but his antagonist. Achilles and Thetis may begin the mourning over his death in the *Iliad*, but the dominant lamentation concerns Hector, while the *Odyssey* mourns not Odysseus, but Achilles, who functions as the former's thematic antagonist.[19] Vergil's epic continues this pattern. Pietro Pucci, writing about female lamentation in the *Iliad*, observes that women there lament not just their dead warriors, but themselves as well; "for the specific female condition . . . their metaphorical death" as slaves ("Antiphonal Lament" 264). Some mourners, however, will not become slaves, but their anguish increases in their awareness that their knowledge will endure as long as their existence, forever. Thetis, one of the Homeric models for Juturna, laments for eternity the death of her mortal son. But for Juturna the pain is greater, for she bought her immortality from the god who raped her and who now consents to her brother's death.

Epics and gods always remember, and the poet, like the goddess, views the action from a distance and ponders its meaning. Homer and Thetis function as an important analogue for Vergil the narrator and Juturna in that the latter pair more subjectively involve themselves in the lament over the fallen hero. Vergil resembles Juturna in the knowledge of what has been given from the gods, the plot, and the frustration over the inability to effect a different outcome. Vergil has already apostrophically expressed this frustration earlier in his lament over the inability of Latins and Trojans to merge peacefully (12.500-4). *Tanton placuit concurrere motu* seems to point back to *tantae molis erat Romanam condere gentem* (1.33), where *condere* may hint at the difficulty that the poet is going to have in "composing" (to the end) his narrative of that foundation.[20] Both Vergil and Juturna ask, "How can I end?" The narrative is required to end but Vergil keeps postponing its conclusion by making Aeneas' conquest of Italy as difficult as possible. Because the epic's length, especially in its last three books, corresponds to the scale of the emotional suffering, its form becomes thematized, and as this is a process Masters (*Poetry and Civil War*) has recently analyzed in Lucan's *Bellum Civile*, perhaps this is another way in which Vergil's epic successor was one of the first and best readers of the *Aeneid*'s poetics. The ending is inevitable, but, especially after its continual postponement, its final specific form is in an important sense arbitrary and artificial. Comments Brooks, "We are frustrated by narrative interminable, even if we know that any termination is artificial, and that the imposition of ending may lead to that resistance to the end which Freud found in his patients and which is an important novelistic dynamic in such writers as Stendhal and Gide" (*Reading for the Plot* 23). The resistance to the end is thus also an important *epic* dynamic in Vergil. Appropriately, then, only Aeneas and Juturna (apart from Jupiter's question to Juno) have an expressed concern with finishing. We find that the sole instances in the entire *Aeneid* of the verb *finire* are Juturna's lament at Turnus' imminent demise, *possem tantos finire dolores* (12.880), and, after Pallas' death, Aeneas' denunciation of what he perceives to be a disparity between Turnus' desire to *bellum finire manu* (11.116) and his reluctance to face Aeneas in battle.[21] But once again Aeneas here misreads the relationship between desire and closure, for Turnus only fails to meet Aeneas because of Juno's decision to interfere in the battle by sending a phantom Aeneas to lead Turnus astray, an event that infuriates Turnus. Juno's achievement of a delay, *mora* (10.622), directly conflicts with Turnus' actions throughout his struggle against the Trojans and with his self-presentation at the beginning of the final book: *nulla mora in Turno* (12.11). The direct echo of Jupiter's temporary stay of death imparts bitter irony to Turnus' assertion, for at this point he is completely right about himself and his situation, since through the linkage of his end and the narrative's he has become the main human force driving the plot towards closure. Juturna, however, cannot finish her "plot."

Vergil has previously given us a tale of unfinished *dolor* in the ekphrastic account of Daedalus' carvings on the temple of Apollo in *Aeneid* 6. Putnam ("Daedalus") traces the clear homology between the narratives of the carvings and of the *Aeneid*. Daedalus, like Vergil, fails to complete the dolorous subject of his art, in Daedalus' case the destruction of youth: "Like Virgil's history of Daedalus [the *Aeneid*] is a brilliantly complete poem ending on premonitions of artistic incompletion" (184). But Vergil underscores this narrative's incompleteness by having Achates interrupt the Trojans' perusal of the carvings (6.33-35):

---

quin protinus omnia
perlegerent oculis, ni iam praemissus Achates
adforet atque una Phoebi Triviaeque sacerdos . . .

They would have read everything through
with their eyes, except that Achates, having already been sent ahead,
appeared, along with the priestess of Phoebus and Trivia . . .

This interruption essentially places the characters as readers of the carvings in the position of the readers of *Aeneid* 12; we know the rest of the myth, but the specific work of art does not narrate it. Thus, Book 6 establishes a model not only for the artist, but also for the reader's experience, thus providing further evidence for James O'Hara's recent discussion ("'Interpreting Character'") of an "implied similitude between the interpreting character in the text, and readers of the poem as interpreters of the text" (104-5).[22] I would add that the case of Achates as an interpreting character is paradigmatic for the reader of the epic as a whole. The inability to finish is a tragedy for the artist and mirrors the discomforting frustration the reader experiences when closure does not occur.

Compared with the healed communities and restored orders of its Homeric and Apollonian models, the *Aeneid*'s sudden stop disrupts narrative pleasure; I shall return to the complicated matter of Vergil's predecessors shortly. Vergil's Masterplot, moreover, moves the mourning given to Hector after his death in the *Iliad* to before Turnus' demise in the form of Juturna's horror, a lamentation Lyne (*Further Voices* 221) calls "proleptic." This dual frustration of the desire for completion is no accident. Since the *Aeneid* closes with its hero returning to the dark emotions of its earlier books and its final lines echo with language from the epic's opening, the narrative repetitiveness enacts the return of the repressed. Aeneas is mastering his past trauma through repetition, but, in the end (literally) it is not Aeneas who repeats parts of the text, but the text which repeats him. The epic proem introduces a set of words that resonate throughout the epic: *dolor, ira, insignis, condere, saevus, memor, profugus.* These words return all together in the last nine lines of the *Aeneid*, but they are given different associations; words which characterized Juno now describe Aeneas, and ones for Aeneas move to Turnus.[23] Angry memory persists from Troy to Rome, passing from Juno to Aeneas. As a form of memory, the epic preserves anger at its end. The repetition of these words and others marks the end of the narrative forces unleashed by the proem, and yet the narrative stops in midstream with Turnus' spirit leaving his body. If we regard the text not as a self-contained object, but as having a dynamic interaction with its readers, then clearly such repetition cannot effect closure as it is experienced by the reader. Don Fowler ("First Thoughts on Closure" 100) thus succinctly observes, "The *Aeneid . . .* notoriously has a surprise ending though many of the systems of meaning within the epic do culminate in the final book." Another recent critic has argued, without much explanation of literary form, that the *Aeneid* has closure simply because Aeneas kills his antagonist,[24] yet if one looks not for wise words providing a moral for story but for some attempt to heal the destructive forces unleashed by the action, one will not find this here.[25]

Generic expectations can help explain how to read this ending. The primary generic model, the *Iliad*, begins its narrative with the word/theme *mênis*, and its plot finds completion only when Achilles' wrath is healed in his meeting with Priam and the hero is reintegrated with society.[26] Compared with the *Iliad*, the *Odyssey* ends more abruptly in a "freeze frame shot,"[27] with Athena intervening to stop the civil war in Ithaca between the island's warring factions, but its hero essentially achieves the task set out by the proem and the main problems articulated by its narrative are solved. Both Homeric models further involve closing rituals; Hector's funeral and the oaths Athena compels Odysseus and the families of the suitors to swear.[28] Indeed, given the role of the Homeric epics in shaping the Vergilian reader's expectations, recalling Athena's role in reminding Odysseus of the need to observe restraint underscores the impact of the return of the Junonian language of anger and violence. The author of the *Aeneid* will not give us a true end, but a stop that one might compare to a symphony's finale recapitulating its main theme, but in the wrong key.[29] The ending of the *Odyssey* thus seems to stand between those of the *Iliad* and the *Aeneid* and indicates that the *Aeneid*'s open-endedness is not developed *ex nihilo*, but drawn and greatly expanded from the hints of dissonances in its epic predecessors. The epic code, affirmed by the *Aeneid*'s proem, incites certain expectations in the reader.[30] The story's lack of progress in escaping *dolor* and *ira* is mirrored in the frustration of narrative desire; the plot's form is thematized.

Narrative repetition may have mastered the characters, but a reader finds its textual energies flung forward into history, unbounded, as for Vergil's epic, in the terms of the Russian Formalists, the plot (*sjuzet*) undermines, not merely arranges, the *fabula*. The *Aeneid*, essentially, lacks a coda which, W. Labov argues, typically has

> the property of bridging the gap between the moment of time at the end of the narrative proper and the present. They [codas] bring the narrator and the listener back to the point at which they entered the narrative.[31] (*Language* 365)

If the reader of the *Aeneid* does not return to where s/he entered the narrative, then where is s/he? Still in the narrative, watching fratricidal civil war, a position that Vergil's original readers might have found very uncomfortable, confronted with "the human stakes of literary form."[32] The narrative order typical of the Homeric epic shares much with the realistic aims of the plots of nineteenth-century novels, an ordered world that Brooks sees scrutinized and dismantled in twentieth-century fiction, a process not unlike the one I see unfolding in the *Aeneid*.[33] Now while I do not want to suggest a Spenglerian cyclical view of history and narrative, or to view Vergil as an Ovidian proto-postmodernist, I hope that Brooks can illuminate for students of ancient narrative the complex relationship among narrative history, the reader's desire for coherence, and a text's capacity to frustrate that desire. But perhaps Vergil is yet another case where the uses of historical literary terms such as "Ancient," "Modern," and "Postmodern" fail as evaluative devices. Modernism, along with its successor, seeks, among other goals, to do away with the idea of narrative endings as natural and necessarily coherent, but as "tenuous, fictive, arbitrary" (Brooks, *Reading for the Plot* 314). It similarly questions the ability of narrative to recover the past by integrating it "within the present through a coherent plot fully predicated and understood as past" (*Reading for the Plot* 311). Narrative thus presents an "incomplete, but not false, image of the universe" (318). Another student of beginnings, endings and the workings of desire, St. Augustine, observing the patent mendacity of the historical promise of *imperium sine fine*, presents an image of Vergil lying to his Roman public through Jupiter's *persona: sicut Deus falsus erat, ita mendax vates.*[34] In O'Hara's words, this account is "crude and inadequate" (*Death and Optimistic Prophecy* 127), but St. Augustine might have avoided such claims had he been a better literary formalist, for Vergil's ending elides falsehood by denying itself.[35]

Notes

1. Given the controversy in some feminist circles over Freud's work, it is interesting to note the resurgence of psychoanalysis in Ancona, *Time and the Erotic*, and Janan, *When the Lamp Is Shattered*, who both finely weave together the concerns of feminism, psychoanalysis and Latin lyric.

2. "Freud's Masterplot: Questions of Narrative." This collection originally appeared as a double issue, numbers 55/56, of *Yale French Studies*. All of my references are to the later book, *Reading for the Plot*.

Before anyone reaches for his or her anti-Freudian revolver, please allow me to make two pre-emptory points in self-defense. First, my main concern here is with

Brooks' narrative theory, which draws on Freud, rather than with Freud's work itself; those with criticisms of Brooks should consult his responses to previous objections in his *Reading for the Plot*, which also includes a perspicuous defense of psychoanalysis itself. Second, this is not the place to hash out yet again the now century-old controversies concerning psychoanalysis. One is tempted to say that Freud might ultimately be proven right by the very continual recurrence of exactly the same arguments. It is obvious where my sympathies lie. Reasonable recent defenses of Freud and psychoanalysis can be found in Zizek (*Metastases*), Wollheim (*The Mind*), and Robinson (*Freud and His Critics*), and a review of the latter two by Thomas Nagel in the *New York Review of Books* (May 12,1994).

3. For a discussion, with bibliography, of closure in ancient literature, see Fowler, "First Thoughts on Closure." My thoughts on the *Aeneid*'s self-consciousness of its form have been ultimately inspired by Stephen Booth's study of *King Lear.*

4. Fowler, "First Thoughts of Closure" 77, with amusing self-deprecation, confesses that his examination is "one of those annoying pieces which suggest that it would be a good idea if somebody else did some work." Those who object to the current article now know whom to blame.

5. I use the term "reader" as shorthand for a more awkward term such as "receiver," or the even more cumbersome "reader/auditor." I am well aware that the ears of Vergil's audience were at least as important as their eyes, and, in fact, greater attention to sound could actually support many of my arguments.

6. See Janan, *When the Lamp Is Shattered*, especially the theoretical first chapter, for an insightful discussion of the role of desire in Roman poetry.

7. Hardie, "Closure in Latin Epic," follows on the lead set by Fowler, "First Thoughts on Closure." I am grateful to Philip Hardie for allowing me to read this work before its publication.

8. On importance of these lines for the epic as a whole, see O'Hara, *Death and Optimistic Prophecy.*

9. However, since *meta* and *finis* are not metrically equivalent in the ablative, *sine meta dedi* cannot fit in a hexameter in that particular order. In Book 12, Vergil also clusters *supremum* (803) and *finis* (793).

10. On the conflict between the text's surface message and a reader's knowledge of history, see Feeney, "Reconciliations."

11. Lyne's comments are apt here: "From the standpoint of Vergil's time, this might seem to have been proved true. But is it not expansive—bland, facile, conveniently omitting to mention the vast amount of blood, sweat and tears the human recipients of his gift will have to expend (not to mention its enemies)?" (*Further Voices* 80-81). See O'Hara, *Death and Optimistic Prophecy* 132-33, on how "Jupiter is carefully tailoring his prophecy to console Venus." One can draw parallels between Jupiter's evasiveness here and his collapse before Juno's demands in Book 12, parallels specifically evoked by the repetition of *olli subridens* from 1.254 to 12.829. On Jupiter in Book 12 see Feeney, "Reconciliations" and Johnson, *Darkness Visible* 123-27.

12. Hardie, "Closure in Latin Epic" writes *a propos* of Jupiter's questions in Book 12: "If *mora* is the concern of actors on earth, the divine characters speak more directly of an end."

13. The alternative reading of *furenti* for *ruenti* does not meaningfully affect my point here since both indicate a loss of control.

14. Nagle, "Open-ended Closure" 263, comments on the "explicit closural allusion" at the end of Book 3.

15. The binding assonance of *fines* and *fides* may be significant as well.

16. On this passage, see Quint, "Repetition" 29-30.

17. From this point in my discussion, "Vergil" signifies "Vergil the narrator."

18. On Juturna see Barchiesi, "Il lamento" and Mitchell, "Violence."

19. See Nagy, *Best of the Achaeans*, on the thematic antagonism between Odysseus and Achilles.

20. On the verb *condere* in the *Aeneid*, see Hexter, "Sidonian Dido" 359.

21. Interestingly, both instances are infinitives used in non-indicative sentences; Aeneas' in a condition, Juturna's in a wish.

22. O'Hara draws on the theoretical work of Naomi Schor.

23. Di Cesare, *Altar and the City* 236, picks up some of these connections and notes the sympathy the poet draws to Turnus by shifting to Turnus in Book 12 some of the language used to describe the helpless Aeneas in Book 1. On the problem of mimetic behavior between Turnus and Aeneas see the studies of Bandera ("Sacrificial Levels") and Hardie (*Epic Successors* ch. 2) which were both influenced by René Girard.

An additional, potentially more disquieting shift can be seen in the description of the Dira's perception of the final array of the two opposing troops—*postquam acies videt Iliacas atque agmina Turni* (12.861)—which recalls Aeneas viewing the monuments in Carthage: *videt Iliacas ex ordine pugna* (1.457). While the repetition of *videt Iliacas* may be coincidental, the poet's choice to use twice an otherwise unique combination of words to describe both a suffering hero mournfully reviewing his past from a distance and a havoc-wreaking goddess about to terrify her last victim is disconcerting, to say the least, and it raises again the homology of epic and divine memory.

24. Springer gives little indication of what narrative closure entails. He argues that *Iliad* 22-24 is, essentially, all unnecessary anti-climax.

25. See Putnam's similar thoughts, "Daedalus" 194-97. Farron, "Abruptness" observes how infrequent violent endings are in ancient literature.

26. See the last chapter of Redfield (*Nature and Culture*), "Purification."

27. I am grateful to Micaela Janan for suggesting this image.

28. However, as Hardie, *Epic Successors* ch. 2, and Mitchell, "Violence," observe, sacrificial imagery dominates the *Aeneid*'s end.

29. One might compare the breakdown of closure in musical narrative in this century; the Sibelius Fourth Symphony merely seems to stop, not end. Similarly, the close of the Ninth Symphony of Gustav Mahler fails to achieve the proper harmonic resolution, although the meaning of this is debatable.

30. On this function of the epic proem, see Conte, *Rhetoric of Imitation* 70-86.

31. I am grateful to Ahuvia Kahane for bringing this passage to my attention. In a currently unpublished study, Kahane observes that "Introductions and codas affect a *deictic shift*, i.e., they bring the audience back to and from the fictional reality."

32. Brooks, *Psychoanalysis* 35. Quint, "Repetition," observes that the "image of civil war" at the end of *Aeneid* "calls its own closure into question" (50).

33. On Homer, Vergil and nineteenth-century fiction, see Johnson, *Darkness Visible* 24-27. However, Johnson is interested in matters of verisimilitude in terms of tone and linguistic surfaces, while I stress here the narrative form as a whole. The two areas, of course, are related.

34. *Serm.* 105, 7, 10. Cited in O'Hara, *Death and Optimistic Prophecy* 126-27.

35. An early version of this paper was given at the 1993 Annual Meeting of the APA in Washington, D.C., for a special panel on psychoanalysis and Roman poetry. For comments and help on its various incarnations, I am grateful to the panel's organizer, Andrew Walker, as well as Martha Davis, Julia Dyson, Don Fowler, Sander Goldberg, Philip Hardie, Sharon James, Micaela Janan, Ahuvia Kahane, Georgia Nugent, James O'Hara and Michael Putnam. I would also like to thank the directors of the Center for Hellenic Studies, Deborah Boedeker and Kurt Raaflaub, for not frowning on my Vergilian studies while I was a Junior Fellow during the 1993-94 year.

Bibliography

Ancona, R. *Time and the Erotic in Horace's Odes.* Durham: Duke University Press, 1994.

Anderson, W. S. "Vergil's Second *Iliad.*" *TAPA* 88 (1957) 17-30.

Bandera, C. "Sacrificial Levels in Virgil's *Aeneid.*" *Arethusa* 14 (1981) 217-39.

Barchiesi, A. "Il lamento di Giuturna." *MD* 1 (1978) 99-121.

Booth, S. *King Lear, Macbeth, Indefinition, and Tragedy.* New Haven: Yale University Press, 1983.

Brooks, P. *Psychoanalysis and Storytelling.* Oxford and Cambridge, Mass.: Blackwell, 1994.

_____. *Reading for the Plot.* New York: A. A. Knopf, 1984.

Conte, G. B. *The Rhetoric of Imitation: Genre and Poetic Memory in Virgil and Other Latin Poets,* translated by Charles Segal. Ithaca: Cornell University Press, 1986.

Di Cesare, M. *The Altar and the City: a Reading of Vergil's Aeneid.* New York: Columbia University Press, 1974.

Duckworth, G. E. *Structural Patterns and Proportions in Virgil's Aeneid.* Ann Arbor: University of Michigan Press, 1962.

Farron, S. "The Abruptness of the End of the *Aeneid.*" *AC* 25 (1982) 136-41.

Feeney, D. C. "The Reconciliations of Juno." *CQ* 33 (1984) 188-203.

Felman, S., ed. *Literature and Psychoanalysis: The Question of Reading: Otherwise.* Baltimore: Johns Hopkins University Press, 1982.

Fowler, D. P. "First Thoughts on Closure: Problems and Prospects." *MD* 22 (1989) 75-122.

_____. "Narrate and Describe: The Problem of Ekphrasis." *JRS* 81 (1991) 25-35.

Gillis, D. *Eros and Death in the Aeneid.* Rome: "L'Erma" di Bretschneider, 1983.

Hardie, P. "Closure in Latin Epic." In *Classical Closure: Endings in Ancient Liter-*

ature, edited by F. Dunn, D. Fowler, and D. Roberts. Oxford: Oxford University Press, forthcoming.

_____. *The Epic Successors of Virgil: A Study in the Dynamics of a Tradition*. Cambridge: Cambridge University Press, 1993.

Hexter, R. "Sidonian Dido." In *Innovations of Antiquity*, edited by R. Hexter and D. Selden. New York and London: Routledge, Chapman & Hall, 1992.

Janan, M. *When the Lamp Is Shattered: Desire and Narrative in Catullus*. Carbondale, Ill.: Southern Illinois University Press, 1994.

Johnson, W. R. *Darkness Visible: A Study on Vergil's Aeneid*. Berkeley and Los Angeles: University of California Press, 1976.

Labov, W. *Language in the Inner City*. Philadelphia: University of Pennsylvania Press, 1972.

Lyne, R. O. A. M. *Further Voices in Vergil's Aeneid*. Oxford: Oxford University Press, 1987.

Masters, J. *Poetry and Civil War in Lucan's Bellum Civile*. Oxford: Oxford University Press, 1992.

Mitchell, R. N. "The Violence of Virginity in the *Aeneid*." *Arethusa* 24 (1991) 219-38.

Nagle, B. R. "Open-ended Closure in *Aeneid* 2." *CW* 76 (1983) 257-63.

Nagy, G. *The Best of the Achaeans*. Baltimore: Johns Hopkins University Press, 1979.

O'Hara, J. J. *Death and Optimistic Prophecy in Vergil's Aeneid*. Princeton: Princeton University Press, 1990.

_____. "Dido as 'Interpreting Character' at *Aeneid* 4.56-66." *Arethusa* 26 (1993) 99-114.

Pucci, P. "Antiphonal Lament between Achilles and Briseis." *Colby Quarterly* 29 (1993) 258-72.

Putnam, M. C. J. "Daedalus, Virgil and the End of Art." *AJP* 108 (1987) 173-98.

_____. "Possessiveness, Sexuality and Heroism in the *Aeneid*." *Vergilius* 31 (1985) 1-21.

Quint, D. "Repetition and Ideology in the *Aeneid*." *MD* 23 (1990) 9-54; reprinted in *Epic and Empire*. Princeton: Princeton University Press, 1993.

Redfield, J. *Nature and Culture in the Iliad: The Tragedy of Hector*. Chicago: University of Chicago Press, 1975.

Robinson, P. *Freud and His Critics*. Berkeley and Los Angeles: University of California Press, 1993.

Springer, C. "The Last Lines of the *Aeneid*." *CJ* 82 (1987) 310-13.

Wollheim, R. *The Mind and Its Depths*. Cambridge, Mass.: Harvard University Press, 1993.

Zizek, S. *The Metastases of Enjoyment*. London and New York: Routledge, Chapman & Hall, 1994.

The Dionysus in Aeneas _____

Clifford Weber

> But Aeneas is not just Augustus. There is also the possibility of his being Augustus' bitter enemy, Marc Antony. Such is the identification we are led to make when, in the fourth book, he has become the consort of Dido, queen of Carthage.
>
> —Adam Parry, "The Two Voices of Virgil's *Aeneid*"[1]

From time to time, a Dionysiac element has been noted in Virgil's portrayal of Aeneas at Dido's court. For example, Brooks Otis, writing in 1964, called attention to "a nuance of Bacchic frenzy" in Aeneas as he is compared to Apollo in *Aeneid* 4.146-50.[2] Some years later, in an article published in the early 1970s, E. L. Harrison observed that the metaphor of the hunt in Books 1 and 4 "changes direction," just as the same metaphor does in Euripides' *Bacchae*.[3] Finally, in a recent book, published in 1997, Michael Paschalis characterizes as "manifestly Bacchic" the features that Apollo's worshipers display in the afore-mentioned simile comparing Aeneas to Apollo.[4]

Isolated observations such as these raise a number of questions that ought to be considered individually and systematically. First, in Virgil's account of Aeneas' dalliance in Carthage, precisely where is this "Bacchic motif," as Otis calls it, to be found? Secondly, does this motif appear only sporadically, or does it undergo a sustained and continuous development? Finally, if an uninterrupted link can be shown to exist between Dionysus and Aeneas at Dido's court, what literary ends might this linkage conceivably serve? The pages that follow will address each of these questions in turn.

As Otis and Paschalis have previously noted, a link between Dionysus and Aeneas in Carthage is first intimated in a most unlikely place, that is, in the simile that likens Aeneas not to Dionysus but to that god's antitype, Apollo.[5] To my knowledge, the degree to which Bacchic elements pervade this simile has never been adequately elucidated. There is thus a good reason for beginning with just this topic. The lines in question (*Aen*. 4.143-50) are these:

> Qualis ubi hibernam Lyciam Xanthique fluenta
> deserit ac Delum maternam invisit Apollo
> instauratque choros, mixtique altaria circum
> Cretesque Dryopesque fremunt pictique Agathyrsi;
> ipse iugis Cynthi graditur mollique fluentem
> fronde premit crinem fingens atque implicat auro,
> tela sonant umeris: haud illo segnior ibat
> Aeneas, tantum egregio decus enitet ore.

Just as when, in winter, Lycia and the streams of Xanthus
are left behind, and his mother's Delos visited, by Apollo,
and he renews dances, and, mingled round the altar,
Cretans and Dryopians and painted Agathyrsians roar;
the god himself walks on the ridges of Cynthus, and with soft
frondage he controls his flowing hair, putting it in place, and entwines
    it with gold.
Weapons rattle on his shoulders. Not slower than he was Aeneas
    going,
and as much splendor radiates from his handsome face.

This simile first compares Aeneas—*ante alios pulcherrimus*[6] *omnis*—to someone of whom it is said, before he is named, *hibernam Lyciam Xanthique fluenta/ deserit ac Delum maternam invisit*. The names Lycia, Xanthus, and Delos would imply Apollo, who in fact proves to be the subject of *deserit* and *invisit* when this subject is finally identified at the end of *Aeneid* 4.144. At the same time, the god who, after an absence abroad in Asia, returns to the Greek land of his mother and there sets his votaries to dancing (*instauratque choros* in 4.145)—this god is first and foremost Dionysus. Indeed, Euripides' *Bacchae* begins with this theme, and it recurs throughout the play.[7] The connection, moreover, between the god's mother and his destination stands out because of its absence from the simile of Apollonius that Virgil is recalling here. In Apollonius, Delos is not "maternal" but ἠγαθέη (*Argon.* 1.308).

Virgil's sole alteration to the next line in Apollonius' simile is to change the modifier of Lycia from εὐρεῖα to *hiberna*. If anything, this detail suits a Bacchic context better than it does Apollo's Lycia. The climate of Lycia is temperate;[8] indeed, in Ovid's *Metamorphoses* 6.339-42, it is hot and dry. Therefore, applied to Lycia in *Aeneid* 4.143, *hibernus* cannot mean "wintry." Out of thirteen other occurrences in Virgil, *hibernus* carries the meaning "in winter" in all cases but two (*Ecl.* 10.20, *G.* 2.339). This usual meaning of *hibernus* is the meaning in *Aeneid* 4.143 as well. Lycia is not Apollo's "winter home" (so R. G. Austin, 1955, ad loc.); on the contrary, it is the place in Asia that in winter the god *leaves behind* for Greece.[9] Yet it is an unfamiliar Apollo who joins his worshipers in the dead of winter. As T. E. Page and Arthur Pease remark (1894-1900 and 1935 respectively, ad loc.), the presence of the visitors named in 4.146 actually rules out winter rites on Delos. The god whose epiphany coincides with winter is rather Dionysus, winter being the season when this god renews his biennial dances on Parnassus and, probably, on Cithaeron as well.[10] Thus, no less than the god's journey from Asia to the Greek land of his mother, the winter setting of this journey suits Dionysus above all.

After leaving Asia and arriving in his mother's land, Apollo is said to "renew dances" (*instauratque choros*) in *Aeneid* 4.145. Dances in honor of Apollo are attested elsewhere,[11] yet they differ in several respects from the dances described here in Virgil's simile. For example, Apollo is elsewhere a spectator, but here he takes the initiative. Secondly, in the cult of Apollo, dancing is but one of several concurrent events,[12] but here it is the sole event. Finally, if the dances on Delos in Virgil's simile reflect the historical Delian festival,[13] celebrated annually, then the simile is remarkably indifferent to the fact that at this festival, the dancers were girls and were led by a bard.[14]

On the other hand, *instauratque choros* suits Dionysus admirably. No mere spectator as others sing and dance in his honor, Dionysus is "the dance god *par excellence.*"[15] In Dionysiac religion, moreover, dance does not share the stage with other, equally prominent forms of worship; rather, it is "the central and essential feature of Dionysiac rites."[16] Finally, the verb *instaurat* in Virgil's simile implies the god's personal renewal of dances performed at regular intervals. Applied to Dionysus, this verb would denote not only the god's participation in his votaries' dances, but in particular the regular celebration of Dionysiac rites in alternate winters. Indeed, this biennial regularity of Dionysiac ritual underlies the technical term ετηρίς,[17] to which Virgil himself refers in *Aeneid* 4.302-3.

In summary, then, the dances renewed by Apollo in Virgil's simile are less than perfectly congruent with the usual form of Apollo's worship; much more do they resemble the dances reinstituted by Dionysus in alternate winters.

In *Aeneid* 4.146, Apollo's votaries are a motley crew. This is explicitly acknowledged in the participle *mixti* (4.145), which Virgil employs elsewhere as well to denote comminglings of heterogeneous groups.[18] Apollo's Cretan worshipers are mainstream Greeks, but the Dryopians are "a rude and predatory Greek tribe."[19] The Agathyrsians are obscure barbarians who here make their debut in Latin poetry, never to be mentioned again by any poet except Juvenal, who, contradicting Herodotus 4.104, thought them uncivilized (*immanes*, 15.125).

Polyglot devotees such as these are out of place in the cult of Apollo, "the most characteristically Greek of all the gods,"[20] and a god who "moved only in the best society," withholding his epiphanies from all except the nobility.[21] Dionysus, on the other hand, is a famously ecumenical god whose worship is open to all, Greeks and barbarians alike.[22] Therefore, whatever may be the analogue in Aeneas' career of the Cretans, Dryopians, and Agathyrsians who roar round Apollo's altar,[23] this heterogeneous mélange of mainstream and marginal Greeks mingling with outlandish foreigners has no place in the elitist cult of

Apollo. Such a retinue of polyglot worshipers would rather be at home in the ecumenical milieu of Dionysus.

The same applies to the tripartition of Virgilian Apollo's votaries into Cretans, Dryopians, and Agathyrsians. Just as Bacchic rites were celebrated every three years (reckoned inclusively) and dubbed τριετηρίδες accordingly, so was a community of the god's devotees divided into three θίασοι. Even if not universal, this was at least the custom in Thebes[24] and so became well known in antiquity. Therefore, when Apollo's devotees fall into three groups in *Aeneid* 4.146, this tripartite organization is consonant with other features that give to these worshipers of Apollo a distinctly Bacchic quality.

Before we turn from the content to the diction and the poetic style of *Aeneid* 4.146, the final two words (*altaria circum*) in the preceding line deserve comment. The specific detail that Apollo's retinue circles the god's altar finds precedent in Theognis and Apollonius.[25] Nevertheless, as "one of the most ancient types of dance . . . especially associated with springs and altars,"[26] a ring dance such as this is by no means confined to the cult of Apollo (or even, for that matter, to Graeco-Roman antiquity). Indeed, arguably its most familiar realizations in Greece are all connected with Dionysus. In Greek theaters, the orchestra contained an altar to Dionysus (the so-called θυμέλη) at its center, and, in the earliest Greek drama, the chorus danced round this altar.[27] Correspondingly, at the City Dionysia in Athens, the dithyramb was performed by a chorus dancing in a ring around the altar in the orchestra.[28] Indeed, Aristophanes routinely treats the circular formation of its chorus as a distinguishing feature of the dithyramb, even as he dubs the dithyrambic poet Cinesias a κυκλιοδιδάσκαλος.[29] Thus, while Apollo's connection with singing and dancing round an altar would appear to be mostly confined to Greek poetry, the same practice in a Dionysiac setting was nothing less than a recurrent and, hence, familiar aspect of Greek cultural and religious life.

If the words *altaria circum* evoke the shape and the locus of the dithyrambic chorus, the meter and the diction of the following line

(*Aen.* 4.146) bring to mind the dithyramb itself. Whatever the dithyramb was in fact, what Virgil's contemporaries perceived it to be—at least in its Pindaric realization—is clear from these lines of Horace (*Carm.* 4.2.10-12):

> seu per audacis **nova** dithyrambos
> **verba** devolvit *numeris*que fertur
> *lege solutis*

For Horace, then, the salient attributes of the dithyramb were neologism and metrical license.[30] That Horace's contemporaries shared this view would seem to follow from the Roman poetry dating to the period of roughly seventy years between the floruit of Catullus and Lucretius and the composition of Ovid's *Metamorphoses*. In the verse surviving from this period, passages having to do with Dionysus, either directly or indirectly, seem to contain more than their share of unprecedented words coupled with metrical mannerisms that, in mimicking Greek practice, violate neoteric and Augustan norms.[31] To cite only a few examples chosen more or less at random, in Catullus 64.252, the epiphany of Bacchus and his retinue is described in a spondaic hexameter containing the compound *Nysigenus*, which is otherwise unattested and quite possibly a neologism:[32]

> cum thiaso Satyrorum et Nysigenis Silenis

In Virgil, *Georgics* 2.5 is a spondaic line in which, moreover, the final syllable of *gravidus* is lengthened in arsis:

> muneribus, tibi pampineo gravidus autumno

Coming from an invocation to Bacchus, this line also contains the epithet *pampineus*, which for us is a Virgilian neologism. It occurs four times in Virgil, and always in connection with Dionysus.[33] Similarly, in *Aeneid* 4.302, comparing Dido to a maenad, the epithet *trietericus* makes its debut in Latin poetry:

> Thyias, ubi audito stimulant trieterica Baccho

In Ovid, *Metamorphoses* 3.530 belongs to a description of a Bacchanal and features *-que* scanned long in the second arsis:

> vulgusque proceresque ignota ad sacra feruntur

Metamorphoses 3.669 is a spondaic line describing the animals that surround Dionysus:

> pictarumque iacent fera corpora pantherarum

The most extreme example of all is to be found in *Metamorphoses* 4.10-13:

> telasque calathosque infectaque pensa reponunt
> turaque dant Bacchumque vocant Bromiumque Lyaeumque
> ignigenamque satumque iterum solumque bimatrem:
> additur his Nyseus indetonsusque Thyoneus

These four lines belong to a description of Bacchic rites and include *-que* scanned long in the second arsis, one hypermeter, and three words (two of them compounds) attested only here: *ignigena*, *Nyseus*, and *indetonsus*.

With these lines that are connected in some way with Dionysus, *Aeneid* 4.146 shares both the neologism and the metrical license that Horace associates with dithyrambs. In *Aeneid* 4.146, both Dryopians and Agathyrsians make their debut in Latin verse, the latter to appear only once again in verse, as was mentioned above, as the *immanes Agathyrsi* in Juvenal 15.125. As far as anomalous prosody is concerned, *Aeneid* 4.146 mimics Greek norms in concluding with a Greek word of ionic-a-minore scansion. In the same line, *-que* is scanned long in the second arsis, just as it is in two of the lines (Ov. *Met.* 3.530, 4.10) quoted above. To be sure, if they occurred in isolation, even these four idiosyncrasies might not suffice to imbue *Aeneid* 4.146 with a dithyrambic coloring. Combined, however, with the other intimations of Dionysus that have already been identified in the preceding lines, two apparent neologisms coupled with two metrical anomalies, all of them Greek,[34] and all concentrated in a single line—these impart to *Aeneid* 4.146 not only a note of generalized "Bacchic frenzy," as Otis observed, but specifically a strong suggestion of the style of the dithyramb.

The resemblance between *Aeneid* 4.146 and dithyrambic style is not the only way in which the meter and the diction of this line acquire a distinctly Bacchic cast. *Aeneid* 4.146 is also composed of words that, in the aggregate, allude to Dionysus as clearly as a comparison to Apollo will allow. Of these words, the most obviously suggestive must be the name *Agathyrsi*, the etymology of which, as it is explained by one Pisander in Stephanus Byzantius (s.v.), would make of these people "the right thyrsic ones." It is difficult in any case to understand why these obscure outlanders are worshiping Apollo on Delos;[35] yet this enigma is compounded when account is taken of their name, which would connect them not with Apollo but with Apollo's antithesis, Dionysus. These Agathyrsians Wilamowitz took for Hyperboreans and explained their name as due to Hellenistic preciosity.[36] That it may be, but it is also a name enhancing, as Paschalis has remarked,[37] the Bacchic coloring of a passage ostensibly concerned with Apollo.

The Bacchic connotations of the Agathyrsians' name also shed light on their characterization as *picti*. Whether this word refers to tattooing or to some other means of coloring the skin or hair,[38] painted or tattooed devotees are out of place in the cult of Apollo. Tattooing the Greeks considered the mark of a slave and, hence, "ugly and dishonorable" (αἰσχρὸν καὶ ἄτιμον[39]). With this judgment "the most characteristically Greek of all the gods" may safely be presumed to have concurred. It is thus hardly surprising that no evidence would appear to exist of either Apollo or his votaries wearing tattoos or otherwise coloring their skin or hair. Yet quite the opposite applies not only to Dionysus himself, but especially to some of his devotees.[40] Thus, *picti* applied to Agathyrsians is, like their name, familiar in the realm of Dionysus but alien to Apollo's world.

To turn from the Agathyrsians to the action in which they engage, Theognis 779 and Callimachus *Hymn to Apollo* 102 will not allow the claim to be made unconditionally that noisy worshipers are out of place in the restrained ambience of Apollonian ritual. Yet the roar that they here emit, though elsewhere unparalleled in the cult of Apollo, is one of the primary attributes of Dionysus and is reflected in this god's epithet "Bromius."[41] Indeed, ancient musicological sources contrast the restraint of the Apollonian paean with the boisterousness of the Bacchic dithyramb,[42] which Aeschylus characterized as μξοβόας (*TGF* 3.355). For Pratinas too, noise (θόρυβος) was one of three attributes distinguishing a Bacchic θίασος (*TGF* 1.18).

In the realm of diction, Virgil's verb *fremere* is something of a *vox propria* for the Bacchic roar, recurring in this connection not only in the *Aeneid* (7.389), but also in Ovid's *Metamorphoses* (3.528). Indeed, *fremere* is probably cognate with Greek βρέμειν and, hence, with Dionysus' epithet Bromius.[43] Together with *Agathyrsi*, then, *fremunt* would create another etymological link, real or apparent, between a word in *Aeneid* 4.146 and one of the hallmarks of Dionysus. Indeed, there may even be a third such case, for the Dryopians share with Dionysus nomenclature connecting them with trees in general and with the oak in particular. As their name contains the stem of Greek δρῦς; ("tree," "oak"), so does Dionysus receive three epithets, all compounded with δενδρ-, that make him Lord of the Trees.[44]

Even if *Aeneid* 4.146 is the most ostentatiously Dionysiac of all the lines in the Apollo simile, intimations of Dionysus persist in the rest of the passage as well. In the phrase *ipse iugis Cynthi graditur*, for example, at the beginning of the next line, Apollo is so unfamiliar a traveler on mountain ridges that Pease, overlooking the *Homeric Hymn to Apollo* 141, cites no parallel for this detail. The noun *iugis* would in any case imply a mountain somewhat higher than the 118-meter hill that Cynthus is. Thus, while *Aeneid* 4.147 suggests both a mountain and a mountain deity, neither Cynthus nor its god meets either requirement particularly well. On the other hand, a mountain god[45] par excellence is to be found in Dionysus, who appears later in the *Aeneid* summoning his maenads to Mt. Cithaeron (4.302-3) and driving his tigers down from Mt. Nysa (6.805). Anacreon has Dionysus "haunting" (ἐπιστρέφεσθαι) mountaintops in *Poetae Lyrici Graeci* 2.4-5; Sophocles has him "dwelling" (ναίειν) there in *Oedipus Tyrannus* 1106; and Phanocles knows him as "mountain-roaming" (ὀρειφοίτης) in fragment 3 in *Collectanea Alexandrina*.[46] Cynthus, then, keeps the phrase *ipse iugis Cynthi graditur* firmly within Apollo's orbit, but otherwise these words suggest a god whose mountain haunts are in general as atypical of Apollo as they are utterly characteristic of Dionysus.

If Apollo walking on mountain ridges is somewhat surprising, what comes next is hardly less so. The rest of *Aeneid* 4.147, and all of the following line, have to do with the god's flowing and carefully coiffed hair. Long hair per se is completely in character for Apollo, as it is for Dionysus. Both gods are eternally young, and hence long hair is a familiar attribute of each of them.[47] Even if Athenians in the 400s B.C.E. contrasted the unrestrained locks of Dionysus with Apollo's style of wearing his hair tied back in a bun,[48] Apollo's untied locks (*crines soluti*) in both Horace *Carmina* 3.4.62 and Propertius 4.6.31 compel the conclusion that in *Aeneid* 4.147-48, Apollo's flowing hair (*fluentem . . . crinem*) is completely appropriate for this god as Augustan poets represent him.

Neither can any significance be attached to *premit crinem*[49] in *Aeneid* 4.148, for elsewhere this expression is applied not only to crowns, helmets, and miters worn atop the head, but also to fillets worn around it (so Sen. *Phaedra* 651, Stat. *Theb.* 10.606). Therefore, although *premere crinem* is used five times of the crown and of the miter that Dionysus typically wears *on* his head (citations in *TLL* 10.2:1169.46-59), it suits equally well the wreath that Apollo wears *around* his head in *Aeneid* 4.148.[50]

At the same time, whatever may be the literal relevance of the epithet *mollis* to Apollo's wreath in *Aeneid* 4.147,[51] this word is also virtually a *vox propria* for objects connected with Dionysus. Beginning in the late 400s B.C.E., an effeminate Dionysus becomes apparent both in art and in drama. In Euripides' *Bacchae* 353, for example, Pentheus refers to the stranger in his city as having the shape of a woman (θηλύμορφος). This aspect of Dionysus' persona becomes universal in succeeding centuries,[52] and it explains why Latin poets so often apply the epithet *mollis* to the god's accoutrements. Indeed, Diodorus Siculus states in 4.4.4 that the delicacy of Dionysus' costume corresponds to the softness (μαλακότης) of the god himself. In Virgil alone, Bacchic objects receive the epithet *mollis* three times: the leaves on the thyrsus in *Eclogues* 5.30-31, the thyrsus itself in *Aeneid* 7.390, and the *oscilla* that Italians hang from pine trees to honor Bacchus in *Georgics* 2.389.[53] Thus, in *Aeneid* 4.147-48, even if Apollo no less than Dionysus can lay claim to long hair, headgear characterized as *mollis* would evoke Dionysus rather than Apollo.

The effeminacy implicit in *molli* in *Aeneid* 4.147 is further suggested by *fingens* in the next line. This participle acquires a degree of emphasis from being somewhat superfluously appended to a clause that is already complete both syntactically and semantically. The nuance that *fingens* adds to the words preceding it can be inferred from the ten other passages in Latin verse (listed in *TLL* 6:772.20-30) in which *fingere* refers to setting the hair. In six of these, the subject is a woman. In the remaining four, the masculinity of the male in question is flawed in one way or another.[54] *Aeneid* 4.148 is thus unique in Latin verse for not applying *fingere* of setting the hair either to a woman or to a male of precarious masculinity. Here *fingens* combines with *molli* in the preceding line to frame *fluentem/ fronde premit crinem*, and both words together imbue the intervening expression with a strong suggestion of the effeminacy that is at once alien to Apollo and intrinsic to Dionysus.[55]

The gold in Apollo's hair in *Aeneid* 4.148 can be—indeed, routinely is—referred to the golden accoutrements for which Apollo, dubbed πολύχρυσος by Callimachus in *Hymn to Apollo* 34, is well known. Yet not every male who wears gold in his hair is a god. On the contrary, one such figure in Statius *Thebais* 5.228 is a weak and tender youth the gold in whose hair is put there by a doting sister. In *Aeneid* 4.148, moreover, the gold in Apollo's hair is combined with a type of headgear that for Virgil is *mollis* and, for Pentheus in Ovid *Metamorphoses* 3.542, betrays men who are men in name only. To be sure, in being compared to an Apollo who wears gold in his hair, Aeneas is made to match the golden queen[56] who is herself compared to Apollo's twin sister in a matching simile. Indeed, Dido's gilt attire is highlighted in *Aeneid* 4.138-39, just before Aeneas is compared to an Apollo with gold in his hair. Nevertheless, the fact remains that Apollo's gold in *Aeneid* 4.148 is such as to evoke not primarily its divine associations, but rather gold as an emblem of luxury and supercivilization. Pease, for example, finds Apollo's "richness of dress" sufficiently striking to merit comment and to require explanation.[57] In a word, the Apollo of this simile exhibits more than a trace of the foppishness that is a hallmark of Dionysus.[58]

It is safe to say, then, that much of the simile comparing Aeneas to Apollo rather gives the impression of likening the Trojan king to Apollo's polar opposite, Dionysus. Nevertheless, the detail with which the simile concludes—*tela sonant umeris* in *Aeneid* 4.149—belongs to Apollo alone. Recalling Homer's description of Apollo bringing death to the Greek army in *Iliad* 1.46-47, weapons rattling on the god's shoulders are incompatible with the peace-loving nature of Dionysus.[59] On the rare occasions when this god appears armed, he and his maenads wield the thyrsus (an "ivied javelin" in Eur. *Bacch.* 25) rather than weapons carried on the shoulders.

Yet it remains a remarkably Dionysiac Apollo to whom Aeneas is compared in *Aeneid* 4.143-49.[60] In causing the polar duality of Apollo and Dionysus to coexist in the persona of his hero, Virgil creates a further correspondence between Aeneas and the Tyrian queen who is metaphorically Aeneas' twin; for Dido is simultaneously identified not only with the chaste Diana, but also with her sensual opposite, Venus. We will return to this point below.

In the pages that remain, limitations of space will allow only an outline of the manifold ways in which Aeneas' assimilation to Dionysus extends beyond the Apollo simile. Nevertheless, though necessarily brief, this outline will at least serve to adumbrate lines of inquiry that further study of this topic could conceivably follow.

Dionysus' aspect as a mountain god has already been documented above. He is also represented as a hunter both in his mythology in general and in Euripides' *Bacchae* in particular.[61] Thus, in *Aeneid* 4.151-59, immediately following the Apollo simile, the dual role of Dionysus as both hunter and mountain god allows the description of the hunt in the mountains to sustain the link between Aeneas and Dionysus that the preceding simile has already established.

The setting of the hunt in the mountains—indeed, in high mountains (*Aen.* 4.151)—receives considerable emphasis, being mentioned in four out of nine lines (151, 153, 155, 159). Yet it is odd for several reasons that this hunt should be set in the mountains at all. First, hunters on horseback (lines 135, 156-57) are incompatible with hunting in the mountains for purely practical reasons.[62] Second, a mountain venue is difficult to reconcile with certain other details. These include the "open plains" (*patentis . . . campos*) in lines 153-54, and Ascanius on horseback "in the middle of the vale" (*mediis in vallibus*) in line 156. Indeed, in lines 153, 155, and 159, the animals being hunted are actually *leaving* the mountains, which has led J. K. Anderson and others to conclude that unmentioned beaters are "somewhere up there among the rocks," while the hunters themselves are down on the plain.[63] Third, a mountain venue is at odds with Juno's forecast in *Aeneid* 4.117-27, where the hunt is twice set in a grove (lines 118, 121), while mountains are never mentioned. For all these reasons, its setting in the mountains is an unexpected and, hence, striking aspect of Virgil's hunting scene. Its effect is to sustain the parallelism between Aeneas and Dionysus. As Dionysus is a mountain god who hunts, Aeneas is a hero who hunts in the mountains.

An additional point merits brief mention in passing. In *Aeneid* 6.804-5, Dionysus drives tigers down from the peak of Mt. Nysa:

> nec qui pampineis victor iuga flectit habenis
> Liber, agens celso Nysae de vertice tigris

Only the first of these lines requires that the god be driving a chariot. The second line, taken by itself, is ambiguous. It could refer to Dionysus hunting[64] and, so interpreted, would recall the similar effect that Aeneas and his hunting partners have on the animals running down from the mountain in *Aeneid* 4.152-59.[65]

Yet the most noticeable point of contact—and surely the most important—between Virgil's hunt and the sphere of Dionysus resides in the fact that the hunting scene in *Aeneid* 4 parallels in both position and function the mountain hunt for Pentheus that is the climax of Euripides' *Bacchae*. Indeed, the counterpoint maintained with this play, both here and in subsequent scenes, duplicates on a smaller scale the sustained allusion to the Homeric epics that characterizes the *Aeneid* as a whole. Beginning in *Aeneid* 1.184-93, where Aeneas goes hunting and kills seven deer, the motif of the hunt constantly reappears, sometimes as reality, sometimes as metaphor, until it culminates in the mountain hunt that leads to the death of the huntress Dido: *ille dies primus leti primusque malorum/ causa fuit* (4.169-70).[66] Likewise, the theme of the hunt has been called the "key metaphor" of the *Bacchae*, permeating the play as an image until the hunt ultimately becomes real and claims the life of the hunter Pentheus.[67]

The hunters in the *Bacchae* number three. The first is Dionysus, identified by Agave as her hunting partner in line 1146 and earlier characterized as a metaphorical hunter of sex (459) and of male spies (731-32). Later, in lines 1189-92, Dionysus is extolled as the actual hunter of Pentheus. Pentheus himself is the second hunter in the play. He hunts maenads (228) and Dionysus (352, 434-35), but for Agave he is inferior to the god as a hunter (1252-53, 1255). Finally, there are the maenads, who are represented as hunting for sex in line 688, but primarily as hunting Pentheus (817, 1183, 1199-1204, 1215, 1241). Toward the end of the play, Agave, as one of their number, boasts that she has renounced housework in favor of the higher calling of hunting with bare hands (1237). Earlier, in lines 731-32, the maenads are figured as Dionysus' hunting dogs.

Aeneas is the Virgilian counterpart of Euripides' Dionysus, as both the hunter who survives the hunt and a stranger newly arrived from Asia. His advent, like that of Dionysus, leads to the death of the reigning monarch. In her role as Aeneas' hunting partner, Dido corresponds to one of Euripides' maenads, together with whom Dionysus is said to hunt in *Bacchae* 1146. Even more salient, however, are the affinities between Dido and Pentheus. Both are reigning monarchs who fall victim to a hunt in the mountains. Indeed, it has not gone unnoticed that Dido and Pentheus play corresponding roles in tragedies in which hunters become the hunted, and vice versa.[68] Finally, it may even be the case that the sexual ambivalence of Euripides' macho king dressed in women's attire is mirrored in the tension between Dido's femininity and her status as a stalwart leader of men. Dido's dual correspondence with both the victim and the partner of Dionysus, contradictory though it may appear, is later confirmed in *Aeneid* 4.301-3 and 469-70, where similes declare that Dido resembles both Pentheus and a maenad respectively.[69]

At the same time, the common metaphor of love as hunting also plays a part in Virgil's hunt in the mountains.[70] This too is paralleled in the *Bacchae*, where Pentheus unkindly represents both Dionysus (459) and the maenads (688) as hunting Aphrodite. In connection with Dionysus, moreover, this metaphor is exploited even more extravagantly in Nonnus' Book 16, devoted in toto to Dionysus' passion for the virgin huntress Nicaea.[71]

In taking to the mountains to hunt in the company of an Aeneas who resembles Dionysus, Dido assumes the role of one of Euripides' maenads. On the other hand, the similarity between Aeneas and Dionysus is further enhanced when the Trojan king withdraws to a cave and there takes part in a grotesque wedding. To be sure, the immediate precursor of this scene is Apollonius Rhodius 4.1128-69, where the marriage of Jason and Medea is consummated in a cave once occupied by Macris, Dionysus' first European nurse. Nevertheless, Virgil's episode in the cave also ties in with the complex of associations linking Aeneas to Dionysus, for in the myth, religion, and iconography of this god above all, caves are central.

The particular instances of Dionysus' connection with caves are too numerous to be presented here.[72] Nevertheless, one stands out as being especially relevant to the cave scene in Virgil. In *Orationes* 9.5, a prose epithalamium, Himerius sets the nuptials of Dionysus and Ariadne "in Cretan caves" (ἐν Κρητικοῖς ἄντροις). Here there is an exact correspondence with the quasi-wedding of Dido and Aeneas in an African cave. To be sure, Himerius is a late source (300s C.E.), but his account is consistent with earlier, graphic portrayals,[73] and Carl Kerényi considers it in any case "the earliest version" of Dionysus' marriage.[74] In addition, the brides Dido and Ariadne are linked once again in Dido's speeches, which repeatedly echo Ariadne's monologue in Catullus.

In Rumor's account of the self-indulgence and lewd behavior of Dido and Aeneas, the reference to the winter season in *Aeneid* 4.193 would apply as well to Dionysus and his women, who, as was mentioned above, stage their orgies in winter. After Rumor has worked her mischief, the correspondence between Aeneas and Dionysus persists, but the Virgilian counterpart of Euripides' Pentheus now ceases to be Dido and becomes instead the Numidian king Iarbas. As Dido's book moves inexorably forward, Virgil's engagement with the *Bacchae* proceeds in the opposite direction, moving backwards from the mountain hunt at the climax of the play to Pentheus' derisive inspection of Dionysus in lines 453-60, and then still farther back to lines 233-41, where Pentheus relates the alarming rumor he has heard.

Beyond the shared situation of a native king inflamed by hearsay and angry that a foppish interloper from the decadent East is seducing the local women,[75] Dionysus and Aeneas as Iarbas represents him exhibit similarities that are remarkable for being both numerous and exact. Specifically, in *Aeneid* 4.215, Iarbas' allegation that the entourage accompanying Aeneas is male only in part (*cum semiviro comitatu*) applies quite literally to Dionysus, whose θίασος in fact consists partly of men, partly of women.[76] In the next line (*Aen.* 4.216), Aeneas is represented as wearing a miter, headgear so typical of Dionysus that in Propertius, the god Vertumnus claims that donning a miter will allow him to pass for Dionysus.[77] In the same line, Iarbas' mockery of Aeneas for hair damp with perfume is paralleled in Pentheus' ridicule of Dionysus for the same affectation.[78]

Finally, in *Aeneid* 4.215-17, Iarbas protests that Aeneas is a Paris redivivus seducing the local women. Pentheus brings a similar charge against Dionysus in the lines cited in note 75 above. Lexicography, moreover, backs Pentheus up, for the partiality that Paris and Dionysus share towards women is reflected in the lexical datum that they also share the epithet γυναιμανής, applied to Paris in *Iliad* 3.39, to Dionysus in *Homeric Hymn to Dionysus* 17 and Nonnus 16.229, 252. For this reason and others, Walter F. Otto finds the same similarity between Paris and Dionysus that Iarbas perceives between Paris and Aeneas.[79] Diodorus Siculus, though mentioning no connection with Paris in particular, nevertheless asserts in 4.4.2 that Dionysus is prone (εὐκατάφορος) to the pleasures of love (αἱ ἀφροδισιακαί ἡδοναί).

No less than in their propensity for love, Aeneas and Dionysus find common ground in the manner and in the object of their love. Unlike his satyr companions and his male kin on Olympus, whose amours tend to be numerous, short-lived, and carnal, Dionysus succumbs to a love that "is ecstatic and binds him to the loved one forever," she being Ariadne above all.[80] As this style of loving is reminiscent of Aeneas' predilections, so are the objects of Dionysus' love. The affinities between Ariadne and Dido are well known. Less familiar is the parallelism between Dionysus' couplings with either Aphrodite or a nymph[81] on the one hand and, on the other, Aeneas' affair with a queen who is figured as each of these women.[82] Dido can thus be connected with the women who play a part in the myth of Dionysus.

These include not only the god's companions, the maenads, but also his exclusively female loves: primarily Ariadne, but nymphs, Aphrodite, and the huntress Nicaea (see n. 71) as well. In turn, Dido's resemblance to each of these women implies a corresponding link between her lover Aeneas and their consort Dionysus.

If Iarbas' description of Aeneas' appearance is liable to seem the distortion of a rival with an ax to grind, the same cannot be said of Aeneas' cloak (*laena*) in *Aeneid* 4.262-64. This the poet himself describes as cascading down from the shoulders (*demissa ex umeris*) and tailored with Tyrian crimson (*Tyrio . . . murice*) and with finely spun gold (*tenui . . . auro*). These particulars duplicate item for item the mantle worn by a statue of Dionysus in a grand procession organized by Ptolemy II Philadelphus.[83] According to the detailed account of this pageant given by Callixeinus of Rhodes (n. 83), the statue of Dionysus, like Virgil's Aeneas, was draped in "a crimson mantle spangled with gold" (ἱμάτιον πορφυροῦν χρυσοποίκιλον). In general, luxurious robes dyed crimson or yellow and trailing down to the feet are thoroughly typical of Dionysus and so figure repeatedly in descriptions of the god beginning with Cratinus and Aristophanes and extending down the centuries to Pausanias.[84] Dionysus' yellow robe even has a name all its own (κροκωτός), yellow being this god's color.[85] Thus, as he is dressed in *Aeneid* 4.262-64, Aeneas could pass for a mortal Dionysus.

If it is the case that, as Adam Parry has written in the epigraph, Aeneas "is" Marc Antony throughout the Dido drama, it stands to reason that in the same episode, Aeneas will also resemble the Dionysus whose mortal counterpart Antony publicly claimed to be. Antony's methods of representing himself in the East as Dionysus reborn are sufficiently well documented to require no summary here.[86] As of 37 B.C.E., when Antony became Cleopatra's consort, two factors in particular furthered his identification with Dionysus. First, as consort of a queen who advertised her connection with Isis, Antony was cast in the complementary role of Osiris-Dionysus.[87] Second, as de facto joint ruler with a Ptolemaic queen whose father, like Antony in Athens, was proclaimed a "new Dionysus," Antony effectively joined a dynasty whose kings claimed descent from Dionysus.[88] Indeed, this propaganda left its imprint on the culture of the entire age, Dionysus being "peculiarly the god of the Hellenistic age."[89] Thus, viewed against the historical backdrop of the Ptolemaic dynasty professing a Dionysiac heritage, Aeneas' assimilation to Dionysus reflects the parallel identification between Antony and the same god. The association between Aeneas and Antony's divine prototype is, then, one of the ways in which Aeneas at Dido's court "is" Antony and emerges by implication as Eastern, monarchical, and distinctly Ptolemaic.

Aeneas' affinities with Dionysus also play a part in the metaphorical representation of Dido and Aeneas as twin sister and brother. This metaphor is based on the fundamental fact that Dido and Aeneas resemble each other in manifold ways. One of these resemblances—their similar fortunes—Dido herself acknowledges in *Aeneid* 1.628. Others have been catalogued by Nicholas Horsfall,[90] and, beyond these, still others exist. For example, justice is a salient trait of both Dido and Aeneas (*Aen.* 1.508, 523, 544-45). They are both wealthy (*Aen.* 1.119, 4.263), and so are Troy and Carthage in general. They both neglect their familial duty, Dido that to her dead husband (*Aen.* 1.719-21, 4.522), Aeneas his to a maturing son (*Aen.* 1.643-46 as opposed to 4.234, 272-76). Dido and Aeneas each present to the other costly things to wear (*Aen.* 1.647-55, 4.261-64), and they are both connoisseurs (*Aen.* 1.119, 455-56). As Dido is *pulcherrima* in *Aeneid* 1.496, Aeneas is *pulcherrimus* in *Aeneid* 4.141. Dido's compassion for a destitute stranger leads to the same ruinous result as the Trojans' compassion for a mendacious Greek: her city like theirs is burned to the ground. Compared to such numerous and wide-ranging similarities as these, not to mention others listed by Horsfall, the differences between Dido and Aeneas are few and insignificant.[91] Indeed, Virgil's foregrounding of Dido and Aeneas' mutual resemblance is later recalled when Plutarch highlights the comparable similarity between Antony and Cleopatra.[92]

The mutual identity of Trojan king and Tyrian queen is also expressed by means of a complex web of interrelated comparisons, images, and allusions. Chief among these are the dual similes that assert the resemblance of Dido and Aeneas to the twin deities Diana and Apollo. The theme of mutual identity is implicit not only in the genetic relationship of Diana and Apollo as twins, but also in the similarity between the similes themselves.[93] In addition to being twin brother and sister, Apollo and Diana are also god and goddess of the sun and of the moon respectively. Likewise, Dido and Aeneas too are linked with the moon and the sun: overtly in *Aeneid* 6.453-54, where a simile likens Dido to a fitful moon, but implicitly as well in *Aeneid* 1.490, 1.742, and elsewhere.[94] The figuring of Dido and Aeneas as sister and brother linked to the moon and the sun is enhanced by the same pair of connections linking their historical counterparts, Cleopatra and Antony. Ruling Egypt as de facto king and queen, Antony and Cleopatra belonged to a dynasty in which a tradition of joint rule was reflected in the appellation of king and queen as brother and sister, which they often were in fact as well.[95] It was assured, moreover, that this tradition would continue into the next generation when, in 40 B.C.E., Cleopatra gave birth to twins by Antony, a boy and a girl whom their names explicitly linked to the sun and the moon. The boy was called Alexander Sun. The girl's name was Cleopatra Moon and so replicated not only the mother's name, but also her public self-representation as the moon goddess.[96] From Olympus, therefore, to mythical Carthage to historical Alexandria, the same typologies persist: twin brothers and sisters, either figurative or real, and in each case their connection with the sun and the moon. The metaphor of Dido and Aeneas as twin sister and brother is thus enhanced by exact parallels both in heaven and in contemporary history.

From the close resemblance between Dido and Aeneas—existing in fact but expressed for the most part metaphorically—it would follow that if a polarity of opposites is embodied in Dido, the same is likely to be found in Aeneas as well. In Dido, such a duality is present in the contrasting figures of Diana and Venus, and ultimately in the opposed principles that these goddesses represent. Correspondingly, as Diana's chastity competes with Venus' sensuality for domination of Dido's soul,[97] so does Diana's male twin, the god of restraint, coexist with— and, for a time, even succumb to—the god of abandon within the soul of Aeneas. To be sure, the possibility of Aeneas' "being" Marc Antony requires the concomitant possibility of his resembling Antony's divine archetype. At the same time, the Dionysus in Aeneas also corresponds to the Venus in Dido. On the level of the microcosm, Artemisian and Apollonian restraint vies with Venusian and Dionysiac abandon to control the individual psyche of Dido and Aeneas respectively. This conflict within individuals finds a macrocosmic analogue in the historical struggle of West against East, waged by Octavian against Antony, for domination of the Mediterranean world.[98] In short, if the complex of polarities to which Aeneas belongs is to be internally consistent, the Apollo in Aeneas requires a Dionysiac antithesis with which to compete for control. Therefore, among several reasons for there being a Dionysus in Aeneas, the most immediate may be the simple fact that Apollo needs a rival to match the Venus who vies with Apollo's twin sister for the soul of Dido. Indeed, when Dido, Aeneas, and their courtiers assemble in Dido's banqueting hall, if only the roles of guest and host were reversed, it could justly be said—as was said in fact when their historical epigones convened on the Cydnus—that "Aphrodite comes in revelry to the side of Dionysus."[99]

Notes

This paper was written to honor the seventy-fifth birthday of my mentor, William S. Anderson, to whom I am pleased to dedicate it *pietatis causa*.

1. Parry 1963, 73.

2. Otis 1964, 74, 76.

3. Harrison 1972-73, 15, and p. 23, n. 34.

4. Paschalis 1997, 153.

5. As one of the referees reviewing this paper has reminded me, the common opinion followed here, that Apollo and Dionysus are polar opposites, is not always taken for granted. Indeed, it has recently been examined in Detienne 2001. Yet Detienne acknowledges a priori that points of contact between the two gods do not vitiate their fundamental opposition, already present "at the origins of Greek religion" (147). When the Apollo worshiped at Magnesia on the Meander causes his votaries to "act as if possessed" (153), this Detienne analyzes as an instance of Apollo's "borrowing" from Dionysus "his apparently most specific trait" (154), and not as a case of the blurring of the contrast between the two gods. Likewise, when ancient iconography depicts Apollo "enveloped in the vine and the bacchanal," for Detienne he "appears completely Dionysiac" (149). This comes very close to my own characterization of Apollo as appearing "remarkably Dionysiac" in Virgil's simile (p. 332 below).

6. Although *pulcher* applies to gods in general (Skutsch 1985, 197), youthful and seductive beauty is routinely ascribed to Apollo and Dionysus in particular. See Bömer 1969-86, 2.20-21, and Williams 1978, 41, both of whom cite many primary sources. Among these, Diod.Sic. 4.4.2 (of Dionysus) and [Tib.] 3.4.25-26 (of Apollo) closely resemble what is said of Aeneas here in *Aen.* 4.141.

7. Viz., in lines 13-20, 55-61, 64-65, 86-87, 234, and 464-65. The suggestion that Apollo's migration in Virgil resembles that of Dionysus in Euripides I owe to the ingenuity of my student, Mr. Bryan Doerries, Kenyon College '98.

8. Cary 1949, 155.

9. Apollo thus replicates Aeneas' abandoning Carthage in winter: see Lewis 1961, 12. Promoting this implication is Virgil's substitution of *deserit* for straightforward εἰσιν in the corresponding part of Apollonius' simile (*Argon.* 1.307). Likewise, in *Aen.* 1.745-46, the same action of Aeneas in the same season is anticipated by Apollo when, in his celestial manifestation as the sun, he hastens to dip himself in Ocean in winter (see Lee 1988, 10-12). As for Dionysus, not only does he travel in winter, but he further parallels Aeneas in traveling by sea (Otto 1965, 63, 93, 156, 163, 198).

10. Dodds 1960, xiii-xiv, 159-60; Farnell 1895-1909, 5:198-200.

11. *Hymn. Hom. Ap.* 149-50; Thgn. 775-79; Callim. *Hymn* 2.8; Ap. Rhod. *Argon.* 1.538-39. Dionys. Per. 527 and Paus. 4.4.1 are inconclusive.

The Dionysus in Aeneas **165**

12. Lonsdale 1994-95, 28-32.

13. So Kerényi (1983, 28), who takes Virgil to be referring to the Hellenistic Delian festival. Kerényi notes, though, that Virgil describes the festival "as if primordial peoples were the attendants."

14. *Hymn. Hom. Ap.* 166-73.

15. Firron 1973, 263. For Dionysus leading his worshipers' dances and participating in them, see Eur. *Bacch.* 62-63 and the sources cited in Dodds 1960, 82-83; Clausen 1994, 162; and Leinieks 1996, 102-4. When Apollo leads a group of dancers, these are the Muses or the Graces (Firron 1973, 256).

16. Leinieks 1996, 58-63; see also Dodds 1960, xiii-xvi.

17. Dodds 1960, xiii-xiv; Pease 1935, 280-81. In Stat. *Theb.* 7.94, *instaurare* occurs together with abl. *trieteris*, which there, however, refers to the biennial celebration of the Nemean Games.

18. Cf. *Ecl.* 10.55; *Aen.* 5.293; 11.134. In Ov. *Met.* 3.529 and Livy 39.13.10, the same participle is applied to women who join men in celebrating Bacchic revels. Similarly, for Aeschylus the dithyramb is μιξοβόας in *TGF* 3.355.

19. Pease 1935, 193. For these Dryopians, see now Strid 1999.

20. Rose 1958, 134. Walter F. Otto is quoted to the same effect in Burkert 1985, 143. That the peoples named in *Aen.* 4.146 are, taken together, unexpected in Apollo's company has even attracted the notice of those whose focus is not literary, e.g., Kerényi in n. 13 above. The qualification "taken together" is important. Individually, a connection between Cretans and Apollo can be traced as far back as the god's prehistory (Burkert 1985, 144-45), and Pausanias 4.34.9 gives to the Dryopians reasons of their own for being specially devoted to Apollo (particulars in Strid 1999, 37-40). Still other Dryopian connections with Apollo are listed in Pease 1935, 193. On the other hand, only the Virgilian scholia ad loc. (and each for different reasons) claim that the Agathyrsians are devotees of Apollo. To others their name rather suggested an affinity with Dionysus.

21. Callim. *Hymn* 2.9, Dodds 1951, 76. William Batstone has reminded me that the Hyperboreans are an exception. One of the referees reviewing this paper objected that the Hellenocentric elitism claimed for Apollo by Dodds and others is refuted by "the international appeal and cosmopolitan atmosphere" of the oracle at Delphi and of the trading post on Delos, not to mention the early and widespread diffusion of Apollo's cult throughout the Mediterranean in general (Burkert 1985, 143-44). In reply, I would stress the important fact that the Apollo of Virgil and Callimachus is not necessarily identical to the historical Apollo in all respects. Nevertheless, even if one adopts a narrowly historical point of view, it does not follow from the internationalism of Delphi and Delos that Greeks and non-Greeks alike worshiped Apollo there. Similarly, in a modern cosmopolis like Manhattan, Jews, Muslims, Christians, and unbelievers interact constantly, yet this interaction has little influence on the religious practices of any of these several groups. As for the diffusion of Apollo's cult in Mediterranean lands, this was due to the migrations of Greek colonists, whose religion cannot be assumed to have won over their non-Greek neighbors. To quote Burkert (loc. cit.), "the worship of Apollo is spread throughout the Greek world." The qualifier "Greek" deserves emphasis.

22. Eur. *Bacch.* 482; Ov. *Met.* 3.529-30. For this distinguishing feature of the Bacchic cult, see Leinieks 1996, 59, 68, 124-25, 327, 330-31, and 345.

23. For this see Lewis 1961, 12.

24. Dodds 1960, 161-62, as opposed to Henrichs 1978, 138 ("may have been a Theban specialty"). See also Theoc. 26.2 (tripartition of worshipers emphasized); and Prop. 3.17.24 (Dionysus' *triplices greges*).

25. Thgn. 779 (not cited in Pease), where shouting (ἰαχή) around Apollo's altar is one of the events honoring the god; and Ap. Rhod. *Argon.* 1.538-39, where young devotees of Apollo gather round his altar and, rather than shout, dance to the accompaniment of the lyre.

26. West 1966, 152.

27. Haigh 1907, 107-8.

28. Pickard-Cambridge 1968, 77.

29. Ar. *Av.* 1403, with which cf. ibid. 1378-79, and frag. 149.10 Demiańczuk (from the *Gerytades*); for the dithyramb characterized as a κύκλιος χορός, Ar. *Nub.* 333, *Av.* 917-18, *Ra.* 366; Xen. *Oec.* 8.20; and Aeschin. 3.232. See Zimmermann 1992, 25-26 and the bibliography cited there.

30. In actual fact as well, these were distinguishing characteristics of both the Pindaric and the "new" dithyrambs, in which neologism tended to assume the form of unprecedented compound adjectives. See Zimmermann 1992, 60, 121.

31. I do not know of any inquiry into a possible link in Roman poetry between Bacchic content on the one hand and, on the other, neologism and metrical license. Such a study would be useful.

32. So Thomson 1997, 422.

33. See Austin 1977, 247.

34. For the Greek flavor of *-que* scanned long in the second arsis, see Clausen 1994, 143; Mynors 1990, 31; and Pease 1935, 192. It is also worth noting that in Verg. *G.* 2.456, where triple *-que* occurs in the same line positions as in *Aen.* 4.146, the context is Bacchic, and the name Rhoecus is unique in Latin verse.

35. "Why Virgil should introduce them into the worship of Apollo is not clear" (Pease 1935, 193).

36. Wilamowitz-Moellendorff 1903, p. 578, n. 2, followed by Clausen 1987, 133.

37. Paschalis 1997, p. 153, n. 18.

38. On this question, Pease (1935, 193-94) leaves no stone unturned, and there is much helpful detail in Dodds 1951, 163-64 as well.

39. Sext. Emp. *Pyr.* 3.202, cited in Pease 1935, 194; and Dodds 1951, 164 (see also 142).

40. Tib. 2.1.55-56 credits the farmer with being the first to have led dances in honor of Bacchus, and to have done so painted red. Thracian maenads are depicted wearing tattoos on several Greek vases (Dodds 1951, 163). Although the practice of applying red paint to statues is widespread, in Greece it was especially statues of Dionysus that received this treatment (Paus. 2.2.6-7, 7.26.11, 8.39.6, 9.32.1; and Versnel 1970, p. 79, n. 5).

41. For the essentials, see Leinieks 1996, 99-100; and Dodds 1960, 74.

42. Rutherford 1994-95, 117.

43. See Chantraine 1968-80, 194; Frisk 1960-72, 1.264-65; Pokorny 1994, 1.143; otherwise Windekens 1986, 49. Damien Nelis has pointed out to me in a letter that in Ap. Rhod. *Argon.* 1.1247 and *Aen.* 9.60, βρέμει and *fremit* correspond in comparable passages.

44. For trees in Bacchic cult and nomenclature, see Detienne 2001, 153-54; Otto 1965, 157-58; Dodds 1960, 80-81.

45. Dionysus is so called in Nisbet and Hubbard 1978, 317.

46. Carl Hosius, followed by R. P. H. Green, was persuaded that in *Idyllia* 10.209-10, Ausonius has transferred *ipse iugis Cynthi graditur* to Dionysus (Hosius 1926, 53; Green 1991, 487). If that were so, it could be taken to imply that the later poet was alert to the Bacchic overtones of Apollo's walking along mountain ridges. Nevertheless, a borrowing from Virgil is very much open to question here.

47. Tib. 1.4.37-38; Ov. *Am.* 1.14.31-32, and *Met.* 3.421; in all of these long hair is said to be common to both gods. See McKeown 1989, 376.

48. For men's hairstyles in fifth-century Athens, see Leinieks 1996, 56; Fitch 1987, 240; Roux 1970-72, 2:405-6.

49. Paschalis (1997, p. 153, n. 18) notes that *crinem* in *Aen.* 4.148 is the last in a series of four words that reappear in the same order in the overtly Bacchic context of *Aen.* 7.390-91. The other three of these words are *choros* (145), *-thyrsi* (146), and *molli* (147). Even if this recurrence is entirely coincidental, it shows how close to the surface of the Apollo simile Bacchic words and themes lie.

50. Conversely, crowns are said to encircle the head in passages too numerous to list. See *TLL* 4:979.23-27, 39-42, 57-60, 980.9.

51. Elsewhere, *frons* receives the epithet *mollis* thrice (Catull. 64.293 [cf. Prop. 1.20.22, another golden line from an epyllion]; Plin. *HN* 8.127, 12.1), *tenera* four times (Verg. *G.* 2.372, *Aen.* 3.449; Ov. *Fast.* 4.398; Columella, *Rust.* 6.9.1; Quint. *Inst.* 2.4.11). The difference between the two epithets would thus appear to be primarily stylistic, *mollis* occurring in verse in exclusively neoteric contexts, *tenera* never so. This distinction is also consistent with the claim advanced below, that *molli* in *Aen.* 4.147 connotes some degree of finesse.

52. See Diod. Sic. 4.4.2, 4.5.2; Ov. *Am.* 3.2.53, *Met.* 3.607, 4.20; Sen. *Hercules furens* 472-76; *Priap.* 36.3; Leinieks 1996, 50-54; Bömer 1969-86, 1.581-82; Otto 1965, 176; Dodds 1960, 133-34.

53. Elsewhere, *mollis* is used of the Bacchic tambourine in Prop. 3.17.33 and in Stat. *Achil.* 1.654-55; the god's garlands in Ov. *Met.* 3.555; Liber's feast in Varro, *Sat. Men.* 443.1 Bücheler-Heraeus; and the hand with which the god wields his thyrsus in Sen. *Hercules furens* 473. It is not always recognized that in all of these instances, *mollis* refers not so much to the objects themselves as to the nature of the god with whom they are associated. Even as early as Euripides, Dionysus' "love locks" (Dodds 1960, 139), soft in themselves, are likely to be called delicate (τρυφερός, *Bacch.* 150) and pretty (ἀβρός, ibid. 493) for the further reason that these words also apply to the effeminate god who wears such locks.

54. See Tib. 1.2.92 (*senex amator*); Manilius *Astronomica* 5.149 (degenerate voluptuaries); Mart. 6.57.1 (a bald counterfeit of Apollo); Stat. *Theb.* 5.228 (a tender youth).

55. Similarly, the two materials adorning Apollo's hair frame *Aen*. 4.148 and enclose a corresponding chiasmus of two verbs. For the elegance of a framed line connoting an elegant appearance, cf. *Aen*. 1.593 (Aeneas beautified by his mother) and Ov. *Met*. 3.556 (Dionysus). Similar to Virgil's double chiasmus of nouns and verbs is Naevius *trag*. 54 Ribbeck, a maximally resolved septenarius (mimicking Dionysus' mincing minions?) framed by the exotic foreign names of the god's glamorous articles of clothing: **diabathra** *in pedibus habebat, erat amictus* **epicroco**.

56. Dido in *Aen*. 1.698, for which see Weber 1998-99, 317-25.

57. Pease 1935, 195.

58. For a similar Apollo in the Corpus Tibullianum, see [Tib.] 3.4.23-38.

59. See Ov. *Met*. 3.553-54 (Dionysus derided by Pentheus for being a "defenseless child" indifferent to wars, weapons [*tela*], and horsemanship); Stat. *Theb*. 7.168-73 (Dionysus protesting that his θίασος knows only revels and not war); Dodds 1960, 109-10, 170.

60. Such a conflation of Apollonian and Dionysiac elements within a single passage has a precedent in Greek in the so-called Ode 16 of Bacchylides, which salutes Apollo's return to Delphi in the poetic form of a dithyramb. See Rutherford 1994-95, 116-18 ("Apollo in Ivy"). For the same conflation in myth and ritual, see Detienne 2001. For Apollo assimilated to Dionysus in other ways, see nn. 77-78 below.

61. Though not attested as an epithet of Dionysus until the 500s C.E., "Zagreus" exhibits the traits of Dionysus as early as Eur. *frag*. 472.11-12 Nauck. The name was etymologized in antiquity as meaning "mighty hunter." In id. *Bacch*. 1189-92, Agave and the chorus praise Dionysus as an accomplished hunter. Finally, two Latin sources have him issuing a summons to the hunt: Plaut. *Men*. 835; and Verg. *G*. 3.43, which have the verb *vocare* in common. See Otto 1965, 109, 191; and Dodds 1960, 225.

62. Anderson 1985, 10, 23.

63. Ibid. 91-92, contradicted by *Aen*. 4.151.

64. See the citations in *TLL* 1:1367.62-70 (hunting) and 1:1367.45-53 (driving a chariot).

65. It would be difficult to argue that *alfa de parte* in *Aen*. 4.153 recalls *parte ex alla* in the Bacchic context of Catull. 64.251, because Catullus shares *parte ex alfa* with Cicero in *Aratea* 367, where the topic is the constellation Orion.

66. For manifestations of the hunting motif from *Aen*. 1.184 through 4.159, see Nelis 2001, 129-35; Lyne 1987, 193-97; Anderson 1969, 43-44; Otis 1964, 75-76. Lyne writes of "Virgilian 'signals' to Dionysus and the *Bacchae*" (p. 197, n. 69).

67. For bibliography on the theme of hunting in the *Bacchae*, see Segal 1997, p. 32, n. 12.

68. For this reversal in the *Bacchae*, see Dodds 1960, 131; and Winnington-Ingram 1948, 70, 107-8. For the same reversal in the *Aeneid*, see Reckford 1995-96, p. 22, and p. 40, n. 38; Lyne 1987, 196; Harrison 1972-73, p. 15, and p. 23, n. 34 (adducing the parallel of the *Bacchae*). It can also be found in the *Argonautica*: Nelis 2001, 129.

69. There are also other similes that confirm prior intimations. For example, the Diana simile in *Aen*. 1.498-502 acknowledges the resemblance between Dido and Diana that is earlier intimated in Aeneas' encounters with a virgin huntress (1.314-37) and with a picture of Penthesilea (1.490-93), she too a virgin and carrying a moon-shaped

shield. Likewise, equating storm winds with rioting citizens, the simile in 1.148-53 confirms the earlier implication that the land of the winds is a *patria* (1.51) with a constitution resembling Rome's (1.54, 62) and a population exhibiting human passions (1.57).

70. See Lyne 1987, 197; and Harrison 1972-73, 15. For the trope of love as hunting, see Green 1996 and Kenney 1970, 386-88. For Dido in particular, see Thornton 1985, 621.

71. Whether or not they indicate direct influence, the points of contact between Nonnus' and Virgil's narratives are many. They include, in addition to the metaphor in question (e.g., 16.232), not only Dionysus' fantasy of Nicaea as his hunting partner, but also the incongruity of Nicaea's embodying, like Dido, both Artemis and Aphrodite simultaneously (16.135).

72. See Ap. Rhod. *Argon.* 2.907-10, 4.1131-38; Callixeinus *FGrH* 627, frags. 1-2; Socr. Rhod. *FGrH* 192, frag. 2.32-33; *Culex* 113; Hazzard 2000, 59-79; Leinieks 1996, 100-102; Merkelbach 1988, 63-66; Rice 1983, 16-17, 60, 81-82; Bérard 1976, 61-62; Roux 1970-72, 2.633-34; Otto 1965, 163-64; Webster 1964, 2, 163, pl. 1a; Boyancé 1960-61, 110-14, 126; Dodds 1960, xxxii, 84, 151, 213.

73. Viz., three sarcophagi cited in Merkelbach 1988, 58-59, 66. They date to the 100s and early 200s C.E. The prototype from which all artistic depictions of a cave-dwelling Dionysus derive is said to be the Chest of Cypselus described in Paus. 5.19.6 (Boyancé 1960-61, 108). For depictions of maenads in or near Bacchic caves, see Merkelbach 1988, pp. 64-65, n. 34; and Boyancé 1960-61, 109.

74. Kerényi 1976, 110.

75. *Aen.* 4.203, 215-17; Eur. *Bacch.* 233-47, 454-59, for which see Dodds' notes.

76. Diod. Sic. 4.2.6 (a στρατόπεδον οὐ μόνον ἀνδρῶν ἀλλὰ καὶ γυναικῶν); Livy 39.13.10 (*permixti viri feminis*); Catull. 64.252-64; Ov. *Met.* 4.25-29. For *comitatus* used of the Bacchic θίασος, cf. Stat. *Theb.* 4.661 (a *comitatus iners*, like that of Aeneas); and Hyg. *Fab.* 191. Corresponding to this is *comes* used of a member of a θίασος in Varro, *Ling.* 7.87; Petron. 133; and Stat. *Achil.* 1.646.

77. Prop. 4.2.31. See also Diod. Sic. 4.4.4; Prop. 3.17.30; Stat. *Achil.* 1.617; Leinieks 1996, 54-55; Ashton 2001, 48, 157. In Nonnus *Dion.* 4.106, Apollo is given the golden miter that belongs to Dionysus in Soph. *OT* 209.

78. Eur. *Bacch.* 235, Ov. *Met.* 3.555. Cf. [Tib.] 3.4.28, where myrrh-scented hair dripping with Syrian perfume belongs to a remarkably epicene Apollo.

79. Otto 1965, 175.

80. Ibid. 176-77.

81. Dionysus and a nymph in Soph. *OT* 1105-9; and Strabo 13.1.12; Dionysus and Aphrodite in Anac. 2; Hedylus in *Anth. Pal.* 11.414; Diod.Sic. 4.6.1; Paus. 9.31.2; *Hymn. Orph.* 55.7; and Serv. ad *Aen.* 1.720. See also Otto 1965, 176.

82. The parallelism between Dido and Homer's Calypso is the most obvious link between Dido and a nymph. Nevertheless, the same association also emerges from the correspondence between the nymphs' cave in Book 1 and the conjugal cave in Book 4. Both are found in the context of Aeneas' taking refuge from storms that are themselves linked when *Aen.* 4.160 echoes 1.124. These caves also occupy essentially the same lines in their respective books, viz., *Aen.* 1.166-68 and 4.165-66. There are thus solid

contextual and structural bases for the suspicion of Pöschl and Kenney that the nymphs residing in the harbor cave prefigure the queen of Carthage: see Pöschl 1962, p. 206, n. 8; and Kenney 1973, p. 153, n. 122.

Dido is identified with Venus primarily through being prefigured in the disguised Venus whom Aeneas encounters in the wilderness, and whom E. L. Harrison has characterized as "a kind of stand-in for Dido" (Harrison 1972-73, 15; see also Reckford 1995-96, 22). This encounter unmistakably recalls the *Homeric Hymn to Aphrodite* and its narrative of the amour between Aphrodite and Anchises. Consequently, Aeneas' encounter with Venus in disguise casts Aeneas in the role of his seduced father, even as Venus as seductress prefigures Dido and her comparable effect on Anchises' son. Venus disguised as a huntress and resembling Diana (*Aen.* 1.329) also anticipates Dido likened to the huntress Diana in a simile (*Aen.* 1.498-502). Conversely, this simile itself recalls in several details the earlier scene with Venus (e.g., Sparta figures both in *Aen.* 1.498-99 and in 1.315-16; in 1.500 and 1.405, either a Greek proper name or Greek prosody creates a bucolic diaeresis coinciding with a sense pause and followed by *ille/-a*). Then, in her exchanges with Ilioneus and Aeneas, Dido fills the interlocutor's role that Venus has previously assumed in her dialogue with Aeneas. Indeed, Ilioneus' speech to Dido concerning Aeneas (*Aen.* 1.522-58) differs in length by only one line from Venus' comparable speech to Aeneas concerning Dido (*Aen.* 1.335-70). As Venus is the golden goddess par excellence, Dido is the golden queen in *Aen.* 1.697-98 (Weber 1998-99, 322). Finally, like Venus in the wilderness, Dido is dressed for the hunt in *Aen.* 4.136-39, which replicates in subject and in order of accoutrements Venus' dress and equipment as these are described in *Aen.* 1.314-20. Even the extraliterary but overt connection between Aphrodite and Dido's epigone Cleopatra (see n. 87 below) enhances the parallelism that Virgil sets up between Venus and Dido herself.

83. Described in Callixeinus *FGrH* 627, frags. 1-2. Text and translation in Rice 1983, 8-25, esp. 16-17, 81-82, now augmented by Hazzard 2000, 59-79.

84. See Cratinus 38.2 Kock (the κροκωτός and the ποικίλον included among four attributes of Dionysus); Ar. *Ran.* 46, Callixeinus *FGrH* 627, frag. 2 (a crimson χιτών and ἱμάτιον worn with a transparent κροκωτός); Naev. *trag.* 54 Ribbeck (a garment called an *epicrocus*); Tib. 1.7.46-47 (Osiris-Bacchus wearing Tyrian *vestes* [cf. Aeneas in *Aen.* 4.262] and a yellow *palla* extending to his "tender" feet); Prop. 3.17.32 (a *vestis* touching the god's "bare" feet); Ov. *Met.* 3.556 (like Aeneas' cloak, a *purpura* and embroidered *vestes* interwoven with gold); Sen. *Hercules furens* 475 (a trailing garment called a *syrma* and resplendent with gold called *barbaricum* [so too the gold of Aeneas' Troy and of Dionysus' avatar Antony in *Aen.* 2.504 and 8.685 respectively]); and Paus. 5.19.6 (a χιτών extending to the feet). In general, see *LIMC* 3.1, p. 414, col. 2, and p. 415, col. 1.

85. See Smith 1913, 336.

86. For the principal sources, see Fraser 1972, 1:205 and 2:348-49, nn. 122, 124. Otherwise, Hölbl 2001, 243-45, 291-99; Meadows 2001, 86; Goudchaux 2001, 137, 139; Ashton 2001, 155; Williams 2001, 193, 238; Pelling 1988, 179-80, 189, 241, 265, 303-4; and Zanker 1988, 57-58. For the association between Antony and Dionysus as reflected in Hor. *Carm.* 2.19, see Stevens 1999, 285-95.

87. Antony's identification with Osiris-Dionysus was in fact, however, utterly overt (see Dio Cass. 50.5, 50.25; Hölbl 2001, 291; Williams 2001, 194; Hazzard 2000, 153; Pelling 1988, 180), and it will have been promoted by Cleopatra's association with Aphrodite (mentioned in n. 82 above and confirmed in Plut. *Ant.* 26.5), who figures as Dionysus' consort in the god's mythology. For the sources documenting the efforts of Ptolemaic queens (especially Arsinoë II, but including Cleopatra VII) to be identified with Aphrodite, see Hölbl 2001, 97-98, 103-4, 290; Higgs 2001, 111, 202; Goudchaux 2001, 134, 137, 139; Williams 2001, 193; Ciampini 2001, 331; Hazzard 2000, 152-53; Whitehorne 1994, 97, 129, 136, 146, 148; Gutzwiller 1992, 363-65; Fraser 1972, 1.197, 238-40; Taylor 1931, 103.

88. Dionysus was represented to be the divine prototype of Alexander the Great. In general, see Hölbl 2001, 283, 289; Hazzard 2000, 8-9, 107, 110, 116, 145, 154-55; Whitehorne 1994, 9; Rice 1983, 43, 48, 67, 83-86, 113, 191-92; Fraser 1972, 1.201-6. For a possible anagram in Callimachus alluding to Ptolemy II and Arsinoë as "dual Dionysians," see Bleisch 1996, 461-68.

89. Webster 1964, 1.

90. Horsfall 1990, 134, which needs some modification. Dido and Aeneas are not only leaders; they are "specifically" reigning monarchs, this shared status reflecting their common Eastern heritage and its penchant for monarchy. The new city that each of them proposes to found is to be sited in the West, and Dido's Carthage in *Aen.* 1.523 has a mission similar to that of Aeneas' Rome in *Aen.* 6.853. Both Dido and Aeneas have recently lost a spouse, but there is more to this too: they are both bereaved in their homeland, and murder and mayhem are responsible in both cases. Finally, they both receive similar instructions from similar apparitions of their departed spouse, but the revelations of Sychaeus are paralleled not in the vision of Hector in *Aen.* 2.289-95, but rather in Creüsa's speech in *Aen.* 2.776-89.

91. *Pace* Horsfall 1990, 134-35. See Pöschl 1962, 69-72; and Otis 1964, 236-37, 265 ("Dido is obviously an *alter Aeneas*").

92. See Pelling 1988, 17, 190.

93. See Pigoń 1991, p. 47, n. 6; Clausen 1987, p. 134, n. 34; Lewis 1961, 9-10; Pöschl 1962, 67-68.

94. See Weber 1999, 133-34, and the sources cited ibid., nn. 21-23.

95. For sibling marriage among the Ptolemies, see Carney 1987, 435-39; and Hopkins 1980, 311-12.

96. Dio Cass. 50.5, 50.25.

97. The opposing principles represented by Diana and Venus are famously chastity and eros respectively. For a somewhat different view of the antinomy between these goddesses as it applies to Dido, see Hardie 1997, 322. For the same duality embodied in Apollonius' Medea, see Nelis 2001, 128-30.

98. The parallelism between Virgil's microcosm and macrocosm was pointed out long ago in Pöschl 1962, 18; and Otis 1964, 233.

99. Plut. *Ant.* 26.5. For Dido's banquet as prefiguring Cleopatra's entertainment of Antony and his Romans on the Cydnus, see Pelling 2001, 295, 298, and Pelling 1988, 17, 190.

Literature Cited

Anderson, J. K. 1985. *Hunting in the Ancient World*. Berkeley and Los Angeles.

Anderson, W. S. 1969. *The Art of the "Aeneid."* Englewood Cliffs, N.J.

Ashton, S.-A. 2001. Identifying the Egyptian-Style Ptolemaic Queens. In Walker and Higgs 2001, 148-55. Catalogue Entries, ibid.

Austin, R. G., ed. 1955. *P. Vergili Maronis "Aeneidos" liber quartus*. Oxford.

_____. 1977. *P. Vergili Maronis "Aeneidos" liber sextus*. Oxford.

Bérard, C. 1976. 'ΑΞΙΕ ΤΑΥΡΕ. In *Mélanges d'histoire ancienne et d'archéologie offerts à Paul Collart*, ed. P. Ducrey et al., 61-73. Lausanne.

Bleisch, P. 1996. On Choosing a Spouse: *Aeneid* 7.378-84 and Callimachus' *Epigram* 1. *AJP* 117:453-72.

Bömer, F., ed. 1969-86. *P. Ovidius Naso: "Metamorphosen."* 7 vols. Heidelberg.

Boyancé, P. 1960-61. L'Antre dans les mystères de Dionysus. *RPAA* 33:107-27.

Burkert, W. 1985. *Greek Religion*. Trans. J. Raffan. Cambridge, Mass.

Carney, E. D. 1987. The Reappearance of Royal Sibling Marriage in Ptolemaic Egypt. *PP* 42:420-39.

Cary, M. 1949. *The Geographic Background of Greek and Roman History*. Oxford.

Chantraine, P. 1968-80. *Dictionnaire étymologique de la langue grecque*. Paris.

Ciampini, E. M. 2001. Catalogue Entries. In Walker and Higgs 2001.

Clausen, W. 1987. *Virgil's "Aeneid" and the Tradition of Hellenistic Poetry*. Berkeley and Los Angeles.

_____, ed. 1994. *Virgil: "Eclogues."* Oxford.

Commager, S., ed. 1966. *Virgil: A Collection of Critical Essays*. Englewood Cliffs, N.J.

Detienne, M. 2001. Forgetting Delphi between Apollo and Dionysus. *CP* 96:147-58.

Dodds, E. R. 1951. *The Greeks and the Irrational*. Berkeley and Los Angeles.

_____, ed. 1960. *Euripides: "Bacchae"*[2]. Oxford.

Farnell, L. R. 1895-1909. *The Cults of the Greek States*. 5 vols. Oxford.

Firron, J. W. 1973. Greek Dance. *CQ*, n.s., 23:254-74.

Fitch, J. G., ed. 1987. *Seneca's "Hercules Furens."* Ithaca.

Fraser, P. M. 1972. *Ptolemaic Alexandria*. 2 vols. Oxford.

Frisk, H. 1960-72. *Griechisches etymologisches Wörterbuch*. 3 vols. Heidelberg.

Goudchaux, G. W. 2001. Cleopatra's Subtle Religious Strategy. In Walker and Higgs 2001, 128-41.

Green, C. M. C. 1996. Terms of Venery: *Ars Amatoria* I. *TAPA* 126:221-63.

Green, R. P. H., ed. 1991. *The Works of Ausonius*. Oxford.

Gutzwiller, K. 1992. Callimachus' *Lock of Berenice:* Fantasy, Romance, and Propaganda. *AJP* 113:359-85.

Haigh, A. E. 1907. *The Attic Theatre*[3]. Rev. A. W. Pickard-Cambridge. Oxford.

Hardie, P. 1997. Virgil and Tragedy. In *The Cambridge Companion to Virgil*, ed. C. Martindale, 312-26. Cambridge.

Harrison, E. L. 1972-73. Why Did Venus Wear Boots?—Some Reflections on *Aeneid* 1.314f. *PVS* 12:10-25.

Hazzard, R. A. 2000. *Imagination of a Monarchy: Studies in Ptolemaic Propaganda*. Toronto.

Henrichs, A. 1978. Greek Maenadism from Olympias to Messalina. *HSCP* 82:121-60.

Higgs, P. 2001. Searching for Cleopatra's Image: Classical Portraits in Stone. In Walker and Higgs 2001, 200-209. Catalogue Entries, ibid.

Hölbl, G. 2001. *A History of the Ptolemaic Empire*. Trans. T. Saavedra. London.

Hopkins, K. 1980. Brother-Sister Marriage in Roman Egypt. *CSSH* 22:303-54.

Horsfall, N. M. 1990. Dido in the Light of History. In *Oxford Readings in Vergil's "Aeneid,"* ed. S. J. Harrison, 127-44. Oxford and New York.

Hosius, C., ed. 1926. *Die Moselgedichte des Decimus Magnus Ausonius und des Venantius Fortunatus*[3]. Marburg.

Kenney, E. J. 1970. Doctus Lucretius. *Mnemosyne*, 4th ser., 23:366-92.

——————. 1973. The Style of the *Metamorphoses*. In *Ovid*, ed. J. W. Binns, 116-53. London.

Kerényi, C. 1976. *Dionysos: Archetypal Image of Indestructible Life*. Trans. R. Manheim. Princeton.

——————. 1983. *Apollo: The Wind, the Spirit, and the God*. Trans. J. Solomon. Dallas.

Lee, M. O. 1988. *Per Nubila Lunam:* The Moon in Virgil's *Aeneid*. *Vergilius* 34:9-14.

Leinieks, V. 1996. *The City of Dionysos: A Study of Euripides' "Bakchai."* Stuttgart.

Lewis, R. W. B. 1961. On Translating the *Aeneid:* Yif that I Can. *Yearbook of Comparative and General Literature* 10:7-15. Later published in Commager 1966, 41-52.

Lonsdale, S. H. 1994-95. *Homeric Hymn to Apollo*: Prototype and Paradigm of Choral Performance. *Arion*, 3d ser., 3:25-40.

Lyne, R. O. A. M. 1987. *Further Voices in Vergil's "Aeneid."* Oxford.

McKeown, J. C., ed. 1989. *Ovid: "Amores."* Vol. 2, *A Commentary on Book One*. Leeds.

Meadows, A. 2001. Catalogue Entries. In Walker and Higgs 2001.

Merkelbach, R. 1988. *Die Hirten des Dionysos*. Stuttgart.

Mynors, R. A. B., ed. 1990. *Virgil: "Georgics."* Oxford.

Nelis, D. 2001. *Vergil's "Aeneid" and the "Argonautica" of Apollonius Rhodius*. Leeds.

Nisbet, R. G. M., and M. Hubbard. 1978. *A Commentary on Horace: "Odes" Book II*. Oxford.

Otis, B. 1964. *Virgil: A Study in Civilized Poetry*. Oxford.

Otto, W. F. 1965. *Dionysus: Myth and Cult*. Trans. R. B. Palmer. Bloomington.

Page, T. E., ed. 1894-1900. *The "Aeneid" of Virgil*. 2 vols. London.

Parry, A. 1963. The Two Voices of Virgil's *Aeneid*. *Arion* 2:66-80. Later published in Commager 1966, 107-23.

Paschalis, M. 1997. *Virgil's "Aeneid": Semantic Relations and Proper Names*. Oxford.

Pease, A. S., ed. 1935. *Publi Vergili Maronis "Aeneidos" liber quartus*. Cambridge, Mass.

Pelling, C. B. R. 2001. Anything Truth Can Do, We Can Do Better: The Cleopatra Legend. In Walker and Higgs 2001, 292-301.

_____, ed. 1988. *Plutarch: "Life of Antony."* Cambridge.

Pickard-Cambridge, A. W. 1968. *The Dramatic Festivals of Athens*[2]. Rev. J. Gould and D. M. Lewis. Oxford.

Pigoń, J. 1991. Dido, Diana, and Penthesilea: Observations on the Queen's First Appearance in the *Aeneid*. *Eos* 79:45-53.

Pokorny, J. 1994. *Indogermanisches etymologisches Wörterbuch*[3]. 2 vols. Tübingen.

Pöschl, V. 1962. *The Art of Vergil*. Trans. G. Seligson. Ann Arbor.

Reckford, K. 1995-96. Recognizing Venus (I): Aeneas Meets His Mother. *Arion*, 3d ser., 3:1-42.

Rice, E. E. 1983. *The Grand Procession of Ptolemy Philadelphus*. Oxford.

Rose, H. J. 1958. *A Handbook of Greek Mythology*[6]. London.

Roux, J., ed. 1970-72. *Euripide: "Les Bacchantes."* 2 vols. Paris.

Rutherford, I. 1994-95. Apollo in Ivy: The Tragic Paean. *Arion*, 3d ser., 3:112-35.

Segal, C. 1997. *Dionysiac Poetics and Euripides' "Bacchae"*[2]. Princeton.

Skutsch, O., ed. 1985. *The "Annals" of Quintus Ennius*. Oxford.

Smith, K. F., ed. 1913. *The Elegies of Albius Tibullus*. New York.

Stevens, J. A. 1999. Seneca and Horace: Allegorical Technique in Two Odes to Bacchus (Hor. *Carm.* 2.19 and Sen. *Oed.* 403-508). *Phoenix* 53:281-307.

Strid, O. 1999. *Die Dryoper: Eine Untersuchung der Überlieferung*. Uppsala.

Taylor, L. R. 1931. *The Divinity of the Roman Emperor*. Middletown, Conn.

Thomson, D. F. S., ed. 1997. *Catullus*. Toronto.

Thornton, M. K. 1985. The Adaptation of Homer's Artemis-Nausicaa Simile in the *Aeneid*. *Latomus* 44:615-22.

Versnel, H. S. 1970. *"Triumphus": An Inquiry into the Origin, Development and Meaning of the Roman Triumph*. Leiden.

Walker, S., and P. Higgs, eds. 2001. *Cleopatra of Egypt*. Princeton.

Weber, C. 1998-99. Dido and Circe *Dorées:* Two Golden Women in *Aeneid* 1.698 and 7.190. *CJ* 94:317-27.

_____. 1999. Intimations of Dido and Cleopatra in Some Contemporary Portrayals of Elizabeth I. *SPh* 96:127-43.

Webster, T. B. L. 1964. *Hellenistic Poetry and Art*. London.

West, M. L., ed. 1966. *Hesiod: "Theogony."* Oxford.

Whitehorne, J. 1994. *Cleopatras*. London and New York.

Wilamowitz-Moellendorff, U. von. 1903. Apollon. *Hermes* 38:575-86.

Williams, F., ed. 1978. *Callimachus: "Hymn to Apollo."* Oxford.

Williams, J. H. C. 2001. "Spoiling the Egyptians": Octavian and Cleopatra. In Walker and Higgs 2001, 190-99. Catalogue Entries, ibid.

Windekens, A. J. van. 1986. *Dictionnaire étymologique complémentaire de la langue grecque*. Louvain.

Winnington-Ingram, R. P. 1948. *Euripides and Dionysus: An Interpretation of the "Bacchae."* Cambridge.

Zanker, P. 1988. *The Power of Images in the Age of Augustus.* Trans. A. Shapiro. Ann Arbor.

Zimmermann, B. 1992. *Dithyrambos: Geschichte einer Gattung.* Göttingen.

The Innocence of Italy in Vergil's *Aeneid*_____

Richard F. Moorton

In one of the most influential essays on the *Aeneid* ever written, Adam Parry argued twenty-five years ago that the coming of the Trojans to Italy ultimately entailed the corruption of the indigenous purity they found there:

> The explicit message of the *Aeneid* claims that Rome was a happy reconciliation of the natural virtues of the local Italian peoples and the civilized might of the Trojans who came to found the new city. But the tragic movement of the last books of the poem carries a different suggestion: that the formation of Rome's empire involved the loss of the pristine purity of Italy.[1]

Subsequent writers have shared Parry's sense that the Trojans brought to a relatively innocent Italy a moral disorder whose metaphors in the scholarship include turbulence and pollution. Thus W. Nethercut speaks of "the upheaval Aeneas must inflict upon the natively tranquil peoples he will contact," while V. J. Rosivach asserts that "the Trojans have come to Latium and in their way they taint the Latin Golden Age themselves long before Juno interferes."[2] In the following paper I intend to challenge the idea advanced by these scholars that the coming of the Trojans somehow vitiated a previously unsullied Italy.

The starting point for Parry's ruminations on the *Aeneid* was the passage in the catalogue of Latin forces in *Aeneid* 7 in which is foreshadowed the death of the warrior-priest Umbro, a man for whom his native landscape itself was to mourn:

> te nemus Angitiae, vitrea te Fucinus unda,
> te liquidi flevere lacus.
>
> (759-760)

For Parry this was an example of a kind of literary passage with a peculiar property akin to revelation: as we reread it, "all at once, as a kind of epiphany, the essential mood of the author seems to be contained in it."[3] Obviously this is a subjective touchstone, and we are entitled to test Parry's contention that his passage reflects Vergil's "essential mood" in the *Aeneid* by interrogating his assessment of its meaning in the light of the rest of the epic. That assessment Parry straightforwardly states:

> Umbro himself is not important. He is no more than a made-up name. The real pathos is for the places that mourn him. They are the true victims of Aeneas' war, and in saying that they weep, Vergil calls on us to weep for what to his mind made an earlier Italy fresh and true.[4]

This is clear enough: Aeneas ruined the innocence of Italy. It is not my intention to deny that the *Aeneid* is, among other things, a lament for lost innocence. But I believe that a close reading of the *Aeneid* will show that Vergil locates the cause for the contamination of Italian innocence not as much in the unparalleled influence of the Trojan newcomers as in the moral imperfections of universal human nature in which, of course, the Italian aborigines and all subsequent immigrants to their shores inevitably shared.

My thesis requires a new look at the pastoral order, which for most scholars is emblematic of the innocence of Italy. Many would accept the statement that in Vergil's *Aeneid*, Italy is a pastoral land characterized by simplicity, innocence, and justice which cannot survive the advent of the Trojans with their complex civilization, martial might, troubled moral heritage and imperial destiny. This conception is an example of what Leo Marx calls the pastoral design, wherein the idyllic vision of the pastoral ideal is juxtaposed with a larger, more complicated order of experience which Marx calls the counterforce.[5] This complex view of pastoralism, designated the pastoral of mind by Marx, in his view transcends in power and penetration sentimental pastoralism, the uncritical idealization of rustic life:[6]

> Most literary works called pastorals—at least those substantial enough to retain our interest—do not finally permit us to come away with anything like the simple, affirmative attitude we adopt toward pleasing rural scenery. In one way or another, if only by virtue of the unmistakable sophistication with which they are composed, these works manage to qualify, or call into question, or bring irony to bear against the illusion of peace and harmony in a green pasture.[7]

Marx views the pastoral world as a middle ground, a kind of compromise or mean, between the wilderness and the city,[8] and as such it is doubly vulnerable:

> We should understand that the counterforce may impinge upon the pastoral landscape either from the side bordering upon untractable nature or the side of advanced civilization.[9]

But the pastoral world is also vulnerable from within to the limitations of human nature. Thus in the seventeenth-century landscape painters, particularly Nicolas Poussin, painted funerary scenes, often including skulls, in pastoral settings with the inscription *Et in Arcadia Ego*, 'I (Death) am also in Arcadia'.[10] Death is a natural evil, but Vergil can also conceive of the existence there of moral evil, which in extreme cases can threaten, even overthrow an enclave of pastoral order or, as R. Poggioli calls it, a "pastoral oasis."[11] Thus in *Aeneid* 7.363-64 Amata recalls to Latinus the shepherd Paris who "penetrated" Sparta and took Helen away to the cities of Troy, thereby starting the great war:

> an non sic Phrygius penetrai Lacedaemona pastor,
> Ledaeamque Helenam Troianas vexit ad urbes?

The irony is radical. Paris, an inhabitant of a pastoral world, the pastures of Phrygia before the Trojan War, invades and corrupts not one urban order but two, an exact inversion of the stereotype of the vulnerability of the pastoral world to corruption from contact with urban influences. By his crime Paris the shepherd destroys his own pastoral serenity from within and drags previously peaceful cities on two continents into a long and ruinous war. This ironic reversal certifies that Vergil's view of the pastoral is subtle and complex. He conceives of the pastoral order at its best as a garden of the virtues, but also understands that human beings are fallible, even in Arcadia or the pastoral oases of Italy. This means that in the world of the *Aeneid*, Italians do not need Trojans to teach them how to sin.

The best evidence for this thesis is the fact that the moral innocence of Italy was compromised before the Trojans ever set foot on its soil. To show this we can begin where Parry does, with the catalogue of Latin heroes in Book 7.[12] As we have seen, he believed that the soulful line and a half in mid-catalogue in which Umbro's Marruvian landscape mourns his death is fundamental to our understanding of the meaning of the *Aeneid*. But is it really more important than the description of the chieftain who appears first, in the emphatic position in the catalogue—Mezentius (647-654)? Mezentius is that worst of all conceivable offenders in Vergil's symbolic world, a *contemptor divum*, and it was already well understood in antiquity that he is placed first in the catalogue to contrast his impiety with the piety of the leader of the Trojans and their Italian allies, Aeneas.[13] In making this contrast Vergil is establishing as foils the monstrous vice of a native Italian captain and the capital virtue of the adventitious Trojan prince, and whatever we conclude about the *pietas* of Aeneas, it is a fact that in Vergil's poem he never expresses contempt for the gods.

We learn more about this prodigy of pre-Trojan evil in Italy in Book 8. There Evander tells Aeneas how Mezentius lost his throne in Etruscan Agyllina (478-495). His reign was characterized by the arrogant power (*superbo*/*imperio*: 481-482) and savage arms (*saevis . . . armis*:

482) with which he kept the city in his grip, and the unspeakable murders (*infandas caedes*: 483) and ferocious tyranny (*facta tyranni/ effera*: 483-484) he inflicted upon his people. Evander calls upon the gods to pay Mezentius and his family back in kind (484), a curse we should remember in assessing the tragic fate of Mezentius' gallant son Lausus. As a crowning example of the horrors of his reign, Evander describes a particularly gruesome form of execution in which Mezentius had the living tied face to face with corpses, and left them to die an agonizing death (485-488). Here, we may surmise, was a practice to make the groves and waters of Tuscany weep. At length the people of Agyllina, exhausted by his outrages, rose up in arms, killed his associates, and set fire to the palace, compelling Mezentius to flee (with Lausus, presumably) for his life. This then is the criminal Italian warlord who leads out the Latin confederacy against Aeneas, the immigrant seen by some as the contaminator of Italian innocence, a conclusion which the very fact of Mezentius' existence and the symbolism of his precedence in the Latin ranks seem to make untenable.

In this same column of doughty Italian warriors, in fact just before the tragic Umbro, march Ufens and his countrymen, the *gens Aequicula*, from the foothills of the Apennines east of Pallanteum. Of these people Vergil observes:

> armati terram exercent semperque recentis
> convectare iuvat praedas et vivere rapto.
>
> (748-749)

These hillsmen live in such a violent world that they plow while armed, presumably so that they can ward off sudden attacks from other Italians. However, the Aequi appear to give as good as they get: they live off the ill-gotten gains of brigandage, and enjoy it (*iuvat*). Of course in Homer plundering strangers was, under certain circumstances, a manly act (resorted to, for instance, by both Achilles and Odysseus), but the Romans had a high regard for private property, and it is unlikely that many of Vergil's Italian readers considered the rapine practiced (and suffered) by the Aequi innocuous, or mourned its eventual outlawry by Aeneas and his successors.[14]

It should be noted that the Aequi are not unique among the Italians in the practice of pillaging. In Book 9, the Italian warrior Numanus Remulus boasts before the Trojan camp that his are a hardy people who live by rapine:

> semperque recentis
> comportare iuvat praedas et vivere rapto.
> (612-613)

The verbatim repetition of the phrase from 7.748-749 almost entitles us to call this an Italic formula. Numanus is so little conscious of the fact that this is a practice of which a morally advanced person might be ashamed that he includes it in his vaunt to the Trojans, opposing this and other hardy habits to the supposedly effeminate ways of his enemies. It is significant that Numanus is the brother-in-law of Turnus (9.593-594), the commander in chief of the forces attempting to annihilate the Trojans. This association confers honor upon neither Turnus nor the Latins whom he leads.

Turnus (783-802) and Camilla (803-817) bring up the rear of the Latin forces in the catalogue in Book 7. The moral position of Turnus in the epic is subject to dispute. Latinus blames Turnus for bringing on the war (7.596-597), and Vergil himself appears to condemn the Rutulian prince for taking the swordbelt of Pallas (10.501-505), but the question of Turnus' culpability in the war is complicated by the invasion of his psyche by Allecto. V. Pöschl has argued that because of Allecto's intervention Turnus *per se* is essentially innocent, while B. Otis has declared that the ultimate cause of the *furor* of Turnus lies in his own character.[15] In my view, the deeds of Turnus before the coming of the Trojans and the onset of Allecto give us reason to question his essential innocence. In his conversation with Aeneas in Book 8, Evander tells him that Mezentius fled from Agyllina to his *hospes* Turnus for protection:

> ille inter caedem Rutulorum elapsus in agros
> confugere et Turni defendier hospitis armis.
>
> (492-493)

At this all of Etruria rose up with just rage (*furiis . . . iustis*: 494) and went to war to bring Mezentius to justice. In the symbolic world of the *Aeneid*, it is highly significant that a bond of *hospitium* should link Turnus and the vicious Mezentius, that Mezentius should turn to Turnus in his richly deserved extremity, and that Turnus should be prepared to plunge his own city into war to protect Mezentius from the just punishment demanded by an outraged people. By befriending a moral monster and defending him against justice, Turnus embraces a position incompatible with innocence, since he thereby acts as a champion of evil.

But just as significantly, Turnus also acts as an enemy of that pure and simple life of which some suppose him to be an exemplar.[16] If any people in Italy can lay claim to embody the pastoral ideal which so many scholars associate with Vergil's pristine Italy, it is Evander and his Arcadian exiles living at Pallanteum on the future site of Rome. As Otis puts it,

> Evander's Pallanteum is at once the golden mean, the primitive, virtuous Arcadia, and . . . a partial *exemplum* of golden age virtues.[17]

If pristine purity exists anywhere in Italy it is here, even more than Latinus' comparatively civilized Latium, with its great walls, its palace of Picus, and its sprawling, wealthy farms. And yet it is precisely against Evander's Arcadian Pallanteum that Turnus, the guest friend and protector of the unspeakable Mezentius, raises his sword.[18] As Evander explains to Aeneas, *hinc Rutulus premit et murum circum-*

---

sonat armis (8.474). Why has Turnus attacked Pallanteum? Evander doesn't say. Probably not because the Arcadians have first attacked him. Both their innate virtue and their sparse numbers would restrain them from aggression against a powerful neighbor. So Turnus' attack would appear to be undeserved, and the simplest way to explain his aggression would be to assume that Turnus wants what little the Arcadians have. This would be entirely compatible with the imperialism which Vergil attributes to Turnus elsewhere in the epic. In 12.22-23, Latinus attempts to console Turnus for the prospective loss of the throne of Latium by pointing out that he has already conquered many towns: *sunt oppida capta/multa manu*. It is natural for Turnus to attempt to add Pallanteum to his empire. So Vergil represents Turnus as afflicting the virtuous Arcadians, enlarging his kingdom through militarism, and succoring the vicious Mezentius. *Pace* Pöschl and all of the other defenders of Turnus, these are not the actions of an innocent man.

Because of Turnus, the Italy to which Aeneas comes is not a peaceable kingdom, but a land sliding into a burgeoning war. The Arcadians are already under attack by Turnus, and the Etrurians are gathering their forces to recover the criminal Mezentius from his protector. As Turnus' Ardea (the center of a growing military empire) is on the plain of Latium, it is obvious that northern Latium, already the site of chronic warfare between the Rutulians and the Arcadians, will soon become involved in a wider conflict. If Turnus marries Lavinia, he can be expected to solicit her father's people to fight his battles. By joining, out of motives of self-defense, the aggrieved parties, the Arcadians and the Etruscans, in this native conflict, the Trojans alter the shape and focus of the war, and some of its outcomes. The most important of these is that Aeneas, not Turnus, becomes the heir to Latinus' throne.

There is reason to believe that this is not inimical to the pastoral order in Italy. It is true that Turnus fights on the side of pastoral Latium, and that in Book 12 rustic divinities of that land, his sister Juturna (138ff.) and his would-be grandfather-in-law Faunus (766ff.), protect him from Aeneas.[19] Because of this, Turnus has been seen as a champion of pastoral Italy.[20] However, he is also a man of innate *violentia*, and violence is a threat to pastoral peace. Therefore it is no surprise that Turnus wages war against pastoral Pallanteum. Of the fourteen similes used to describe him in the *Aeneid*, six, nearly half, liken Turnus to beasts of prey, natural enemies of the pastoral order.[21] In 9.59 Turnus is compared to a wolf hungry for lambs; in 9.564 to an eagle, or (566) a wolf which has stolen a lamb from its mother; in 9.792 to a lion assailed by a group of men; in 10.454 to a lion gazing at a bull; and in 12.6 to a wounded lion. By contrast, only once is Aeneas compared to a beast of prey (2.355), a wolf with other wolves (Trojan warriors on the night Troy fell), foraging because of hunger and the needs of their young. The emphasis is on obligation, not predation, and Pöschl describes the essential mood as one of "despair out of love."[22]

However, Aeneas is three times likened to a shepherd (2.308, 4.71, 12.587) in similes which led W. S. Anderson to the following conclusion:

Pastor Aeneas has perforce left his pastoral world, descending among the troubles of his people and compromising his abstract ideals in the process. However, within that compromised person lives an affection for pastoral values that makes the recapture of *Saturnia regna* at least a remote possibility. What he has experienced since the loss of innocence will make that goal far more meaningful than it was for the *inscius pastor.*[23]

In Book 1 of Plato's *Republic* Socrates demonstrates to a surly Thrasymachus that the good shepherd *qua* shepherd is concerned not with his own good but with the good of his sheep (343a-345d). This is an important reason why Aeneas can be thought of as a man of pastoral values. Distinguished for his *pietas*, Aeneas acts usually if not invariably for others, rather than himself, and hence R. A. Brooks rightly calls his epic quality "the heroism of obligation."[24] Turnus on the other hand strives for personal ends, for marriage to Lavinia and the kingdom of Latium, to expedite the attainment of which he is prepared to see his fellow Italians sacrifice their lives in war. Vergil therefore never likens Turnus to a shepherd, but to the predators which prey upon sheep in the pastoral world. By repeatedly comparing Aeneas to a shepherd and Turnus to beasts of prey Vergil makes a statement on the relationship of the two men to the pastoral order. Aeneas, a shepherd of men who has lost his own pastoral world, comes to Latium, another pastoral world, which is imperiled by Turnus, the predacious warrior expanding his empire in northern Latium through war and seeking through marriage to Lavinia to add the kingdom of Latinus to his holdings. Since by turning it into a battleground Turnus threatens the pastoral world from the side of civilization with the violence of art, military technology, it is appropriate for Vergil to liken him to the beast of prey which threatens the pastoral world with natural violence from the primitive world of the wilderness. The war between Aeneas and Turnus over Latium is therefore aptly symbolized on the figurative plane of the poem as the war between the shepherd and the predator over the flock. Aeneas precisely defines his relationship to the pastoral order by forming an alliance with Evander's uncorrupted pastoral people against the marauding Latins, whose peaceful world has been deranged by Juno and Turnus, her violent client. Turnus' war against Evander's Arcadians reaches a symbolic culmination when he slays Pallas, the only royal scion of the indigenous pastoral order in all of Italy, a prince whom Vergil compares to a *pastor* (10.406) soon before he is cut down by Turnus. For this offense Aeneas, the warrior with pastoral aspirations, will kill him at the end of the epic.

Last in the catalogue comes Camilla, the virgin queen of the Volscians. As much as any character in the *Aeneid*, this huntress of Diana represents wild Italy. But for all of her immense appeal, a close analysis of Camilla will reveal good reason not to idealize too much either this warrior-maid or the untamed Italy for which she stands. As Otis observes, "her primitivism is, in the last analysis, a most ambiguous and fatal thing."[25]

The weapon Camilla carries is a myrtle shepherd's staff fitted with a spearhead: *pastoralem praefixa cuspide myrtum* (817). M. C. J. Putnam has this to say of Camilla's weapon:

> This is not so much a symbol of the Italian shepherds (they too were at peace before the Trojans came) as it is the final emblem of the perversion of pastoral into violent, of love misguided into war, of Venus' myrtle into a weapon of Mars.[26]

We must say at the outset that the shepherds of Ardea, Pallanteum and Tuscany were not untouched by war when Aeneas arrived, nor were the Aequi, who plow armed, not the *gens* of Numanus Remulus, who also live by rapine. We may also point out that Mars seems to come more naturally than Venus to Camilla. However, Putnam is right to be struck by the fusion of the pastoral and the violent suggested by Camilla's staff-spear. This pastoral weapon symbolizes an ironic tension in the pastoral order, since to maintain its dream of peace shepherds must make war against wild nature: to preserve the lives of their flocks shepherds must take the lives of wild predators which would prey on their sheep. Therefore the fusion of the pastoral and the violent in the spear-staff is not inappropriate to a sophisticated appraisal of the pastoral order. However, Camilla carries the war against wild nature one step further. Though her life has things in common with a pastoral existence, since she lives away from cities and her father herds sheep, Camilla's patron Diana is not a shepherd, and we have no reason to believe that Camilla herds sheep in Italian pastures. Rather she hunts animals in the deep woods, not in the defense of flocks but as a way of life.[27] She lives at the margin of the pastoral world and wild nature. Therefore the fusion of the pastoral and the violent in her weapon has a particular appropriateness to her marginal status in life. Neither Camilla the hunter nor the shepherds defending their flocks do moral wrong in the killing of animals. Pastoral war becomes perverse when the violence is directed against human beings, and this, I assume, is the point of Putnam's interpretation of the meaning of the spear.

It would appear that Diana, Camilla's patroness, blames Camilla for her martial perversion of her venatic life in the service of the goddess. In Book 11, as Camilla and Turnus are preparing to ambush Aeneas while he drives on Laurentum, Diana says this of Camilla's part in the action:

> vellem haud correpta fuisset
> militia tali conata lacessere Teucros:
> cara mihi comitumque foret nunc una mearum.
> (584-586)

Diana deplores the fact that Camilla is engaging in such military activity (*militia tali*), while attempting to *provoke* (*lacessere*) the Trojans. *Lacessere* implies irritation, attack, aggression. Vergil could easily have used a different infinitive to represent the action as defensive rather than aggressive. *Repellere*, for instance, would be an exact metrical equivalent of *lacessere*, but Diana uses an expression which portrays Camilla as acting provocatively in a war from which she should stand apart. The clear suggestion is that Diana faults Camilla rather than the Trojans for her estrangement from the wilderness and the goddess' band.

The story of the compromise of the purity of Camilla, the princess of Italian nature, is a complex one with important implications for my thesis. Commentators have taken 11.584-586 to mean that Camilla's campaign against the Trojans was her first military experience.[28] This seems to conflict with the characterization of Camilla which Vergil presents in the catalogue of Book 7.

> bellatrix, non ilia colo calathisve Minervae
> femineas adsueta manus, sed proelia virgo
> dura pati. . . .
> (805-807)

Here Vergil introduces Camilla as a woman warrior (*bellatrix*) accustomed to undergo harsh battles. Whether or not Vergil is technically guilty of a contradiction, there is something very fitting about this description of Camilla. In combat she proves to be a *bellatrix* indeed, and even if she has not fought men before, her life in the wild prepared her for the experience of war. Nursed on the milk of wild animals[29] and armed from infancy, Camilla knew what it was to take life, the life of wild animals, from her earliest years (11.570-580). She was prepared by the physical rigors and violence of her incessant hunting for war as surely as male aristocrats in antiquity were prepared by the chase, preferably after powerful beasts, for the encounter in combat with that most dangerous game, man. In turning from the woods to war Camilla was not turning from tranquility to violence, but from the killing of animals to the killing of human beings. Her avidity for battle was undoubtedly related to her joy in the hunt.

But nothing in the *Aeneid* is more important in explaining the nature and fate of Camilla than the career of her father Metabus, a review of which will still further qualify the pristine purity seen by Parry as the condition of Italy before the Trojans came. Metabus had been the king of Privernum, a major town of the Volscians, who was, like Mezentius, driven out by his own people because of their resentment of his arrogant exercise of power: *pulsus ob invidiam regno virisque superbas* (11.539). Like Mezentius, he escaped a violent insurrection (*media inter proelia:* 11.541) to go into exile with his child. When a river blocked Metabus' way, he first offered to consecrate the infant Camilla to Diana if the goddess would safeguard the child, and then threw the infant, lashed to his spear, across the Amasenus, and finally swam to join her on the other side. No city would take them in, nor would he have accepted such hospitality due to his savageness, and hence he led the life of a shepherd in the mountains:

non illum tectis ullae, non moenibus urbes
accepere (neque ipse manus feritate dedisset),
pastorum et solis exegit montibus aevum.

(567-569)

Although Metabus herds sheep, he does not inhabit the pastoral world, a tranquil landscape hospitable to the simple virtues, but a wilderness in which fierce natures too savage for social congress can live a solitary life.

In the mountains Metabus raised his daughter. The wildness she inherited from her father did no harm in the solitude of nature, where her innate aggressiveness was channeled into hunting:

tela manu iam tum tenera puerilia torsit
et fundam tereti circum caput egit habena
Strymoniamque gruem aut album deiecit olorem.

(578-580)

Besides her outcast father, her only companions in this secluded life were Diana, another fierce and unapproachable virgin, and her nymphs. Like the purity of Diana, Camilla's purity was a function of a formidable independence in which violence was always implicit. While she remained sequestered in the wilderness, that purity was innocent in the sense that it did humankind no hurt. But eventually, perhaps because of the war, the opportunity came for Camilla to rejoin the human community under the only circumstances her father had been able to tolerate, as the leader of their people, the Volscians. With her decision to do so she became her father's daughter even more fully than before. As he had been a *bellator* (11.553) rather than the keeper of the *pax Latina*, so she became a *bellatrix* (7.805). As he had ruled his people in his pride and might, so did she. Her self-confidence verges on audacity, as we see when she tells Turnus, her commander in chief, that she will meet the Trojans and Etruscan forces alone while he stays behind and guards the walls of Laurentum (11.502-506). In his courteous reply, Turnus addresses the terrible virgin (*horrenda . . . virgine:* 507) as the glory of Italy, *o decus Italiae virgo* (11.508). In this we can concur without losing a sense of Camilla's limitations. Her prowess is breathtaking, and her brilliant aristeia is terminated only by Arruns' cowardly arrow, but we have reason to doubt that as a peacetime ruler she would have been able to govern herself with any more success than her father had in ruling his own wild nature on the throne of Privernum. Camilla entered the service of Diana with the spear of her father and left it with her own. That symmetry reminds us that the violence of Camilla's end was foreshadowed in the violence incited by her fierce sire when she was an infant, and that the primitivism of her life was a not inappropriate period of incubation preparing Camilla to take from her father, Metabus, the *bellator*-king of Privernum, her patrimony of war and dominion as monarch of the Volscians. Therefore it is wrong to say that Aeneas and the Trojans introduced the alien realities of war and political discord into the pristine Italy of Camilla. These, at any rate, were part of her family heritage.

Finally we may note that the positioning of the three most morally problematic personalities in the catalogue, Mezentius, Turnus, and Camilla, at the emphatic positions in that catalogue, the beginning and end, stresses the fact that the early Italy for which they stand and to which Aeneas came was not innocent of moral evil.

This survey of Vergil's catalogue of Italian forces in Book 7 has been, by design, select. It has said nothing of the deep affection for an earlier, simpler Italy with which Vergil composed these lines because that quality is obvious to all. What is less evident to some is the dark side of pristine Italy also implicit in this passage, and it is this more troublesome dimension of the catalogue which I have attempted to document in the first half of this paper.[30] My preliminary results show that Italy before the coming of the Trojans was no primitive Eden, but rather a postlapsarian land inhabited by a complex, non-uniform human population in which immorality and violence were indigenous if not predominant. If, when Parry said that the formation of Rome's empire entailed the loss of the pristine purity of Italy, he meant that the coming of Aeneas and its consequences introduced moral evil to a land which previously knew it not, then his thesis is not consonant with the facts of Vergil's text. But in making my case thus far I have said very little about Latinus, the pacific king of Latium, and the golden age of his great grandfather Saturn of which he is in some sense the heir. The dynasty of Saturn in Latium is obviously crucial to the moral history of Hesperia, so in the second half of this paper I will investigate the question of the problem of evil in Italy with especial emphasis on the placid kingdom of Latinus.

Aeneas first learns that Italy will be the new home of the Trojans from the dream of the Penates in Book 3 (148-171). The Penates tell Aeneas that Italy is militarily powerful, *potens armis* (164), and therefore we may infer that it is no stranger to the evils of war. We also learn a salient fact vital to my thesis, that the pioneer Dardanus, the founder of Troy and the Trojan line, emigrated from his original home in Italy to Asia Minor (167-168). This reality is important because often the Trojan immigrants and the residents of Italy are distinguished with a misleading neatness. Hence K. J. Reckford speaks of the coming of the Trojans as "the invasion of Latium by foreigners from across the sea,"[31] Putnam writes that "Turnus stands for the world of Italy . . . which Aeneas destroys,"[32] and Nethercut sees the Trojans throughout their odyssey and especially in Italy as aggressive aliens.[33] In fact the Trojans come to a culturally diverse Italy as the latest in a long series of immigrants which include the westward moving Etruscans from Lydia (8.479-480), the Ausonians (8.328), the Sicanians (8.328), and of course various Greek contingents, Evander's Arcadians, the Argive ancestors of Turnus, and Diomedes: the eastern coast of Italy is so heavily colonized by hostile Greeks that Helenus advises Aeneas and his Trojan companions to avoid it altogether (3.396-398). All of these populations intermingled with the aborigines Evander describes in

8.315ff. Whatever the "pristine purity" of Italy might mean, it does not mean ethnic purity. To this ethnic melange the Trojan immigrants come with more right to settle than most, for their race sprang from Dardanus, an Italian. Far from being alien invaders, the Trojans with Aeneas are coming home to the land of their roots after an ill-fated sojourn of several generations in Asia Minor. This is why the idea that the Trojans come to Italy as its destroyers is so paradoxical. In fact nothing of the sort happens. In the end Aeneas and his men are so totally merged with the Italy from which their forefathers sprang that they lose their Trojan language and national identity, as Jupiter himself proclaims in Book 12:

> sermonem Ausonii patrium moresque tenebunt,
> utque est nomen erit; commixti corpore tantum
> subsident Teucri. morem ritusque sacrorum
> adiciam faciamque omnis uno ore Latinos.

> (834-837)

The Trojans know before they reach Italy that they must face war upon arrival (*ventura . . . bella*: 3.458). This prophecy of Helenus seems to be confirmed by their first sight of Italy, where they see four white horses grazing. Anchises interprets the omen complexly, as a sign that Italy portends for the Trojans both war, since horses are equipped for war, and peace, since horses have peaceful uses, and these horses are white:

> et pater Anchises "bellum, o terra hospita, portas:
> bello armantur equi, bellum haec armenta minantur.
> sed tarnen idem olim curru succedere sueti
> quadripedes et frena iugo concordia ferre:
> spes et pacis" ait.

> (3.539-543)

This interpretation portrays Italy not as a peaceful Eden, but as an ambivalent land whose potentials include both conflict and concord, and this portrayal is in precise accord with the Italy the poem gradually reveals to Vergil's reader.

In the course of time the Trojans land in Latium, where old King Latinus rules Laurentum in long-standing peace:

> rex area Latinus et urbes
> iam senior longa placidas in pace regebat.
> hunc Fauno et nympha genitum Laurente Marica
> accipimus; Fauno Picus pater, isque parentem
> te, Saturne, refert, tu sanguinis ultimus auctor.
>
> (7.45-49)

Vergil intentionally stresses the tranquillity of Latinus' rule, and the rustic sanctity of his pedigree, stretching back through a line of sylvan deities, his father Faunus, his grandfather Picus and his great grandfather Saturnus, the founder of the *Saturnia regna*, the golden age in Latium. In emphasizing the peaceful aspects of Latinus' kingdom, Vergil prepares for a tragic contrast between Latium at peace and Latium at war. But it is vital to realize that here the poet is, by design, showing us only part of the picture in Latium, not to mention Italy. Metabus' Privernum was in Latium and had within living memory known civil war, and Rutulian Ardea under Turnus and Pallanteum, two cities in the territory of Latium, were at war. And as we have seen, the Aequi bordering Latium apparently lived on a perpetual war footing. Moreover, the peace of Latinus does not necessarily descend unbroken from the age of Saturn, since Latinus' grandfather Picus is depicted in Book 7 as a martial horseman (*equum domitor*: 189) who bears the shield of Mars (188).

When the Trojan deputation under Ilioneus makes its way to Laurentum, what they find is a far cry from a sleepy, harmless rustic village. Latinus' capital is a great city circled by a wall (7.161) and fortified by towers (7.160). Cities in antiquity built walls and towers not for ornamentation but for defense. So it is not surprising that the young men of Laurentum should be discovered riding horses, training chariot steeds, shooting the bow, hurling the javelin, and running and boxing before the city walls (7.160-165). These young cadets are honing their fighting skills in a world in which war is absent but clearly not unthinkable. Latinus receives the Trojan emissaries in the *regia Pici*, an enormous building on the citadel of Laurentum full of images of Latin kings and war heroes and the trophies of war:

> quin etiam veterum effigies ex ordine avorum
> antiqua e cedro, Italusque paterque Sabinus
> vitisator curvam servans sub imagine falcem,
> Saturnusque senex Ianique bifrontis imago
> vestibulo astabant, aliique ab origine reges,
> Martiaque ob patriam pugnando vulnera passi.
> multaque praeterea sacris in postibus arma,
> captivi pendent currus curvaeque secures
> et cristae capitum et portarum ingentia claustra,
> spiculaque clipeique ereptaque rostra carinis.
>
> (7.177-186)

Here Vergil deliberately complicates and qualifies the sylvan picture of the Latin past he gave in 7.45-49. The pastoral quality of that picture is not abandoned—rustic figures like Sabinus, Saturn, and Janus still are present in the catalogue—but now the pastoral ideal finds its place in a pastoral design where peace is juxtaposed with war. The *regia Pici* is a testament to the fact that the Latins have a complex and changeful past; that is, the Latins are the children of history. Rosivach finds the revelation disquieting:

Earlier Latinus' ancestry was traced but three generations to Saturn, the "sanguinis ultimus auctor" (49). Now it is as if a veil were lifted and we see

Latinus' ancestors with Saturn in the relative foreground of a line of kings stretching back to the vanishing point in time. The earlier genealogy emphasized Latinus' peaceful roots. The later genealogy emphasizes war.[34]

Rosivach sees in this contrast a deliberate contradiction engineered by Vergil to show that by coming to Latium the Trojans "taint the Latin Golden Age."

But surely Vergil does not mean to say that the Trojans have changed the realities of the Latin past merely by setting foot on the soil of Latium. I propose a different interpretative approach. It is possible to view the genealogy of Latinus in 7.45-49 and the contents of the *regia Pici* not as the two terms in a contradiction, but as complementary opposites. The genealogy of Latinus emphasizes, as it were, the quietism of the Latins, the innocuous, inactive, quasi-feminine aspect of Latium of which Latinus is the incarnation. This dimension is benign but incomplete, as symbolized by two deficiencies in Latinus. First Vergil tells us with pointed significance just after his account of Latinus' genealogy that the gentle Latinus has been unable to produce a male heir hardy enough to survive to maturity:

> filius huic fato divum prolesque virilis
> nulla fuit, primaque oriens erepta iuventa est.
> (7.50-51)

The male line of Saturn will end with Latinus. However, in accordance with his nature he has begotten a daughter, Lavinia, who has reached marriageable age, and the necessity to seek a son-in-law, a surrogate for the son Latinus does not have, leads to a tragic contention between more vigorous men. The second sign of Latinus' deficiency is his inability to control what are in part the consequences of the first. When Latium, with Lavinia's suitor Turnus in the vanguard, demands an unnecessary and unjust war, Latinus knows that this conflict is wrong but lacks the strength to prevent it. His entirely characteristic response is first to exclaim that events are out of his control—*"frangimur heu fatis" inquit "ferimurque procella!"* (7.594)—then to place all of the blame on others, his Latin subjects and Turnus, and finally to shut himself away and surrender the reins of state:[35]

> nec plura locutus
> saepsit se tectis rerumque reliquit habenas.
> (7.599-600)

The pacific civility of Latinus is a real good, but one which, if unsupplemented, will not be sufficient to the conduct of life in all of its seasons.

To the quietism of Latinus' influence in Latium the effigies and trophies in the *regia Pici* counterpose the dynamism, the active, quasi-masculine, potentially violent principle, in the Latin people. Like its complement, this principle is a good thing, but deficient in isolation. This active, sometimes violent and potentially evil quality is in the Latin people not because Aeneas and the Trojans have tainted them with an alien impurity but because the Latins are human beings. The tragedy of the Latins is not that they possess this natural energy, but that, seduced by the dark powers, Juno and Allecto, they suffer it to overwhelm the calm wisdom of Latinus with which it should remain in harmonious balance. The Latins are vulnerable to this catastrophe not because of an adventitious corrupter but because of the lability of their own precarious human nature, a weakness to which all mortals in Vergil are heir.

To put the finishing touches on the incipient conflict, Juno sends Allecto to goad the hounds of Ascanius into flushing Silvia's pet stag, which the young archer then shoots (7.476ff.). For this act some have blamed Ascanius, on fire with the love of glory—*eximiae taudis succensus amore* (7.496)—but it is hard to see how a desire for that great distinction which given credence to authority is a flaw in a teenager who will one day be the leader of his people.[36] It is important to notice that Vergil takes care to distance Aeneas from the incident of the wounding of the deer, which provides the spark for the war. It is, after all, not Aeneas but his adolescent son who shoots Silvia's pet. Aeneas is not even mentioned in this action or the battle it inspires. Furthermore, Ascanius is unaware that this animal is anyone's pet, let alone that of the family of the *armentarius* of King Latinus. As Vergil portrays him, Ascanius is incapable of knowingly offending the people who have hospitably received the Trojans, and so he must be duped by the machinations of Juno into committing a *faux pas* which triggers the impetuous and disproportionate wrath of the Latin farmers.

The stricken stag runs to Silvia bleating like a crying human being, an instance of Vergilian pathos meant to plausibly motivate the vindictive rage of the farmers who are, after all, prepared to massacre, no questions asked, a group of men under the protection of their own king for the act of wounding in the woods an apparently wild animal which only prescience could have told them was tame. Vergil's text embodies ironies subversive of the stereotype of the violation of pastoral innocence from the outside which it ostensibly presents. Ascanius' deed, though destructive, is not culpable, since he acts with neither malice nor negligence. The Latin's violent response, on the other hand, is unjust on two counts: it is directed without reflection or investigation against those who in fact meant no offense, and it is absurdly out of proportion to the provocation, since the Latins mean to take human life in revenge for an animal's injury. Allecto is at work in the souls of the pastoral rustics: *pestis enim tacitis latet aspera silvis* (7.505).

Creating a striking parallel to Camilla's pastoral spear, Vergil reiterates the violent potential of the pastoral world by having Allecto give on a shepherd's horn the signal for the rustic Latins to mobilize: *pastorale canit signum cornuque recurvo/ Tartaream intendit vocem* (7.513-514). *Canere signum* is a standard military phrase, and the use of *pastorale* to modify *signum* is proof that the pastoral world of the Latins is not ignorant of conflict. At the signal the Latins, understanding its import perfectly well, arm themselves immediately and prepare for combat.

The reinforced Trojans resist their assailants with such spirit that they put them to rout, and the angry Latins, who now have corpses to count, bring on the war. In so doing they do not make trial of a new or foreign evil, but one in their patrimony, as Vergil indicates when he says that as the Latins arm they retemper their fathers' swords: *recoquunt patrios fornacibus ensis* (7.636). By thus fusing pastoralism with rustic bellicosity in his picture of Latium Vergil yet again ironically qualifies the placid vision of Latinus' world he presented at the beginning of Book 7. In accordance with an ancient Latin custom attesting to the antiquity of war in Latium, Juno herself rips open the gates of the temple of Janus as a sign that war has come again to the land as it had so many times before (7.601-622). Her own work of inspiring the madness of war in Italy done, Allecto returns to hell through a cave in the Italian valley of Ampsanctus—notorious for its toxic exhalations—which links the upper world of Italy with the subterranean horrors of Hades (7.561-571), evidence that Hesperia need not rely on Trojan middlemen for access to the infernal powers which symbolize the human impulse to do evil.

E. Vance has rightly called the killing of Silvia's deer a "false tragedy."[37] The real moral catastrophe begins when the furious Latins foist a murderous melee on the Trojans. It is true that the attackers are incited by Allecto, but G. Duckworth has shown that in the *Aeneid* divine impulsion and human inclination generally converge.[38] As with Amata, Turnus, and the dogs of Ascanius, Allecto's incitement of the Latin farmers implies a demonic capacity in the hearts she inflames, and when she departs they persist in their folly. In so doing the Latin rustics bring down their pastoral world from within. This fall is possible because in Vergil's deep conception of the human predicament the ultimate threat to the community of justice symbolized by the pastoral order is to be found in the destructive impulses of the human soul, whether inside or outside of the pastoral enclave.

In Book 8 Aeneas travels to Pallanteum to seek help from Evander, and there he acquires a complex new understanding of Italy which I wish to examine in this paper's final section.

As Aeneas beaches his boats on the shores of the Tiber, Pallas greets the Trojans with a drawn sword, and a question as to whether the strangers bring peace or war, for, as we have already seen, the Italy he knows is a dangerous place in which newcomers may be hostile (8.110-114). This day the Arcadians are celebrating the victory of Heracles over the monster Cacus (8.185-270). The allegorical significance of Cacus has been much discussed,[39] and without necessarily repudiating the interpretations of other scholars I wish to suggest that whatever else he might be, Cacus is a personification of the dark side of Italian primitivism. Like the more barbarous of the Italians, his humanity is morally rude, and he lives by violence, not peaceable toil. Cacus the thieving murder is an indigenous evil destroyed by Hercules, a heroic newcomer to Italy. In this mythological paradigm Italian pastoralism is not tainted by outside violence but purged of a native violence by an outside vindicator. This paradigm has certain generally recognized parallels to the situation of Evander's own people when they welcome Aeneas as their champion against the *violentia* of Turnus.

The next day Evander gives Aeneas a capsule history of Italy. The very fact that all of Italy, like Latium, has a history, a chronicle of change, ill accords with the static calm of the pastoral world which is, for some, the essence of pre-Trojan Italy. Here at last is the key to the assessment of the moral evolution of Italy, and the passage is worth quoting in full:

> haec nemora indigenae Fauni Nymphaeque tenebant
> gensque virum truncis et duro robore nata,
> quis neque mos neque cultus erat, nec iungere tauros
> aut componere open norant aut parcere parto,
> sed rami atque asper victu venatus alebat.

primus ab aetherio venit Saturnus Olympo
arma Iovis fugiens et regnis exsul ademptis.
is genus indocile ac dispersum montibus altis
composuit legesque dedit, Latiumque vocari
maluit, his quoniam latuisset tutus in oris.
aurea quae perhibent illo sub rege fuere
saecula: sic placida populos in pace regebat,
deterior donec paulatim ac decolor aetas
et belli rabies et amor successit habendi.
tum manus Ausonia et gentes venere Sicanae,
saepius et nomen posuit Saturnia tellus;
tum reges asperque immani corpore Thybris,
a quo post Itali fluvium cognomine Thybrim
diximus; amisit verum vetus Albula nomen.

(8.314-332)

The aboriginal Italians were people as hard as the trees from which they sprang. They had neither tradition (*mos*) nor civilization (*cultus*), but lived the life of primitive hunter-gatherers. Civilization came to Italy from the fugitive Saturn who gathered the scattered wild people together and gave them laws, *leges*, through whose influence the golden age came to Italy.

This seems at first to contradict the characterization of the Latin people given by Latinus in 7.202-204:

ne fugite hospitium, neve ignorate Latinos
Saturni gentem haud vinclo nec legibus aequam,
sponte sua veterisque dei se more tenentem.

According to Latinus, his people are just not through constraint of law or penalty, but follow the model of Saturn by their own free will. Servius ad 8.322 explains the apparent contradiction by remarking that Saturn gave laws through obedience to which the Latin people became

---

just by nature. However, Fordyce has noticed from 7.170-174 that the kings of Latium assume the rods and axes of the *fasces*, a symbol of the enforcement of law through discipline which impugns Latinus' sanguine assessment of the moral perfection of his people.[40] Must we then assume that Latinus is lying? That is unnecessary. Latinus is projecting his own just nature onto his people. He assumes that his will and that of his people are one, and so they are, until the Latin race must choose between war and peace. In accord with his nature Latinus makes the right choice, but his people are more impetuous than he, and opt for war. Ultimately pre-Saturnian savagery and post-Saturnian moral decline prevail even in Latium, the last remaining enclave in Italy of the first *Saturnia regna*.[41] This catastrophe had been foreshadowed by ominous events on the fringes of the Latin plain, the military adventurism of Turnus, the brigandage of the Aequi, and civil war in Privernum. In their willful war against the Trojans, the agents of the plan of Jupiter, the moral relapse of the Latins is complete.

If we need proof that Vergil's concept of evil is more complex than the simple model of innocence corrupted, it lies in the mystery of the golden age which Saturn created. Saturn in the *Aeneid* is a Latinized *Kronos*, in Hesiod a figure of barbaric savagery, a tyrant cannibal who devours his own children and must be cast down by force. Hence Saturn is referred to by Vergil as fleeing the arms of Jove, *arma Iovis fugiens* and an exile stripped of his kingdom, *regnis exsul ademptis* (8.320). Tempered by defeat at the hands of his more potent and civilized son, Saturn offers mankind a unity and order which lifts it from savagery. To leave savagery, human beings must lose one kind of innocence (which they have shared with animals), the ignorance of the difference between right and wrong, and acquire another, higher innocence founded on knowledge. For both Saturn and humanity this higher innocence, benign placidity, is not a primeval birthright, an aboriginal purity, but rather an attainment which must be learned. In the Saturnian world innocence is not the ignorance of evil but the absence of evil achieved by the wisdom to live in concord, not discord. This humane knowledge must govern the soul's energetic, potentially savage nature for innocence to prevail. In the Saturnian order natural evils, death and accident, remain, but moral evil can be suppressed in man by *leges*, rules encoding knowledge of the human good, which guide the conduct of life. The essence of the *Saturnia regna* in the *Aeneid* is not effortless living in a spontaneously opulent nature, but a communal life according to justice which is at the very heart of the true pastoral order. Saturn creates humane society by giving savage humanity a moral order. However, the aboriginal wildness of humanity is not thereby expunged, merely controlled. Should the rule of law falter, a fall from innocence, a decline to moral savagery (which need not involve a decline in technology) remains a possibility. This moral savagery will be different from the innocent savagery of pre-Saturnian man in that it exists in spite of, not in the absence of, the knowledge of right and wrong which is the legacy of the *leges* of Saturn. Pre-Saturnian humanity lacked the knowledge to commit moral wrongs. But by the very nature of his felicity, founded as it is on the knowledge of good and evil, Saturnian man becomes capable of a fall into immorality.

So it happened in Italy. Saturn's golden age was gradually replaced by a tarnished era (*decolor agitas*: 326) marked by the accession of the madness of war (*belli rabies*: 327) and greed (*amor . . . habendi*: 327). Vergil does not explain the mechanism of change, but we know that Saturn eventually left Italy, and it is reasonable to conclude that in the absence of the lawgiver the hold of the laws on the people grew less sure. Then the Ausonians and the Sicanians came to Italy, and Italy, the Saturnian land (*Saturnia tellus*), often changed its name (329), that is, Italy became less Saturnian. The decline was uneven. Latium, the center of Saturn's rule, ultimately remained as the last stronghold of the *Saturnia regna*, and even here, as we have seen, the general deterioration had made inroads. Saturn's pastoral kingdom was receding towards its center.

Tum reges. The era of decline was marked by kings, some good, like Picus and Faunus, some morally problematic, like Turnus, Mezentius, and Metabus. As a sign of the coarsening of Italy, Evander mentions violent Thybris, from whom the Tiber took its new name. Servius ad 8.330 cites various explanations for Thybris. Of these, he gives as his first, apparently preferred gloss the identification of Thybris as a Tuscan king who died fighting by the river. One of the other traditions Servius mentions makes Thybris a robber who outraged his victims on its banks. In any case, this violent (*asper*) man gave his name to a river forming the northern boundary of Latium, which thereby lost its first, true name, the "White River": *emisit verum vetus Albula nomen* (332). Servius ad 8.332 tells us that the river was so-called because of its white color, caused, we know, by the sulfur springs which feed its waters, but the symbolism of the change transcends mineralogy. The "White River," symbolic of the purity of the *Saturnia regna*, is renamed for a man of violence as a sign of the creeping corruption of Italy. Here we have unmistakable evidence of the symbolic contamination of the very waters of Italy which Parry took as the symbolic repository of Italian purity. When Aeneas arrived in Hesperia, the *decolor aetas* had spread like a stain on the map of Italy right up to the borders of Latium, and beyond. The golden age in Italy was dying a natural death.

My conclusion is that in the last, most monumental portrait of his beloved Italy in a brilliant literary career, the ambiguous and realistic strain in Vergil's rich intelligence found full expression. Hesperia in the *Aeneid* is no idyllic land outside of time on which Aeneas unleashes the corrupting forces of history, but a country as dynamic and diverse as Greece, Asia, or North Africa. The Italians Aeneas encounters are sometimes peace-loving, hospitable, courteous, generous, courageous, and hardy, but Italy has also known the evils of greed, rapine, tyranny, torture, murder, insurrection, and war. These vices are a sign of a post-Saturnian moral degeneration in Italy which is encroaching on Pallanteum and Laurentum, the most important pastoral enclaves still remaining on Italian soil. This is the crisis which confronts Aeneas, a man driven by destiny to Italian shores where he must continue his long and uneven struggle to keep his integrity in a world he never made. To win Lavinia, the bride destined to bear him an Italian son whose name, Silvius, portends a pastoral future in Italy as Silvia's name signifies a pastoral heritage there, Aeneas must reluctantly draw his sword in a shepherds' war, a bitter paradox which the *Aeneid* presents unflinchingly. In the end, Vergil's moral conception of Italy is as problematic, complex, passionate, and unsentimental as his view of the long-suffering hero after whom his epic is named.[42]

Notes

1. Adam Parry, "The Two Voices of Virgil's *Aeneid*," *Arion* 2 (1963) 68.
2. W. Nethercut, "The Imagery of the *Aeneid*," *CJ* 67 (1971-1972) 123; V. J. Rosivach, "Latinus' Genealogy and the Palace of Picus (*Aeneid* 7.45-9, 170-91)," *CQ* n.s. 30 (1980) 151.
3. Parry (n. 1 above) 66.
4. Parry (n. I above) 68.
5. L. Marx. *The Machine in the Garden* (New York 1964) 25.
6. Marx (n. 5 above) 5ff., esp. 32.
7. Marx (n. 5 above) 25.
8. Marx (n. 5 above) 23.
9. Marx (n. 5 above) 25-26.
10. Cf. Marx (n. 5 above) 26; see also the discussion of death in Arcadia in R. Poggioli, "The Oaten Flute," *Harvard Library Bulletin* Vol. 11, No. 3 (1957) 164-165.
11. Poggioli (n. 10 above) 155.
12. For two useful studies of this passage, with pertinent bibliography, see R. D. Williams, "The Function and Structure of Virgil's Catalogue in *Aeneid* 7," *CQ* n.s. 11 (1961) 146-153; and C. F. Saylor, "The Magnificent Fifteen: Vergil's Catalogues of the Latin and Etruscan Forces," *CP* 69 (1974) 249-257.
13. See, e.g., Servius ad 7.647.
14. For the Roman attitudes towards private property, see G. E. M. de Ste. Croix, *The Class Struggle in the Ancient Greek World* (Ithaca 1981) 329-330, 425-426. For Roman attitudes towards banditry (*latrocinium*), see B. D. Shaw, "Bandits in the Roman Empire," *Past & Present* 105 (1984) 3-52.
15. V. Pöschl, *The Art of the Aeneid: Image and Symbol in the Aeneid*, trans. G.

Seligson (Ann Arbor 1962) 91ff.; B. Otis, *Virgil, A Study in Civilized Poetry* (Oxford 1963) 377-378.

16. The following statement by Parry (n. 1 above) is typical: "Thus the plot of the closing books of the poem center on Turnus, Aeneas' antagonist, who is made the embodiment of a simple valor and love of honor which cannot survive the complex forces of civilization" (p. 68).

Still more telling is this assertion by M. C. J. Putnam in *The Poetry of the Aeneid* (Cambridge, Mass. 1965): "Turnus stands for the world of Italy, that strange combination of wildness and pastoral order" (p. 192).

17. Otis (n. 15 above) 337.

18. Hence Putnam's characterization of Evander's realm as representing "the pastoral life beyond the bounds of actual human strife" (n. 16 above, 109) is too sanguine a view of the perilous situation of the Arcadians.

19. For a good analysis of the compromised morality of Juturna's actions on Turnus' behalf, see V. Castellani, "Anna and Juturna in the Aeneid," *Vergilius* 33 (1987) 49-57.

20. See Putnam (n. 16 above) 165ff., 188-192.

21. For a tabular review of similes representing Turnus and Aeneas in the *Aeneid*, see Pöschl (n. 15 above) 98-99.

22. Pöschl (n. 15 above) 98.

23. W. S. Anderson, "*Pastor Aeneas:* On Pastoral Themes in the Aeneid," *TAPA* 99 (1968) 17.

24. R. A. Brooks, "*Discolor Aura.* Reflections on the Golden Bough," *AJP* 74 (1953) 266-267.

25. Otis (n. 15 above) 364.

26. M. C. J. Putnam, "*Aeneid* VII and the *Aeneid*," *AJP* 91 (1970) 419.

27. For the anti-pastoral dimension of Diana and the hunting life, see Poggioli (n. 10 above) 152.

28. Cf. P. *Vergili Maronis Opera*³, III, eds. J. Conington and H. Nettleship (London 1883) 85 ad 806: and P. *Vergili Maronis Aeneidos Libri VII-VIII* with commentary by C. J. Fordyce, ed. J. D. Christie (Oxford 1977) 203 ad 807.

29. It is important to notice that Camilla was nursed with the milk of a wild *mare*. In 3.539-543, Anchises points out that horses portend both peace and war, and thus mare's milk is a highly fitting nutriment for Camilla the future *venatrix/bellatrix*.

30. For a perceptive account of the negative side of the Latin catalogue, see Saylor (n. 12 above) passim, esp. 254 (very good on Turnus and Camilla).

31. K. J. Reckford, "Latent Tragedy in 'Aeneid' VII, 1-285," *AJP* 82 (1961) 258.

32. Putnam (n. 16 above) 192.

33. W. R. Nethercut, "Invasion in the *Aeneid*," *G & R* n.s. 15 (1968) 82-95.

34. Rosivach (n. 2 above) 151.

35. It is interesting to notice that each of the males in Latinus' family tree appears to relinquish the throne prematurely: Saturn mysteriously gives way to Picus, Picus is transformed to a woodpecker by Circe, Faunus dwindles to an oracular voice, and Latinus retires in the face of events he cannot control.

36. E.g., Putnam (n. 26 above) takes a dim view of Ascanius here (422). For a more

ambivalent though still essentially "pessimistic" reading of the episode see E. Vance, "Silvia's Pet Stag: Wildness and Domesticity in Virgil's *Aeneid*," *Arethusa* 14 (1981) 127-137.

37. Vance (n. 36 above) 128.

38. G. Duckworth, "Fate and Free Will in Vergil's *Aeneid*," *CJ* 51 (1956) 357-364.

39. For a concise bibliography of the scholarship see Fordyce (n. 28 above) 227 ad 184-279. See also Putnam (n. 16 above), who sees Cacus as an incarnation of *furor impius* (131-132), and G. K. Galinsky, who in "The Hercules-Cacus Episode in *Aeneid* VIII," *AJP* 87 (1966) 18-51, sees Cacus as a symbol of Turnus.

40. Fordyce (n. 28 above) 106 ad 203f.

41. On the fragility of the Latin commitment to pastoral values, see Vance (n. 36 above) 133.

42. I must record my thanks to Professor Robert Proctor, who thoughtfully read an intermediate draft of this paper, and particularly to Professor Dirk Held, whose penetrating critique of that draft prompted a dramatic improvement of the argument. Nonetheless, I bear the sole responsibility for judgments and imperfections of this article.

Vergil and the Sibyl of Cumae _____

It is nowadays almost generally assumed that Vergil found a visit by
Aeneas to the Sibyl of Cumae recorded in the legend of his hero.[1]
However, if we seek for evidence, we soon discover that the rightness
of this supposition is usually taken for granted. As far as I know, an
elaborate argument for this assertion is only given by Norden in his famous commentary which is the base of all studies devoted to the sixth
book of the *Aeneid*. So it seems appropriate first to examine this
scholar's discussion of the question.

On p. 350 of his commentary Norden writes: "Was Vergil darüber
(i.e., about the time spent by the Trojans on the coast of Campania) in
der Legende vorfand, war nicht viel: die Begegnung des Aeneas mit
der Sibylle (s. den Kommentar S. 148 f.) sowie Tod und Bestattung des
Misenus." On pp. 148/149 this assertion is supported by an argument
which may be summed up in the following way:

"In vss. 83/97 which contain the Sibyl's prophecy to Aeneas, several details may be observed which have parallels in the *Oracula
Sibyllina* or similar texts. This leads us to the assumption that for the
contents of this prophecy Vergil drew upon on existing *oraculum
Sibyllinum*; this supposition is supported by the fact that corresponding details occur in the prophecy of the Cumaean Sibyl to Aeneas
in Tibullus II, 5, 39/64, among which details the announcement of
Aeneas' death in the waves of the Numicus[2] is particularly remarkable.
Now Tibullus for this prophecy cannot have drawn upon Vergil, since
he mentions several facts omitted by the latter poet, e.g., the foundation of Rome; so we may conclude that the prophecy as given by
Tibullus derives from the same *oraculum Sibyllinum*. On account of
resemblances in the most important details it seems probable that eventually this oracle drew its material from Lycophron *Alexandra* 1226/
1282, in which passage Cassandra prophesies Aeneas' rescue from
Troy, his wanderings, and his settlement in Italy; both Roman poets

208   Critical Insights

may have become acquainted with the oracle through the intermediary of a common authority, perhaps Alexander Polyhistor." At the end of this argument Norden adds that it is based on the assumption defended by Friedrich Leo[3] that by the anonymous Sibyl who delivered a prophecy to Aeneas Tibullus meant the Sibyl of Cumae.

Let us begin by examining whether the base of the argument is sound. According to Leo, Tibullus in the passage under discussion cannot have thought of the Sibyl of Troy, since immediately after the prophecy (mss. 67/68) the latter's name (*Marpessia Herophile*) occurs in an enumeration of four Sibyls who are opposed to the first-mentioned. A further argument is found by him in vss. 41/42 (*iam tibi Laurentes adsignat Jupiter agros,/ iam vocat errantes hospita terra lares*), which he takes to imply that at the moment of the prophecy Aeneas' wanderings had come to an end. Finally, the circumstance that Tibullus does not furnish any indication of the place in which the Sibyl delivers her prophecy, induces him to assume that only such a place could be meant which in Augustus' time would occur to every Roman at once, viz., Cumae.

This interpretation has two consequences which do not tend to increase our faith in its probability. Firstly, in vss. 21/22 (*Nec fore credebat* (viz., Aeneas) *Romam, cum maestus ab alto/ Ilion ardentes respiceretque deos*) the reading *Roman* can not be maintained: if the prophecy was delivered at Cumae, then Aeneas immediately after leaving Troy (*cum ... deos*) could not yet know anything about the future foundation of Rome. Hence Leo reads *Troiam* and translates: "und er glaubte nicht, dass Troja wieder erstehen würde." Secondly, in vss. 19/20 (*haec dedit Aeneae sortes, postquam ille parentem/ dicitur et raptos sustinuisse lares*) a most tortuous explication of the use of *postquam* becomes necessary.[4]

More than sixty years ago already Ernst Maass[5] has exposed the weak points of Leo's argument. His chief objection is indeed conclusive: *Nec fore credebat Troiam* cannot possibly give the sense required: "and he did not believe that Troy would resurge": in all the parallel passages quoted by Leo in support of his conjecture this idea of a resurrection of Troy in Rome has been fully expressed (*recidiva Pergama, Troica Roma, melioris moenia Romae*, etc.). Hence the conjecture is unacceptable and the original reading *Nec fore credebat Romam* has to be maintained. From this Maass rightly concludes that the prophecy must have been delivered to Aeneas before he left the Trojan soil (*Nec fore credebat Romam, cum maestus ab alto/ Ilion ardentes respiceretque dens*);[6] his second conclusion, viz., that Tibullus must have thought of the Sibyl of Marpessus here, is less probable, cf. below p. 48. For a refutation of Leo's second argument, cf. *op. cit.*, 324; with regard to the third, it need hardly be pointed out that the use of *iam* in vss. 41/42 does not at all imply that at the moment of the prophecy the foundation of Rome belonged to the immediate future: in every prophecy the time which separates the announcement from its fulfillment is considered to be of secondary importance.

On the other hand, serious consideration is required for Leo's first argument (*op. cit.*, 9): "Die 'Marpessia Herophile' wird aber von Tibull v. 67 unter den der 'Sibylla' entgegengesetzen Seherinnen genannt. Das wendet schon Dissen ein, und in der That ist hiermit deutlich gesagt, dass unter des Sibylle des Aeneas nicht die troische verstanden ist." According to Maass,[7] Tibullus must have made an error in distinguishing the Sibyl of Troy from *Marpessia Herophile*, which error, however, in his opinion finds both an excuse and an explanation in the fact that Herophile is also the name of the Sibyl of Erythrae. Afterwards he preferred a different solution, viz., that Tibullus deliberately left his Sibyl nameless, lest he should be obliged to take sides in the discussion whether it was the Sibyl of Marpessus or of Cumae who delivered the prophecy to Aeneas.[8]

It seems to me that both remarks by Maass lead us to the truth without, however, reaching it. Let us begin by examining the verses under discussion. In most editions they are now given in this form:

> *quidquid Amalthea, quidquid Marpessia dixit*
> *Herophile, Phyto Graia quod admonuit,*
> *quasque Aniena sacras Tiburs per flumina sortes*
> *portarit sicco pertuleritque sinu.*

If we adopt this text, the words *Marpessia Herophile* indeed clearly indicate that Tibullus means a definite prophetess, the Sibyl of Troy, and in that case the fact that she is thus mentioned immediately after a prophecy given by a Sibyl in Troy[9] cannot be explained satisfactorily. However, it is more than doubtful that Tibullus should indeed have written this. In vs. 68 all manuscripts give *Herophile Phoebo grata quod admonuit*, *Phyto* being a conjecture by Huschke, *Graia* one by Lachmann. The cause which gave rise to these alterations is clear: it was regarded as certain that, just as everybody else, Tibullus considered *Marpessia* to be an adjective, and hence connected it with *Herophile*, the name of the Trojan Sibyl; thus after the last-mentioned word a comma had to be put and the words *Phoebo grata quod admonuit*, which did not give a complete sentence, needed remedy.

However, this argument is far from convincing. First of all, it should be remembered that Herophile was the official name of the Sibyl of Erythrae,[10] whereas only two passages from ancient literature mention it as the name of the Trojan Sibyl, viz., Pausan. X, 12,5 and Mart. Capella II, 159.[11] When, moreover, we think of the close—though not always friendly—connections between the Sibyl (or Sibyls) and Apollo, we cannot but conclude that Rossbach was right in retaining the reading of the manuscripts: *Herophile Phoebo grata quod admonuit*.[12] In that case the first line must run—and as to the form of the verse this is certainly much more satisfactory—: *quidquid Amalthea, quidquid Marpessia dixit*. The conclusion is obvious that Tibullus wrongly regarded *Marpessia* as being on one level with *Amalthea* and *Herophile*, i.e., as a substantival proper name. Nor had he any motive to improve his knowledge in this respect, for, as Michaelis has pointed out,[13] in his eyes the four Sibyls enumerated in vss. 67/70 were greatly inferior to his 'great Sibyl' who prophesied the fate of Aeneas and—in connection with it, cf. p. 51—the foundation of Rome.

Thus, if by his 'great Sibyl' Tibullus meant the Sibyl of Marpessus, as was originally assumed by Maass, the fact that the poet mentions her twice (vss. 19 and 67) is sufficiently explained by the circumstance that he did not realize this himself: he did not know that *Marpessia* was a denomination of the Sibyl of Troy. However, it is much more probable that Maass's second hypothesis (cf. note 7) was right, viz., that Tibullus purposely left his Sibyl unnamed in order that he should not be obliged to choose between the Sibyls of Troy and of Cumae. The probability of this hypothesis is supported by the following fact: in vs. 15 (*te*, viz., *Apollo, duce Romanos nunquam frustrata Sibylla est*) *Sibylla* can only refer to "Sibylline literature in general"[14] which implies an association with the Sibyl of Cumae. Now in vs. 19 *Haec* refers to *Sibylla* in vs. 15; consequently, the 'great Sibyl', though clearly represented as delivering her prophecy before Aeneas' departure from Troy, i.e. in Troas, is most likely to have been left unidentified to preserve the connection with Rome, too, intact.

At all events, Leo's view that in vs. 19 Tibullus can only have meant a prophecy delivered at Cumae may be regarded as refuted. One additional argument may be added: Tibullus' list eventually derives from the list of Sibyls drawn up by Varro, as is evident from his mentioning the Sibyl of Tibur;[15] hence, if Leo objected to identifying Tibullus' 'great Sibyl' with the Sibyl of Troy on account of *Marpessia Herophile* in vss. 67/68, he should also have considered it impossible to identify her with the Sibyl of Cumae, for, according to Varro, *Amalthea* was one of the names of the latter,[16] and this name also occurs in vs. 67.

Thus it has become impossible to agree with Norden that Vergil and Tibullus in every respect should have drawn on the same authority concerning the prophecy of the Sibyl to Aeneas. Of course they partly deal with the same material, which for a long time had already formed part of the legend,[17] but Tibullus does not say anything about a prophecy by the Sibyl of Cumae.

Now the question arises whether before Vergil's time such a prophecy formed part of the legend of Aeneas besides the version preserved by Tibullus and Dionysius of Halicarnassus[18] or whether Professor Butler was right indeed.[19]

As we have seen (p. 43), Norden's argument primarily bears upon the existence of a Sibylline oracle concerning Aeneas which for the chief part of its contents was borrowed from Lycophron and which became known to both Roman poets through the intermediary of a common authority, perhaps Alexander Polyhistor. Though in the exposition of this argument Norden does not mention the Cumaean Sibyl, the fact that he declares it to be based on the supposition that Tibullus' great Sibyl should be the Sibyl of Cumae, shows that, in his opinion, the 'common authority' and the 'Sibylline oracle', and probably also Lycophron, localized the Sibyl's prophecy to Aeneas at Cumae. At all events, as to the passage in Lycophron this has frequently been taken for granted, as is shown by the words of Ernst Maass, who, after proving that Tibullus must have meant a prophecy delivered in Troy, continues:[20] "Es ist zunächst beachtenswert, dass er (i.e., Tibullus) die ältere, den Römern geläufige Erzählung von der italischen[21] Sibylle verworfen und sich dadurch in Widerspruch zu dem Vater dieser Sage Timaeus[22] und der von ihm vertretenen Chronologie gesetzt hat. Timaeus knüpfte die Gründung Roms direct an Troias Untergang. Dem entsprechend liess er seinen Aeneas mit der auf die neunte Olympiade fixirten erythräisch-cumanischen Sibylle in Italien zusammentreffen, obwohl vier Jahrhunderte zwischen beiden liegen."

So let us first examine the text of Lycophron[23] in which the Sibyl of Cumae is mentioned. Cassandra prophesies that Aeneas is to found a city (τύρσιν)

> μακεδνὰς ἀμφὶ Κιρκαίου νάπας
> Ἀργοῦς τε κλεινὸν ὅρμον Αἰήτην μέγαν,
> λίμνης τε Φόρκης Μαρσιώτιδος ποτὰ
> Τιτώνιόν τε χεῦμα, τοῦ κατὰ χθονὸς

δύνοντος εἰς ἄφαντα κευθμῶνος βάθη,
Ζωστηρίου τε κλίτυν, ἔνθα παρθένου
στυγνὸν Σιβύλλης ἐστὶν οἰκητήριον
γρώνῃ βέρεθρον συγκατηρεφές στέγῃ.

(vss. 1273-1280)

It is only when surveying this enumeration in its entirety and not only its last three lines that we see that Lycophron's words do not at all imply a visit of Aeneas to the Cumaean Sibyl. For, if we should indeed draw this conclusion from the fact that the Sibyl and her cave in the acropolis of Cumae are mentioned here, we are likewise obliged to assume that the version of the legend of Aeneas known to Lycophron should have contained visits of Aeneas to the other places mentioned in the enumeration; but this is out of the question in the case of the river Titon, the lake of Phorce in the country of the Marsians, and the Κιρκαῖοι νάπαι. As to the last place, cf. Holzinger's note *ad loc.* (p. 345): "Beachtenswerth scheint mir, dass die Erwähnung von Circeji und Cajeta aus der Darstellung der Argonautenfahrt (nicht aus einer "Reise des Aeneas") herrührt."[24]

A further argument may be added: that Lycophron wished to allude to, or even ever heard about, a prophecy of the Cumaean Sibyl to Aeneas, is improbable on account of the very fact that in this poem it is Cassandra who delivers the prophecy. It is well known that in later times Cassandra the prophetess and the Sibyl of Troy were considered to be so strongly related to each other that the former is frequently called a Sibyl (for evidence, cf. Bouché-Leclercq, *op. cit.*, 148/153. 175₅. 175₄); it is even probable that the characteristics of one of the two figures derive from the other (according to Bouché-Leclercq, *op. cit.*, 148/153, and Picard, *Claros et Ephèse*, 419/421, the figure of the Sibyl is secondary; the contrary opinion is held by Buchholz, art. *Sibylle*, Roscher 4, 797). Now in vss. 1464/1465 Lycophron calls Cassandra Κλάρου Μιμάλλων (i.e., Βάκχη) ἢ Μελαγκραίρας κόπις/ Νήσους θυγατρός (*schol. ad loc.*: Μελαγκραίρα δὲ ἡ Σίβυλλα, παρὰ τὸ μελαίνειν τὴν φράσιν καὶ το ς χρησμούς. Νησὼ δέ, μήτηε Σιβύλλης), in other words, he compares her to the Sibyl. It seems indeed plausible that Lycophron knew both the identification of Cassandra with the Sibyl of Troy and the tradition adopted by Dionysius of Halicarnassus and others (cf. p. 48 and note 26) which declared this Sibyl to have prophesied the *fata Aeneae*.

Finally, it should be remarked that in this context a prophecy by the Cumaean Sibyl would be plainly superfluous, as Cassandra is already prophesying everything that was to be prophesied, the 'Italian part' of the *fata Aeneae* included.

Nor is it more plausible that a 'Sibylline' oracle prophesying the adventures of Aeneas should have presented itself as a revelation by the Cumaean Sibyl. First of all it should be pointed out that the parallels advanced by Norden in his commentary on vss. 83/97[25] are by no means sufficient to make it probable that such an oracle should have existed: they only serve to prove that in several of these verses Vergil wanted to give a formal imitation of the style of Sibylline oracles, but not one of them contains a concrete allusion to the legend of Aeneas. But even if such an oracle existed—and indeed some indications of its having existed may perhaps be found[26]—it is much more probable, as is already shown by the passages quoted in note 26, that it should have presented itself as a prophecy by the Sibyl of Troy: if 'a prophecy by the Sibyl of Cumae' should have already been current before the days of Vergil and Tibullus, it would be hard to explain why Tibullus and Dionysius of Halicarnassus adopted a different version, whereas in the inverse case the reason for Vergil's alteration of the tradition is obvious (cf. p. 57).[27]

Having thus established that neither Lycophron nor Tibullus say anything about a prophecy of the Cumaean Sibyl to Aeneas and that it is also improbable that such a prophecy should ever have formed part of a Sibylline oracle containing the *fata Aeneae*, we now turn to examining a different version of the legend adopted by Roman authors, which indeed mentions a visit of Aeneas to an Italian Sibyl.

In the list of Sibyls drawn up by Varro in his *Antiquitates divinae*[28] and preserved by Lactantius (*divin. instit.* 1, 6) we read: *quartam Cimmeriam in Italia, quam Naevius in libris belli Punici, Piso in Annalibus nominat.* To this testimony we must add a passage from the *Origo gentis Romanae* (ch. 10) which is best quoted in full: *"Addunt praeterea quidam Aeneam in eo litore Euxini cuiusdam comitis matrem ultimo aetatis affectam circa stagnum, quod est inter Misenon Avernumque, extulisse, atque loco inde nomen inditum, qui etiam nunc Euxinus sinus dicitur: cumque comperisset ibidem Sibyllam mortalibus futura praecinere in oppido, quod vocatur Cimbarionis, venisse eo sciscitatum de statu fortunarum suarum aditisque fatis vetituin, ne is cognatam in Italia sepeliret Prochytam, cognatione sibi coniunctam, quam incolumem reliquerat. Et postquam ad classem rediit, repperitque mortuam, in insula proxima sepelisse, quae nunc quoque eodem est nomine, ut scribunt Vulcatius et Acilius Piso."*[29]

Now it is indeed highly probable that Piso, if he mentioned the burying by Aeneas of his relative Prochyta,[30] also spoke about Aeneas' visit to the Cimmerian Sibyl, who was said to live near the Avernan lake.[31] Accordingly, Varro's words *quam . . . Piso in annalibus nominat* are likely to refer to a report of this visit; and since we know that Naevius in the first two books of his *Bellum Punicum* treated the legend of Aeneas and, moreover, in the first book mentioned Prochyta as a relative of Aeneas (Serv. Dan. *ad Aen.* IX, 712), the same conclusion may be drawn from the sentence in Varro.[32]

It has frequently been asserted, e.g. by Alexandre[33] and Bouché-Leclercq,[34] that this Cimmerian Sibyl must have been regarded as identical with the Sibyl of Cumae; the circumstance that Varro explicitly distinguishes between them (in his list the former occupies the fourth, the latter the seventh place) is explained as 'a scholar's invention'. Apart from the fact that such an argument does not sound very convincing where two figures so well-known are concerned, and that the distance between Cumae and the Avernan lake must have seemed more important to popular belief than to the creative mind of Vergil, the seat of the Cimmerian Sibyl was regarded as wholly different from the Sibyl's cave in the acropolis of Cumae, as was first elucidated by Corssen.[35]

It is told by Ephorus (*ap.* Strabo V, 4, 5 = frag. 134 Jacoby), Cicero (*Tusc. disput.* 1, 37), and Maximus Tyrius (*dissert.* 8, 2, p. 88 Hobein) that once a famous νεκυομαντεῖον, already visited by Odysseus,[36] existed near the Avernan lake, and Corssen has made it highly probable that in Naevius' *Bellum Punicum* Aeneas' visit to the Cimmerian Sibyl led to a consultation of this oracle, which may have culminated, or consisted, in an *evocatio* of the spirit of Anchises.[37] From this Corssen drew the conclusion that the Sibyl's function as Aeneas' guide through Hades is a modification by Vergil of her function as priestess of the νεκυομαντεῖον in Naevius, and that by calling his Sibyl *Phoebi Triviaeque sacerdos* (vs. 36) the poet announced that this figure combined the features of the priestess of Apollo at Cumae and of the priestess of Hecate (= *Trivia*) at the Avernan lake. Unfortunately, Corssen did not say whether he thought a prophecy by the Cumaean Sibyl to Aeneas to have formed part of the legend before Vergil, and Norden, who took this for certain, by adopting Corssen's view arrived at the conclusion that Vergil took the prophecy of the Cumaean Sibyl from the legend of Aeneas, her connection with Hades from Naevius.[38]

From what has been said in the foregoing pages it is clear that Vergil's alteration of the material which he found before him was more radical. In fact he combined the features of three Sibyls into one:[39]

(a) the Sibyl of Cumae, who at the time when Vergil was working on his epic had become the object of general interest on account of the deposition of the *libri Sibyllini* in the new-built temple of Apollo on the Palatine (28 b. Chr.) and of the restoration of the temple and the cave at Cumae by Augustus and Agrippa. The wish to mention these books and the holy places of Cumae in the *Aeneid* (VI, 71/76) obliged Vergil to make this Sibyl a contemporary of Aeneas, whereas it was generally believed—and Varro had done much to popularize this belief—that she had offered her books to Tarquinius; it is for this reason that Vergil, by emphasizing her advanced age already at the time of Aeneas' visit (vs. 764), represents her as a being almost beyond time (cf. Servius ad vs. 36).

(b) the Sibyl of Troy, who for a long time had been believed (a belief still mentioned by Dionysius of Halicarnassus) to have prophesied the *fata Aeneae*.

(c) the Cimmerian Sibyl mentioned by Naevius, Piso, and Varro whose connection with the ψυχομαντεῖον at the Avernan lake suggested to Vergil the idea of making his Sibyl the guide of a Κατάβασις Αἰνείου.

In spite of—or perhaps on account of—the threefold function deriving from this combination Vergil's Sibyl has by no means become a predominating figure in the structure of the sixth book of the *Aeneid*: she prophesies Aeneas' adventures in Italy—but the hero knows them already and only asks for her confirmation;[40] as authoress of the *libri Sibyllini* she is acquainted with the *fata Romae*—but it is Anchises who prophesies them owing to a most elaborate *inventio* (metempsychosis), whereas, if the Sibyl had given this prophecy, no difficulties would have existed;[41] by far her most important function is that of guiding Aeneas through Hades—but for the plot this guidance is only important because it shows the way to Anchises. Perhaps a confirmation of our view may be found in the fact that it is the 'typically Cumaean' element in Vergil's Sibyl (the connection with the *libri Sibyllini*) which of all three components has remained the most anaemic. Norden thought it improbable that the prophecy by the Cumaean Sibyl to Aeneas should be a 'fiction by Vergil', because he considered such a function to be contrary to the poet's usual method of working.[42] However, the only 'fiction' to be assumed is the localization of Aeneas' visit to the Sibyl at Cumae, an alteration far less serious than the introduction into the legend of a Κατάβασις Αἰνείου, which Norden accepts without comment. We may rather regard this connection of the legend with Cumae as a confirmation of Mr. Jackson Knight's judicious statement:[43] "He (i.e., Vergil) seems to try to neglect tradition as little as he can, but to take every chance to alter it and combine versions together."

Notes

1. An exception is to be made for H. E. Butler, who in his commentary (*The Sixth Book of the Aeneid,* Oxford 1920) writes (pp. 85/86): "Vergil, in view of the important part played by the Sibylline books at Rome, may have been the first to introduce the Sibyl of Cumae into the Aeneas legend, one of his many devices for introducing national colour into his epic." Unfortunately he does not give any argument. J. Perret (*Les Origines de la Légende troyenne de Rome,* thesis Paris 1942, 101/104), with whom I agree in several respects, only remarks (*op. cit.,* 103; cf. below p. 55): "Il n'existe aucun indice que cette localisation d'Enée à Cumes et sur l'Averne ait préexisté à Naevius" without even mentioning Norden's commentary in this context.

2. Verg. vs. 88 (*Simois,* cf. Servius *ad loc.*), Tib. vss. 43/44.

3. *Zu Augusteischen Dichtern* (Philol. Unters., 2. Heft, Berlin 1881), 9/12.

4. *Op. cit.,* 10/11: "Wir verstehen demnach *postquam* v. 19 nicht perfectisch ('nachdem er grade getragen hatte'), sondern es hebt aoristisch die rühmlichste und bekanteste That des Mannes heraus."

5. *Hermes* 18 (1883), 323/337.

6. I regard it as certain that in vs. 22 *respiceret* is meant in the literal sense of the word (cf. the similar situation in Verg. *Aen.* V, 3/4: ([Aeneas] *moenla respiciens quae iam infelicis Elyssae collucent flammis*); then Aeneas at the beginning of his journey was acquainted with the future foundation of Rome. From this it follows that the prophecy must have been delivered in the time between Aeneas' escape from burning Troy (19 *postquam . . . 20 Lares*) and his departure from the Trojan soil, i.e., in the time described in *Aen.* III, 1/11. That *nec* in vs. 21 opens a new sentence and has adversative force, in my opinion, is evident from its connection with *nondum* in vs. 23: "Aeneas received a <glorious> prophecy after his flight from Troy. However, he did not believe much of it, when <shortly after> he looked back from his ship to burning Troy. <Nor is this incredulity surprising, for nothing had yet happened which could give him confidence:> Romulus had not yet," etc. Vss. 21/22 are the introduction of the ἔκφρασις given in vss. 23/38.

7. "Sind die beiden Seherinnen in Wirklichkeit identisch, und sind sie trotzdem im Gedicht unterschieden: so folgt für mich und jeden Unbefangenen daraus mit unabweisbarer Notwendigkeit, dass Tibull die Unterscheidung selbst gewollt, d.h. sie irrtümlich begangen hat. Zur Entschuldigung des Irrthums aber lässt sich Folgendes anführen, das zugleich zu seiner Erklärung dienen mag. Es giebt, wie schon erwähnt, zwei Sibyllen des Namens Herophile, bei denen die Bezeichung erythraea stehend ist,

---

das eine Mal als Ethnicum von Erythrae, das andere Mal . . . hergeleitet von der ἐρυθρῇ Μαρπήσσος." The hypothesis of Maass that the Sibyl of Marpessus should have been 'invented' by Demetrius of Scepsis, has sufficiently been refuted by Corssen, *Athen. Mitteil.* 39 (1913), 9, and Buchholz, *Roscher* 4, 793.

8. E. A. F. Michaelis, *Philologus* 73 (1914-1916), 387/388: "In diesem Streit (viz., whether Tibullus meant the Sibyl of Troy or of Cumae) Partei zu nehmen, ist um so weniger meine Absicht, als Tibull sich vielleicht grade durch die Namenlosigkeit seiner Sibylle einer solchen Fragestellung hat entziehen wollen" (38$_{11}$: "Nach einer brieflichen Anregung von Herrn Geh R. Maass").

9. Which does not yet mean that she is the Trojan Sibyl, cf. below p. 48.

10. The only exception occurs in Mart. Capella II, 159, where she is called Symmachia which, however, may be a surname (cf. A. Bouché-Leclercq, *Histoire de la divination dans l'antiquité*, 2 (Paris 1880), 167).

11. The latter passage is no more than a faint echo: *Herophilam Troianam Marmensi filiam.* Maass, *De Sibyllarum indicibus* (thesis Greifswald 1879), 27, instead of *Marmensi* reads *Marpessi.* However, it is doubtful whether this conjecture is necessary, cf. already Heyne's note on Tibullus, *loc. cit.*

12. Cf. e.g. the first line of the epitaph of the Sibyl of Alexandria (Pausan. X, 12, 6): ἄδ᾽ ἐγὼ ἁ Φοίβοιο σαφηγορίς εἰμι Σίβυλλα.

13. *Op. cit.* (cf. note 8), 388: "Das scheint mir schon aus dem Ton von v. 39-64 hervorzugehn, dass dies die 'grosse Sibylle' sein soll, der gegen-über Amathea, Marpessia e tutte quante nur zweiten Ranges sind." It should be noted that in this correct paraphrase of Tibullus' nonchalance Michaelis unawares treats *Marpessia* as a substantival proper name.

14. *Sibylla* (not the plural *Sibyllae*) is frequently found in the sense of 'Sibylline literature' or (more restricted) 'the *libri Sibyllini*', e.g. Cic. *pro Rab. Post.* 4; *ad fam.* I, 7, 4; *divin.* II, 110-112; Liv. X, 8, 2; Tac. *Ann.* VI, 12; Lact. *div. instit.* I, 6, 13. For these quotations and for the reference to the importance of vs. 15 in this context I am indebted to Professor H. Wagenvoort.

15. Cf. C. Alexandre, *Oracula Sibyllina*, 2 (Paris 1856), 23 *seqq.*; Buchholz, s.v. *Sibylle*, Roscher 4, 803. Perhaps a second specimen of Tibullus' carelessness may be adduced. About the Sibyl of Tibur Varro's catalogue says: *Decimam Tiburtem nomine Atbuneam quae Tiburi colitur ut dea iuxta ripas Anienis cuius in gurgite simulacrum eius inventam esse dicitur tenens in manu librum; cuius sortes senatus in Capitolium transtulerit.* Vss. 69/70 are usually edited as quoted, but it should be noted that the readings *Aniena* and *Tiburs* only occur in the Italian manuscripts of the fifteenth century, in which an endeavour to make the text harmonize with Varro (quoted by the much-read Lactantius!) is by no means impossible. The better manuscripts read *albana* and *ti(y)beris*, which gives a wholly different verse (we should only change *albana* into *Albuna*, a form found in CGL IV 307, 17 and V 590, 44): *quasque Albuna sacras Tiberis per fluminis undas.* If this is really the exact reading, the substitution of the Anio by the Tiber in this context may be one more proof of Tibullus' carelessness.

16. Varro *ap.* Lact. *div. instit.* 1, 6: *Septimam Cumanam nomine Amaltheam, quae ab allis Demophile vel Herophile nominatur.* Bouché-Leclercq (*op. cit.*, 160) supposes

that originally Amalthea was the name of the Thesprotian Sibyl; in this he follows Klausen who, moreover, assumed (*Aeneas und die Penaten*, 222) that the name became known to Campania through the intermediary of the Leucadians.

17. Vergil mentions Lavinium, the war in Italy, Aeneas' death in the Numicus, Turnus, Iuno, Lavinia, and the help from a Greek city; Tibullus enumerates Laurentum, the Numicus, the final victory, a fire in the Rutulian camp, Turnus and his death, Lavinium, the foundation of Alba Longa by Ascanius, Ilia and Mars, and the foundation of Rome. With one exception (the somewhat mysterious fire in the Rutulian camp) all details are certain to have formed part of the legend before the time of both poets; most of them are mentioned in the fragments of Cato's *Origines* (for further evidence, cf. e.g. Schwegler, *Röm. Gesch.*, 1, 279 *seqq.* and Malten, *Aineias*, ARW 29 (1931), 33/59). It is probable that in vss. 96/97 (*via . . . urbe*) Vergil followed a tradition of Sibylline literature (cf. Heinze, *Hermes* 33 (1898), 478, n. 1); however, we should remember that this imitation only extends itself to the form of the prophecy (cf. note 22): as to the contents of these verses, Diomedes' reconciliation with the Trojans also had its place in the legend (cf. Pausan. I, 11, 7). I fail to see why the mentioning of Aeneas' death in the waves of the Numicus should be regarded as particularly important (thus Norden, *op. cit.*, 148): it was already recorded by Cato (Serv. *ad Aen.* IV, 620), probably also by Ennius (*id., ib.* VI, 777). I agree with B. Riposati, *Introduzione allo Studio di Tibullo* (Como-Milano 1945), 216/220, that Tibullus is not likely to have drawn upon Vergil directly in this passage.

18. *Antiq. Rom.*, I, 55.

19. Cf. note 1.

20. *Hermes* 18 (1883), 329/330.

21. This must refer to the Cimmerian Sibyl mentioned in this context by Naevius and Piso (cf. p. 54), who was and is usually identified with the prophetess of Cumae; cf. p. 55.

22. It may indeed be regarded as certain that Lycophron's description of the Sibyl of Cumae is borrowed from Timaeus; cf. e.g. Maass, *De Sibyllarum indicibus*, 36/37; Geffcken, *Timaios' Geographie des Westens* (Berlin 1892), 1/4; 145/146.

23. The opinion of P. Cauer (*Rhein. Mus.* 41 (1896), 387, and *Neue Jahrb. Suppl.* 15 (1880, 128 *seqq.*) and others that Lycophron vss. 1226/1280 are an interpolation, has been refuted by Wilamowitz, cf. Geffcken, *op. cit.*, 41.

24. According to Vergil, too, Aeneas sails past Circei, *Aen.* VII, 10: *Proxima Circaeae raduntur litora terrae* (Vergil follows Varro, who asserted that in Aeneas' time Circe's dwelling-place was still an island (Hom. *Odyss.* X, 135) which afterwards became connected with the continent).—It should be noted that Caieta, besides Cumae the only place from this enumeration which is mentioned in the *Aeneid* as having been visited by Aeneas, is here connected with the legend of the Argonauts.

25. Verg. vss. 77/80 ~ *Orac. Sib.* III, 5 *seqq.* τυπτόμενος μάστιγι; vs. 94 *externi . . . thalami* (indefinite plural) ~ *ib.* VII, 98. 270, etc.; vs. 102 *quierant* ~ *ib.* III, 3 ἄμπκυσον; vss. 96/97 (*via. . . . urbe*) ~ oracle preserved by Phlegon (Diels, *Sibyll. Blätter*, 115): Τρὼς δῆτ' ἐκλύσει σε κακῶν, ἅμα δ' ᾽Ελλάδος ἐκ γῆς (cf. Heinze, *Hermes* 33 (1898), 478₁). In addition to the details deriving from the legend and from this formal imitation, a third important factor in the moulding of this passage is the cor-

respondence of the Sibyl's answer to Aeneas' prayer (vss. 56/76), as was first pointed out by J. van Ooteghem, *L'oracle de la Sibylle au chant VI de l'Enéide*, Et. Class. 9 (1940), 14/17.

26. This may perhaps be deduced from two facts: a) with regard to the famous prophecy in the *Iliad* (XX, 307/308: νῦν δὲ δὴ Αἰνείαο βιὴ Τρώεσσιν ἀνάξει | καὶ παίδων παῖδες, τοί κεν μετόπισθε γένωνται) the *scholia Townleyiana (Schol. gr. in Iliad.*, ed. Dindorf, VI, 325, 21/22) observe: οἳ μὲν διὰ ῾Ρωμαίους φασίν, ἅπερ εἰδέναι τὸν ποιήτην ἐκ τῶν Σιβύλλης χρησμῶν; cf. also *id. ad* XIII, 460, and Eustathius *ad. loc.*: λέγει δὲ καὶ, ὅτι᾽ ἤδη γὰρ . . . οἳ μετόπισθεν γένωνται᾽. τοῦτο δὲ λέγεται διὰ τὴν τῶν ῾Ρωμαίων ἀρχὴν, ἥν, φασιν, εἰκὸς εἰδέναι τὸν ποιήτην ἐκ τῶν τῆς Σιβύλλης χρησμῶν, ἢ καὶ αὐτὸν οἴκοθεν εἰδότα. Though unfortunately it is impossible to say anything definite about the origin of this interpretation—it may, however, have been known to Aristarchus, cf. Maass, *Hermes* 18 (1883), 331—so much at least is clear that a tradition existed according to which Homer had taken this prophecy from 'the Sibyl'—probably the Sibyl of Troy; b) *Orac. Sib.* XI, 144 *seqq.* contain a prophecy of the *fata Aeneae* which mentions the escape from Troy, the wanderings on sea, the foundation of a city in the country of the Latini, and the death in the Numicus. In view of the power of tradition in this kind of literature this passage (which belongs to the youngest parts of the collection, cf. Alexandre, *op. cit.*, 2, 415 *seqq.*) is likely to derive from an older oracle which, just as the passage under discussion, on account of its first part (the wanderings on sea) could not possibly have been pronounced by the Cumaean Sibyl. Cf. also Diod. Sic. IV, 66.

27. We should bear in mind that an inclination to adopt less known versions of myths or even to make alterations has never been found in Tibullus, whereas for Vergil this practice is typical; cf. the last sentence of this article.

28. Lact., *loc. cit.* (in the introduction to the list): *M. Varro . . . in libris rerum divinarum quos ad Caesarem pontificem maximum* (47 b. Chr.) *scripsit, cum de XV viris loqueretur, Sibyllinos libros ait non fuisse unius Sibyllae*, etc.

29. It is certain that Piso the annalist was quoted in this context (cf. e.g. Alexandre, *op. cit.*, 2, 54; H. Peter in the *Prolegomena* to his edition of the *Origo*, Ber. sächs. Ges. d. Wiss., Philol-histor. Kl., 64 (1912), 88/89). Jordan reads *Acilius et Piso*, Peter maintains the *lectio tradita (op. cit.*, 91, n. 2 and 93, n. 1). Probably the author of the *Origo* did not realize whom he was speaking about. See also Perret, *op. cit.*, 105, n. 3.

30. Bouché-Leclercq, *op. cit.*, 188, seems to believe that in the *Origo Prochyta* is said to be the name of the Cimmerian Sibyl; this curious error is probably due to his not having read the entire passage quoted above, for the words *Et postquam ad classem rediit, repperitque mortuam* plainly exclude this interpretation. Cf. also Dion. Hal., I, 53.

31. Plin. *nat. hist.* III, 61: *lacus Lucrinus et Avernus, iuxta quem Cimmerium oppidum quondam.*

32. A similar argument is given by Perret, *op. cit.*, 100/101: "Le fait que Varron distinguât nettement cette Sibylle (i.e., the Cimmerian Sibyl) de celle de Cumes nous parait exclure que Naevius ait mis en oeuvre son personnage à propos de l'épisode où intervient traditionnellement la Sibylle de Cumes, celui de la remise à Tarquin des livres fatidiques de Rome. Dès lors, on voit mal à quel propos Naevius aurait pu

évoquer une Sibylle italienne sinon dans l'histoire d'Enée; la tradition latine ultérieure n'a jamais fait intervenir de Sibylle en d'autres circonstances."

33. *Op. cit.*, 2, 54: "Certissimum igitur est, Cimmeriam Naevii et Pisonis, a Varone memoratam, non aliam esse quam Cumanam Vergilii."

34. *Op. cit.*, 184/188. Cf. also Buchholz, Roscher 4, 801, Peter, *op. cit.*, 142, and note 38.

35. *Die Sibylle im sechsten Buch der Aeneis*, Sokrates, N.F. 1 (1913), 1/16.

36. Strabo, *loc. cit.*: ἐμύθευον δ'οἱ πρὸ ἡμῶν ἐν τῷ Ἀόρνῳ τὰ περὶ τὴν νεκυῖαν τὴν Ὁμηρικήν. καὶ δὴ καὶ νεκυομαντεῖον ἱστοροῦσιν ἐνταῦθα γενέσθαι καὶ Ὀδυσσέα εἰς τοῦτ' ἀφίκεσθαι. Of course this belief is based upon Hom. *Odyss.* XI, 14: ἔνθα δὲ Κιμμερίων ἀνδρῶν δῆμός τε πόλις τε.

37. This supposition finds support in the following words of Maximus Tyrius: Ἐνταῦθα ὁ δεόμενος ἀφικόμενος, εὐξάμενος, ἐντεμὼν σφάγια, χεάμενος χοάς, ἀνεκαλεῖτο ψυχὴν ὅτου δὴ τῶν πατέρων ἢ φίλων.

38. *Op. cit.*, 118. Corssen's view has been contested by W. Hoffmann, *Wandel und Herkunft der sibyllinischen Bücher in Rom* (thesis Leipzig 1933), 35, n. 6. Hoffmann starts from Norden's correct observation (*op. cit.*, 154) that Vergil must have been the first to introduce the Κατάβασις into the legend of Aeneas and hence also the first to make the Sibyl his guide through Hades, so that it is impossible that Piso and Naevius should already have mentioned this function in the case of the Cimmerian Sibyl. From this, however, Hoffmann concludes that both these authors can only have described the latter Sibyl as a prophetess, not as servant of Hecate as well; and from this conclusion again he infers that the Cumaean Sibyl must have been 'wesensgleich' with the Cimmerian (and hence identical, as he does not say explicitly in his argument, but takes for granted in his conclusion). In the first case he forgets that the Cimmerian Sibyl may quite well have led Aeneas to the ψυχομαντεῖον (cf. the parallel scene in *Silius Italicus* XIII, 385 *seqq.*), in the second the prematurity of the conclusion is obvious. Perret (*op. cit.*, 102/103) writes: "il est assez vraisemblable que Naevius, précurseur de la combinaison que nous trouvons réalisée dans *l'Enéide*, aura mêlé à des réminiscences 'cimmériennes' de la *Nekyia* homérique, les légendes de la Sibylle propres à Cumes"; from this he concludes: "La Sibylle qui intervient dans ses (i.e., Naevius') vers est donc selon nous la Sibylle de Cumes," and assumes that Varro distinguished the Cumaean from the Cimmerian Sibyl for reasons of chronology. But if this Cimmerian Sibyl was indeed only a 'poetic invention' of Naevius, it does not seem right to say that "she was the Sibyl of Cumae."

39. In his article *La Sibylle de Cumes et Virgile* (Symbol. Osl. 24 (1945), 88/120) S. Eitrem writes (p. 109): "Les rapports de la Sibylle Cuméenne avec les Enfers et le ψυχομαντεῖον, de longue date localisé au lac d'Averne, ont parus à Properce si naturels et si bien établis dans la littérature qu'il écrit, IV, 1, 49: *Avernalis tremulae cortina Sibyllae.*" I can agree with this view, if the words "bien établis dans la littérature" refer to the *Aeneid*.

40. Vss. 66/67: *d a-non indebita posco/ regna meis fatis-Latio considere Teucros.* Cf. Norden's note *ad loc.* and especially on vss. 103 *seq.* (pp. 153/154). Probably Vergil assumed Aeneas' knowledge to derive from a prophecy given by Cassandra (cf. p. 52) to Anchises (*Aen.* III, 182/185).

---

41. However, a prophecy of the *fata Romae* by the Sibyl would have been one more curious innovation. In Lycophron and Tibullus the prophetesses confine themselves to the *fata Aeneae* (the *foundation* of Rome was considered to form part of these, since Hellanicus and others had asserted that this event took place very soon after the destruction of Troy). The 'Italian' tradition (Naevius, Piso) could not mention such a prophecy, since, as Hoffmann (cf. note 38) has demonstrated, it was not before 217/216 b. Chr. that the Sibylline books were consulted for the purpose of knowing the future, and since it is improbable that this new estimation should have already found its expression in Naevius' *Bellum Punicum*. Hoffmann might have added a confirmation from the *Origo gentis Romanae* (cf. p. 54): (*Aeneam*) *venisse eo* (viz., *ad oppidum Cimbarionis*) *sciscitatum de statu fortunarum suarum*.

42. *Op. cit.*, 149.

43. *Roman Vergil*[2] (London 1945), 109.

The Golden Bough for the Student of Vergil[1]_____

Mary Randall Stark

After one has taught a subject for some time, especially a subject of fixed content like the works of our ancient writers, there is an almost fatal tendency to become stereotyped in attitude towards the subject matter. Either we do not see the breadth of the forest of the work in our efforts to explain the trees of difficulty, or in our zeal for the forest we neglect the trees and ultimately find that growth stops for lack of roots. It behooves us, then, as teachers (and all the more as students) of the great master whose life and work we are recalling today to pause occasionally, take account of stock, and see whether we ourselves are approaching our subject in the attitude of Aeneas of old, *rerum cognoscere causas*.

Whether the student comes to "the stateliest measure ever moulded by the lips of man" for the first time or after years of painstaking classroom work, he finds certain difficulties confronting him in the unusual constructions and artificial structure demanded by the hexameter verse. Even the mature student of Latin feels the sharp difference between the sonorous periods of Cicero and the apparently irresponsible order and lack of agreement in the parts of a Vergilian line. The vocabulary, too, presents trouble. New endings appear, proper nouns increase, and endless allusions are presented that lead the reader astray into all the bypaths of mythology, to say nothing of the broad highways of history and geography.

To meet these difficulties, two courses are open to him. He can equip himself with numerous texts, all more or less carefully edited, and proceed to swallow and digest the notes; or he can get his major interpretation from the Latin itself and the various sources it suggests. Both of these methods lead to the same fountainhead of authority, viz. to a knowledge of Greek. The thoughtful student of Vergil, the one who seeks to read between the lines and is not content to take the vocabulary rendering of the words and call it a translation, can no more avoid the issue of Vergil's debt to Greek than the student of English Literature can shut his eyes to the part played by Latin in his mother tongue. As one of our English commentators says of Vergil, "The cultured circle for whom he wrote would probably have turned aside with contempt for a poem which relied wholly on native vigor and did not conform, at any rate outwardly, to one of the accepted standards of literary excellence."[2]

The touchstone, then, the Golden Bough, that opens to the appreciative reader the wealth of imagery and the delicate shades of meaning, marking the poet as a painter of pictures in words instead of a raconteur or powerful advocate, is a practical, working knowledge of Greek.

We delight in the *Eclogues*, which follow the *Idyls* of Theocritus so closely that one can easily imagine the pleasure that Vergil took in reproducing the older thought in a modern setting. We enjoy the *Works and Days* of Hesiod through the Italian atmosphere of the *Georgics*. We admire the skill with which the first six books of the *Aeneid* reproduce for us the wanderings of the "much-enduring" Odysseus, and the last six the martial tone of the *Iliad*. We check by means of translations the parallel accounts of the visit to Orcus (in the sixth book of the *Aeneid* and the eleventh of the *Odyssey*), the funeral games at the tomb of Anchises (*Aeneid* V) and those at the burial of Patroclus (*Iliad* XXIII), the making of the armor for Aeneas (*Aeneid* VIII) and for Achilles (*Iliad* XVIII), the final single combat of Aeneas and Turnus (*Aeneid* XII) and that of Achilles and Hector (*Iliad* XXII), etc. Some of us may even wish to trace such obscure allusions as the *dea—dignata cubili est* of the fourth *Eclogue* (*Odyssey* XI, 601). Allowing for the necessary loss in vividness and spirit which is always the price of translation, such studies are fascinating and indispensable to the student who would get a genuine understanding of Vergil's work and give him a fair rating among the great poets of the world. It is not our wish to accuse Vergil of "want of originality." Voltaire's terse retort to the charge that Homer wrote Vergil, "If such is the case, 'tis unquestionably his grandest work," needs no vindication. The Forum stirs the heart and the imagination no less because the Acropolis is behind it.

But it is not enough to recognize Vergil's debt to his Greek precursors as sources for his material. Entirely apart from matters of plot and character portrayal, in the very form of his verse Vergil is often dependent on the Greek. Time would fail even to list the forms or turns of expression that are decidedly not Latin but which are mere commonplaces in Greek verse. The following illustrations are drawn from the *Aeneid* as being more familiar to the average student of Vergil and as presenting the comparison with Homer, whose work perhaps lingers more in our minds than that of Theocritus or Hesiod.

Of necessity many of the proper nouns have the Greek form, and until the reader knows his Greek declensions he will be a slave to vocabulary markings. His study, too, must not stop with names but must include many common nouns with their more musical vowel endings. He must understand from the first introduction of the hero's name the principle of pronunciation underlying all Greek words, so different from that of the Latin.

In sentence structure the older form is often followed, and parataxis becomes a matter of course; but it is in the syntax of the sentence that the Homeric influence is most apparent. The dative of reference (so common in Homer) and the dative used with its original force as in *Aeneid* II, 85:

> Demisere neci, nunc cassum lumine lugent,

are pitfalls for the unwary to one unfamiliar with the older tongue. The accusative often vaguely referred to as the "Greek accusative" reflects two Homeric constructions, one the part affected as in VII, 60:

> Sacra comam multosque metu servata per annos,

and the other the object of a middle verb as in I, 320:

Nuda genu nodoque sinus collecta fluentis.

Tenses frequently borrow the Homeric force, especially perfect passives used without the time element like the Homeric aorist, e.g.

Discite iustitiam moniti et non temnere divos,
[VI, 620]

and the future to express purpose as in II, 46f

Aut haec in nostros fabricata est machina muros
inspeetura domos venturaque desuper urbi.

Infinitives occur frequently in the epexegetic, or explanatory, use of Homer with nouns as in II, 10:

Sed si tantus amor casus cognoscere nostros,

or with adjectives as in the description of Camilla in VII, 807:

Dura pati, cursuque pedum praevertere ventos,

or with verbs in the familiar passage, *Dederatque comam diffundere ventis* (I, 319). The student gains little in his understanding of this usage from the comment of grammars that the infinitive is used loosely in poetry, often to express purpose; but he finds it a construction of beautiful simplicity when comparing it with Homer's

Αὐτὰρ ὁ αὖτε Θυέστ᾽ ᾽Αλαμέμνονι λεῖπε φορῆναι
[*Il.* II, 107]

"Then he in turn, Thyestes, left it to Agamemnon to bear." The omission of the subject of the infinitive, as when Palinurus *negat discernere caelo* (III, 201), seems only natural to the Greek student.

The movement of the verse offers many parallels. The frequent di-aeresis in the first foot, so often imitating the ὣς φάτο, is very convenient to set out a thought for special attention and gives a touch of life to what might otherwise be conventional artificiality:

> Dixerat, et pariter gressi per opaca viarum.
> [VI, 633]

The occasional monosyllable at the end of the line, which Homer uses to throw his emphasis on some important word as in *Iliad* I, 508:

> ἀλλὰ σύ πέρ μιν τῖσον, Ὀλύμπιε μητίετα Ζεῦ,

is equally effective in such lines as III, 375:

> Auspiciis manifesta fides, sic fata deum rex.

The convenient lengthening of a short ultima before a pause appears in the striking line:

> Sancta ad vos anima atque istius inscia culpae,
> [XII, 648]

and the shortening of a long final vowel by semihiatus is occasionally adopted, notably in the line

> Nomen et arma locum servant; te, amice, nequivi.
> [VI, 507]

The common use of couplets as in

> Involvens umbra magna terramque polumque
> [II, 251]

---

reechoes such lines as *Iliad* III, 298:

Ζεῦ κύδιστε μέγιστε καὶ ἀθάνατοι θεοὶ ἄλλοι,

while the occasional rhyme as in

Arma rogo, genetrix nato, te filia Nerei
[VIII, 383]

reminds us of such passages as

Ἀθανάτων ἀέκητι θεῶν ἐριδαινέμεν οἶος.
[*Od.* I, 79]

This may have been accidental on Homer's part, as Professor Seymour thinks,[3] but it doubtless lingered in Vergil's mind and reappeared in his verse.

A bare mention of one or two figures of speech which are brought over most strikingly is all that time allows: such periphrases as *rotarum lapsus* (II, 235f) recalling the Πριάμοιο βίην (*Il.* III, 105); and the *odora canum vis* (IV, 132), the μένος ἡμιόνοιιν (*Od.* VII, 2); and the adding of a descriptive adjective at the end of a sentence to make the subject stand out more vividly, which is an exact counterpart of Homer:

Litoreis ingens inventa sub ilicibus sus . . .
alba solo recubans
[III, 390 and 392]

Ἄγριον ἐν στήθεσσι θέτο μεγαλήτορα θυμὸν
σχέτλιος
[*Il.* IX, 629f]

Tmesis, or (better) the use of prepositions as adverbs, occurs commonly, especially with adverbs of place, and seems to follow Homer's ἔπι, κάτα, etc., while the use of *ceu* after its noun in *inde, lupi ceu* (II, 355) is a direct copying of οἵ σε θεὸν ὥς (*Il.* IX, 302).

The stereotyped expressions that Vergil either adopted bodily or adapted to his Roman point of view make a story by themselves and offer endless opportunities for comparison and study. The *magnanimus Aeneas* and the μεγάθυμος son of Tydeus, the *equum donnitor Lausus* and the Ἕκτορος ἱπποδάμοιο, the *lacrimabile bellum* and the θυμαλγὴς πόλεμος, the μώνυχες ἵπποι and the *cornipedes equi* are too similar to be accidental.

Finally, only the briefest mention can be made of the allusions, so many of which lend the real meaning to the lines. If the reader is familiar with the alpha privative, he sees at a glance the aptness of Vergil's explanation of the name of Avernus. If he has the most elementary Greek vocabulary, the Harpies become allegorical figures and not merely birds with queer names. Hesperia itself takes on a different nature as the name brings a picture of the coming of evening. *Pater Anchises* is no longer a shadowy figure when one reads

> Then had Aeneas, king of men, been slain—
> Had not Zeus' daughter, Aphrodite, marked
> Swiftly his plight. Her son was he and born
> By her unto Anchises, pasturing his herds.
> [*Il.* V, 311-13; Lewis' translation]

Neptune appears as the well-known "earth-shaker" in the words

> Muros magnoque emota tridenti
> fundamenta quatit;
> [II, 610f]

and the part of the gods in the conflict as portrayed in the following:

Not the loathed charms of Sparta's dame,
Nor Paris, victim of your blame—
No, 'tis the gods, the gods destroy
This mighty realm, and pull down Troy.

[II, 601-03; Conington]

takes on added meaning to the one who is familiar with Homer's account of the Olympian Council.

These, then, are some of the aids that a knowledge of Greek brings to a student of Vergil. In the words of Mr. Conway in his delightful *Vergilian Age* the Golden Bough "kept him [Aeneas] living in a region where all else was dead."[4] For all of us who, like Aeneas, are called to preserve and hand on the treasures of the ancients this Golden Bough is waiting to be plucked.

Yet none may reach the shades without
The passport of that golden sprout.

[VI, 140f; Conington]

We need no Sibyl to guide us to the magical tree, if we will but remember her words:

Ergo alte vestiga oculis, et rite repertum
carpe manu, namque ipse volens facilisque sequetur
si te fata vocant.

[VI, 145-47]

Therefore go seek it with uplifted eyes!
And when by will of Heaven thou findest it,
Reach forth and pluck: for at a touch it yields,
A free and willing gift, if Fate ordain.

[Williams]

Shall we not then pluck the Golden Bough and pass it on to the earnest seeker after knowledge that he may enter the Elysian Fields of true literary appreciation and find the narrow way and the strait gate even though few go in thereat?

Notes

1. Read before the twenty-fifth annual meeting of the Classical Association of New England at Yale University on April 5, 1930.

2. Cf. T. E. Page, *P. Vergili Maronis Bucolica et Georgica*, London, Macmillan and Co. (1926), p. x.

3. Cf. Thomas D. Seymour, *Introduction to the Language and Verse of Homer*, Boston, Ginn and Co. (1886), 15.

4. Cf. R. S. Conway, *The Vergilian Age*, Cambridge, Harvard University Press (1928), 46.

Daedalus, Virgil, and the End of Art_____

Michael C. J. Putnam

My text is Virgil's version of the story of Daedalus, from the open-ing of *Aeneid* 6.[1] Aeneas confronts this tale on reaching Cumae in search of the Sibyl. It is told in a series of tableaux on the doors of a temple dedicated to Apollo by the artisan-sculptor himself after his safe arrival in Italy. This is the only occasion in ancient literature where an artist is described as constructing his literal, which in this case is also to say his spiritual, or psychic, biography. As such I take it as a metaphor for the progress of any artist, for his imaginative diary, as it were. My thesis will be that in certain essential ways the tale of Daedalus, crafted by himself, sets up a typology that is mirrored in the ethical artistry practised by Aeneas from standards set him by his fa-ther toward the end of the same book. After parading before his son a host of future Roman heroes, most of them distinguished for their mili-tary prowess, Anchises summarizes what he foresees as Rome's spe-cial genius. It will not lie in any unique brilliance as sculptors in bronze or stone, or as orators or astronomers, but in their accomplishment as governing warriors, in their moral usage of political power:

> "tu regere imperio populos, Romane, memento
> (hae tibi erunt artes), pacique imponere morem,
> parcere subiectis et debellare superbos."[2]

This is the Roman "artistry" set up for Aeneas to model himself against in the epic's second half.

But I would go still further in drawing analogies from the *vita* of Daedalus and suggest that it reveals something, first, of the narrator's spirit as he outlines Aeneas' progress, and then also of the intelligence of the poet Virgil working within the demands of a strict generic tradition. Aeneas who has himself, like Daedalus, just completed an extraordi-nary journey, is not allowed by the Sibyl to meditate on even the most simplistic parallels between himself and the Cretan inventor. She brusquely whisks her charge away from what she styles *spectacula*, sights presumably purveying only aesthetic delight. But Virgil's reader, with his privileged, unheroic leisure for contemplation, is under the obligation to respond not only—as Aeneas might have—to the sculptured encapsulation of an artist's life but to what Aeneas does not know, to the emotions of the artist in the crafting and of the narrator in the telling. Here is the story as told by Virgil at *Aeneid* 6.14-37:

> Daedalus, ut fama est, fugiens Minoia regna
> praepetibus pennis ausus se credere caelo   15
> insuetum per iter gelidas enauit ad Arctos,
> Chalcidicaque leuis tandem super astitit arce.
> redditus his primum terris tibi, Phoebe, sacrauit
> remigium alarum posuitque immania templa.
> in foribus letum Androgeo; tum pendere poenas   20
> Cecropidae iussi (miserum!) septena quotannis
> corpora natorum; stat ductis sortibus urna.
> contra elata mari respondet Cnosia tellus:
> hic crudelis amor tauri suppostaque furto
> Pasiphae mixtumque genus prolesque biformis   25
> Minotaurus inest, Veneris monimenta nefandae,
> hic labor ille domus et inextricabilis error;
> magnum reginae sed enim miseratus amorem
> Daedalus ipse dolos tecti ambagesque resoluit,
> caeca regens filo uestigia. to quoque magnam   30
> partem opere in tanto, sineret dolor, Icare, haberes.
> bis conatus erat casus effingere in auro,
> bis patriae cecidere manus. quin protinus omnia
> perlegerent oculis, ni iam praemissus Achates
> adforet atque una Phoebi Triuiaeque sacerdos,   35
> Deiphobe Glauci, fatur quae talia regi:
> "non hoc ista sibi tempus spectacula poscit; . . ."

The story divides itself into five parts: introduction (Daedalus' arrival in Italy), first segment of sculpture devoted to events at Athens, counterbalancing Cretan exploits, the story of Ariadne and the address to Icarus. There is a climactic heightening of emotion on the part of both artist and the narrator of his tale as the story progresses, leading in the final episode to the artist's inability to create. Let us watch this happening by examining each section in more detail.

At the start, through the phrase *ut fama est*, the narrator seems hyperconscious of putting things before us. By recreating someone else's report and not, it would seem, inventing his own version of the Daedalus story, he distances us in time while apparently disclaiming any direct involvement on his part in the telling.[3] Yet even in this introduction the narrator betrays a certain empathy with his version of Daedalus which suggests a deep understanding of his subject's imaginative ways. Daedalus, as the Cretan vignette makes clear, is a dealer in duplicity, an inventor of hybrid objects that cater to the furtive in their recipients and in their turn create further hybrids—a fake beast enclosing a true human (Pasiphae inside the replica of a cow) that begets a man-animal, the Minotaur. The narrator anticipates this proclivity even now in his own poetic inventiveness. He replaces visual duplicity with verbal contrivance, exchanging the craftsman's dualistic artifact with the poet's ambiguous metaphor by seeing Daedalus, the human aviator, as swimmer through the heavens. The terrestrial creature, though airborne, is made poetically to deal (like Aeneas for much of the preceding story of his epic) with a watery element, and dedicate on return to earth the oarage of his wings.[4]

The narrator is a discerning critic of Daedalus' adventures in two other ways. One is a simple matter of rhetoric. By apostrophizing Apollo he, as it were, mimics Daedalus, claiming himself to share the emotion Daedalus felt on safe return to earth and voiced in gesture of thanks to Phoebus Apollo. But address to the god as Phoebus proves the narrator privy to the myth of Daedalus on a deeper level. Daedalus ends his adventuring on a spot sacred to Apollo, where Aeneas will hear prophecy of his, and Rome's, future through the god's mouthpiece, Deiphobe, the Sibyl. But Apollo the sun god played an important role in Daedalus' recent life. By steering a course toward the chill Bears, Daedalus saved himself from the fate of Icarus, whose wings melted as he drew too near the sun's heat. The artisan of hybrids, who turns himself and his offspring into men-birds, loses his son in the process of artistic experimentation.

But there is also a hint, in the verb *enavit* and the very phrase *gelidas Arctos*, of a certain insouciance on the part of Daedalus. By swimming free of danger toward northern cold he followed the proper procedures for survival, but his child Icarus either was not taught, or at least was not able to practise, them.[5] To put it another way, both Daedalus within this initial segment of the narrative and the narrator expounding his tale, seem in different senses careless—and leave the reader thus far unaware—that more than one person was involved in this strange itinerary. Because there is no mention of Icarus and no hint of Daedalus' role as father, the reader remains with the impression, which the narrator's metaphors abet, that Daedalus thinks largely of his invention and the clever manipulation of it, not of its human consequences.

The narrator therefore gives us a foretaste of circularity in his rendering of the tale, preparing us for the address to Icarus at the end. But neither at the start nor at the conclusion of the episode is the actual death of Icarus mentioned, a fact which invites the reader to fill in the text, to exercise his own imagination recreating and contemplating the most poignant incident in Daedalus' biography. In his role as father Daedalus is a double artistic failure, first incapable of completely imitating nature, then unable to mime the disastrous results of this inadequacy.

Though they now forthrightly continue the theme of sons killed or sacrificed, the initial sculptures proper, devoted to events in Athens, are treated as matters of fact, save in one respect. There is no word for the act of crafting and the only object mentioned, the urn, was not of Daedalus' making. The exception is the exclamation *miserum* (alas!

dreadful!). From its placement in the middle of line 21 and therefore at the center of the three lines, it serves as emotional commentary on the whole segment. But to whom the emotion is imputed remains ambiguous. Is it that experienced by the suffering Athenians? Is it Daedalus' response as he contemplates the results of his handiwork (or, in his mind's eye, the events themselves), or Aeneas', examining the sculpture? Is it the reaction of the narrator sharing the same sensations, or of the reader being taught them in his turn? For one verbal moment, even in the most "detached" segment of Daedalus' tale, narrator, characters and audience are united in empathy.[6]

The first Cretan segment is even more nominal, but now the list of characters and emotions concentrates specifically on Daedalus' art. His is an inventiveness which articulates subterfuge and doubleness, that tangibly fosters sexual perversity, and harbors its results, a man-bull, in a labyrinthine dwelling that is both *labor* and *error*.[7] It exemplifies the intensity of craftsmanship that imprisons the misformed product of human-animal passion in a maze symbolizing, like its contents, the troubling results of a "wandering" of the emotions. Pasiphae's double "error" receives its artistic complement from Daedalus' tricky fabrication.[8] Thus far in his tale Daedalus' art is dangerous only for its receivers.

The second Cretan scene brings a series of abrupt changes. Though the labyrinth remains an essential part of the plot, we turn from one queen, Pasiphae, to another, her unnamed daughter, Ariadne, and from a cruel love to another labelled simply "mighty." But the viewer-reader is also appropriately disoriented. We know from what follows that the Ariadne episode is part of the tableaux of sculptural reliefs. But Daedalus has suddenly, and Virgil brilliantly, led us from his *curriculum vitae* as guileful artisan to his role as apparently dispassionate reappraiser of the effects of that art. He becomes the undoer of his own trickery, an undoing we can hear in the sound of line 29:

> Daedalus ipse dolos tecti ambagesque resolvit, . . .

Daedalus, who reprojects his artistic self through *se dolos*, the labyrinth's wiliness, now straightens its windings and lightens its darkening ways. But dispassionate is far too mild a word. Through poetry's magic Daedalus actually becomes Ariadne. She is the *regina* and she it was who, through Daedalus' gift of thread, directed the steps of Theseus out from the maze after killing the Minotaur.[9] Yet, according to Virgil-Daedalus, we find him *regens*, taking her emotional and physical role by linguistic sleight of hand. The reason for this empathy, as the artist unwinds his own artistry and forgoes his own self-made heritage of deception, is pity. Pity is the response that transforms the apparently aloof artistic deceiver into the emotional resolver of his own deceits. It is this response in himself that he would now monumentalize.[10]

His own poet-monumentalizer is equally forward. He puts no word of crafting into his own presentation. Nothing intervenes to prevent the reader from the stated actuality of Daedalus' experience.[11] By contrast to the preceding episode, then, this tableau is *vivant*. Frozen representation yields to active experience, as we are made to share directly in the artist's suffering. We are Daedalus but, because he is one with his protagonist, we are Virgil as well, uttering through the power of words what cannot be expressed in sculpture.

Finally, we leave the triply fictive world of poet imagining artist crafting himself in art to look more simply at the artist's inability to create. We find him unable to bring to aesthetic completion the delineation in sculpture of an event which in itself, to the artist as experiencer, remained a subject of sorrow, rousing emotion unsatisfied and therefore incomplete. As an interested third party, Daedalus could be shown to share in Ariadne's feelings, ruling with her out of pity her lover's steps. The death of Icarus is a deeper matter. It is the death of a son from the misuse of his father's artistry and for which the father's artistic but duplicitous heroizing must bear some responsibility. As he did in the case of Ariadne, the narrator draws a lexical connection between artist and subject. But the artist who there rules the queen he depicts (*regina-regens*) now fails in his vocation. Because of Icarus' attempt to emulate his father as man-bird, he suffered a mortal fall, and the contemplation of this mischance (the Latin *casus* plays on both literal and figurative senses) caused his father's hands twice to fall as he attempted to monumentalize it.[12]

Here the empathy of the narrator, which has been building from the opening segment, is most fully expressed. As in the initial apostrophe to Phoebus Apollo, he seems to adopt the voice of Daedalus. There his cry was in thanksgiving. Here his words are uttered in sorrow. But in fact so strong is the narrator's involvement that he replaces Daedalus entirely so as to address Icarus directly in explanation of his father's artistic failure. In so doing, in replacing the sculptor-father, the poet's narrator becomes a Daedalian figure, bringing Icarus and his father's frustrating grief before us in the permanence of words.

We have therefore, in one of Virgil's richest poetic moments, a study in artistic incompletion that is extraordinarily complete as a poetic act. The incompletion, the tale within the tale, is Daedalus' and it results from a gradual heightening of his emotional participation. In the last three episodes of Daedalus' story as Virgil tells it, the only ones where the artisan is directly involved, we watch him first as aloof artificer of duplicity, constructing monsters to create further monsters. His empathy grows, and his characterization as artist disappears, as he shows himself (and is shown) pitying Ariadne and as a result unravelling his own artistic stratagems (which, I take it, is not only to show himself powerful over his own art but also, perhaps, even to admit fallibilities in that art). Finally he becomes the victim of *dolor*, of the spasm of grief for his lost son, and this distress results in his inability to create at all. Death renders this artist artless. Daedalus' final honesty, his deepest response to natural feelings, brings artistic barrenness as well as a final powerlessness. But this very gesture of unfulfillment becomes, through Virgil's narration of it, the perfecting element of a poet's holistic enterprise. One artist's failure through passion is the subject of another's successful finishing of his art.

My thesis is that this treatment by one artist of the spiritual biography of another serves as paradigm of the Virgilian career and of the equally tripartite division of the *Aeneid* as a poetic entity, and that it is particularly enlightening for the reader probing the meaning of the epic's conclusion. It is important for my argument to remember that the *Aeneid* begins and ends with acts sparked by *dolor*. At line 9 of the first book we find Juno, Aeneas' divine arch enemy and emblem of irrationality, *dolens*, aggrieved, as she launches this hero, noteworthy for his *pietas*, into a sea of troubles. Sixteen lines later we are told in greater detail of the *causae irarum saevique dolores*, the sources of her wrath and fierce anguish that now spur her on to violence. In balance, eight lines from the epic's conclusion we learn of the *saevus dolor*, the fierce anguish which Aeneas experienced at the death of Pallas. Recollection of this event, aroused by sight of the belt Pallas had worn, now on the suppliant Turnus, who had killed him earlier in battle, drives Aeneas to a frenzy of rage (he is described as "set aflame by furies and terrible in his wrath"). In this paroxysm he slays his antagonist whose soul flees under the shades as the epic comes to its abrupt end. I have proposed elsewhere, from several angles, that Aeneas' final deed turns him into a Juno figure, in other words that he becomes a personification, not of his much touted *pietas* based on his father's injunction to *clementia* for the beaten down, but of its opposite, Junonian anger.[13] The subsequent pages will further defend this contention.

First, Daedalus and the Virgilian career, and Daedalus and the structure of the *Aeneid*. In two cryptic lines near the start of the second book of his *Georgics* Virgil in his own voice addresses his patron Maecenas:

> . . . non hic te carmine facto
> atque per ambages et longa exorsa tenebo.[14]

This definition of casuistic poetry may apply to work Virgil anticipates for his later career, but more likely it is his way of looking back to his first work, the *Eclogues*. Certainly no other poems in Latin, with their many layers of symbolism and multivalent masquerades, could more justly claim the epithets fictive and ambiguous. The rich later history of pastoral poetry as a vehicle for necessary indirection of statement looks back in honor to its primarily Virgilian source.

As Virgil, Daedalus-like, leads his poetry out of the *ambages* of pastoral and into the greater openness and availability of didactic, his poetic voice moves from playful to serious and he from poet as implicit deceiver to poet as explicit pitier. His opening prayer to Augustus asks Caesar to nod approval to his bold beginnings

> ignarosque viae mecum miseratus agrestis
> ingredere . . .[15]

Pity creates poetry with the Daedalian power of Ariadne's thread, capable, through teaching, of directing those unsure of the path they tread. The immediate result, as the poet and his farmer set out on their interactive labors, is that new spring arrives, snow melts and "the crumbling clod has broken itself up" (*resolvit*) under the power of the west wind.[16] Pity's poetry has also Daedalus' power to resolve nature's seasonal dilemmas and set the farmer firmly on his arduous road.

Last in the Virgilian career comes the poetry of *dolor*. The *Aeneid* seems the impersonal epic of one man's pious journey toward accomplishment, mirroring *in parvo* the future achievements of imperial Rome as it rises to unparalleled greatness under Augustus. But it is also, as we have seen and will further observe, a passion-ridden poem whose final deed of violence stemming from anguish and anger leaves open as many questions as it answers. It leaves dissatisfied the reader's expectations of praise for Aeneas' most memorable action as model for Rome's glorious enterprise to come, and instead completes a cycle based on *dolor*, that is, on an emotion founded in discontent and battening on deprivation. Like Virgil's history of Daedalus it is a brilliantly complete poem ending on premonitions of artistic incompletion.

For the *Aeneid* itself also has the rhythms of a Daedalian undertaking. As one of the most highly ordered of poems, the possibilities for imaginative structuring it offers to the reader are numerous. We gain pleasure, as we approach the epic in linear fashion, from sensing books grouped as pairs or trios, or from savoring a balance between the epic's halves, as they open out in clear echoes of book 1 in book 7. We may also acknowledge Virgil's grand chiasmus, where opening anticipates closure. We then focus centrally on the powerful linkage between books 6 and 7 which begins with address to Caieta, Aeneas' nurse, another in the host of those, especially prominent in the preceding book, who gain real death and dubious immortality for being in Aeneas' entourage.

I would like here to reconsider what has long been observed as the *Aeneid*'s tripartite division.[17] We could distinguish the three movements as follows: books 1-4, which take us topographically and temporally from Troy to Carthage and revolve on Aeneas' meeting with Dido; books 5-8, as we move from Sicily, to Cumae, to Tiber-mouth, which contain Aeneas' two great revelations of the future, from his father in the Underworld and on the shield of Vulcan; books 9-12, which deal primarily with the war for supremacy in Latium and, in particular, with Aeneas' confrontation with Turnus.

After the pattern Virgil has Daedalus establish for himself, the first segment of the *Aeneid* is rich with exemplification of deceit. As recreated for us in Aeneas' words, the wooden horse, Troy's equivalent of Pasiphae's cow, is, save for the shield of Aeneas, the single most memorable artifact in the *Aeneid*, notable for its Daedalian duplicity and duality.[18] (It is at once alive and dead, a wooden object, fashioned as an animal, pregnant with a human brood. As objects both cow and horse are marvelous on the outside, deceptive on the inside. They can, even should, be viewed as Virgil's epic can be read. Past a veneer of artificial charm—in regard to the *Aeneid* the veneer is partially manufactured of our idealizing expectations—lie, in all cases, terrible truths.) The second part of Aeneas' narrative is also riddled with the monstral and the biform, with a plant that drips with human blood, Harpies who are at once birds or maidens or goddesses, Scylla (part human, part fish, part wolf), the man-mountain Etna and the mountain-man Polyphemus.

But it is the story of Aeneas, especially as it merges with Dido's, to which I want to call attention.[19] Venus, divinity of love and mother of Aeneas, arrives on the scene in the disguise of the virgin-goddess Diana. She soon hides her son in a cloud, as he makes his way into Carthage, and his beauty is said to be his mother's artifice (grace added by craftsmen to ivory is the poet's simile, gold embellishing silver or marble) as he bursts from its enclosure. But counterfeiting is once again her province, her "new arts" (*novas artis*) in the narrator's words, as she replaces Ascanius with Cupid in preparation for the temptation of Dido.

The pretendings of Aeneas, as orchestrated by Virgil, are more elaborate. The most patent example is his gift-giving. He offers to Dido Helen's cloak and the scepter of Ilione, which is to say his presence brings her, from Helen, illicit love leading to her city's symbolic razing by fire, from Ilione, suicide. His relation to the sculptures on Juno's temple which he sees in Carthage's midst is more subtle. They depict scenes from Troy's fall which summarize Homer or intervene between the story line of the *Iliad* and Aeneas' own tale. Aeneas and Achates take them as evidence of Dido's sympathy for human suffering. The reader, aware of their connection with Juno and her vengeful proclivities, looks at them in other ways. Their great figure is Achilles. He appears directly in three of their episodes, indirectly in three others, primarily as a killer, of Troilus, Hector, Memnon and Penthesilea. By the end of the epic, Aeneas will become in part an Achilles, pitilessly killing his Latin Hector, Turnus. The equation here is more understated. By continuing on the tale of Troy in his narrative to Dido, Aeneas becomes active as well as passive, participant in events but their passionate recaller as well. His verbal artisanship, in other words, takes up where the sculptures left off yet also becomes part of the seduction of Dido.[20] The destruction of Troy, which he suffers as a character within his narrative, leads inevitably to the destruction of Dido which his very act of narration helps to cause.

The lexical, symbolic or imagistic continuum from the end of book 1, through Aeneas' narrative, to the masterful delineation of Dido's downfall in the fourth book needs only brief documentation. Cupid's fake words (*simulata verba*, 1.710) lead directly to the faking of the wooden horse (*simulant*, 2.17), which in turn anticipates Aeneas' attempts at dissimulation (*dissimulant*, 4.291) which Dido unmasks in her first words addressed to him after his decision to depart:

> "dissimulare etiam sperasti, perfide, tantum
> posse nefas . . . ?"[21]

It is an easy transition from the *doli*, the wiles of Venus and Cupid, in book 1, to the deceits of the Greeks in book 2 as executed by Sinon and the horse, to the deception of Aeneas which Dido uncloaks. The symbolic flames with which Venus plans to gird Dido become the destructive arson of Troy and then the triple fires of book 4—the metaphoric ardor of her love, her literal burning on the pyre which, as we have seen, is visualized as the burning of Carthage, the queen as city demolished by a concatenation of circumstances.

It is not necessary to argue yet again the moral fine-points of a tragic adventure where ignorance and knowledge play intermeshed roles, and human weaknesses make its characters easy prey for divine machinations as well as self-deceptions. I want only to suggest that in detail and in general the constancy of deceit in the story-line of *Aeneid* 1-4 finds its parallel in the exploits of Daedalus as artificer. The particularities and their consequences press the connection between Pasiphae and Dido. Pasiphae's love is *crudelis* and this is the adjective Dido twice applies to her absconding lover. Just as the Cretan queen's erotic adventure is based on a stratagem which is also a hiding (*furto*), so also, in the narrator's words, Dido ponders a furtive love (*furtivum amorem*), and it is against accusations of trickery (*furto*) from her that

Aeneas must defend himself. Finally, the Minotaur, symbol of Pasiphae's "unspeakable passion" (*Veneris monimenta nefandae*) has its more tangible counterpart in Aeneas' trappings and their marriage, "all the reminders of that unspeakable man" (*nefandi/cuncta viri monimenta*) which Dido will set aflame along with herself.

The generalities, on the other hand, center as we have seen on the artificers rather than on their products. They define Aeneas, and the narrator of his tale, as Daedalus figures. Both particular points of contact and more broad equations persist in the second segment of Virgil's scheme. Critics have remarked on the abruptness with which Ariadne is introduced into the narrative at line 28. She is not named and, though she was a princess, she was certainly not, at least not at that moment in her eventful life, a *regina*. This apparent discontinuity, however, is actually a brilliant transition when we pursue our projection of the plot of Daedalus' psychological progress on to the *Aeneid*'s triple divisions. For, if in the life of Daedalus we move from Pasiphae to Ariadne, in the artistic development of the *Aeneid* we stay with Dido, who need not be renamed and who remains the poem's great *regina*.[22] The difference is that, in the second movement of the *Aeneid*, her *crudelis amor* (now become *magnum amorem*) is resolved. When Aeneas sees her in the Underworld, in the company of those "whom harsh love has gnawed through with cruel wasting" (*quos durus amor crudeli ta be peredit*), she scorns him, fleeing into a shady grove:

> . . . coniunx ubi pristinus illi
> respondit curis aequatque Sychaeus amorem.[23]

Differentiation leading to suicide has yielded, in book 6, to reciprocation and balance.

Yet we have been readied for this denouement earlier. At the conclusion of book 4, as we prepare to leave the epic's initial third for its central articulation, we have Virgil's first, enormously moving example of pity for suffering leading to its resolution. The moment is Dido's death:

Tum Iuno omnipotens longum miserata dolorem
difficilisque obitus Irim demisit Olympo
quae luctantem animam nexosque resolveret artus.[24]

At the end pity releases the troubled queen from her enmeshed body, which is to say from the deceits of what Anchises is soon to call the blind prison which confines us within the toils of our destructive emotions.[25] There is another Daedalian resolution, centering on book 6, that belongs more exactly to Aeneas. The literal labyrinth of Daedalus' manufacture (*hic labor ille domus*) becomes now symbolic, but equally present, in the hero's effortful life as he faces the prospect of descending, alive into the world of the dead and returning whence he came. *Hoc opus, hic labor est* "this the task, this the effort," says the Sibyl.[26] As preparation for this undertaking, Aeneas must attend to the *horrendas ambages*, the fearful enigmas of the seeress' utterances which correspond to the palpable but no less devious windings (*ambages*) of the Minotaur's dwelling. The Daedalian "threads" that bring resolutions to Aeneas' quandary are manifold. They consist not only in a growing clarity to the Sibyl's words but in the person of the Sibyl herself who will serve as guide through the Underworld's paths. He is, however, given further assistance by a series of talismans, first, the birds of his mother, then the golden bough—a very Daedalian object, serving now to open out rather than close in, to undeceive instead of dupe—his chief passport, to which the birds direct his traces. Finally we have the words of the poet Musaeus to whom the priestess turns for help in the search for Anchises.

If deceit is the chief impulse behind Daedalus' initial fabrications, pity rules him in their undoing. Though Aeneas does address Dido in his first words to her as the only person to have taken pity on the Trojans' sufferings, it is a virtue noticeably absent from the first four books. Yet here once more it is our changing viewpoint on the figure of Dido that helps us make the transition from segment to segment. At 4.369-70 she speaks to her former lover as if he were already absent:

num fletu ingemuit nostro? num lumina flexit?

num lacrimas victus dedit aut miseratus amantem est?[27]

This, we remember, is exactly what Aeneas does do here in the Underworld, though she refuses to respond to his plea for words:

prosequitur lacrimis longe et miseratur euntem.[28]

Aeneas has now performed the great act of which Dido had earlier found him negligent. He himself has—at last, and too late—also pitied the queen's love (*reginae . . . miseratus amorem*).

He had come to this emotion, for the first time in the epic, in the fifth book, which opens the *Aeneid*'s second of three divisions. There, at the end of the foot-race, Aeneas pities the unfortunate Salius who had slipped during the competition.[29] It is an emotion that he must receive as much as offer during this middle segment of the epic. He pities the unburied who are forced to wait at length before crossing the Styx. Yet he is also himself subject to three notable acts of pity during these books, from Jupiter, who saves his fleet, from the Sibyl and her inspirer, to both of whom he must pray, and from the Tiber in book 8. For this reach of the epic is Aeneas' most extended period of dependence which proves at the same time to initiate him, and the reader of his saga, into the most elaborate revelations of the future. Pity of Sibyl and of river god lead him, one, to his father, the other, to the site of future Rome. Anchises parades before him future Roman heroic greats and gives him his ethical commission. Evander's tour of Pallanteum anticipates the grand city to come, and the shield, which Venus brings to Aeneas at Caere, concludes book 8 with another series of visions into heroic action, the *ennarrabile textum* of Roman history.

In details, then, and from a larger viewpoint, during the second segment of the epic Virgil has his hero put behind him the deceitful, artifice-ridden atmosphere of the initial quartet of books. He replaces it with a portrait of the artisan-hero as pitier. Aeneas undoes his own dissimulations, or those thrust upon him, while the mazey mysteries that lead him to Rome's future are tantalizingly unravelled for him by others who offer him their rich solace in turn.

The last third of the epic can be treated more briefly. Its plot is the war in Latium, but the narrator tells a singularly purposeless tale. The omniscient reader knows from occasional prophecies that Aeneas will become overlord of Latium and marry Lavinia. But the fullness of the narrative dwells on the relentless futility and unceasing loss that war engenders. It furnishes a catalogue of deaths, especially those of the young whose lives have been cut off near their starts. We think immediately of Nisus and Euryalus, of Pallas and Lausus, of Camilla and finally of Turnus. The rampage of slaughter that Aeneas embarks on after Pallas' death, in which he kills with equal indiscrimination suppliant and priest, takes its last victim in his primary antagonist who is wearing Pallas' belt. Yet for all his *violentia* and pride our sympathies lie at the end with Turnus, not with the titular hero, with Turnus beaten down by Jupiter's minion Fury and by the inner furies which set Aeneas at the last ablaze.

One of the framing emotions of this last quartet of books, as it is of the epic as a whole, is *dolor*. We find it in Turnus near the opening of book 9 as he casts a greedy eye on the leaderless Trojans penned within their camp:

> ignescunt irae, duris dolor ossibus ardet.[30]

Or, soon again, in a speech of exhortation to his colleagues:

> "sunt et mea contra
> fata mihi, ferro sceleratam excindere gentem
> coniuge praerepta; nec solos tangit Atrides
> iste dolor, solisque licet capere arma Mycenis . . ."[31]

It is remarkable how much of the same language recurs in the counter-balancing moment of anger with which the epic concludes. Aeneas, in his final words, accuses Turnus of possessing *scelerato sanguine*, criminal blood. The reader could presume that a variation of the reason Turnus gives for his own *dolor*—that Lavinia, his Helen, has been torn from him—is applicable also now to Aeneas, poised to kill because of the *dolor* aroused by the death of Pallas. In any case, though the last appearance of *dolor* doubly rounds out the epic to a splendid rhetorical and psychological moment of closure, it is, in senses that transcend mere personal feelings, an extraordinarily unfulfilling, not to say devastating, emotion. Turnus asks for pity and Aeneas does hesitate, as if he were preparing to respond with sympathy and practise *clementia*.[32] For Aeneas to grant pity through clemency, though it might appear an unheroic act by Homeric standards, would be for Virgil to round out the poem spiritually. He does not—cannot, perhaps—allow himself the luxury.[33]

I would like, in conclusion, to look in more detail at reasons why *dolor* leaves Aeneas-Daedalus-Virgil with his (their, if you prefer) heroic-artistic-poetic fabrication unfinished. First Aeneas-Daedalus. The ethical artistry imposed on Roman might, pursuing its political ends, was summarized, as we have seen, by Anchises to his son near the end of their meeting in the Underworld. The nub of his command, which he addresses to Aeneas as *Romane*, ancestor of and paradigm for his distinguished race, is to remember to spare the suppliant and war down the proud. By the end of the poem proud Turnus has been battled into abject submission, but, for whatever deep-seated reason, Aeneas does not spare him. He does not, finally, recall his father's admonition. Instead, in the narrator's words, he drank in the reminders of his fierce grief (*saevi monimenta doloris*) and, in an access of fury and rage, buries his sword in his opponent's chest. *Dolor* initiates Aeneas' final act. In so doing it gives the lie to Roman pretensions toward clemency, toward an artistic morality that reincorporates an antagonist, abased but living, into the civic community. Aeneas' attack of *dolor* proves the impossibility of realizing in fact Anchises' exhortation. In this case to complete is to idealize, to idealize is to dream untruths.[34]

Secondly we must pursue the analogy of Virgil, the creator of the *Aeneid*, and Daedalus. We are not now concerned with Aeneas' emotions as they undermine Roman political artisanship but with the imagination that shapes such an ending. My thesis is that Virgil deliberately leaves his poem incomplete, vis-à-vis the epic genre as he inherited it, as if the *Aeneid* were to serve as one final, magnificent metaphor—one masterful artistic symbol—for the incompletions in Roman, which is to say human, life. Let me illustrate my point with brief reminders of the plot endings of four other epics of which three (the *Iliad*, the *Odyssey* and the *Argonautica* of Apollonius Rhodius) precede the *Aeneid*, while the other, Statius' *Thebaid*, follows.

First the *Iliad*. The bulk of its last book is taken up with the reconciliation scene between Priam and Achilles, but its last moments are devoted to the aftermath of the burning of Hector's body:

And when they [the people of Troy] were assembled together, first they quenched with flaming wine all the pyre, so far as the fire's might had come upon it, and thereafter his brethren and his comrades gathered the white bones, mourning, and big tears flowed over down their cheeks. The bones they took and placed in a golden urn, covering them over with soft purple robes, and quickly laid the urn in a hollow grave, and covered it over with great close-set stones. Then with speed heaped they the mound, and round about were watchers set on every side, lest the well-greaved Achaeans should set upon them before the time. And when they had piled the barrow they went back, and gathering together duly feasted a glorious feast in the palace of Priam, the king fostered of Zeus. On this wise held they funeral for horse-taming Hector.

The completion of a life demarcates the completion of a poem. The careful rituals of burial and feast, that bring the funeral of Hector to conclusion with communal ceremony, are complemented by the perfection of the epic that describes them, by poetry's own exacting ritual.

The twenty-fourth book of the *Odyssey* finds its hero taking revenge with bloody slaughter on the suitors of Penelope. But the ending turns this thirst for vengeance around. Zeus says to Athene in heaven:

> "Now that goodly Odysseus has taken vengeance on the wooers, let them swear a solemn oath, and let him be king all his days, and let us on our part bring about a forgetting of the slaying of their sons and brothers; and let them love one another as before, and let wealth and peace abound."

Thus, as Odysseus is preparing to kill the suitors' relatives bent, in their turn, on revenge, Athene speaks to him, bringing the epic to end:

> "Son of Laertes, sprung from Zeus, Odysseus of many devices, stay your hand, and make the strife of equal war to cease, lest haply the son of Cronos be wroth with you, even Zeus, whose voice is borne afar."
> So spoke Athena, and he obeyed, and was glad at heart. Then for all time to come a solemn covenant betwixt the twain was made by Pallas Athene, daughter of Zeus, who bears the aegis, in the likeness of Mentor both in form and in voice.

Forgiveness, reconciliation, a commitment to peace and a statement by the narrator of an eternal pact to assure it—these are the gestures with which the *Odyssey* ends. Reintegration of society betokens poetic wholeness, and vice versa. Content and imagination are one.[35]

The ending of the *Argonautica* is simpler still as the singer speaks in his own voice:

> For now I have come to the glorious end of your toils; for no adventure befell you as you came home from Aegina, and no tempest of wind opposed you; but quietly did you skirt the Cecropian land and Aulis inside of Euboea and the Opuntian cities of the Locrians, and gladly did you step forth upon the beach of Pagasae.

Just as the argonauts bring their journey to completion by returning whence they started, so the singer, proclaiming direct control over the matter of his verse, brings his own poetic voyage to a parallel stop.

Unfortunately we lack the final lines of any pre-Virgilian Latin epics. We must therefore jump in our survey to silver Latin and in particular to Statius who, at the end of his only completed epic, the *Thebaid*, directly acknowledges his indebtedness to Virgil. He finishes with an address to his own book:

> vive, precor; nec tu divinam Aeneida tempta,
> sed longe sequere et vestigia semper adora.
> mox, tibi si quis adhuc praetendit nubila livor,
> occidet, et meriti post me referentur honores.

The ending of the narrative proper, which precedes the speaker's *sphragis*, is equally important for our purposes. After the hideous carnage of civil strife and Theseus' killing of Creon (the equivalent moment to the end of the *Aeneid*), who had refused to allow the dead to be buried, the warring factions forge a treaty as the women rejoice in the Athenian leader's calming presence. The epic's plot ends with due display of mourning for the fallen and with some of Statius' most beautiful (and most Virgilian) lines. I could not tell, says the speaker, even if I had a hundred voices, of all the cries of grief:

> Arcada quo planctu genetrix Erymanthia clamet,
> Arcada, consumpto servantem sanguine vultus,
> Arcada, quem geminae pariter flevere cohortes.
> vix novus ista furor veniensque implesset Apollo,
> et mea iam longo meruit ratis aequore portum.[36]

Though he gives them new turns, especially in his elaboration of the autobiographical "seal," Statius essentially clings to the closure patterns of his generic inheritance. In fact he combines elements from the endings of all three Greek epics—ceremonies of lamentation from the *Iliad*, the *Odyssey*'s call for forgiveness and reconciliation, and Apollonius Rhodius' self-projection as traveller, appropriately completing at once his poetic journey and the heroic voyage it had sung.

It is important to notice not so much how influential Greek epic remains upon Statius' conclusion but how clearly the *Aeneid*'s finale is absent as an imaginative force on this most Virgilian of poets while he wrote his *envoi*. Hence to my point. In terms of its Greek epic past and its Roman poetic progeny, Virgil's *Aeneid* is a strikingly incomplete poem.[37] Its ending is equivalent to Achilles' killing of Hector, to the death of the suitors in the *Odyssey* or of Creon in the *Thebaid*. No Iliadic mourning breaks the spell of Aeneas' inexorable blood-lust.[38] Reconciliations akin to the *Odyssey*'s are mouthed in heaven but form no part in human action, as victor kills suppliant. Turning to the end of the *Argonautica*, which has its spiritual kinship to the *Odyssey*'s conclusion, we do not find in the *Aeneid* any equivalent satisfactions. No wife is given Aeneas in a marriage ceremony that might give the epic's quasi-tragic ending a comic twist. Nor is there a speaking "I," proud of his accomplishment, who could at least abstract us at the end from the lived experience of the violence his story tells into the imagination that fostered it.

We will never know what Daedalian *dolor* within Virgil caused him to leave his epic so generically incomplete. (The ancient lives tell us that at his death Virgil had failed only to apply his *ultima manus*, his finishing touch, to the poem, not that it remained deficient in any substantial way.) But I have a suggestion. Critics have long since, and quite correctly, sensed a parallel between Icarus and the many people who die as they follow in the wake of Aeneas. I listed earlier the most prominent losses in the last quartet of books and it is well to remember that books 2 through 5 all end with deaths, of Creusa, Anchises, Dido, and Palinurus. The clearest parallel structurally, however, is with the death of Marcellus, the son of Augustus' sister and his adopted heir, whose funeral is described at the end of the sixth book.[39] It is as if the poet were saying that the Roman mission cannot go forward without loss of life, that the reality of death ever looms as a counterbalance to progress.

What critics have not stressed is the concomitant parallel between Aeneas and Daedalus. To do so is to turn from deaths suffered as the price of empire to placing responsibility for those deaths.[40] The artisan loses his son from his overreaching. Aeneas loses Pallas but he also kills Turnus. These deaths receive the final emphasis which is on causes as much as on results, on the perpetrator as much as on its victims.

The conclusion of the *Aeneid*, then, doubly uncloaks the deceptiveness of art. Aeneas cannot fulfill his father's idealizing, and therefore deceptive, vision of Rome, and Virgil, the artisan of his tale, cannot show him as so doing. Aeneas' final killing of Turnus differs from Daedalus' loss of Icarus essentially for being active instead of passive. Each demonstrates nature's final, Pyrrhic, triumph over art.

We may be meant to think that, as he crafted the *Aeneid*, in the process of writing, of practising his own art, Virgil followed his own voyage of self-discovery and came with full assurance to see *dolor*, the immediacy of suffering, frustration, resentment, as an overriding presence in human life and therefore in his creative life. His plotline, which mimes and reproduces the artist's growing inwardness, suggests a paradox: when, in the course of his experience an artist forgoes his natural role as trickster, and relieves his art of duplicity, in favor of truth of expression, his artifact, as his life's work, is an apparent failure. To idealize is to envision wholeness in self and society, to claim consistency in their patternings. It is to twist the tragic divisiveness of life's irrationality into comic returns, reconciliations, renewals. But Virgil, by ending his epic with two consequential acts of resentment, the one resulting in violence, the other from having to accept that violence, does not finally idealize. His final artifice is the sham of forgoing art.

In sum, Virgil does, idiosyncratically, complete the *Aeneid* just as he completes with growing emotion the tale of Daedalus' inability to create. This carefully, brilliantly flawed wholeness is perhaps his passionate way of saying that art's feigned orderings do not, cannot, claim to control the uncontrollable. For a poet of consummate honesty the truths of nature, Virgil would seem to say, are ever triumphant over the soothing trickery of art, however seductively its practitioners pattern their wares. For the art that supplants deceit with honesty, that composes life's imperfections, that unthreads its own labyrinthine text, not piety, or even pity, is possible, only the final, perfecting deficiencies of anger and sorrow.[41]

From *American Journal of Philology* 108:2 (Summer 1987): 173-198. Copyright © 1987 by The Johns Hopkins University Press. Reprinted with permission of The Johns Hopkins University Press.

Notes

1. The most recent discussions of the Daedalus episode are by V. Pöschl ("Die Tempeltüren des Dädalus in der *Aeneis* [6.14-33]," *WJA* n.f. 1 [1975] 119-33), who sees it as exemplifying the failure of art when the artist confronts the truth of his suffering; C. Weber ("Gallus' Grynium and Virgil's Cumae," *ARCM* 1 [1978] 45-76) for whom the sequence serves as model for a miniature epyllion; and W. Fitzgerald ("Aeneas, Daedalus and the Labyrinth," *Arethusa* 17 [1984] 51-65). Fitzgerald's important essay views the two major segments of the tale as illustrating the change from "a finished work of art" to "the narrative of Daedalus, unfrozen and released into history" (54). In his earlier discussion (*Die Dichtkunst Virgils* [Innsbruck 1950] 244-46 = *The Art of Vergil*, trans. G. Seligson [Ann Arbor 1962] 149-50), Pöschl draws analogies between Aeneas and Daedalus. Both are exiles, both offer pity at crucial moments (Daedalus for Ariadne, Aeneas for Dido), both exemplify *pietas* (Daedalus' love for Icarus is parallel, according to Pöschl, to Aeneas' yearning for Anchises with whom he is soon to be reunited). See also Weber, op. cit., 40, n. 33.

Such analogies are further developed by C. P. Segal in his sympathetic analysis of these lines ("*Aeternum per saecula nomen*, the golden bough and the tragedy of history: Part I," *Arion* 4 [1965] 617-57, especially 642-45). For Segal Daedalus "foreshadows the sufferings of the individual in the *mythical*, not the historical world, sufferings which lead to no lasting fruition in history, hence no transcendence of death."

The legend of Daedalus has been treated in depth by F. Frontisi-Ducroux (*Dédale: mythologie de l'artisan en grèce ancienne* [Paris 1975]) and by J. K. Koerner (*Die Suche nach dem Labyrinth* [Frankfurt 1983]), who draws analogies between Daedalus and the modern mind dealing with its labyrinthine past while at the same time drawn toward self-sufficient flights into the a-historical and the novel. Cf. also the remarks on Daedalus as typifying "the artist as magician" by E. Kris and O. Kurz in *Legend, Myth, and Magic in the Image of the Artist* [New Haven 1979] 66-71.

2. 6.851-53.

3. The authoritative discussion of the phrase *ut fama est* is by Norden (*P. Vergilius Maro: Aeneis Buch VI* [repr. Stuttgart 1957] *ad loc.*). The variations on tradition which it implies are numerous. Foremost is the connection of Daedalus with Italy. Writers of the generation before Virgil return Daedalus to earth either in Sicily (Dio. Sic. 4.78) or Sardinia (Sall. *Hist.* fr. 2.7 [Maurenbrecher] from, among others, Servius on 1.14). By having him aim directly for Cumae, Virgil emphasizes the parallel with Aeneas which will gradually grow clearer as the ecphrasis evolves.

By feigning to repeat tradition unemotionally and then significantly varying it, the narrator claims control over the history of his subject. The poet does the same generically. Virgil's model for Aeneas' arrival at Cumae as prelude to his visit to the underworld is the opening of book 11 of the *Odyssey* where Odysseus reaches the land of the Cimmerians and immediately conjures up the spirits of the dead. No ecphrasis intervenes (re. G. Knauer, *Die Aeneis und Homer* [*Hypomnemata* 9: Göttingen 1979] 130, n. 1). Therefore, even where Daedalus seems as yet indifferent to, or even unaware of, his loss, the narrator-poet is very involved with the tale so as to mould Daedalus, to make the sculptor his own artifact, to impress his stamp of originality on his artisan-hero. If Daedalus deepens his emotional involvement in his subjects over time, as he sets about the crafting of his psychic biography, the narrator has a deep imaginative commitment from the start.

4. According to R. G. Austin (ed., *P. Vergili Maronis: Aeneidos Liber Sextus* [Oxford 1977] on 18, following Norden on 18f.) the dedication to Apollo "marks his gratitude for a safe landing and also his retirement from air-travel, in the manner of many Greek dedicatory epigrams. . . ." But these strange oar-wings are also an offering for passing safely through the god's province in which men do not ordinarily trespass. (Virgil's only other use of the phrase *remigium/remigio alarum* is to describe the means of Mercury's descent from heaven at *Aen.* 1.301. The repetition here suggests a momentary equivalence between god and mortal who ascribes to the supernatural.) The overreacher might be expected to pay a penalty for challenging Apollo in his territory. The passive *redditus* implies that throughout this stage of his adventures Daedalus has in fact been the god's subject. Virgil may portray him as flying *praepetibus pinnis*, but Horace, in an ode of which Servius twice reminds us (on 15 and 18), sees the means of his journey as *pinnis non homini datis* (*c.* 1.3.35). Perhaps the implication is that Phoebus Apollo does claim recompense, in the form of Icarus, for earth-bound man's sally into the skies, for momentary human arrogation of divinity. As god-man, the ultimate in spiritual hybridization, the Orphic artist, fulfilling for an instant his imagination's divine claims, suffers a profound human loss.

By forcing us even here to meditate on the negative demands of progress, Virgil reminds us that, in the unfolding epic story, it has not been long since Neptune exacted *unum caput* (5.815), one life for the safe completion of Aeneas' journey to Italy through the god's watery element.

5. OLD (*s.v.* 1b) would translate *enavit* here as "to fly forth," but it is more enrich-

ing within the context to take the meaning as a metaphorical example of the dictionary's first definition: "to swim out or forth; (esp.) to escape by swimming; swim to safety." But, since Daedalus escaped the danger and the (pointedly) unnamed Icarus did not, the reader should rightly sense ambiguities in *praepetibus* and *levis*.

The first is an augural word, discussed in detail in relation to these lines by Aulus Gellius (*N.A.* 7.6). It appears four times in Ennius (Gellius mentions two instances) and lends a tone of majesty to the description of the artisan's epic accomplishment. As a term in augury it means "propitious," the opposite (according to Gellius' source, Figulus' *Augurii Privati*) of *infera* which he defines as a low-flying, less auspicious appearance. Its etymology is from *prae-peto*, "forward-seeking." As Gellius (followed closely by Servius on 6.15) expounds the meaning, the word becomes closely complementary to *enavit:*

> idcirco Daedali pennas "praepetes" dixit, quoniam ex locis in quibus periculum metuebat in loca tutiora pervenerat.

The reader, wondering why the narrator does not have Daedalus here include Icarus in his daring, sees *praepes* as "well-omened" (at least for Daedalus!), as "flying directly ahead" (without a concern for the tragic events occurring behind?), and as "lofty" (unlike Icarus who, after rising too high, fell into the sea?). *Levis*, then, while primarily defining Daedalus' nimbleness, hints at a certain fickleness as well. Physical dexterity (or artistic talent, for that matter) does not necessarily ally itself with stability of mind.

6. Even here Virgil may possibly be alluding to Aeneas' tale. The seven bodies (*septena corpora*) of sons sent to Crete each year by the Athenians are reviewed shortly later in the *septem iuvencos* (38), the seven bullocks and the same number of heifers which Aeneas must now present to Apollo and Trivia. As the two myths follow their parallel progress, human offering is replaced by animal but in each case sacrifice is essential.

7. The standard article on Daedalus' labyrinth and its resonances for Virgil is by P. J. Enk, "De Labyrinthi Imagine in Foribus Templi Cumani Inscripta," *Mnemosyne*, ser. 4.11 (1958) 322-30.

8. The language is close to *Aen.* 7.282-83 where the horses given by Latinus to Aeneas are described as coming

> illorum de gente patris quos daedala Circe
> supposita de macre nothos furata creavit.

Aen. 6.24 and 7.283 document Virgil's only uses of the perfect participle of *suppono* in a sexual sense, and *furata* (7.283) echoes *furto* (6.24). The connection is further secured by Circe's epithet *daedala*. Circe is prone to the same erotic supposititiousness and "thievery" as the Athenian artificer. This supposititiousness is both literal and figurative. To "put under" sexually is fraudulently to replace the usual with the unexpected. The resulting miscegenation is, in book 7, between mortal and immortal (in the animal kingdom), in book 6, between human and animal. In each case generic mixing, as performed by Circe and Daedalus and recreated by the latter in sculpture, is typically Daedalian. Circe's hybrid horses anticipate the figures on the armor of Turnus: a Chimaera on his helmet (7.783-84) which, like Circe's horses (*spirantis naribus ignem*, 281), spouts fire (*efflantem faucibus ignis*), and Io in the process of metamorphosis from human into animal, *iam saetis obsita, iam bos*. Hybridization and metamorphosis complement each other in both instances. The latter, especially metamorphosis down from a higher to a lower sensibility, typifies book 7 as a whole (lines 660-61, e.g., offer an example of the furtive "mixing" of god and mortal). I trace the book's patterns of metamorphosis in further detail in "*Aeneid* 7 and the *Aeneid*," *AJP* 91 (1970) 408-30 = *Essays on Latin Lyric, Elegy, and Epic* (Princeton 1982). On the association of Turnus and the Minotaur see P. duBois, *History, Rhetorical Description and the Epic* (Cambridge, England 1982) 39f., part of a thoughtful discussion of Daedalus' sculptures.

9. It remains deliberately ambiguous whether *caeca vestigia* refer to the unseeing steps of Theseus or to the Labyrinth's dark path. Support for the former proposition comes from Catullus' reference to Theseus' *errabunda vestigia* (64.113) and from later imitations (re. Austin on 30), for the latter from Virgil's earlier description of the Labyrinth with its dark walls (*caecis parietibus, Aen.* 5.589) and from the sentence structure whose logic suggests a sequence from *ambages* to *caeca vestigia*. In either case the artisan is directly involved though his duplex activity lends different shades of meaning to *regens*. He becomes Ariadne and empathetically "leads" her lover to safety, or "straightens" the windings of his Labyrinth, unravelling the unravellable out of pity. *Inextricabilis* (27), Varro's coinage to describe Porsena's Etruscan labyrinth (Pliny *H. N.* 36.91), helps define the Labyrinth's puzzlement and toils, and adds a further dimension to Catullus' parallel, *inobservabilis* (64.115, itself a coinage), whose point is absorbed into Virgil's *caeca*. Virgil's Daedalus first creates, and then solves, the problems of his "text."

The influence of Catullus 64 on the Daedalus episode as a whole, most recently treated by Weber (op. cit. 47, 50-51), deserves still further study. It begins with similarities between the Argonauts and Daedalus through the primacy of their daring (there is a common emphasis on nimbleness, oarage and swimming in both initial episodes), develops in close parallels between the poets' treatments of Androgeos (64.77-83; *Aen.* 6.20-22) and the Labyrinth (64.113-15; *Aen.* 6.28-30), and concludes with loss. In Catullus the loss is double. Ariadne loses Theseus, Theseus Aegeus. In Virgil Daedalus misses Icarus alone.

10. Perhaps the artist unravels his artistry, out of manifest pity, to abet the love of others for fear that it might bring doom on himself. At the least his uniting of two other lovers anticipates the loss of love in his own life. (For the relation of pity and fear, see P. Pucci, *The Violence of Pity* [Cornell 1980] especially 169-74.)

11. This point is valid for the ecphrasis as a whole. We are earlier made aware of the placement of the sculptures (*in foribus*), of the dynamic interrelationship between episodes (*respondet*), of the specifics of location within a scene (*hic . . . hic*). The absence of a word for crafting in the Ariadne vignette is particularly telling. Because the Icarus scene could not be started we assume that Ariadne's story, which precedes it, was brought to completion, but nothing in the narrative attends to this. Instead, while Daedalus implements the penultimate, and the second most emotional, episode in his

artistic biography, the narrator of his tale shows him in the emotional act of unravelling his past art, not in the dispassionate formation of it. Even here, though we are led to presume one act of artistic fulfillment, emotion directly undoes the mind's creation.

12. Though Virgil on three other occasions repeats *bis* in a line or between adjacent lines (*Aen.* 2.218; 6.134; 9.799-800), only once elsewhere does he employ it in anaphora at the opening of contiguous verses, 11.629-30, which is also the only instance where the two uses of *bis* contrast with rather than reinforce each other. The context is the ebb and flow of war which in turn, if we look at the last four books as a whole, analogizes its futility.

The parallel with 6.134-35, where the Sibyl remarks on Aeneas' *cupido*

> bis Stygios innare lacus, bis nigra videre
> Tartara . . .

no doubt strengthens the bond between Daedalus and Aeneas. Though Aeneas does in fact complete his underworld journey, where Daedalus fails to finish his sculpture, the verbal interconnection may be one of Virgil's several subtle ways in book 6 of questioning the success of Aeneas', or Rome's, enterprise. There is, however, a later moment in book 6 with an even richer correlation to lines 32-33. When Aeneas finally reaches Anchises, son tries to embrace father (6.700-701):

> ter conatus ibi collo dare bracchia circum;
> ter frustra comprensa manus effugit imago . . .

The lines are repeated from book 2 (792-93) where Aeneas fails in his attempt to clasp the ghost of Creusa. Both events document the hero's inability throughout the epic to achieve emotional fulfillment (he does embrace his mother at 8.615 but at her insistence, not his). As critics note, Daedalus' inability to sculpt Icarus after two attempts may be modelled on Odysseus' triple attempt, and triple failure (*Od.* 11.206-208) to embrace the spirit of his mother (re. Pöschl, "Die Tempeltüren," 121; Fitzgerald, 63, n. 18). This, of course, was Virgil's model in the episodes of book 2 and 6 (the imitation, in the case of the latter, has most recently been noted by Austin ad loc.). But further potential meanings of this last anticipation in the Daedalus story of the later narrative of book 6 must not be overlooked. If Daedalus cannot perfect the loss of his son in art, can Aeneas finally fulfill the *pietas* owed to Anchises, especially given the strong need for *dementia* with which his father overlays his future loyalty?

It is noteworthy that the fall of Icarus is alluded to only by paronomasia in the word *casus*. The fall of Daedalus' hands, however, suggests that now, finally, the artisan experiences a version of his son's misfortune. Father becomes son. The son's physical fall is reiterated in the father's emotional collapse. Empathetically, literal death is the death of art.

13. I examine the reasoning behind Aeneas' actions at this crucial moment in "The Hesitation of Aeneas," *Atti del Convegno mondiale scientifico di studi su Virgilio* (Milan 1984) 2.233-52.

Critical Insights

14. *Geo.* 2.45-46.

15. *Geo.* 1.41-42.

16. *Geo.* 1.44.

17. See especially G. Duckworth, "The *Aeneid* as a Trilogy," *TAPA* 88 (1957) 1-10, revised and expanded in *Structural Patterns and Proportions in Vergil's Aeneid* (Ann Arbor 1962) 11-13.

18. The parallels between the wooden horse and Daedalus' cow and Labyrinth are noteworthy. In each case they include *doli* (2.44), accompanied by the supportive wiles of Thymoetes, Sinon, Epeos—the Daedalian *doli fabricator* (264)—and the Greeks (34, 62, 152, 196, 252), trickery (18, 258), and *error* (48). In both instances a hybrid animal produces a monstrous birth. Both the cow and horse are mounted on wheels as they implement their subterfuge (Dio. Sic. 4.77, Apollodorus 3.1.4, for the cow; *Aen.* 2.235-36, for the horse). Daedalus' gift to Pasiphae therefore resembles the Greeks' gift to Minerva, the *innuptae donum exitiale Minervae* (2.31), which the art of the goddess has helped produce (*divina Palladis arte*, 15). At this stage of his career and in this particular instance, Daedalus anticipates both duplicitous Greeks and crafty Minerva as they bring into being the *machina . . . feta armis* (2.237-38), the horse and its destructive brood.

19. Allusions to deceit begin, in book 1, at 130 where Neptune becomes aware of the *doli* and *irae* of his sister Juno. Out of 18 uses of *dolus* in the *Aeneid*, 10 arc in books 1-4.

20. Dido, in this matter as in others, is an accomplice in her own downfall, asking, at the end of book 1 (750-52), for Aeneas to retell the known as well as the novel in Troy's demise, and reiterating the request as her tragic love deepens (4.77-79).

Yet, whereas the sculptures of book 1 lead diachronically toward Aeneas' narrative, as he "sculpts" Troy's fall and manages Dido's death, and the shield of book 8 details Rome's future in linear progression, Daedalus' artistry analogizes the whole of the epic on several levels, offering a series of synchronic paradigms. The two longer ecphrases, by dwelling, in the first instance, on Aeneas' response, in the second, on Vulcan's craftsmanship, retain a strong specific point of focus that the Daedalian sculptures, with their lack of concern with the crafter at work or the viewer reacting, carefully forgo.

Aeneas' perception of the sculptures on Juno's temple is discussed, with great sensitivity, by W. R. Johnson (*Darkness Visible* [Berkeley 1976] 99-105). By contrast with the earlier episode, the narrator does not allow us to learn how far in his examination of Daedalus' sculptures Aeneas had proceeded (*quin protinus omnia perlegerent oculis, ni . . .* , 33-34), though we presume that his "reading" was near to completion. In any case only narrator and reader, not the poem's protagonists, know of Daedalus' final suffering (see p. 180 above). But perhaps a similar event will occur in Aeneas' life. At the moment in book 8 when Aeneas is about to set out from Pallanteum, taking himself and Pallas to war, we find him "pondering many hardships in his sad heart" (*multa . . . dura suo tristi cum corde putabant*, 8.522). To break his spell of contemplation Venus sends as sign a lightning-bolt and resounding thunder (*iterum atque iterum fragor increpat ingens*, 527). Aeneas will not explain what *casus* (533) this betokens, only that he must go into battle. But he may already sense the loss of Pallas with its many ramifications of incompletion in his life. It is a *fragor* (493), three times heard in Avernus, which, in the fourth *Georgic*, signals Eurydice's death caused by the *furor* (495) of Orpheus. The reader schooled in Virgil's symbolic modes is prepared to await a parallel misfortune as the *Aeneid* draws to a close and Aeneas, potential artist of Rome, undoes his work by his own version of madness.

21. 4.305-306.

22. Looked at within the bounds of books 1-4, the story of Dido shares common ground with that of Daedalus and, partially, of Aeneas. It begins with double artistic accomplishment—an extraordinary city being built with a magnificent temple at its heart, a disciplined civilization arising to bring order to the territory around it—and ends with a series of *dolores* (419, 474, 547, 679, and the death agony at 693; cf. the uses of *doleo* at 393 and 434). These destroy, literally, the queen and, symbolically, the city she had founded. Pöschl (*Die Dichtkunst*, 246 and note = *The Art of Vergil*, 150 and 207, n. 17) recognizes the parallel between Ariadne and Dido *regina*. See n. 1 above.

23. 6.473-74.

24. 4.693-95.

25. The complex *resolveret* is simplified shortly later in *solvo* (703). For Dido here, as for Pasiphae, passion creates the need for subterfuge, for *doli* (663) which only augment and finalize the *doli* of Venus and Juno which initiate her tragedy (95, 128) and of Aeneas who furthers it (296, the narrator's word). In Daedalus' artistic, which is to say psychic, life, *doli* precede *dolor*. For Dido *dolor* both anticipates and is precipitated by her resort to *doli* (see n. 22 above). The release of Dido from her entrapment, cares and body unmeshed at once (*me . . . his exsolvite curis* she cries to Aeneas' *dulces exuviae*, at 652) is the reader's release into the second third of the epic. Aeneas is the major Daedalian figure in Dido's life, but it is Virgil who frees her from his text.

26. Fitzgerald (63, n. 13) sees a probable connection between Labyrinth and underworld. The link is strengthened by appeal to the Sibyl's definition of Aeneas' *labor* (128):

sed revocare gradum superasque evadere ad auras . . .

Though Aeneas' "mad enterprise" (*Insano . . . labori*, 135) works on the vertical plane while the Labyrinth presents a horizontal complexity, the parallels between the two adventures, where the hero must enter treacherous territory, engage in an arduous challenge or challenges, and return out alive, are suggestive. They are supported by the narrator's striking, ironic designation—and presumably Daedalus' depiction—of the Labyrinth as a *domus*. It will not be long before Aeneas will cross the *atri ianua Ditis* (127) and enter the *vestibulum* (273) in order to make his way *per . . . domos Ditis* (269).

Among the monsters Aeneas must soon thereafter pass by are *Scyllae biformes* (286). (Virgil's only two uses of the word are at 25 and here.) It will not be long before he crosses the *inremeabilis unda* of the Styx (425), an adjective used of the *error* of the Labyrinth at 5.591 and akin to the rare *inextricabilis* at 6.27. These difficulties past,

Aeneas, as we shall see, continues his Daedalian enterprise with his pity for Dido and with his manifold inability to embrace his father.

27. Cf. also Dido's plea to Aeneas at 4.318—*miserere domus labentis*—and her later command to Anna, *miserere sororis* (435).

28. 6.476.

29. 5.350-54.

30. 9.66.

31. 9.136-39.

32. See n. 13 above.

33. If we pursue the analogy between Daedalus and Aeneas as we reach the poem's conclusion, we could say that in terms of life's terminations the two are successful. Each has reached a goal. Daedalus gains Cumae and constructs a notable artifact (*immania tempia*), an awesome temple to Apollo. Aeneas, too, has come to Italy and defeated the enemy who, presumably, has stood in the way of his founding the Roman race. But to turn biographical completions into art, to make them appear as art, is for each a different, highly inconclusive matter.

34. By the end of his epic Aeneas could also be seen as an Icarus figure, the most palpable sign of his father's failed artistry, realistic proof of how idealizing are Anchises' notions of *dementia*. (We remember that it is Anchises, not Aeneas, who initiates the sparing of Achaemenides in the epic's third book.) Daedalus' *dolor*, yearning for his lost son which may well include resentment and self-hatred also, results only in artistic incompletion. Aeneas' *dolor*, where loss is directly linked to the Furies' fires, to *saevitia* and *ira*, leads to a resentful, passionate killing with far more complex intimations of failure.

Forgetful Aeneas is made to mimic careless Icarus with the forceful difference, of course, that Aeneas lives on. For him, in Virgil's richly ironic narrative, survival is the equivalent of over-reaching Icarus' plummeting into the sea, and this survival means the end of his father's art.

The "celestial" plot of the *Aeneid* concludes with Jupiter yielding to Juno's demand that all things Trojan submerge their identity in the Latin present and future. What follows, therefore, up to the epic's last lines, is in fact the intellectual birth of Rome, as Aeneas becomes, according to his father's definition, *Romanus* (6.851). Two actions are paramount. First, Jupiter coopts the Dirae to warn Juturna and her brother of the latter's impending death. Second, Aeneas kills Turnus. In the first deed heaven summons hell to motivate earthly doings for the last time in the epic but for the first, one could surmise, in Virgil's Roman history, as history's cycle starts anew. The second, Aeneas' concluding deed, becomes the initial Roman action. Motivated by inner furies, it betokens a continuum of passion and anger, portending the impossibility of any new aesthetic or ethical wholeness.

35. The case for the authenticity of the *Odyssey* from 23.297 to the end is argued persuasively by C. Moulton, "The End of the *Odyssey*," *GRBS* 15 (1974) 153-69.

36. 12.803-808. His beloved Virgil is here on Statius' mind, but the Virgil not of the *Aeneid* but of *Georgic* 4 (525-27).

37. The abrupt conclusion of *De Rerum Natura* offers the closest parallel in earlier literature to the end of the *Aeneid*. I strongly support the view of Diskin Clay

(*Lucretius and Epicurus* [Ithaca 1983] 251) that Virgil's "grim and unresolved" finale deliberately echoes both the style and tone of his great predecessor.

38. The reversals of the *Iliad* in the *Aeneid* deserve separate study. The *Aeneid* ends in one respect where the *Iliad* begins. Achilles' anger at the start of the *Iliad* turns to forgiveness at the end. The story of Aeneas, on the other hand, begins with the hero's suppression of *dolor* (1.209), for hardships experienced in the past, and ends with his outburst of *dolor* over the loss of Pallas. In at least one episode of the *Aeneid* the reversal directly concerns Achilles. In Pyrrhus' vengeful killing of Priam, Achilles' anger lives on. It too, of course, is an emotion that spurs on Aeneas to his final deed (*ira terribilis* is the narrator's characterization of Aeneas immediately before his final speech, 12.946-47). Is it mere coincidence that Helenus bestows the *arma Neoptolemi* (3.469) on Aeneas as his parting gift?

39. The parallel is developed with sensitivity by C. P. Segal ("*Aeternum* per saecula nomen, the golden bough and the tragedy of history: Part II," *Anon* 5 [1966] 34-72, especially 50-52). Cf. also H. Rutledge ("Vergil's Daedalus," *CJ* 62 [1967] 311) and Pöschl ("Die Tempeltüren," 120).

40. Fitzgerald (note 1 above, 54) rightly notes that Daedalus' tale delivers him "from the past [that his artwork first encapsulated] into the painful and unfinished world of history." He pursues his insight by concluding that Aeneas, as Daedalus, is forced into a tragic history "that forfeits the comfort of closure."

41. The truth of Aeneas' emotions at the end of book 12, as in the Helen episode in book 2, leads to artistic inconclusions, in the first instance because the text (2.567-88) would be expunged by, and nearly lost because of, Varius and Tucca, in the second because it leads not to potential elimination but to aspects of incompletion. The first episode suggests, too early and too strongly, it might have been said, the truth of the hero's emotionality. The second cannot be argued away, though its author sought to destroy it as part of his whole epic. It forms a special complement to the first. Virgil stops at a moment of the greatest honesty which demonstrates Anchises' model to be one based on wishful thinking while Aeneas' violent response to Turnus and the emotional thrust behind it speak the truth. This truth brings about, literally and splendidly, the end of art.

Mathematical Symmetry in Vergil's *Aeneid*___

George E. Duckworth

This article is a brief summary of some amazing discoveries which I have made in recent years concerning the structure of Vergil's *Aeneid*. During the academic year 1957-58 I was engaged upon a general book on *Vergil as the Poet of Augustan Rome*,[1] and in April, 1958, my analyses of the individual books (for a chapter on the structure of the *Aeneid*) revealed unexpectedly the basic symmetry of the poem. The symmetry is mathematical: each book reveals, in small units as well as in the main divisions, the famous numerical ratio known variously as the Golden Section, the Divine Proportion, or the Golden Mean ratio.

As a result of this discovery, my original work was laid aside for the time being, and I have now completed a new book, neither planned nor anticipated, with the title: *Structural Patterns and Proportions in Vergil's Aeneid*. The subject is a technical one, but it has the excitement of a journey into new and uncharted territory. If the presence of exact or approximate Golden Mean ratios everywhere in the *Aeneid* seems improbable or even fantastic, I can assure the reader that it seemed so likewise to me when I first discovered their existence. Each step in my investigations led to new and equally surprising results. In this resumé I shall first describe how my earlier work led me to the mathematical proportions; then I shall explain what they are, *how* and *why* (if possible) Vergil employed them to the extent that he did, and finally—most important of all—I shall attempt to show the significance of the proportions for our understanding of many problems concerning the text of the poem.

I

The *Aeneid* of Vergil is the great national epic of ancient Rome; it portrays the journey of Aeneas and the Trojans from Troy to Italy and their trials and victories after they reach their "promised land"; it gives the archaeology and topography of early Latium and Rome, and by means of prophecy and foreshadowing it presents the outstanding events of Roman history and the achievements of Augustus in Vergil's own day. The miracle of the poem is Vergil's ability to treat three different topics simultaneously—the legendary narrative of Aeneas, themes and personages of Roman history, and the praise of Augustus who has brought a new era of peace to the Roman world. The epic rises far above the patriotic and historical level in the poet's dramatic treatment of character and event and in his introduction of loftier themes of philosophy and religion; it is an epic not only of Rome but of human life as well. Vergil's superb poetic power, as seen in imagery, sound effects (such as alliteration and assonance), and complex metrical patterns, contributes to the greatness and splendor of the poem. The *Aeneid* is one of the most consciously planned and carefully constructed poems of world literature.

In a work of such magnitude, with so many threads firmly and harmoniously interwoven, it should occasion no surprise that one or more basic designs of symmetry and variety, of parallelism and contrast, underlie the composition of the poem, both as a whole and in its separate parts. All readers of the *Aeneid* are conscious of these qualities to a degree, but the extent to which structural pattern and architectonic design dominate the epic has not been realized fully. Moreover, these structural features are not merely an adornment for their own sake but are devised to emphasize and make more significant the meaning of the poem; structure and content go hand in hand, and Vergil's artistry in combining the two is an additional proof of his supreme achievement as an epic poet.

The *Aeneid* reveals a conscious attention to various structural devices: alternation, parallelism by means of similarities and contrasts, concentric or framework patterns, tripartite divisions; these appear both in the epic as a whole and in the individual books. This in itself is not surprising, for earlier poetry, both Greek and Roman, had been composed with a similar devotion to structural design. Throughout the *Iliad* of Homer there exists a most elaborate correspondence of parts, in which, as Whitman says, "episodes, and even whole books, balance each other through similarity or opposition."[2] The fact that many or most in the Homeric audience would not be conscious of this elaborate design is no argument against its existence. A great poet, or artist, or musician, always puts more into a work than is ordinarily realized, and this is even truer of Vergil than of Homer.

In the *Aeneid* as a whole we find three definite structural patterns:

1. The alternation of the books, those with even numbers being of a more serious and tragic nature than those with odd numbers, which are lighter and serve to relieve the tension. The famous books which stand out in the reader's memory are even-numbered: II, the fall of Troy; IV, the tragedy of Dido; VI, the trip to the underworld; VIII, the visit to early Rome; X, the great battle, with the deaths of Pallas, Lausus, and Mezentius; and XII, the final conflict and the death of Turnus. Vergil has stressed the significance of these books by means of the alternating rhythm.

2. The second pattern is the parallelism, by similarity and contrast, between the books in each half, I and II and VIII, III and IX, etc. I have discussed this elsewhere,[3] and therefore shall list only a few examples. The similarities between I and VII are very numerous; in each the Trojans arrive in a strange land and are welcomed after a speech by Ilioneus; in each Juno stirs up trouble with divine or infernal assistance—in I, the storm at sea, and in VII, the war in Latium. Book II is the fall of Troy and VIII the birth of Rome; at the end of II Aeneas carries on his shoulders from Troy his father—a symbol of the past; at the end of VIII he raises to his shoulder the shield portraying scenes of Roman history—symbolic of the future. Book IV is the tragedy of Love, and X is the tragedy of War. One of the best parallels I have noted only recently: at the end of VI Anchises recommends *clementia* and *iustitia* in the famous verse (853):

parcere subiectis et debellare superbos;

at the end of XII when the wounded Turnus appeals for mercy, Aeneas is about to show *clementia* and spare him, when he sees the swordbelt of Pallas. In X Vergil had referred to Turnus as *superbus* both before and after the killing of Pallas (445, 514), and so now, at the very end of the poem, Aeneas cannot yield to clemency; *iustitia* demands that Turnus die.[4]

3. Vergil combines with the alternation of the books and their division into two corresponding halves a third and most important architectonic device—a tripartite division of the epic into three groups of four books each.[5] The *Aeneid* is the story of Aeneas, but it is also the story of the destiny of Rome under Augustus. This latter provides much of the central core of the poem (V-VIII) and concludes with the victories and triumphs of Augustus as described on the shield at the end of VIII. The *Aeneid* is thus a trilogy with the first four books, the tragedy of Dido, and the last four books, the tragedy of Turnus, enclosing in a framework pattern the central portion, where long Homeric episodes (games, trip to underworld, catalogue, description of a shield) are reworked and transformed for the glorification of Rome and its history, the portrayal of ancient Italy, and the praise of Augustus and the new Golden Age. This division of the poem into three parts is undoubtedly a deliberate attempt on Vergil's part to avoid too sharp a break into an "Odyssey" of wanderings and an "Iliad" of battles, and it enables him to emphasize the story of Rome and Augustus in the very center of the epic[6]; we have here an excellent illustration of the manner in which structure and content are combined.

In the individual books likewise, Vergil introduces effective contrasts by means of alternation; e.g. in the contests in V where the first (boat race) and the third (boxing match) are longer and contain more details of characterization than the second (foot race) and the fourth (archery match).[7] The poet's use of alternation is especially striking in the catalogue of Latin warriors (VII.641-807); the leaders alternate between major figures (Mezentius and Lausus, Messapus, Turnus and Camilla)

Critical Insights

and those of less significance, the latter being arranged in three groups of three each[8]; also, there is an interesting geographical variety, with the warriors from local areas enclosing pairs from the north (Messapus and Clausus), the south (Halaesus and Oebalus), and the east (Ufens and Umbro); i.e. we have two types of alternation in the same passage.

A second design is that of a balanced symmetry around an important central passage or focal point; this is called a framework or concentric or recessed panel pattern. Mendell has pointed out several examples in various books of the *Aeneid*,[9] but he does not cite VI.56-123, where we find an almost perfect balance of passages about the words of the Sibyl (83-97)—an important speech which arouses suspense concerning the events of VII-XII:

56-76	Speech of Aeneas
77-82	Description of the Sibyl
83-97	Speech of the Sibyl
98-102	Description of the Sibyl
103-123	Speech of Aeneas

This symmetrical framing of the Sibyl's speech underlines its importance for the later action of the poem.[10] *Aeneid* IV as a whole may be viewed as a series of loosely corresponding episodes about a focal point.[11] The speeches of Dido and Anna at the end balance those at the beginning, and Mercury appears to Aeneas twice and urges him to depart. In the very center we have the following sequence:

279-304	Narrative.	Preparations for departure
305-30	Dido's speech	
331-33a	Aeneas' emotions	
333b-61	Speech of Aeneas	
362-64	Dido's emotions	
365-87	Dido's speech	
388-415	Narrative.	Preparations for departure

The famous defense of Aeneas in 333b-61 is the focal point about which the corresponding passages revolve. However much modern readers may sympathize with Dido, it is evident that Vergil looked upon the queen as a danger to be resisted; Aeneas' duty lay elsewhere, and the poet has emphasized the rightness of Aeneas' decision by placing his speech in the very center of the book.

The third structural device is the use of tripartite divisions everywhere. Sinon in II makes three speeches (77-104, 108-44, 154-94), each with its appropriate effect on his listeners. The activity of Allecto in VII is threefold: she incites Amata (341-405), Turnus (406-74), and the hounds of Ascanius (475-510), and the results of her actions are described in reverse order in 572-82 (shepherds, Turnus, Amata). In IX the tragic story of Nisus and Euryalus is a miniature drama in three parts: the scene in the Trojan camp (176-313), the slaughter in the camp of the enemy (314-66), their departure and death (367-449).

An examination of the twelve books of the *Aeneid* reveals that every book falls naturally into three main divisions,[12] and each main section is usually subdivided into three parts. Book II illustrates well Vergil's interest in tripartite structure:

A. 1-249.   Sinon (57-194), Laocoon (40-56, 195-227), and the wooden horse (on shore, 1-39; in city, 228-49).[13]

B. 250-558.   Return of Greeks (250-369), capture of Troy (370-505), death of Priam (506-58).

C. 559-804.   Aeneas-Venus episode (559-633), Aeneas at home (634-729), departure and loss of Creusa (730-804).

In III the threefold division and the tripartite subdivisions are indicated even more clearly: we have nine episodes (or stops) on the journey from Troy to Sicily, divided into three main groups: Aegean area (1-191), western Greece (192-505) and Magna Graecia (506-718); the third episode in each group (Crete, 121-91; Helenus and Andromache,

294-505; the rescue of Achaemenides, 588-691) is more important and narrated at greater length.[14]

I add in outline form the tripartite divisions and subdivisions of Books IV (Tragedy of Love) and X (Tragedy of War):

IV. A. 1-172   Dido's love and its consummation
    1.   1-89   Growth of Dido's love
    2.   90-128   Juno-Venus scene
    3.   129-172   Hunting scene and "coniugium "
  B. 173-449   Aeneas' determination to leave
    1.   173-278   Fama—Iarbas—Jupiter—Mercury
    2.   279-415   Narrative; speeches of Dido, Aeneas, Dido; narrative
    3.   416-449   Attempted reconciliation fails
  C. 450-705   Aeneas' departure and Dido's suicide
    1.   450-552   Magic rites and Dido's lament
    2.   553-583   Aeneas' departure
    3.   584-705   Dido's curses and suicide
X. A.   1-361   Return of Aeneas
    1.   1-117   Council of the gods
    2.   118-255   Return of Aeneas; catalogue of ships
    3.   256-361   Landing and battle
  B. 362-688   Death of Pallas
    1.   362-478   Aristeia of Pallas
    2.   479-605   Death of Pallas and effect on Aeneas
    3.   606-688   Removal of Turnus from battle
  C. 689-908   Deaths of Lausus and Mezentius
    1.   689-746   Aristeia of Mezentius
    2.   747-832   Death of Lausus
    3.   833-908   Death of Mezentius

It is important to note how frequently Vergil uses the central position in each book—the second subdivision of the second main division—for material of special significance. In II it is the capture of Troy (370-505), in III the stop at Actium (274-93)—an important Roman theme. We have seen above that the speeches of Aeneas and Dido are at the very center of IV and Aeneas' decision leads to Dido's suicide at the end of the book[15]; in like manner the death of Pallas in X.479-605 is the focal point of the entire book and is decisive for the death of Turnus at the conclusion of the poem; cf. XII.940ff. These passages, so important for the action of the *Aeneid*, receive added emphasis from their central position in each book, a position resulting from Vergil's arrangement of his material into tripartite divisions and subdivisions.

II

I have given above a brief analysis of the *Aeneid* as a whole and have discussed the structure of individual books for two reasons: (1) the mathematical proportions in the poem are achieved by the use of alternating, tripartite, and framework patterns very similar to and often identical with those already described, and (2) it was only when I had determined the tripartite divisions of the books that the mathematical ratios appeared. The main divisions were of very uneven length, and it occurred to me that these inequalities might be intentional. Then I made the amazing discovery (amazing to me, at any rate, as I had no idea what would develop) that the line totals of at least two of the three main divisions in each book (and often of all three) were always in the same approximate proportion; also, the subdivisions not only contained the same ratios but in most instances combined to produce a similar ratio in each main division. Additional investigation revealed that within the divisions and subdivisions were smaller narrative units composed of others still smaller (episodes and speeches), all in the same proportion, the exact or approximate Golden Section, or Golden Mean ratio; in other words, each book of the *Aeneid* is constructed on the basis of mathematical symmetry, with the proportions in the short passages combining into larger units until we reach the ratios in the subdivisions and main divisions of each book.

The Golden Section, famous in mathematics, in art and architecture, in aesthetic theory, is that ratio according to which the greater part is to the lesser as the sum of the two is to the greater. This is the extreme and mean ratio of Euclid 2.11 and 6.30. The two parts, greater and lesser, are usually called major and minor. If we denote the major by M and the minor by m, $M/m = (M + m)/M = 1.618$, and $m/M = M/(M + m) = .618$. These total $2.236 = \sqrt{5}$; $1.618 = 1/2(\sqrt{5} + 1)$ and $.618 = 1/2(\sqrt{5} - 1)$. In my calculations I have regularly divided the smaller number by the larger, as the mathematics is somewhat simpler, and the ratios which I give below result from the division of the major by the sum of major and minor, i.e. $M/(M + m)$.[16]

We can reach the Golden Section most quickly by a mathematical series named after the thirteenth-century Italian mathematician Fibonacci, where each number is added to the second to produce the third, beginning with 1 and 1; i.e. 1, 1, 2, 3, 5, 8, 13, 21, 34, 55, . . . ; 21/34 or 34/55 or 55/89 = .618. But we can take any two numbers, 1 and 3, or 1 and 4, or 1 and 5, or 2 and 5, and these also produce series which lead eventually to the Golden Section, e.g. 1, 5, 6, 11, 17, 28, 45, 73, 118, 191, . . . ; 118/191 = .618; or 2, 5, 7, 12, 19, 31, 50, 81, 131, . . . ; 81/131 = .618. Here we necessarily go to much higher numbers than in the case of the Fibonacci series.[17]

If Vergil writes an episode with two passages of unequal length, e.g. of 25 and 75 lines, $M/(M + m) = .750$; if the two passages are 45 and 55 lines, $M/(M + m) = .550$; these are far from the Golden Section. But in the *Aeneid* the ratio in the short episodes and speeches, in longer narrative units, and in the subdivisions and main divisions of each book is almost always in the approximate area of .618. This cannot be chance. In a passage of 100 lines, even if we eliminate the extremes of 1-19 and 99-81, we have a possible range for $M/(M + m)$ from .800 (80/100) to .500 (50/100); 61/100 produces a ratio of .610, 62/100 that of .620, and 63/100 that of .630. In a series from 20-80 to 80-20 these three ratios each occur twice; the probability of their appearance is six out of sixty times or once in ten times. A range from .610 to .626, a variation of .008 from the perfect .618, would thus be extremely difficult to achieve accidentally, and a perfect .618 is impossible. And yet Vergil has many perfect ratios of .618, most of them in short passages of from 30 to 70 lines, and in most instances he reaches this perfect ratio by the numbers 13 and 21, or 21 and 34; i.e. he is using the numbers of the Fibonacci series. This series and its multiples, e.g. 26, 42, 68 (= 2 × 13, 21, 34) or 40, 65, 105 (= 5 × 8, 13, 21), appear in the *Aeneid* more than 300 times, and the next simplest Golden Mean series (1, 3, 4, 7, 11, 18, 29, 47, 76, . . . ; 47/76 = .618) occurs about 90 times. The other series, such as 1, 4, 5, 9, 14, 23, . . . or 1, 5, 6, 11, 17, 28, . . . likewise appear, but only 15 to 30 times each; in other words, the Fibonacci series occurs about three and one-half times as often as 1, 3, 4, 7, 11, 18, . . . and this in turn is three times as frequent as any of the others.

This would seem to rule out not only chance but also intuition or poetic instinct. Friends with whom I have discussed Vergil's use of the Golden Section suggest that he had a feeling for this particular ratio but that he did not deliberately count lines. But when these various mathematical series appear again and again, with the simplest and quickest series used so much more frequently than the others, I cannot believe that we have here merely a subconscious desire for proportion and symmetry. It seems far safer to assume that Vergil purposely introduced Golden Mean ratios into all parts of the *Aeneid* by means of these mathematical series. We must keep in mind Suetonius' statement in his *Life* of Vergil (15) that the poet as a student gave special attention to the study of mathematics.

III

Before I present typical examples of the proportions in the *Aeneid*, I wish to point out that the same Golden Mean ratio is found in both the *Eclogues* and the *Georgics*. The first to reveal Vergil's knowledge and use of the Golden Section was Father Le Grelle who in 1949 explained the troublesome structure of Book I of the *Georgics* by means of the numerous ratios which he found therein.[18] Le Grelle accepts the division of the book into "Works" (43-203 = 161 lines) and "Days" (204-463a = 259.5 lines); these parts as minor and major produce the Golden Section; $M/(M + m) = 259.5/420.5 = .617$.[19] The prologue (5b-42) and the epilogue (463b-514) combine to form a major of 89 lines, which, with the central astronomical passage ("foyer astronomique," 204-58) of 55 lines as minor, reveals the perfect Golden Section: $55/89 = 89/144 = .618$. We have here a tripartite framework design with *a* and c enclosing *b*, in the pattern $b/(a + c)$, and the totals are higher numbers in the Fibonacci series, . . . 13, 21, 34, 55, 89, 144, . . . In each of numerous smaller units, which he terms "chrysodes," he likewise finds a major and a minor part which are in proportion, e.g. 100-117 (18 = m) and 118-46 (29 = M) produce the ratio .617 (29/47), and 100-146 (47) is the major of a larger unit, with 147-75 (29) the minor; the ratio here is the exact .618 (47/76) and the numbers are those in the series 1, 3, 4, 7, 11, 18, 29, 47, 76, . . .

Le Grelle's discovery of the Golden Mean ratios in *Georgics* I is confirmed by the many similar examples which I have detected elsewhere in the *Georgics* and also in the *Eclogues*. These were brought to my attention purely by chance. While working on the *Georgics* for my original book, I happened to read the statement of Wili that less than half of the *Georgics* is composed of didactic material, the greater part consisting of "Bild und Reflexion," the descriptive passages praising Italy, country life, Octavian, etc.[20] Curiosity led me to check the statement. Wili is quite wrong, for the technical sections on farming have much the greater extent, the ratio being 1352 verses to 835.[21] It was amazing to find here the exact Golden Mean ratio; $M/(M + m) = 1352/2187 = .618$.[22] The possibility of this being accidental (in a poem of 2187 verses) would be at least one chance in 500.

I next turned to many short passages in *Georgics* II, III, and IV, especially those of a non-technical nature, and again the Golden Section appeared; e.g. (1) the praise of country life in II.458-540 (four parts in a chiastic arrangement): country life (459-74) and the poet's ambition (475-89) as minor (32 lines), the *felix-fortunatus* passage (490-94) and the advantages of country life with the new Golden Age in Italy (495-540) as major (51 lines); 51/83 = .614; (2) the plague in III.478-566, which divides into three stages: 478-502, 503-36, and 537-66 (the third stage beginning with the reversal of nature—almost a Golden Age in reverse); the ratio is tripartite in a framework pattern, with the first and third stages, 478-502 and 537-66 (a total of 55 lines = M) enclosing the second stage, 503-36 (34 = m); 34/55 = 55/89 = .618, again the perfect Golden Section in the Fibonacci series 34, 55, 89; (3) the Aristaeus and Orpheus stories in IV.281-558: (a) Aristaeus, 281-452 (171) as M; (b) Orpheus and Eurydice, 453-529, and (c) the restoration of the bees, 530-58, as m (77 + 29 = 106); 171/277 = .617.[23]

The Golden Mean ratio appears likewise in the *Eclogues*, e.g. in X: 1-30 (introduction, nymphs, shepherds, Apollo, Pan) provide the minor, the major consisting of 31-77 (song of Gallus, conclusion); 47/77 = .610. The recessed panel construction of *Eclogue* I was analyzed above[24]; the focal point (40-45) and the two Tityrus passages which frame it (27-39, 46-58) provide the minor of 32 verses; the balancing passages at the beginning and the end of the poem (1-26 and 59-83) are the major of 51 verses; 51/83 = .614. Similarly, in II, the focal point of 28 lines (28-55, invitations to Alexis and gifts offered) is the minor and is framed by 1-27 (introduction; Corydon reproaches Alexis) and 56-73 (Corydon reproaches himself; conclusion) which provide the major of 45 lines; 45/73 = .616. In both I and II the patterns of thought, the recessed panel or framework construction, and the Golden Mean ratios are subtly interwoven.

Much has been written about the structure of the *Eclogues* as a group; especially significant are the reverse parallelism of I-IV and VI-IX about V as the central poem (with X, the poet as a shepherd, added to balance V, the shepherd-poet as a god), and the arrangement of the poems in triads with the central triad (IV-VI) on more cosmic themes

Critical Insights

and X combining the themes of all three triads.[25] Golden Mean ratios appear in the collection as a whole, and the corresponding poems may be grouped into major and minor units, as follows:

I + II = m (156); VIII + IX + X = M (253);   253/409 = .619;

III = M (111); VII = m (70);   111/181 = .613;

IV + VI = M (149); V = m (90);   149/239 = .624.[26]

The existence of these proportions in the *Eclogues*, especially in the two corresponding responsive songs III and VII, and in IV-VI, where IV ("the world to come") and VI ("the world that was") enclose V (the death and deification of Daphnis) is most impressive. The relation between the major and minor poems may be diagrammed as follows:

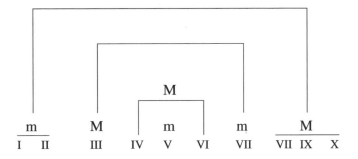

If we view the *Eclogues* as composed of three triads and a final poem which blends the shepherds and the realism of Triads One and Three with the gods and the fantasy of Triad Two, the Golden Section is likewise present; the first two Triads (I-III, IV-VI) form a major of 506 lines, and the final Triad plus X a minor of 323 lines; 506/829 = .610. The proportions thus support both the concentric arrangement of the *Eclogues* about V (Daphnis) and the triadic structure, and they illustrate the complexity of Vergil's compositional patterns.

Although Vergil's use of mathematical proportions in the *Eclogues* and the *Georgics* was now clearly evident, I still had no idea that the same exact or approximate Golden Mean ratio would appear everywhere in the *Aeneid* and, strange to say, it did not occur to me to look for it. When, however, I had completed my structural analyses of the *Aeneid*, with each book divided into three main divisions, and with these in most instances falling into three clearly-marked subdivisions, the unequal length of the main divisions aroused my interest; then I discovered that in every book at least two and often all three main divisions were in proportion; e.g.:

A. Two divisions in proportion:

III.1-191 (m = 191),   192-505 (M = 310.8); 310.8/501.8 = .619;[27]

IV.1-172 (m = 171.4),   173-449 (M = 275.2); 275.2/446.6 = .616;

VII.1-285 (M = 284.2),   641-817 (m = 175.8); 284.2/460   = .618;

IX.1-175 (m = 171.4),   176-449 (M = 273.4); 273.4/444.8 = .615;

X.1-361 (M = 358.8),   689-908 (m = 217.8); 358.8/576.6 = .622;

XII.289-696 (M = 405.2), 697-952 (m = 256);   405.2/661.2 = .613.[28]

B. All three divisions in proportion:

II.1-249 and 559-804   (M = 488 .8),   250-558   (m = 307.9);

488.8/796.7 = .614;

IV.1-172 and 450-705   (M = 425 .4),   173-449   (m = 275.2);

425.4/700.6 = .607;

VI.1-235 and 236-547   (M = 545 .6),   548-901   (m = 353.7);

545.6/899.3 = .607;

VIII.1-369 and 370-453   (M = 451 .4),   454-731   (m = 276.6);

451.4/728 = .620;

X.1-361   (m = 358.8),   362-688 and 689-908   (M = 543.6);

543.6/902.4 = .602.

It is interesting to note that in five of the six even-numbered books (those of greatest significance), all three main divisions combine to produce the approximate Golden Section. In Books II and IV the second division is enclosed by the first and third in a framework pattern.

I next examined the main divisions (36 in the 12 books) and found that each contained a Golden Mean ratio and that this was usually produced by the already-determined subdivisions (most often tripartite) of each main section, e.g.:

I.223-296	(m = 74),	297-417
		(M = 121); 121.0/195.0 = .621;
II.250-369	(m = 119.2),	370-505 and 506-558
		(M = 188.7); 188.7/307.9 = .613;
559-633 and 730-804		(M = 147.7),
framing 634-729		(m = 94.6); 147.7/242.3 = .610;
III.506-547 and 548-587		(m = 81.4),
588-718		(M = 129.6); 129.6/211.0 = .614;
IV.173-278	(m = 105),	279-415 and 416-449
		(M = 170.2); 170.2/275.2 = .618;
VII.286-322 and 540-640		(m = 138),
framing 323-539		(M = 216); 216.0/354.0 = .610;[29]
VIII.454-596 and 597-625		(M = 170.6),
626-731		(m = 106); 170.6/276.6 = .617;[30]
IX.450-589	(m = 137.8),	590-671 and 672-818
		(M = 228.1) 228.1/365.9 = .623;
X.1-117 and 256-361		(M = 220.8),
framing 118-255		(m = 138); 220.8/358.8 = .615;[31]
362-478 and 606-688		(M = 200),
enclosing 479-605		(m = 125.8); 200.0/325.8 = .614;
XI.1-99 and 100-138		(M = 138)
139-224		(m = 86); 138.0/224.0 = .616.

As I worked from the main divisions and subdivisions to shorter narrative units, more and more Golden Mean proportions appeared. As I shall show below, my line-divisions are not arbitrary but are based upon the natural units of speech and action. I have made no attempt to discover every single ratio in the *Aeneid*, but my completed tables, arranged by patterns, contain 1044 proportions, from 75 to 100 a book, ranging from .60 to .636, and of these 622, about 60 per cent, are in the area from .610 to .626, i.e. within .008 of the exact .618. Every verse of the *Aeneid* (except the interpolations) appears in at least one, and usually in three, four, or more proportions. Moreover, 300 ratios are in what I consider an almost perfect area, from .615 to .621, and 45 are exactly .618.

Suetonius (*Vita* 23) states that Vergil made a prose outline of the *Aeneid* arranged in twelve books and then wrote *particulatim*—in small sections—as he pleased, taking nothing in order. These small sections are his units of composition, and they all contain exact or approximate Golden Mean ratios. As in the case of the main divisions and subdivisions listed above, Vergil achieves the Golden Section by a variety of patterns. I shall present sample ratios of each type and show how the units of speech and narrative combine in the proportions:

1. Two passages, *a* and *b*, with *a* either major or minor:

I.	8-33	(a) Juno's hostility	$(m = 26)$,
	34-75	(b) Juno's lament and speech to Aeolus	$(M = 42)$; $42/68 = .618$;
	34-75	(a) Juno's lament and speech to Aeolus	$(M = 42)$,
	76-101	(b) Aeolus' reply, the storm and Aeneas' words	$(m = 26)$; $42/68 = .618$;
	227-253	(a) Venus' complaint to Jupiter	$(m = 27)$,

254-296	(b) Jupiter's prophecy	($M = 43$);	$43/70 = .614$;
586-595a	(a) Aeneas appears before		
	Dido	($m = 9.4$),	
595b-610a	(b) Aeneas' speech	($M = 15.2$);	$15.2/24.6 = .618$;
II.506-525	(a) Priam and Hecuba at		
	the altar	($m = 20$),	
526-558	(b) Priam slain by Pyrrhus	($M = 33$);	$33/53 = .623$;
567-574	(a) Aeneas sees Helen	($m = 8$)	
575-587	(b) Aeneas thinks of		
	killing Helen	($M = 13$);	$13/21 = .619$;[32]
679-686	(a) the first omen	($M = 8$)	
687-691	(b) Anchises' words	($m = 5$);	$8/13 = .615$;
IV.160-164	(a) the storm	($m = 5$),	
165-172	(b) the cave and the		
	"coniugium"	($M = 8$);	$8/13 = .615$;
522-533	(a) Dido's last night	($m = 11$),	
534-552	(b) Dido's lament	($M = 19$);	$19/30 = .633$;
672-692	(a) Anna's lament	($M = 21$),	
693-705	(b) Iris releases Dido's		
	spirit	($m = 13$);	$21/34 = .618$;[33]
VI.789b-800	(a) Augustus and the		
	Golden age	($M = 11.6$),	
801-807	(b) Augustus compared to		
	Hercules and Bacchus	($m = 7$);	$11.6/18.6 = .624$;
VII.323-329	(a) description of Allecto	($m = 7$)	
330-340	(b) Juno's instructions	($M = 11$);	$11/18 = .611$;
670-677	(a) Catullus and Coras		
	from Tibur	($m = 8$),	

678-690	(b) Caeculus from		
	Praeneste	(M = 13);	13/21 = .619;
IX.590-620	(a) the taunts of Numanus	(m = 31),	
621-671	(b) Numanus slain by		
	Ascanius	(M = 51);	51/82 = .622;
X.791-816	(a) conflict between		
	Aeneas and Lausus	(M = 26),	
817-832	(b) Lausus' death and		
	its effect on Aeneas	(m = 16);	26/42 = .619;
888-895	(a) Mezentius' horse slain	(m = 8),	
896-908	(b) death of Mezentius	(M = 13);	13/21 = .619;
XII.919-939	(a) the wounded Turnus		
	appeals for mercy	(M = 21),	
940-952	(b) Aeneas sees the		
	sword-belt of Pallas		
	and slays Turnus	(m = 13);	21/34 = .618.[34]

Vergil's use of the Fibonacci series, . . . 5, 8, 13, 21, 34, . . . (or multiples thereof) is seen in many of the ratios listed above. It is worth noting that the most perfect ratios appear usually at the beginning and the end of the books; this suggests that Vergil wishes the attentive listener to be conscious of the mathematical symmetry of the poem and perhaps to detect more readily the approximate ratios elsewhere in each book. Or the hearer may be expected to derive a subconscious pleasure from the harmony of the proportions.

The use of two passages to produce Golden Mean ratios occurs less frequently than that of three or more.

2. Tripartite (non-framework): three passages, *a*, *b*, and *c*, with a + b or b + c either major or minor. Actually, this is a variation of the first, or bipartite, pattern, with *a* or *b* subdivided into two parts, episodes or speeches. E.g.:

I.34-39	(a) Juno's lament	(m = 16),	
50-64	(b) description of Aeolus		
65-75	(c) Juno's words to Aeolus	(M = 26);	26/42 = .619;
76-80	(a) Aeolus' speech		
81-91	(b) the winds released	(M = 16),	
92-101	(c) Aeneas' lament	(m = 10);	16/26 = .615;[35]
586-612	(a) Aeneas appears before Dido and speaks	(m = 27),	
613-630	(b) Dido's welcome		
631-656	(c) banquet preparations and gifts	(M = 43.6);	
			43.6/70.6 = .618;
723-735	(a) conclusion of banquet and Dido's words	(m = 13),	
736-747	(b) song of Iopas		
748-756	(c) Dido urges Aeneas to speak	(M = 21);	21/34 = .618;
II.730-744	(a) departure and loss of Creusa		
745-770	(b) search for Creusa	(M = 40.2),	
771-795	(c) vision of Creusa	(m = 24.7);	
			40.2/64.9 = .619;[36]

III.472-481   (a) farewell of Helenus

482-492   (b) Andromache's farewell (M = 21),

493-505   (c) Aeneas' parting words (m = 13);   21/34 = .618;

IV.90-104   (a) speech of Juno   (m = 15),

105-114a (b) Venus' reply

114b-128 (c) Juno's second speech (M = 24);   24/39 = .615;

Dido's speech to Anna in 416-436:

416-423   (a) Aeneas trusts Anna   (m = 8),

424-428   (b) Anna should entreat Aeneas

429-436   (c) Dido wants Aeneas'

            departure postponed (M = 13);   13/21 = .619;[37]

VI.756-807 (a) Alban kings, Romulus,

            Augustus   (m = 52),

808-853   (b) Roman kings and heroes

854-892   (c) Marcellus passage   (M = 84.7);

                                  84.7/136.7 = .620;

X.439-478   (a) Turnus against Pallas (m = 40)

479-509   (b) death of Pallas

510-542   (c) effect on Aeneas   (M = 63.6);

                               63.6/103.6 = .614.[38]

3. Tripartite framework: three passages, *a*, *b*, and *c*, with a + c as major or minor enclosing b, the focal point. The ratios in this category are twice as numerous as those in the second group. The focal point (b) may be a speech framed by two other speeches or by two episodes, or it may itself be narrative, but in most instances it is a passage of special significance; e.g.:

I.335-370a (b) speech of Venus,
                enclosed by   (M = 35.4),
   326-334 (a) speech of Aeneas
   372-385a (c) speech of Aeneas   (m = 22.6);

$$35.4/58 = .610;[39]$$

III.320-343 (b) Andromache's speech,
               framed by   (m = 23.4),
   294-319 (a) Aeneas meets Andromache
   344-355 (c) Helenus welcomes
               Aeneas   (M = 37.6); 37.6/61 = .616;

IV.331-361 (b) Aeneas' defense,
               framed by   (m = 30.6),
   303-330 (a) Dido's speech
   362-387 (c) Dido's speech   (M = 52);   52/82.6 = .630;

   648-671 (b) final speech and suicide
               of Dido, enclosed by   (m = 24),
   630-647 (a) Dido prepares for suicide
   672-692 (c) lament of Anna   (M = 39);   39/63 = .619;

VI.77-103a (b) description of Sibyl and
               prophecy, enclosed by   (m = 26.2),
    56-76 (a) speech of Aeneas
  103b-123 (c) speech of Aeneas   (M = 41.4);

$$41.4/67.6 = .612;$$

868-886a	(b) Anchises' speech about	
	Marcellus, framed by	$(m = 18.2)$,
854-867	(a) Aeneas sees Marcellus	
886b-901	(c) instructions and	
	departure	$(M = 29.8)$; $29.8/48 = .621$;
VIII.337-358	(b) Evander's description	
	of early Rome,	
	enclosed by	$(m = 22)$,
313-336	(a) history of Latium	
359-369	(c) Aeneas at Evander's	
	home	$(M = 35)$; $35/57 = .614$;
675-713	(b) battle of Actium,	
	framed by	$(m = 39)$,
626-674	(a) scenes of history of	
	Rome; ocean	
714-728	(c) triumphs of Augustus	$(M = 64)$; $64/103 = .621$;
IX.324-356	(b) aristeia of Nisus and	
	Euryalus, enclosed by	$(M = 33)$,
314-323	(a) in the camp of the enemy;	
	Nisus suggests slaughter	
357-366	(c) taking of spoils	$(m = 20)$; $33/53 = .623$;
XII.18-45a	(b) speech of Latinus,	
	framed by	$(M = 27.2)$,
10-17	(a) speech of Turnus	
45b-53	(c) speech of Turnus	$(m = 16.8)$; $27.2/44 = .618$.[40]

4. Four or five passages, usually interlocked, with b + d as major or minor alternating with a + c or a + c + e. Both major and minor passages are not infrequently bound together by similarity of theme or identity of speaker; e.g.:

IV.129-172, the hunting scene:

129-135 (a) preparation for hunt
136-150 (b) description of Dido and Aeneas
151-159 (c) the hunt
160-172 (d) the storm and the "coniugium"
The two Dido and Aeneas passages (b + d)
provide the major (28), the scenes concerning
the hunt the minor (16); $28/44 = .636$;

279-415, the central core of Book IV, discussed above:

279-304 (a) preparation for departure
305-330 (b) Dido's speech
331-361 (c) Aeneas' defense
362-387 (d) Dido's response
388-415 (e) preparation for departure
The Aeneas passages (a + c + e) form the
major (84.2), the Dido speeches (b + d)
the minor (52); $84.2/136.2 = .618$;[41]

VII.406-474, the Allecto-Turnus scene:

406-434 (a) Allecto visits Turnus and speaks
435-444 (b) reply of Turnus
445-457 (c) action and words of Allecto
458-474 (d) effect on Turnus
The two passages of the major (a + c = 41.6)
concern Allecto, those of the minor (b + d =
26.4) concern Turnus; $41.6/68 = .612$;

IX.184-223, alternating speeches:
　　184-196　　(a) speech of Nisus
　　197-206　　(b) speech of Euryalus
　　207-218　　(c) speech of Nisus
　　219-223　　(d) speech of Euryalus
　　　　　　　The two speeches of Nisus are the major
　　　　　　　(a + c = 25), those of Euryalus the minor
　　　　　　　(b + d = 15);　　　　　　　　　　　　　　　　25/40 = .625.

The amazing feature about the ratios in this pattern is that the major (a + c, or b + d) is so often composed of speeches which are linked together by similarity of theme or identity of speaker, or by the second speech being an answer to or a development of the first; e.g.:

　　II.650-678　　(four-part); M = 18:
　　　　657-670　　(b) Aeneas' speech
　　　　675-678　　(d) Creusa's words;　　　　　　　　　18/29 = .621;

　　III.84-101　　(four-part); M = 11:
　　　　84-89　　(a) Aeneas' prayer to Apollo
　　　　94-98　　(c) reply of oracle;　　　　　　　　　11/18 = .611;

　　　　472-492　　(five-part); M = 13:
　　　　475-481　　(b) Helenus' farewell
　　　　486-491　　(d) Andromache's farewell;　　　　　13/21 = .619;

　　V.700-745　　(five-part); M = 28:
　　　　708-718　　(b) advice of Nautes
　　　　724-740　　(d) words of Anchises;　　　　　　　28/46 = .609;

　　VIII.370-406　　(five-part); M = 22.6:
　　　　374-386　　(b) Venus' words to Vulcan
　　　　395-404a　　(d) Vulcan's words to Venus　　　　22.6/37 = .611;

IX.224-280a (four-part); M = 35.4:
  234-245 (b) Nisus to Trojans
  257-280a (d) Ascanius to Nisus;   35.4/56.4 = .628;

X.846-871 (four-part); M = 16.2:
  846-856a (a) Mezentius reproaches himself
  861-866 (c) Mezentius speaks to his horse;   16.2/26 = .623;

XII.134-160 (four-part); M = 17:
  142-153 (b) Juno to Juturna
  156-160 (d) Juno to Juturna;   17/27 = .630.

The relative frequency of the four patterns illustrated above is as follows: (1) bipartite, 394; (2) tripartite (non-framework), 138; (3) tripartite framework, 276; and (4) four or more parts, usually interlocking, 236—a total of 1044 ratios.[42] Also, in the *Aeneid* as a whole, I-IV and VII-X are the major (a + c = 6223.4) and V-VI and XI-XII the minor (b + d = 3628.8); 6223.4/9852.2 = .632.[43] In each half the first four books are the major, the last two the minor, and if we view the *Aeneid* as a trilogy, with I-IV and V-VIII the major, another approximate Golden Mean ratio appears.

I said above that Vergil's use of the Fibonacci and the other mathematical series seems convincing evidence that the Golden Mean ratios throughout the *Aeneid* could not be the result of intuition or a subconscious desire for this particular proportion, but reveal a deliberate arrangement of the parts of each book. This conclusion is supported by the fact that in every book there is an amazing correlation between the narrative units, the short passages with ratios, and the component parts of the main divisions. As a typical example I give the second main division of Book VII with its tripartite subdivisions, and then present a chart of the passages containing proportions (with the ratios in parentheses).[44]

VII.286-640:

   (1)   286-322   Juno's lament

   (2)   323-539   The Allecto episode:

             323-340   Juno summons Allecto

             341-539   Threefold activity of Allecto

                  341-405   Maddens Amata

                  406-474   Maddens Turnus

                  475-539   Maddens hounds of Ascanius

   (3)   540-640   Outbreak of the war

The ratios in 286-640 are as follows:

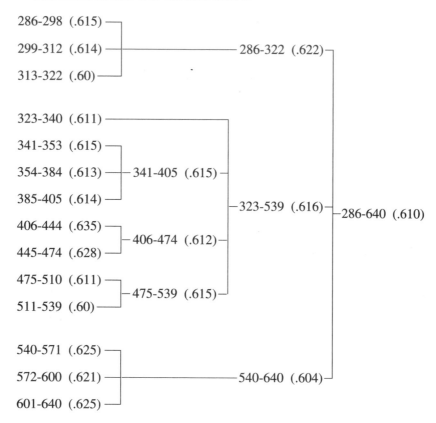

286-298 (.615)

299-312 (.614) ——— 286-322 (.622)

313-322 (.60)

323-340 (.611)

341-353 (.615)

354-384 (.613) — 341-405 (.615)

385-405 (.614)

                           323-539 (.616) — 286-640 (.610)

406-444 (.635)

445-474 (.628) — 406-474 (.612)

475-510 (.611)

511-539 (.60) — 475-539 (.615)

540-571 (.625)

572-600 (.621) ——— 540-640 (.604)

601-640 (.625)

In this one main division I find 21 proportions, the smaller narrative units combining into larger passages until we reach the main division, 286-640. The ratio in this passage (.610) is derived from 323-539 as major, which is framed by 286-322 and 540-640 as minor, and these three passages are identical with the tripartite subdivisions listed above. This section of *Aeneid* VII illustrates the manner in which the narrative units, small and large alike, coincide with the Golden Mean proportions. When such a striking correspondence appears in almost every division of every book throughout the *Aeneid*, we can only conclude that Vergil intentionally composed his narrative units in mathematical ratios and used them as building blocks to form the major or minor parts of the larger proportions.

V

We have seen *how* Vergil achieves the Golden Section by means of bipartite, framework, and alternating patterns and the extent to which he carefully combines structure and content in the proportions. To explain *why* Vergil composed his narrative by mathematical symmetry is more difficult—unless, with many Vergilian scholars, we believe that he was a Neopythagorean. Some, like Le Grelle and Maury, find number symbolism in both the *Georgics* and the *Eclogues*, especially in the use of the mystical numbers 333 and 666; Carcopino sees Pythagoreanism everywhere in the Fourth *Eclogue*; Boyancé and others believe that the *felix* passage in *Georg.* II.490ff., refers not to Lucretius but to Pythagoras; still others find Pythagoreanism in *Aeneid* VI.[45]

If we could accept the view that Vergil was a Pythagorean, his interest in—almost obsession with—mathematical ratios could be explained more readily; but I do not believe that his use of the Golden Section proves his Pythagoreanism, for a very simple reason: *he was not the only Roman poet to compose by Golden Mean ratios.* Catullus 64, the wedding of Peleus and Thetis enclosing the story of Ariadne, contains 31 examples of the Golden Section.[46] The books of Lucretius, in spite of the uncertainty of the text, are in proportion with I-IV the major (4675) and V-VI the minor (2747); 4675/7422 = .630; each book divides into four or five main divisions which produce ratios ranging from .608 to .620.[47] I have examined Book I in detail; it contains 62 ratios with a correlation between the proportions and the units of thought very similar to that appearing everywhere in the *Aeneid*. The structure of Horace's *Ars poetica* has been much debated, but there is general agreement that 1-294 concern poetry and 295-476 the poet and critic.[48] The major divided by the total, i.e., 294/476, equals .618, the perfect Golden Section, and the totals, 182, 294, 476, are multiples (by 14) of 13, 21, 34, the Fibonacci series which we find so often in the *Aeneid*.[49] Many Golden Mean ratios appear elsewhere in Horace's hexameter poems, e.g. *Sat*. I.10: 1-35, criticism of Lucilius (m = 35) and 36-92, Horace's own ideal (M = 57); 57/92 = .620. If we retain the disputed eight verses which most editors reject, the ratio changes to .570 (57/ 100); the presence of the Golden Section in the tenth satire thus strengthens the view that the initial eight verses are not by Horace. An interesting illustration of the four-part interlocked pattern occurs in *Sat*. II.3.82-295, where four vices are described: (a) avarice, 82-157 (b) ambition, 158-223 (c) self-indulgence including that of lovers (224-80), and (d) superstition (281-95). It is appropriate that avarice and self-indulgence, the two vices condemned by Horace so frequently elsewhere in his poetry, should form the major (a + c = 133); 133/214 = .621.

Mathematical symmetry based on the Golden Section thus seems a regular feature of the structure of Roman poetry in the first century B.C. In Book I of Lucretius I find an average of one ratio to every 18 verses, in Catullus 64, one to every 13.2 lines, but in Vergil's *Aeneid* one to every 9.4 lines. Vergil, with his interest in mathematics, has apparently carried the use of the Golden Section much farther than have the other Latin poets. But why?

The Golden Section has been viewed by many modern artists as one of the secrets of beauty and has played an important role in attempts to reduce beauty of proportion to a mathematical formula.[50] Almost a hundred years ago the German philosopher and psychologist Gustav Theodor Fechner conducted a most interesting experiment. By a kind of "pre-Gallup" poll he requested opinions, both likes and dislikes, from a large number of men and women about the innate beauty in a series of rectangles of different shapes. One rectangle had a far greater appeal than any other—absolutely no rejections and 35 per cent of the preferences—and this was the rectangle constructed on the Golden Section, with its sides 21 to 34, giving the exact ratio .618; the two rectangles closest to the "Golden Rectangle" each received over 19 per cent of the preferences.[51] Thus the "Golden Rectangle" and the two nearest to it in proportion received 74 per cent of the votes. This implies that the Golden Mean ratio has the most beauty on its own merits.

Did Vergil likewise believe that poetic passages or groups of passages bearing this same ratio, exact or approximate, had a mathematically formal beauty which could contribute to the perfection of his epic structure? I can think of no other explanation which will account for the presence of the Golden Section everywhere in the *Aeneid* and elsewhere in his poetry.

VI

Finally, are the proportions of significance for the text of the *Aeneid*? This is the most important question of all, and, in my opinion, the answer is a strong affirmative. The dozens and hundreds of Golden Mean ratios in the poem provide us with a control for a number of textual matters, and in this article I can enumerate these only briefly and in outline form; I shall give only a few of the many examples which illustrate each of the following categories.

1. Half-lines, such as we find in the *Aeneid*, appear in no other hexameter poetry, Greek or Roman. Some Vergilian scholars believe that these, or at least many of them, were deliberate, being rhetorically or emotionally effective[52]; but most think that Vergil in his final revision

would have replaced them all by whole lines.[53] In determining the ratios, was I to count the hemistichs as fractions or as whole lines? Since the *Aeneid* was meant to be heard, the half-lines would strike the ear as fractions of a line, and I therefore counted them as such to the nearest decimal, .2, .3, .4, .6, or .7. Then I discovered that dozens of proportions were more accurate with the half-lines so treated and included several perfect .618 ratios. E.g. in V.315-26 (m = 318-22), with 322 (*tertius Euryalus*) as .4, the ratio is .614 (7/11.4) but with 322 as a whole line, we have an impossible .583 (7/12); similarly, in X.1-17 (M = 6-15, Jupiter's speech), with 17 (*pauca refert*) as .2, the ratio is .617 (10/16.2), but with 17 as a whole line it changes to .588 (10/17). VIII.469 (*rex prior haec* = .2) appears in three short proportions (454-80, 454-93, 469-519) with ratios .618, .617, .618 respectively; with 469 as a whole line, the ratios are less exact: .630, .625, .608.

On this mathematical basis about three-fourths of the half-lines may be viewed as intentional. The remaining hemistichs not only provide more exact ratios if we count them as whole lines but also, when they are so treated, the major and the minor in these passages become numbers in the Fibonacci and the other Golden Mean series which appear so often elsewhere in the proportions in the *Aeneid*. These half-lines would probably have been replaced by whole lines in the final revision; e.g.:

Half-lines	Value as fraction	Passage with ratio	Ratio as half-line	Ratio as whole line	Numbers in Golden Mean series
II.640	.4	634-49	.610	.625	3, 5, 8 (× 2)
		624-49	.606	.615	5, 8, 13 (× 2)
		624-91	.623	.618	13, 21, 34 (× 2)
II.787	.7	771-804	.614	.618	13, 21, 34
III.640	.2	613-54	.631	.619	8, 13, 21 (× 2)
VIII.41	.4	36-65	.613	.621	11, 18, 29
		18-65	.612	.617	18, 29, 47
VIII.536	.4	520-40	.608	.619	8, 13, 21[54]

It thus seems possible to determine mathematically, to some degree at least, both the half-lines which were deliberate and those which would have been revised.

2. The ratios are helpful also for the problem of interpolations and so-called spurious passages. They support the rejection of individual lines which do not appear in the best MSS. and which are therefore bracketed as interpolations on MS. evidence[55]; they do *not* support the rejection by editors of lines or groups of lines on subjective grounds. E.g. Mackail speaks of the clumsy phrasing and the needlessness of IV.256-58; these lines occur in passages with the following ratios: .610, .625, .610, .60; with the three verses removed, the ratios become .544, .595, .659, .584. Ribbeck brackets VIII.42-49a, joining the remainder of 49 to the half-line in 41; with this passage omitted, five ratios change from .613, .612, .617, .618, .608 to .500, .550, .586, .591, .592. The removal of the many passages suggested by Ribbeck, Mackail, and other editors produces like results and in most instances any approximation to the Golden Section disappears.

Certain passages are lacking in the MSS., but we have ancient testimony concerning their authenticity. Most editors reject I.1a-1d, the four verses preceding *arma virumque cano* which, according to Suetonius (*Vita* 42), were removed by Varius after Vergil's death; but Hirtzel seems correct in accepting them as genuine. I include these four lines in my proportions as their omission changes three ratios from .623, .631, .628 to .592, .663, .640.[56]

The famous Helen passage in II.567-88, omitted in the best MSS. but preserved by Servius, has been considered spurious by Heinze and others, but many scholars defend the passage as genuine.[57] This episode, itself a Fibonacci ratio of .619 (13/21) is also the minor of a proportion which of course vanishes if we reject the passage.[58] In II.559-663, the major (44.8) is 588-633, the minor (29) is 559-87; the ratio of .607 (44.8/73.8) becomes .848 (44.8/52.8) with the passage omitted. Every main division of every book in the *Aeneid* reveals the approximate Golden Section. But in the third main division of II (634-729, Aeneas at home, as minor, framed by 559-633, Helen and Venus episodes, and 730-804, departure from Troy), where we have a ratio of .610 (147.7/242.3), the removal of the Helen passage produces an impossible .571 (125.7/220.3). It seems hardly likely that 35 out of 36 main divisions would contain the Golden Section and that the one exception would appear in this much discussed passage. We have here a strong argument for retaining the Helen episode as authentic. It is possible that Vergil was dissatisfied with the passage and planned to revise it, but the substitute version would necessarily have been similar and of the same approximate length.

3. Many editors suggest the transposition of lines or groups of lines. But if a passage is transferred from one series of proportions to another, several more or less perfect ratios may disappear. *We have here a useful control against editorial whim and wild conjecture.* E.g. in the catalogue of warriors in Book VII, Fowler suggests transposing six verses, 664-69, from Aventinus to Ufens, i.e. after 749.[59] Fowler's arguments have never impressed me as convincing, and certainly Aventinus, son of Hercules, should wear the lionskin of Hercules rather than Ufens. The Aventinus passage is a part of five proportions with ratios of .609, .622, .636, .618, .620, but with the removal of the six verses these same ratios become .529, .548, .579, .575, .568. If we add 664-69 to the Ufens passage, five other ratios change from .616, .615, .630, .615, .608 to .685, .653, .652, .634, .639. We have here additional arguments against Fowler's proposed transposition.

I have examined nine transpositions suggested by Ribbeck, Mackail, and others, with the following results. The removal of these passages from their contexts and their insertion elsewhere destroys 48 Golden Mean ratios and produces proportions ranging from .503 to .590 and from .650 to .780. Many examples of the Fibonacci series vanish, including five perfect .618 ratios. In other words, the mathematical structure of the poem gives no support to the transpositions proposed by modern editors but confirms the text of the poem as it has come down from antiquity.

4. I have in general followed the paragraphing in Hirtzel's Oxford edition, but I departed from it on occasion where the sense and the ratios indicated a different division; also, in many instances (especially in short passages) I made logical divisions where no paragraphs appeared. I now find that 187 of these new divisions, 99 between proportions and 88 between major and minor within proportions, are identical with the paragraphing in one or more of the following editions: Ladewig-Schaper-Deuticke-Jahn, Mackail, and Sabbadini.[60] This is an indication that these editions, and especially Mackail's, reproduce most faithfully the pattern of Vergil's thought, and they in turn support the proportions which are based on these same units of speech and narrative.

There are a number of places where editors disagree as to the beginning and the end of narrative units. Here the Golden Mean ratios may help to decide where the paragraphs are to be introduced. In Book II, e.g., the ratios favor new paragraphs after the lines listed in column 1 rather than those in column 2:

227 (J)	233 (S)
317 (JHS)	313 (M)
346 (S)	335 (JM)
436 (M)	437 (J)
623 (JHS)	620 (M)
670 (JHS)	672 (M)
795 (H)	794 (JMS)

The break between the end and the beginning of proportions indicates in many places where a paragraph might well be introduced into the text. Two important breaks occur after VIII.596,[61] and III.273; the latter concludes the second subdivision of the second main division of the book; 274 rather than 278 (JHS) marks the beginning of the Actium episode, and several proportions end with 273 or begin at 274. The ratios also favor paragraphs after the following: I.706 (not 708 with S); III.492 (not 491 with JM); V.853; VI.312, 449, 607, etc.

Mackail states that over-paragraphing which disturbs the continuity is to be avoided.[62] Most editors err in the opposite direction. A new edition of Vergil, based on narrative units as determined by the Golden Section, would combine the best features of the paragraphing in the Oxford text, Mackail's edition, and that of Sabbadini, and should produce the most readable text of the *Aeneid* to date.

5. Many suggestions made concerning Vergil's proposed revision of the poem appear in a new light when we consider the symmetrical arrangement of the proportions; e.g. Mackail thinks that Vergil contemplated discarding XII.593-611 and leaving Amata's end in silence.[63] I disagree. Amata's suicide is a necessary part of the tragedy of Turnus; his failure to face Aeneas leads her to believe him dead and she carries out her threat of XII.61-65.[64] Structurally also we should miss the episode; several Golden Mean ratios vanish, including that in the second subdivision of the second main section of the book, where the ratio changes from .621 to .718. An examination of other proposed revisions shows that they likewise disrupt the structure of the poem.

Book III has been called "the most incomplete and the least coherent in the whole Aeneid,"[65] and many believe that it would have undergone a thorough revision had Vergil lived longer; others have defended the book and have shown how the episodes were executed with meticulous care.[66] My own findings support the latter view. The close correlation of the narrative units and passages with ratios (as accurate as in I, IV, and VII, and more so than in V, VI, and XII) prove that Book III is constructed with far greater artistry than has usually been believed.

We shall never know what changes in wording and poetic expression Vergil would have made in his final revision, but the numerical symmetry of the *Aeneid* enables us to assert that he would *not* have done many of the things which have been suggested—such as the change of all half-lines to whole lines, the deletion of various passages, and the transposition of others. Thus, however fantastic the mathematical composition of the poem may seem, it favors a conservative treatment of the text.

There are two other aspects of the Golden Mean ratios which I touch upon very briefly.

1. The problem of the *Appendix Vergiliana*: the longer poems in the collection contain Golden Mean ratios, many of them in the Fibonacci series, and reveal also a close correlation between the proportions and the narrative units. This would mean Vergilian authorship if he were the only one who composed in this fashion. But when we find ratios corresponding to narrative units in Lucretius, Catullus, and Horace, we can not argue in favor of the authenticity of the so-called "minor poems."

Certain results may be stated, however. The structure of the *Ciris* and the *Aetna*, each with four main divisions, resembles that of Lucretius I rather than that in the books of the *Aeneid*, and this might argue against the post-Vergilian authorship of the poems. The ratio in the *Dirae* as a whole includes 104-83, the lines considered by many to be a separate poem named *Lydia*, and thus gives support to those who maintain that the poem is a unity.[67]

The *Culex* has the strongest claim to Vergilian authorship, not only on the basis of external evidence, but also from the standpoint of composition; it has a tripartite structure similar to that in the books of the *Aeneid*, and the three main divisions (1-41, prooemium; 42-201, the shepherd, the serpent, and the gnat; 202-414, lament of the gnat; tomb and inscription) combine in a framework pattern ($a + c = M = 254$) to produce the Golden Section; $254/414 = .614$. Also, the story itself as minor (158.6) is in proportion with the descriptive passages as major (255.4); $255.4/414 = .619$.[68] This procedure is so similar to that in the *Georgics* as a whole where the technical and the descriptive sections are in proportion that the *Culex* seems less likely to be the work of a later imitator or forger than the work of a youthful Vergil who later used the same alternating technique in the composition of the *Georgics*.

2. The metrical patterns analyzed by Knight several years ago seem to go hand in hand with the smaller proportions. Knight's patterns are based upon heterodyne (clash of ictus and accent in the fourth foot) and homodyne (agreement of ictus and accent in the fourth foot).[69] I have examined many of these in passages where Golden Mean ratios appear, and the interesting result is this: in numerous proportions, the major has one type of metrical pattern, the minor another.[70] We have here triple correlation between narrative units, mathematical symmetry, and metrical structure—an added argument to support my view that Vergil's procedure throughout was deliberate.

To conclude, these various aspects of the mathematical structure of the *Aeneid* show conclusively, I believe, how important the Golden Section is both to the structure and to the content of the epic. Our increasing knowledge of Vergil's method of composition by narrative units coinciding with Golden Mean ratios may lead to a new and better text of the *Aeneid* and perhaps even indicate more clearly the nature of the poem as he would have left it, had he lived to give it the final revision.

From *Transactions and Proceedings of the American Philological Association* 91 (1960): 184-220. Copyright © 1960 by the American Philological Assocation. Reprinted with permission of The Johns Hopkins University Press.

Notes
1. Freedom from academic duties in 1957-58 was made possible by a leave of absence granted by Princeton University and a Fellowship awarded by the John Simon Guggenheim Memorial Foundation.

2. C. H. Whitman, *Homer and the Heroic Tradition* (Cambridge [Mass.] 1958) 258.

3. G. E. Duckworth, "The Architecture of the *Aeneid*," *AJP* 75 (1954) 1-15.

4. Among other similarities and contrasts not listed in my 1954 article (above, note 3) the following may be mentioned:

> I. Trojans *laeti* (35), and VII. Trojans and Aeneas *laeti* (36, 130, 147, 288);
> I and VII. Juno laments her lack of power;
> I. Pictures of Trojan past, and VII. Statues of Latin past;
> I. Closing of gates of war (in Jupiter's prophecy), and VII. Opening of gates of war;
> II. Luxury of Priam's palace, and VIII. Simplicity of Evander's home;
> II and VIII. Venus as goddess appears to Aeneas;
> II. Gods against Troy, and VIII. Gods for Rome (at Actium);
> III. Apollo helps Aeneas, and IX. Apollo advises Ascanius;
> III. Astyanax-Ascanius equation (489ff.), and IX. Euryalus-Ascanius equation (297ff.);
> IV. Jupiter intervenes, and X. Jupiter refuses to intervene;
> IV. Aeneas sheds tears, but fate prevails (449), and X. Hercules sheds tears, but fate prevails (464 f.) [On the *lacrimae* of IV. 449, as the tears of Aeneas, see A. S. Pease, *Publi Vergili Maronis Aeneidos Liber Quartus* (Cambridge [Mass.] 1935) 367 f.; V. Pöschl, *Die Dichtkunst Virgils* (Innsbruck 1950) 76ff.];
> V. Cavalry display (*ludus Troiae*), and XI. Cavalry battle;
> V. Juno sends down Iris, and XI. Juno sends down Opis;
> V. Palinurus killed by minor deity (Somnus), and XI. Arruns killed by minor deity (Opis);
> VI. Meeting with Dido concludes Dido-story (IV), and XII. Avenging of Pallas concludes Pallas-story (X).

5. For details, see G. E. Duckworth, "The *Aeneid* as a Trilogy," *TAPA* 88 (1957) 1-10.

6. The temple to honor Octavian which Vergil describes in *Georg.* III. 13ff. is usually believed to refer to an historical epic in which he intended to praise the deeds of Octavian; cf. 16:

> in medio mihi Caesar erit templumque tenebit.

It is significant that Vergil achieved the same result in his mythological epic about Aeneas and the Trojans. When we view the *Aeneid* as a trilogy, it becomes apparent that his desire to have Caesar *in medio* has been fulfilled. Augustus is at the very heart and center of the poem (VI.788-807), and the central portion (V-VIII) concludes with the scenes on the shield describing his victory at Actium and his triumphs at Rome (VIII.675-728). It should be noted also that on the shield itself Augustus occupies the central position; cf. *in medio* (VIII.675).

7. I do not include among the contests the *ludus Troiae* (545-603) which is a separate spectacle not previously announced (cf. 64-70); see below, note 12.

---

8. See E. A. Hahn, "Vergil's Catalogue of the Latin Forces: A Reply to Professor Brotherton," *TAPA* 63 (1932) lxii f.

9. C. W. Mendell, "The Influence of the Epyllion on the *Aeneid*," *YCIS* 12 (1951) 222ff. For similar patterns in Catullus 64, the longer poems of the *Appendix Vergiliana*, the *Eclogues*, and the *Georgics*, see L. Richardson, Jr., *Poetical Theory in Republican Rome* (New Haven 1944).

10. The numerical symmetry in VI.56-123 (21, 6, 15, 5, 21) resembles that which appears in several of the *Eclogues*, e.g. in I:

5	1-5	Introduction
21	6-26	Good fortune of Tityrus
13	27-39	Tityrus in Rome
6		40-45 Benefits from the youth (focal point)
13	46-58	Tityrus at home
20	59-78	Plight of Meliboeus
5	79-83	Conclusion

Cf. Richardson (above, note 9) 122f.

11. See Pease (above, note 4) 30.

12. *Aeneid* V is often divided into two main sections: 1-603 (arrival and contests) and 604-871 (burning of the ships, departure, and death of Palinurus). But the *ludus Troiae* (545-603) was a spectacle, not a contest, and it was not included among the games announced by Aeneas in 64-70; also, it is the most Roman element in the book which begins the Roman and Augustan portion of the poem (V-VIII). If we look upon the *ludus Troiae* as a main division, V has the normal tripartite structure of the other eleven books: 1-544, arrival and contests; 545-603, *ludus Troiae*; 604-871, burning of ships and departure. The fact that the Trojan spectacle is short (59 verses) is not a valid reason against accepting it as a main division; the second section of VIII (370-453, the night scene of Venus and Vulcan and the making of the armor) is almost as short (84 verses).

13. The three parts of the first main division are here arranged in a recessed panel pattern (a b c b a), with the story of Sinon as the focal point. For the division after 227, see A. Cartault, *L'Art de Virgile dans l'Énéide* (Paris 1926) 181, 184.

14. See R. B. Lloyd, "*Aeneid* III: A New Approach," *AJP* 78 (1957) 136ff. K. Büchner, *P. Vergilius Maro, der Dichter der Römer* (Stuttgart 1956) 336, with less plausibility views the journey to Italy (506-47) and Scylla and Charybdis (548-69) as one episode and lists Drepanum (707-15) as the ninth and final episode.

15. The meeting of Aeneas and Dido in the underworld (VI.450-76) is, appropriately, the second of the three encounters (Palinurus, Dido, Deiphobus) in the second main division of VI (236-547).

16. I omit the ratio of m/M, as this can always be deduced from the slightly more accurate M/(M + m); e.g. if the major is 75 lines and the minor is 46 lines, M/(M + m) = 75/121 = .620, a variation of .002 from the perfect .618; the variation in the ratio m/M is about two and one-half times as great in the opposite direction, i.e. 46/75 = .613. It is therefore unnecessary to list both ratios. On this and other matters connected with the

Golden Section, I am deeply indebted for advice and assistance to Professor William Feller of the Department of Mathematics, Princeton University. Also, although I frequently refer to the perfect .618, there is of course no such thing; ½(√5 – 1) is an irrational number which approaches .618034. Since I carry the ratios only to the third decimal, I use the terms "exact .618" and "perfect .618" to distinguish the more exact ratio from approximate ratios such as .610 or .625.

17. On the Golden Mean ratio and the Fibonacci series, see R. C. Archibald, "Golden Section" and "A Fibonacci Series," *Amer. Math. Monthly* 25 (1918) 232-38, reprinted with corrections and additions in J. Hambidge, *Dynamic Symmetry. The Greek Vase* (New Haven 1920) 152-57; D. W. Thompson, "Excess and Defect: or the Little More and the Little Less," *Mind* 38 (1929) 43-55, reprinted in *Science and the Classics* (Oxford 1940) 188-213; cf. also V. Capparelli, "Ludus Pythagoricus e divina proporzione," *Sophia* 26 (1958) 197-210. On the Fibonacci series in nature, e.g. in the spirals of fir-cones and flowers (phyllotaxis), cf. D. W. Thompson, *On Growth and Form*[2] (Cambridge 1942) 2.921-33. For the use of the Golden Section in art and architecture, see M. C. Ghyka, "The Pythagorean and Platonic Scientific Criterion of the Beautiful in Classical Western Art," in F. S. C. Northrup (ed.), *Ideological Differences and World Order* (New Haven 1949) 90-116; M. Borissavlievitch, *The Golden Number and the Scientific Aesthetics of Architecture* (New York 1958). Earlier items are listed by G. Le Grelle, S.J., "Le premier livre des *Géorgiques*, poème pythagoricien," *Les études class.* 17 (1949) 145, note 4.

18. Le Grelle (above, note 17) 139-235.

19. Le Grelle regularly divides the total of major and minor by 1.618 to derive the major part, i.e., 420.5/1.618 = 259.88, a variation of a fraction of a line from the actual major (204-463a = 259.5). Since my procedure throughout is to divide the major by the total in order to derive the Golden Mean ratio (in this instance .617, a variation of .001 from the perfect proportion), the range of the proportions in the area of .618 is more easily discerned.

20. W. Wili, *Vergil* (München n.d.) 54.

21. The descriptive passages are the following: I.5b-42, 125-46, 231-58, 463b-514; II.1-8, 136-76, 319-45, 380-96, 458-542; III.1-48, 242-83, 284-94, 339-83, 478-566; IV.1-7, 116-48, 315-558. The section about the rebirth of bees (IV.281-314), although actually the beginning of the Aristaeus story, is itself of a technical nature and is not included among the descriptive passages. Also, the introductory statement of the plan of the poem (I.1-5a) and the final recapitulation (IV.559-66) are properly classed with the didactic portions.

22. These totals do not include IV.338, bracketed as an interpolation by Hirtzel and other editors. If we retain the verse, the ratio is not affected: 1352/2188 = .618.

23. Each of these parts likewise contains a ratio: (a) 281-386 (105) as M, and 387-452 (66) as m; 105/171 = .614; (b) 453-98 and 528-29 (48) as M, and 499-527 (29) as m; 48/77 = .623; (c) 530-47 (18) as M, and 548-58 (11) as m; 18/29 = .621. In the Aristaeus story I omit verse 338; cf. above, note 22. The ratios listed here are composed of smaller units also in proportion; I have detected 22 ratios in IV.281-558.

24. See above, note 10.

25. For discussion and bibliography, see Duckworth (above, note 3) 3f.; cf. also E. A. Hahn, "The Characters in the *Eclogues*," *TAPA* 75 (1944) 239-41.

26. For these three ratios I am indebted to Edwin Brown, now completing a Princeton doctoral dissertation, "Studies in the *Eclogues* and *Georgics* of Vergil."

27. In establishing my line totals I have omitted bracketed lines which do not appear in the best MSS., and I have counted the half-lines as fractions to the nearest decimal, e.g. 5/12 as .4, 7/12 as .6; see below, 213. Partial lines are treated likewise when speeches or episodes end within a verse.

28. In general I have followed the paragraphing in Hirtzel's Oxford text. Mackail (edition of 1930) seems correct, however, in indicating a paragraph after 288 rather than after 286 (Hirtzel) or 282 (Sabbadini,[2] 1937), and he is supported by several shorter proportions which end with 288 or begin at 289.

29. See below, 209, for a detailed analysis of this division.

30. It is strange that most editors fail to indicate a paragraph after 596, which ends the first subdivision of the third and final portion of Book VIII. Fairclough in his Loeb edition (1916) begins a paragraph with 597 in both text and translation, as do Humphries (1951) and Guinagh (1953) in their translations. The departure from Pallanteum ends with 596; 597ff. describe the arrival near Caere, many miles and certainly several hours on horseback from the site of Rome. The division after 596 is supported by the ratio in the third main section of the book and also by several shorter proportions.

31. Mackail seems correct in beginning a new paragraph with 256 rather than 260 (as do Hirtzel and Sabbadini); see Cartault (above, note 13) 725, 727.

32. This passage concerning Helen (II.567-87) is the minor (21 lines) of a larger proportion, the major consisting of 588-623, the Venus-Aeneas scene (34.8 lines); 34.8/55.8 = .624. The existence of these two ratios is an indication of the authenticity of the much discussed Helen passage; see below, 215, and note 57.

33. Sabbadini begins a new paragraph with 672.

34. Modern editors punctuate with a semicolon at the end of 939, but a full stop seems advisable as it places more stress on the *clementia* of Aeneas in 940, before he sees the sword belt. (See above, 186f., on the close relationship between the conclusion of XII and that of VI, where Anchises in 853 recommends both *clementia* and *iustitia*.) The beginning of 940: *et iam iamque* as a new sentence is recommended also by the fact that editors so frequently start a new sentence (and often a new paragraph) with *et iam* and *iamque*; for *et iam* (Hirtzel's text), cf. Aen. I.223, 302; II.254; IV.584, etc.; for *iamque*, cf. I.419, 695; II.132, 567, 730, 789, 801; III.135, 356, 521, etc. Finally, for three hundred years prior to 1775, almost every Vergil edition (including the Aldine, Juntine, Elzevir, and Ruaeus texts) had a full stop at the end of 939, and in several (e.g. the editions of 1533 and 1540 by R. Stephanus and the Venice editions of 1539, 1555, 1566, and 1582) line 940 began not only a new sentence but also a new paragraph. The punctuation with a full stop after 939 is found as late as the mid-nineteenth century, cf. e.g. F. Bowen (Boston 1842), J. G. Cooper[12] (New York 1863), E. Benoist (Paris 1872). The semicolon first appears regularly in Heyne's editions (1775, 1789, 1793), is adopted by Wagner, Forbiger, Conington, and Ribbeck in the nineteenth century, and accepted by present-day editors. There seems no reason to fol-

low Heyne here; both structure and sense favor the punctuation of the earlier editors. Perhaps in the future it might even be advisable to begin a new paragraph with 940; this would give proper emphasis to Aeneas' thought of *clementia*.

35. These two passages (I.34-75 and 76-101) are the major and minor respectively of the second proportion listed under the bipartite pattern.

36. Both Sabbadini and Mackail begin a new paragraph with 730.

37. The ratio is the same if we view a + b as the major, but the shift in thought seems greater at line 424. Also, it should be noted that 424-28 is minor both to 416-23 and 429-36; these smaller units produce two additional ratios of .615 (8/13).

38. As is regularly the case with larger units such as these, several smaller proportions combine to form the larger ratio. The smaller units in X.439-542 may be charted as follows (with the ratios in parentheses):

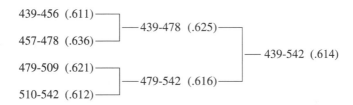

See below, 209, on VII. 286-640.

39. Venus' speech in 335-70a itself subdivides into a framework pattern, with 343-64 (b), story of Dido, Sychaeus, and Pygmalion (M = 22), framed by 335-42 (a), introduction, and 365-70a (c), conclusion (m = 13.4); 22/35.4 = .621. The thought in 365f. (*nunc ingentia cernes moenia surgentemque novae Karthaginis arcem*) takes us back to the first section (cf. 338; *Punica regna vides, Tyrios et Agenoris urbem*).

40. The totals in this ratio (16.8, 27.2, 44) are numbers in the Fibonacci series: 21, 34, and 55 × .8, hence the exact Golden Section.

41. This passage is so symmetrically constructed that the approximate Golden Section also appears if we view the three speeches (b + c + d) as major (82.6) and the framing passages concerning Aeneas' departure (a + e) as minor (53.6); 82.6/136.2 = .606.

42. Whereas I believe that Vergil deliberately introduced the Golden Section into all parts of the *Aeneid*, I do not maintain that he was conscious of the existence of all the 1044 ratios which I have detected. Many of these may have been, and undoubtedly were, the more or less accidental result of ratios in smaller or larger passages; e.g. if two passages appear side by side with a as minor and b as major in each, the combined passages may be in proportion in the familiar interlocked four-part pattern, with a + c as minor and b + d as major; conversely, if we have the framework pattern with b as minor enclosed by a + c, a and b or b and c are often in proportion.

43. The total lines of the *Aeneid* include I.1a-1d; see below, 215.

44. In the work of which this article is a summary I have prepared similar charts for each book of the *Aeneid*, with the passages in each chart keyed to the tables describing the various ratios.

45. See Le Grelle (above, note 17), especially 152ff., 159ff., 222ff.; P. Maury, "Le

---

Mathematical Symmetry in Vergil's *Aeneid*   **305** secret de Virgile et l'architecture des Bucoliques," *Lettres d'humanité* 3 (1944) 71-147, especially 111ff.; J. Carcopino, *Virgile et le mystère de la IVe Églogue*[2] (Paris 1943); P. Boyancé, "Sur quelques vers de Virgile (*Géorgiques*, II, v. 490-492)," *Rev. Arch.* 25 (1927) 361-79; P. Scazzoso, "Reflessi misterici nelle 'Georgiche' di Virgilio," *Paideia* 11 (1956) 5-28.

46. For the three main divisions of the poem I follow C. Murley, "The Structure and Proportion of Catullus LXIV," *TAPA* 68 (1937) 308: 1-51, wedding of Peleus and Thetis; drapery; 52-250, story of Ariadne; 251-408, drapery; wedding of Peleus and Thetis. 1-51 and 52-250 provide the major; 250/408. = .613. The ratios in the main divisions are tripartite framework, as follows: (a) 12-30, love of Thetis and Peleus (m = 19), enclosed by 1-11 and 31-51 (M = 32); 32/51 = .627; (b) 116-237, lament and curse of Ariadne; earlier speech of Aegeus (M = 122), framed by 52-115 and 238-50 (m = 77); 122/199 = .613; (c) 323-83, song of the Parcae (m = 60), enclosed by 251-322 and 384-408 (M = 98); 98/158 = .620.

47. E.g. Book I; I use Bailey's text of 1947, adding one line for each lacuna indicated. Leonard and Smith (1942) seem correct in viewing 921-50 as the introduction to the final division: 1-145 (a) and 635-920 (c) as minor (434), and 146-634 (b) and 921-1117 (d) as major (687) in a four-part interlocking pattern; 687/1121 = .613. In Book III (Bailey's divisions), 1-93 (a) and 94-416 (b) are the minor (417), with 417-829 (c) and 830-1094 (d) the major (677); 677/1094 = .619. Also in III the first three divisions are in proportion in a framework pattern, with 1-93 (a) and 417-829 (c) as major (505); 505/829 = .609; also 417-829 (c) is the major (412), with 830-1094 (d) the minor; 412/677 = .609.

48. For discussion and earlier analyses, see W. Wili, *Horaz und die augusteische Kultur* (Basel 1948) 316 (and note 2), 325; G. Stégen, *Les Épîtres littéraires d'Horace* (Namur 1958) 8, 166ff.

49. This ratio in the *Ars poetica* was discovered also by K. Gantar, "De compositione Horatii 'Epistulae ad Pisones,'" *Ziva Antika* 4 (1954) 277, but he does not mention the presence of the Fibonacci series.

50. Cf. G. Sarton, *A History of Science: Ancient Science through the Golden Age of Greece* (Cambridge [Mass.] 1952) 443; H. Weyl, *Symmetry* (Princeton 1952) 72; C. Ottaviano, "Nuove ricerche intorno all'essenza del bello," *Sophia* 22 (1954) 3-46.

51. See G. T. Fechner, *Vorschule der Aesthetik*[3] (Leipzig 1925) I.184-202.

52. Cf. e.g., J. Sparrow, *Half-lines and Repetitions in Virgil* (Oxford 1931) 23-46; W. W. Fowler, *Virgil's "Gathering of the Clans"*[2] (Oxford 1918) 93f.

53. See O. Walter, *Die Entstehung der Halbaerse in der Aeneis* (Giessen 1933) 67; Büchner (above, note 14) 404.

54. The ratios with the half-lines as fractions are the ones which I list in my tables. The other hemistichs which would probably have been changed to whole lines are II.767; III.661; IV.516; V.574, 653, 815; VI.835; X.284, 876; possibly II.623. Such a revision would have increased the number of perfect and almost perfect Golden Mean ratios.

55. E.g. two ratios in which II.76 occurs move from .615 and .606 respectively to .583 and .593 if we retain the verse. The other lines to be rejected as interpolations are III.230; IV.273, 528; VI.242; VIII.46; IX.29, 121, 151, 529; X.278, 872; XII.612-13. I

have omitted these verses in determining the ratios and have also ignored the second part of the line in V.595; XI.391, XII.218; these are more accurate when treated as hemistichs.

56. The ratios do not support the retention of III.204a-204c, and VI.289a-289d, as Vergilian.

57. Vergilian authorship is denied by R. Heinze, *Virgils epische Technik*[3] (Berlin 1915) 45ff.; E. Norden, *P. Vergilius Maro. Aeneis, Buch VI*[3] (Leipzig 1926) 261f.; H. Liebing, *Die Aeneasgestalt bei Vergil* (Kiel 1953) 44, 189f. Those who defend the authenticity of the passage include H. R. Fairclough, "The Helen Episode in Vergil's *Aeneid* ii. 559-663," *CP* 1 (1906) 221-30; J. Gerloff, *Vindiciae Vergilianae: Quaestiones criticae de Aeneidis libri II 567-588* (Jena 1911); M. M. Crump, *The Growth of the Aeneid* (Oxford 1920) 44ff.; F. W. Shipley, "The Virgilian Authorship of the Helen Episode, Aeneid II, 567-588," *TAPA* 56 (1925) 172-84; W. F. J. Knight, *Vergil's Troy* (Oxford 1932) 45ff.; L. R. Palmer, "Aris invisa sedebat," *Mnemosyne* 6, 3rd Ser. (1938) 368-79; and, most recently, Büchner (above, note 14) 331ff.; N. L. Hatch, "The Time Element in Interpretation of *Aeneid* 2. 575-76 and 585-87," *CP 54* (1959) 255-57. Palmer views the sacrilege committed at altars as a *leitmotif* of Book II; his conclusion (379) ". . . not merely that the Helen episode is authentic, but that it constitutes the spiritual crisis of the second book" seems correct.

58. See above, note 32.

59. Fowler (above, note 52) 46ff.; see also Mackail on 664-65.

60. E.g. in Book III new paragraphs agreeing with my ratio divisions begin in the texts of Jahn (J), Mackail (M), or Sabbadini (S) after the following verses: 101 (M), 131 (M), 153 (M), 171 (JMS), 208 (JMS), 244 (JS), 257 (M), 267 (S), 283 (M), 319 (JS), 343 (JM), 380 (M), 395 (M), 409 (M), 432 (M), 440 (M), 460 (M), 612 (M), 668 (S), 706 (M). Hirtzel (H) paragraphs at none of the above places. For specific points connected with paragraphing, see above, notes 28, 30, 31, 33, and 36.

61. See above, note 30.

62. *The Aeneid*, lxiii.

63. *The Aeneid*, 463; cf. 517 f.

64. Cf. XII.598f. See G. E. Duckworth, "Fate and Free Will in Vergil's *Aeneid*," *CJ* 51 (1955-56), 361f., and note 32.

65. Mackail, *The Aeneid*, 89; cf. Crump (above, note 57) 115: "Vergil had intended to give three years to the final revision of the Aeneid. . . . The most important task was the rewriting of III."

66. See e.g. Lloyd (above, note 14) 133-51, and "*Aeneid* III and the Aeneas Legend," *AJP* 78 (1957) 382-400.

67. The ratio in the *Dirae* as a whole is derived from four alternating parts: (a) 1-47 (b) 48-81 (c) 82-103, and (d) 104-83, with b + d the major (114); 114/183 = .623. For the divisions after 47 and 81 (1-47, imprecation by fire; 48-81, imprecation by water), see C. Van der Graaf, *The Dirae, with Translation, Commentary and an Investigation of its Authorship* (Leiden 1945) 133. Van der Graaf argues against the view that the so-called *Lydia* is a separate poem.

68. The actual narrative of the *Culex* is limited to 42-57, 98-122, 157-231a, and 372-414, a total of 158.6 verses.

---

69. See W. F. J. Knight, *Accentual Symmetry in Vergil* (Oxford 1939); cf. his "Table of Fourth-Foot Texture" which follows p. 108: Catullus in 64 and Lucretius in Book I had used fourth-foot homodyne 61.25 and 51.49 per cent respectively; Vergil in his authentic works reduces the amount of fourth-foot homodyne to the following percentages: *Eclogues*, 37.27; *Georgics*, 33.45; *Aeneid*, 35.95. The *Culex* has 35.59 per cent, and in this respect also is Vergilian. (On the *Ciris*, see Knight, 42, 53.)

70. The following ratios will illustrate the correlation of narrative units, mathematical symmetry, and metrical patterns (= "accentual symmetry"). I.124-141: 124-30, Neptune sees the effect of the storm (m = 7), 131-41, Neptune rebukes the winds (M = 11); 11/18 = .611. The minor consists of a heterodyne sequence, the major of a framework and alternation (a = heterodyne, b = homodyne):

m = 124-130; b a a a. a a a.

M = 131-141; a a a b a. a b a b a b.

II.402-36: 402-23, temporary success of Trojans (M = 22), 424-36, the Trojans slain (m = 13); 22/35 = .629. The major contains what Knight calls "one of the most elaborate symmetries of pure expanded alternation" (*Accentual Symmetry*, 66), the minor consists of simple alternations:

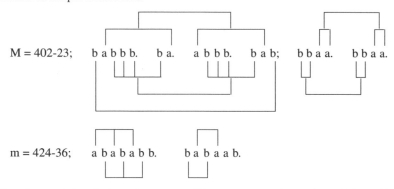

M = 402-23; b a b b b. b a. a b b b. b a b; b b a a. b b a a.

m = 424-36; a b a b a b b. b a b a a b.

The minor ends in a "released movement," i.e. two or more heterodynes followed by a homodyne (for the importance and the frequency of this pattern, see Knight, 48ff.). The conclusion of the minor with a released movement in 434-36 (a a b) indicates that the punctuation with a full stop after 436, as in Mackail's edition, is correct; see above, 217.

Dryden's Virgil
William Frost

The year 1982-1983 marked, and was celebrated as, the two-thousandth anniversary of Virgil's death in 19 B.C.; the year 1984 marks another Virgilian anniversary, the first partial appearance of the most read English translation ever made of his work. Dryden began publishing his Virgil translation in 1684—two eclogues only—and finished with his second (revised) edition of Virgil's complete works fourteen years later, in 1698. He began, that is, at age fifty-two or -three, and finished at age sixty-six or -seven—one way of looking at it. Or you could say he began in the last year of the reign of Charles II, for whom he had served, on occasion, as poetic spokesman; and finished in the tenth year of the reign of William III, to whom he refused to dedicate his Virgil despite his publisher's wish that he do so, but whose likeness he nevertheless could not prevent his publisher from building into the lavishly illustrated volume by an alteration of Aeneas's appearance in the plates inherited from Ogilby's 1668 Virgil—a blatant "nose-job" to make the profile of the hero instantly recognizable as the well-known physiognomy of the king. Virgil was thus part of Dryden's life; and part, too, of the life of late seventeenth-century England.

Part of Dryden's life. When he began translating Virgil in 1684, a beginning he followed up next year with some *Aeneid* extracts in the miscellany *Sylvae*, Dryden had completed all the work—or almost all—for which he is now most remembered: I mean by this his satires *MacFlecknoe* and *Absalom and Achitophel*, his "Essay of Dramatic Poesy," and his play *All for Love*. That play was one of almost twenty he had authored or co-authored by 1684; there were to be only three more from his pen, plus two operas long unremembered today. 1684 was also the year of his elegy to Mr. Oldham, now regarded by some as his finest single poem; and at least since the death of John Wilmot, second earl of Rochester, in 1680, Dryden had obviously lacked any possible rival for the title of the best living poet writing in English. He had in fact, in

1684, been officially the poet laureate for sixteen years. As an author, Dryden's situation was such, in 1684, that he could approach Virgil if not on equal terms—that would have been a presumptuous idea indeed—at any rate in some kind of momentarily comparable league.

But ten years later, when Dryden took his third step in Virgil translation by contributing a version of *Georgics* III to Tonson's Fourth Miscellany of 1694, his circumstances had radically altered in ways he could not have foreseen. Theatrically, he had already written his last play and was about to be replaced as England's leading playwright; Congreve, as he correctly foresaw and predicted in print, would shortly be *that*. Ideologically, from having been a national leader of triumphant public opinion in the Popish plot days of the early 1680s, Dryden had become no more than the clearly committed spokesman for a tiny discredited minority, those who were *both* practicing Roman Catholics (he had become one in 1685), *and* loyal to the dethroned James II rather than to the popular national hero King William, who would soon be seen, because of his military successes against Louis XIV, as "the first man in Europe." Financially and officially, Dryden had been for six years replaced in the laureateship and historiographer royalship—and in the emoluments from these two offices—by unworthy successors of a different political stripe. Poetically, his *The Hind and the Panther* (his longest poem yet written) was being thought notable, I suppose, chiefly for its unexpected result of catapulting into national attention a new Cambridge graduate of previously only local fame, Matthew Prior, aged twenty-three, co-author of "The Hind and the Panther Transvers'd to the Story of the Country-Mouse and City-Mouse." This was a burlesque response to Dryden, which many contemporary readers probably found as devastating as Buckingham's *Rehearsal* had been, sixteen years earlier, in responding to the "heroic plays" Dryden had been famous or infamous for in his thirties. Poetically, financially, officially—politically, theologically, and theatrically—Dryden in 1694 at age sixty-three, as he signs a contract with Tonson to translate Virgil's entire works, 12,000 lines of high-wrought Latin verse, is either in eclipse or at least in sharp decline. The comparison sometimes made with Milton, at least equally eclipsed under Charles II yet publishing *Samson Agonistes* at the same non-youthful age a generation earlier than Dryden, might be thought too honorific for either the quality of Dryden's verse or the nature of Dryden's project, translation rather than original new work; but what *Paradise Lost* represented to the Milton whose life circumstances had pushed him into an uncomfortable corner in 1674, it is easy to believe that Dryden's *Aeneis* was going to have to represent to Dryden.

Thus Virgil became *quite* a part of Dryden's life. But he would not have undertaken the commission if it had not been evident, both to him and to his publisher Tonson, that Virgil could also count in the life of England in the 1690s. Considering Dryden's situation as man and poet in his and the century's last decade, it was inevitable that his Virgil, like Milton's *Samson* a generation earlier, would be read in a certain light: not simply as the restatement, or re-presentation, of old Rome, but also as related, directly or obliquely, to much more recent, local, and urgent matters.

Obvious features of the 1697 Virgil would have reinforced such expectations at once. The *Georgics* dedication refers to specific circumstances of the Austro-Turkish war then going on. In *Pastorals* IV and *Aeneis* I Dryden smuggles into his translation loaded political terms like "banishment," "restoration," and "succession," and even adds a line (666) to *Aeneis* VIII that updates ancient political theory to accord with more modern notions of a "mixed state" where executive and populace share in decisions. Dryden's long dedication—i.e., preface— to his *Aeneis* derives partly from Segrais's preface to his 1668 French version, but unlike Segrais, Dryden introduces much political discussion with implied, if glancing, modern analogies. Segrais doesn't do this, his France being from our point of view politically an underdeveloped nation in comparison to Dryden's England.

Most obvious of all, many of the full-page illustrations in Dryden's Virgil have been coordinated with choices of dedicatees (the 101 plates were sold to 101 rich or noble donors whose names and coats of arms were affixed)—coordinated so as to place well-known contemporaries of Dryden, like the painter Kneller, in clearly appropriate Roman contexts, contexts sometimes politically pointed. The Laocoön plate, for example, symbolizing hopeless minority resistance to treacherous foreign incursion, celebrated a dedicatee who had been impeached eight years earlier for Roman Catholicism and high treason. (Are the serpents the House of Commons?) The Virgil volume was elaborately dedicated, furthermore, to three significantly chosen noblemen—*Pastorals* to Clifford, *Georgics* to Chesterfield, *Aeneis* to Normanby; significantly because each was in one way or another a noted *non*-Williamite—while in his *Aeneis* preface Dryden acknowledges the frequent and significant help in preparing the translation itself of another nobleman, Lauderdale, who had died abroad, a Jacobite author and exile, two years before Dryden's Virgil appeared.

Prefaces, notes, and the translation itself took extra life from contemporary concerns. When Dryden refers to Aeneas as "an elective [i.e., selected] King" who didn't claim the throne "during the life of his father-in-law" the allusion to father-in-law James and son-in-law William could hardly be clearer. When Dryden says that Virgil wrote at a time "when the Old Form of Government was subverted, and a new one established. . . . In effect by force of Arms, but seemingly by consent of the Roman people," he enunciates the interpretation of the 1688 Revolution held in his time by moderate Jacobites. And when he suggests that Virgil "shows himself sufficiently to be a Commonwealth's man" or terms him "still of Republick principles in his Heart," he leaves it open to his reader to reflect that Virgil's *translator's* heart was still loyal to a former order of things in the English nation. By contrast with Segrais, Dryden professed an aim "to make Virgil speak such English as he would himself have spoken if he had been born . . . in this present Age"—rather than, as Segrais had put it, "if he had been born a subject of our glorious monarch."[1] For Segrais, the monarch, for Dryden, the age, deserves a Virgil.

In the text of the translation, contemporary references or importations were sometimes less muted. At *Pastorals* I, 16 and 18, the advantages of true succession are reinforced by explicit rhetorical parallelism not in the original Latin. In *Georgics* IV, 134, the rivalry between two "monarchs" for control of the beehive (bee-rulers were taken to be male in Dryden's patristic period, instead of being seen as queens, as in our more feminist and zoologically authentic times) is made more topical by Dryden's having rendered Virgil's *melior* ("better") as "lawful": "Then to the lawful King restore his right." In *Aeneis* II, 752, "And on the Sacred Pile, the Royal Victim laid," Dryden's emotional epithet for Priam, "the Royal Victim"—language added to Virgil—deepens the implication of sacrilege as well as regicide, as though Priam were an earlier Charles I. At *Aeneis* VI, 824-5, Dryden, who two years earlier had turned a deaf ear to appeals to come up with a funeral elegy for Queen Mary, follows his predecessor the Jacobite Lauderdale's version (at that time unpublished—Dryden saw it in manuscript) in consigning the deceased queen to Virgil's Tartarus for usurping a throne rightfully her (half-) brother's; and a few lines further on, Dryden's and Lauderdale's addition "foreign" in the phrase "Imposing Foreign Lords" (line 846) invests her Dutch husband William with a similar whiff of brimstone. In *Aeneis* VII, King William's desire for a standing army is obliquely mocked in imagery of "boist'rous Clowns." Probably most blatant and anachronistic of all is Dryden's unliteral line 587 in *Georgics* III: "The savage Scythian, and unwarlike Dutch."

I would be giving a false impression, however, if I did not immediately add a reminder that Virgil's major poetry—however much a translator might call the original poet a "republican at heart"—can hardly be taken as subversive of the political order (gradual replacement of a republic by imperial monarchy), which was developing during the ancient poet's lifetime. In his *Pastorals* dedication to Clifford, Dryden may be somewhat rueful or even ironic when he says that young Clifford (unlike Dryden) "may live to enjoy the benefits" of William's recently concluded Peace of Ryswick; but it would not need a preternaturally alert reader of Virgil to realize that Virgil's early poetry, leading up to the conclusion of the *Georgics* and beyond, reflects ideals of "peace, unity and nationhood," to quote John Chalker's analysis,[2] emerging out of a long period of instability, cruelty, and danger. However many reservations Dryden's *Aeneis* dedication may evince toward the Augustus whom Chetwood, in the Life of Virgil published as part of the Virgil volume, even treated as the Oliver Cromwell of his times,[3] it remains true that neither the preface nor the translation can possibly be read as incitements to the "civil discord" mentioned in Dryden's version of some phrases in *Eclogue* I, 71-72: "What dire effects from Civil Discord flow." At an early point in the translation, when the English, but not the original Latin, attributes to the "Ignoble Crowd" an "innate Desire of Blood," Virgil seems to be being made more anti-populist than he probably was. Later on, in Book VII, the picture of the anarchic Bacchantes is so rendered by Dryden as to emphasize a continuing order-disorder contrast; and in Dryden's preface the monarch Latinus, who resists these Bacchantes like the wise orator calming the crowd in Book I, is contrasted to a certain tyrant named Mezentius, who figures in the last half of the epic. Dryden's language about Mezentius, who he says was "expell'd" because he "govern'd arbitrarily," would (I suggest) have been slightly easier for a Williamite to read as alluding to James II than for a Jacobite to take as a cautionary message to William III. (I may add that I have just finished reading Frank Kermode's book, *The Genesis of Secrecy*, and am perhaps specially sensitive to possible enigmas embedded in kerygmas.)

Also, against Dryden's choice of non-Williamite, or even anti-Williamite, dedicatees for the *Pastorals*, *Georgics*, and *Aeneis*, we do have to set his mention, in very friendly terms, of three other noblemen in his "Postscript to the Reader" at the end of the whole volume. These three were the Earl of Peterborough, the Earl of Derby, and the Duke of Shrewsbury—all pro-Williamite peers of long standing, and the third, an ex-Roman Catholic, a holder of high office under William. Whatever reservations Dryden may have had about Augustus Caesar as a grasper of supreme power by force—in his dedication he uses the phrase "though of a bad kind [nevertheless] the very best of it"—in his notes to *Aeneis* V he links poet, patron, emperor, and literary father, and a note on Book VI portrays Virgil as tactful in condemning Augustus's imperial course and as using "the authority of a parent" (Virgil was in fact all of seven years older than Augustus) to convey peaceable advice to the ruler.

If that sort of stance toward poetry vis-à-vis politics strikes us today as a little complacent, or even blindly romantic, something else Dryden says in his *Aeneis* dedication may please us better. Comparing his own preface with its model, Segrais's thirty years earlier, Dryden notes the contrast between the rather freely political nature of much of what he says as compared with the more ideologically inert French preface; and he remarks, only a decade after Louis XIV showed how arbitrary he could be by revoking the Edict of Nantes and causing the expulsion of many French Protestants, that he is able to dwell on matters which Segrais "durst not touch: for 'tis dangerous to offend an Arbitrary Master; and every Patron who has the Power of Augustus has not his Clemency." These words speak volumes for Dryden's view of the government of William III. If it is true that all the evidence, on balance, as W. J. Cameron puts it, seems to show that Dryden, like Pope later on, "owed deeply felt allegiance to the *de jure* 'King over the water' while holding strong opinions about the necessity for a stable society that forced them into equally strong allegiance to the *de facto* monarch of England," if Dryden was indeed, in George Watson's words, perhaps the first Jacobite to realize that the 1688 Revolution was irreversible,[4] then the obvious initial anti-Williamite aspects of the 1697 Virgil volume might perhaps have served a purpose similar to one purpose of the disrespectfully farcical treatment of Charles II at the opening of *Absalom and Achitophel*—that is, to assert the poet's detachment and independent status as commentator so as to leave him all the freer to celebrate order without the odium of subserviency. Some people have said that Dryden so framed the Virgil volume politically that there would be "something in it for everybody." To this consumer-oriented analysis I obviously prefer the contrast W. J. Courthope drew eighty years ago between the *Absalom* and the Virgilian periods of Dryden's career when he wrote that in the 1690s the poet's "sense of personal dignity must have been raised by the consciousness that, in the sphere of letters, he was no longer the poet-attorney of the Crown, but the free representative of the nation."[5]

Politically then, insofar as it *had* a political component, Dryden's Virgil could be said to represent a new departure for the poet, a complicated adjustment of poetry and translation to a changing national scene. I now pass on to another aspect of the poet's situation, one which has implications well beyond Virgil or William III, I mean the financial aspect. Dryden was in fact able to realize by his four years' labor (1693-97) on the bulk of Virgil's poetry an income quite comparable to what the stage and the laureateship would have brought him per annum during the best years of the Drydenian ascendancy, as the early 1680s might be called; and that income is a fact significant well beyond Dryden's particular pocketbook or career. It signalizes a technological change of truly McLuhanesque dimensions. How *did* poets—how did *writers*—make a living in the sixteenth and seventeenth centuries on the threshold of modern times? Up to the 1690s there had been three answers (unless the writer had, like the Earl of Rochester, independent means): the stage (Shakespeare's route), patronage (Spenser's), or politics. Up to the 1670s and '80s an author could support himself, if at all, only by the first two of these means; in the last quarter of the century, politics, the attempt by print to sway public opinion, began to open up a new avenue, as was shown clearly by King Charles's in effect commissioning Dryden's satire *The Medal* just after the great success of *Absalom and Achitophel*. Events like these of course foreshadowed much in the subsequent professional literary careers of Addison, Defoe, and Swift.

Beginning with the Dryden-Tonson miscellany of 1684, however, in which the first brief Virgil versions by Dryden saw the light of print, it became apparent that a reading—and buying—public now existed, and that this public was keenly interested in verse translations of ancient classic poetry by versifiers of a quite different order of competence from the prosaic and literal John Ogilby, who had published well-known and widely circulated versions of Virgil and Homer in the 1650s and '60s. A decade later, Dryden's Virgil became the first instance in history of a work of imaginative literature, costing years of a distinguished author's time and effort, to be directly funded by a reading public, rather than by theater audiences, noble patrons, or a political faction; and the £1,400 which the enterprise brought its author turned out to be the direct harbinger of the £9,000 which, two decades later, would not only reward Pope handsomely for his Homer, but also, by so doing, free him, for life, from dependence on any source of income but his pen, earning him the sobriquet sometimes bestowed on him of "the first English man of letters."

I have stated the matter bluntly and starkly, because it seems to me a blunt and stark economic and sociological fact. This seems so despite the fact that Dr. Johnson's calling the Virgil "the first considerable work for which this expedient [subscription publication] was employed"[6] takes no account of Tonson's having brought out the fourth edition of *Paradise Lost* by this method in 1688, or the further fact that subscription publication began with an etymological work in 1617 and by the 1690s had already been used for sermon collections, atlases, algebras, music books, polyglot Bibles, Bible commentaries, royal genealogies, various classics, and the works of Charles I, as well as—in direct ancestry to Dryden—John Ogilby's second edition, 1654, of *his* Virgil (whose plates later adorned Dryden's), *and* Ogilby's edition of the Latin original, also with these plates, for three-quarters of Ogilby's subscription list in 1658, *and* Ogilby's large illustrated folio translations, the *Iliad* and the *Odyssey* in 1660 and 1665. We must put in these forerunning events to keep the record straight and to account for the obvious inspiration of Tonson's and Dryden's breakthrough; but that it *was* a breakthrough nonetheless Alexandre Beljame's pioneer study of the public and men of letters in the Augustan Age (1660-1744) amply showed when published a century ago. Whatever Ogilbys, sermon-writers, atlas-makers, and assorted miscellanea may have preceded him, Dryden was the first author of any stature as an author of original works to attempt such a method, and his success with it is symptomatic of a change in the conditions of authorship, a change as significant, I would say, as the change occasioned by the introduction of reading and writing on a general scale in fifth century B.C. Athens: the first appearance in history of a reading public—a general, non-specialized, non-priestly reading public—as can be shown by the evidence of scenes on contemporary Attic vases, as well as by such other evidence as a reference to a place "where the books are on sale" in a fragment of a contemporary of Aristophanes, dated probably about 425 B.C.[7] I see the history of these matters in terms of two revolutions, the Periclean (to use a catch-phrase) in antiquity, and the Gutenbergian in post-medieval times; and the fulfillment of the Gutenbergian, the turning point at which the potentialities of print first became apparent, is signalized best, I believe, by Dryden's Virgil. Just in case a new McLuhanesque revolution impends, as, for the first time in England, breakfast television is challenging the morning newspaper, we might take a retrospective glance at this aspect of the enterprise in the mid-1690s.

Dryden's Virgil, then, had the effect of putting the English-speaking people in the forefront of all peoples in respect to demonstrating that print could mean a new relationship between an author and a large reading public, not a viewing public or a theater-going public, but a reading public—a new relationship in which the author could go to the public for support rather than to a noble patron, the government, the theater audience (after all, a limited local group), or a political party. The careers of very influential authors—Voltaire, Goethe, Byron, Victor Hugo—are foreshadowed by the notable, unprecedented financial success of Dryden's Virgil, which was also an important work, quite apart from its financing, in the history of Virgil-translating, classics-translating, and translation in general.

Strictly speaking, English Virgil translation began at least as early as Chaucer, if not among the Anglo-Saxons or Anglo-Normans; but the first milestone in the British Isles is Gavin Douglas's famous rendition of the *Aeneid* into Middle Scots. Douglas completed his version on July 22, 1513, and it was still admired in the 1690s as indeed it is still admired today. Douglas wrote in quasi-Chaucerian rhymed couplets. Later in the sixteenth century Surrey incorporated a lot of Douglas's work in his own versions of *Aeneid* Books II and IV, a landmark because in writing them Surrey invented, or discovered, blank verse for England. Rhyme, however, remained the standard vehicle for the many English Virgils, which by Dryden's time had included complete *Aeneids* by the Elizabethan team Phaer and Thyne and the Caroline John Vicars; five complete versions of the *Eclogues* and three of the *Georgics*; and numerous translations—some significant—of a single book, poem, or passage from Virgil. Altogether at least fifty-six Englishmen or Scotsmen before Dryden had tried their hands at translating at least *some* Virgil, and since none of them, beginning with Surrey, hesitated to borrow from others, and since a good version of a phrase or line was often regarded, I think, as being just as much a discovery as a creation—you couldn't put a patent or copyright on the Straits of Magellan—it is hardly surprising that Dryden's version turns out to include identifiable traces of the work of many previous Virgilians who translated into English, or Middle Scots, or even French (it has long been known that he studied Segrais), or Italian (he mentions the famous Italian version of Annibale Caro in his preface). With Lauderdale, whose help he acknowledges in his preface, "traces" is an understatement; for the *Aeneid*, at least, he used Lauderdale so extensively that the great question for scholarship may well be not so much whether a particular Dryden passage derives from Lauderdale, as which manuscript of Lauderdale Dryden was looking at! Lauderdale's heirs brought out two printed editions of Lauderdale's Virgil some years after the deaths of both translators; these editions differ from each other and also (since Lauderdale, like Pope later, was a compulsive reviser of his own works) from the seven manuscripts which, lodged in various libraries or in private hands, today contain small or large parts of the Earl's Virgil translation in pre- or post-printed form.

Whichever manuscript he looked at, there is no question that Dryden often depended heavily for initial suggestions (e.g., rhyme words) on the Earl; and there is little question that Dryden had had a look at the work of at least forty of the fifty-six previous Virgil translators. There is a question, however, about the earliest of these, Bishop Gavin Douglas, that distinguished member of a distinguished Scottish clan. Modern scholarship has tended to suppose that Dryden did not know Douglas, whose approach to Virgil's sense is obviously more respectfully literal than Dryden's, and whose poetic methods as a composer of rhyming couplets show the influence of Chaucer at Chaucer's most garrulous, whereas Dryden's are strictly in the tighter tradition of such influential seventeenth-century Virgil translators as John Denham, Edmund Waller, and the brilliant minor poet Sidney Godolphin, who shared with Waller the authorship of a version of *Aeneid* Book IV, the Dido story, published in 1658. Since almost two centuries—not to mention two distinct languages—separate Dryden and Douglas, and since we know that Douglas's *Eneados*, though still reputable, was hard to come by in the 1690s (it was long out of print), the notion that Douglas had an impact on Dryden seems initially improbable.

I am, however, suspicious of this improbability. There is lots of evidence—some of it supplied by Dryden himself, evidently proud of his own thoroughness—that Dryden made at least some use of translators much less talented or devoted than Douglas; there is some evidence that Lauderdale, Dryden's most immediate predecessor, looked at Douglas, and a lot of evidence that Surrey did, back in the sixteenth century. Therefore I have noted with interest enough cases of Dryden-Douglas parallels—including parallels in which both poets depart from, or at least modify, Virgil's plain sense in similar ways—to raise, I think, a real suspicion that Dryden had somehow got his hands on a copy of the Scotsman's work.

The most interesting evidence is linguistic, parallels of language appearing despite the differences between English and Middle Scots as languages, and within the linguistic evidence the two oddest bits are (I think) the most revealing. Virgil, in *Aeneid* Book II, says that the serpents that slay Laocoön and his sons spray Laocoön's robes with "black venom" (*atro veneno* in line 221) which Dryden translates in his line 291 as "blue venom," a color selected by no previous English translator of Virgil and never used by anybody to translate *ater* from Latin except possibly in expressions like "black and blue." Even more mysterious is Dryden's translation of *sacra* 'sacred things' in Book VIII, line 665, as "odorous gums" in a passage of the Latin about whose meaning many commentators seem uncertain, though none, as far as I know, has ever suggested "gums." In the first case, Gavin Douglas in his Middle Scots says that the serpents were "blaw with venom," meaning that their cheeks were swollen, blown up, with venom; in the second, he says that the matrons in the ritual procession were "Ledand" (leading) "gammys festuall," meaning (no doubt) that they were conducting ritual games, an interpretation that might just possibly fit *ducebant sacra* 'led sacred things' in Virgil's line 665. It looks to me as though Dryden took his "blue" in "blue venom" from the first Douglas translation, and from the second his "gums" in the line "odorous gums in their chaste Hands they bear." In the context of much other suspicious evidence about the translations, these details seem to me the least likely to have arisen from mere coincidence; and in fact if Dryden doesn't get his "blue" in "blue venom" from Douglas's "blaw" or his "odorous gums" from Douglas's "gammys," then I can't account for either of these very specific details in his version. "Odorous" seems to me especially a smoking pistol; it is a kind of midrash, or interpretative addition, to Douglas's potshot, or what Dryden thought was Douglas's potshot, at the meaning of some cryptic Latin. "Gums" by itself would be too puzzling; "odorous" ones could be frankincense, or something similar.

There is evidence, then, that Dryden's Virgil in some way subsumes aspects of the previous history of British Virgil-translating up to and especially including his own time. I say, especially including his own time since he was himself responsible for some of the most recent work he sponsored, for example, a joint version of the ten eclogues in 1684, to which (as I began by mentioning) he himself contributed two, the fourth and the ninth. Others who contributed were John Caryll, uncle of the dedicatee, twenty-eight years later, of *The Rape of the Lock*; and Sir William Temple, who preferred to have his contribution remain anonymous, though he did let Swift publish it among his Works, which Swift edited, some years after his death. In Dryden's 1684 collection, this contribution appeared under the rubric "Translated, or rather Imitated, in the Year 1666," possibly because Temple, envoy in Brussels in 1684, preferred to have himself thought of as doing something more important on the Continent than rendering Virgil's tenth eclogue in elegant couplets. In any event, Dryden somehow extracted the contribution from Temple, and several others from other translators, titled or untitled, and later incorporated good bits of his collaborators' work in his own eventual complete Virgil, as he incorporated bits of the work of forty or fifty others, and as later translators of Virgil into English were sometimes to incorporate bits of *his*. As one might expect, this indebtedness to Dryden has been shown to be especially heavy in certain eighteenth-century Virgil translations; but even in our time I have come across a passage in which the standard twentieth-century Loeb version runs for an entire clause word for word identical with Dryden, despite its being theoretically in the most literal prose.

From the moment of its first appearance Dryden's Virgil was—and has continued to be—subject to vigorous attacks, both general and specific. Up to now its most distinguished antagonists, by far, have been Swift and Wordsworth. Swift apparently wrote all or most of his *A Tale of a Tub* during the 1690s (it came out in 1704), and some of the stimulation for that brilliant work is sometimes thought to have been a supposedly slighting remark—"Cousin Swift, you will never be a poet"— that Dryden is said to have made about a turgid early ode, Swift's first publication, which came out in 1692.[8] Whether the remark was ever made or not, what *is* clear is that *A Tale of a Tub*, locating itself ostensibly in the late 1690s, about the time Dryden's Virgil appeared, takes aim at Dryden (in his late sixties, Swift being then in his late twenties) as the target of choice to be toppled, and pays eloquent tribute to the instant prominence of Dryden's Virgil by the superb wit and imaginative energy of its reiterated assaults—the drama of the situation being of course much enhanced for us today by Swift's double role as a youthful Williamite (the king is supposed to have offered him a captaincy in the Cavalry) and as a lifelong proponent of the Anglicanism Dryden had so notably renounced for Roman Catholicism during James II's recent reign. Tremendously popular and at once widely read, the *Tale*'s intended demolition fell short of actually demolishing and may even have contributed to Dryden's sales. By 1710, when the *Tale*'s fifth edition came out, equipped this time with footnotes, the translation supplied for the *Aeneid* motto on Section I's opening page turned out to be Dryden's.

As for Wordsworth, he was like Swift a youthful—well, fairly youthful—revolutionary a century later when Scott was preparing his great edition of Dryden's works and Wordsworth wrote to Scott that "whenever Vergil can be fairly said to have had his *eye* upon his object, Dryden always spoils the passage."[9] This incisive-sounding put-down may well have been prompted by a remark in Dryden's *Aeneis* preface where (echoing Segrais) he says that Virgil's *mollis amaracus* in *Aeneid* IV cannot be translated literally: "if I should Translate it Sweet Marjoram, as the word signifies, the Reader would think I had mistaken Virgil: for those Village-words, as I may call them, give us a mean Idea of the thing." And so, like Segrais, he changes marjoram (an herb used in cooking) to myrtle, a plant symbolic of Aeneas's mother, the goddess Venus, and hence (perhaps) more appropriate to the passage at the end of Book I, where Cupid is being substituted for the boy Ascanius at Dido's dinner table. All this may well have justified Wordsworth's ire. "Village words" indeed!

Many other objections to Dryden's Virgil have arisen from a refusal to consider, or to accept, Dryden's premises; he stated explicitly that he was steering "betwixt the two extremes of Paraphrase and literal Translation" and gave notice that "Some Things too I have omitted, and sometimes added of my own." "But by what Authority?" asked Luke Milbourne angrily, in his *Notes on Dryden's Virgil* (1698), detailing objections to nearly six hundred separate passages in the *Pastorals* and *Georgics* and supplying many alternatives in the form of his own or Ogilby's renderings (he says of Ogilby's that "The words are not so well plac'd, but his *meaning* is the *same* with *Virgil's*"). If Dryden renders *obscura ferrugine* ('dusky darkness') by "Iron Clouds," Milbourne objects that *obscura Ferrugo* was never so construed before; if he renders *Lucifer* as Hesperus, this shows Dryden can't tell the morning from the evening star; if Dryden's Orpheus, crossing the Styx, sits "in the leaky Sculler," this must mean "in Charon's lap," since Milbourne either doesn't know, or won't admit, that the noun "Sculler" can mean vessel as well as navigator.[10]

The Milbourne tradition, with less spleen but using at least a couple of Milbourne's illustrations, was later carried on by Pope's friend Spence in *Polymetis* (1747), an illustrated mythology book containing numerous objections to Dryden—for example that the Dryden-Lauderdale description of the Minotaur as "the lower part a Beast, a Man above" (a description added to Virgil in *Aeneis* VI, 37) is the reverse of the usual assumption.[11] (Spence does not allow for allegorizing.) In more recent times Dryden's excellent editor Noyes has objected to Dryden's anachronistic introduction of a "wheel" (i.e., spinning wheel) into a domestic scene in *Georgics* IV.[12]

A continuing line of attack on the Virgil has been for crudity, vulgarity, or (the reverse) over-gentility, in situations where an attacker assumes that delicacy, reverence, reticence, or bluntness would have fitted Virgil, or his subject matter, better than what Dryden has given us. Spence dislikes such "low expressions, and mean lines" as occur when Dryden's Juno "sail[s] on the wind" (at *Aeneis* XII, 243) or his Apollo "bestride[s] the clouds" at a point where the more decorous Loeb has him "cloud-enthroned" (IX, 873).[13] More recently E. M. W. Tillyard judges that by adding a graceful walk, and dishevelled hair that reaches the ground, to Virgil's account of Venus revealing herself to Aeneas (*Aen.* I, vv. 402-09), Dryden "transforms a goddess into a competitor in a beauty competition."[14] Another commentator begins an account of Dryden's "coarsening of [Virgil's] tone" by stigmatizing Dryden's heightened picture of Cassandra's sufferings at the hands of Greek soldiers (*Aeneis* II, 543-51) as "newspaper work in verse."[15]

The fact is, however, that publication records show Dryden's Virgil to have long been a punching bag that springs back after being hit, or a corpse that refuses to stay dead. By 1710, the year of *A Tale of a Tub*'s fifth edition, the third edition of Dryden's Virgil had been out one year; by the time of Spence's *Polymetis* in 1747, the seventh had already appeared. By the eighteenth century's end, Dryden's Virgil had appeared at least twenty-four times, mostly in London but also in Glasgow, Edinburgh, and Perth. Nineteenth-century editions, numbering more than fifty, included appearances in Baltimore, Philadelphia, New York, and Chicago, while its eleven twentieth-century reincarnations include five in the World's Classics, three in editions of Dryden's poems, and a one-volume reprint in 1961.

I have been speaking of the total Virgil—*Pastorals*, *Georgics*, and *Aeneis*. The *Aeneis*, the heart and body of Dryden's Virgil, began to come out on its own in Baltimore in 1818, and has since appeared independently upwards of thirty times, including a polyglot French-Italian-English *Aeneid* in Paris and London in 1838, the Harvard classics edition in 1909, the Heritage Press and Limited Editions illustrated reprint in 1944, Robert Fitzgerald's annotated edition in 1965, and a cheap paperback in 1968 and 1980. Considering its well over one hundred appearances since 1697, it seems fair to say of Dryden's *Aeneis*—called a "distinguished failure" in the only twentieth-century book devoted to it[16]—that, except for its two successors (and imitators), Pope's *Iliad* and *Odyssey*, and except for the 1611 King James Bible, it is far and away the most successful version, judged by continuous reader acceptance in the face of much spirited competition, of any foreign major work ever translated into English. Its one obvious Virgilian rival in a modern language, Annibale Caro's Italian version (which Dryden studied) seems to have been reprinted distinctly less than half as frequently, despite having come out more than a century before Dryden's and despite having been used, till the early twentieth century, as a textbook in Italian schools. (Perhaps many Italians tend to read Virgil in Latin.) My own guess is that except for "Alexander's Feast" and the "Song for St. Cecilia's Day" Dryden's *Aeneis* has probably been more often read, and given more readers more pleasure, than anything else Dryden ever wrote.

Perhaps I may instance my own experience. Two long poems that, through deficiency of education, I had never read even until after getting a Master's Degree at age twenty-five, happened to be Wordsworth's *The Prelude* and Dryden's *Aeneis*, and each came to me as a big surprise. I approached *The Prelude* with reverence because of the impression made by many of the author's shorter poems, and was soon amazed at how anyone could write so much, and so flatly, and still retain any readers; after long poems like *Troilus and Criseyde* or *Paradise Lost*, *The Prelude* initially seemed to me the biggest lead balloon in English literature. Later, of course, I got to know it better and came to see some of its strengths; but my first impression was of almost incredible unreadability.

My experience with Dryden's *Aeneis* was the opposite. Assigned it in a graduate class, I approached it with skepticism, having liked the original well enough when an adolescent to regard the *Aeneid* as essentially untranslatable, and knowing Dryden well enough to suppose that he was probably the wrong man to have tried the impossible task anyway.

The reading was, however, the reverse of boring; the version was electric with life. How can I express my sense of discovery better than by instancing a passage which for Virgil, and I think for Dryden too, was invested with meaning and emotion: the picture of Charon in the sixth (Dryden's favorite) book of the *Aeneid:*

> Hence to deep *Acheron* they take their way;
> Whose troubled Eddies, thick with Ooze and Clay,
> Are whirl'd aloft, and in *Cocytus* lost:
> There *Charon* stands, who rules the dreary Coast:
> A sordid God; down from his hoary Chin
> A length of Beard descends; uncomb'd, unclean:
> His Eyes, like hollow Furnaces on Fire:
> A Girdle, foul with grease, binds his obscene Attire.
> He spreads his Canvas, with his Pole he steers;
> The Freights of flitting Ghosts in his thin Bottom bears.
> He look'd in Years; yet in his Years were seen
> A youthful Vigour and Autumnal green.
> An Airy Crowd came rushing where he stood;
> Which fill'd the Margin of the fatal Flood.
> Husbands and Wives, Boys and unmarry'd Maids;
> And mighty Heroes more Majestick Shades.
> And Youths, intomb'd before their Fathers Eyes,
> With hollow Groans, and Shrieks, and feeble Cries:
> Thick as the Leaves in Autumn strow the Woods:
> Or Fowls, by Winter forc'd, forsake the Floods,
> And wing their hasty flight to happier Lands:
> Such, and so thick, the shiv'ring Army stands:
> And press for passage with extended hands.
>
> (lines 410-32)

If the power of poetry is both to present a subject matter in such a way that it comes alive and at the same time to impart a sense that more is meant than meets the eye—that revisiting these cadences will reward a reader with news unsuspected on a first reading, with "news that stays news"—then I think the energies of Dryden's Virgil show that it does merit, at least to some degree, the title of a poem. And if it is not itself a poem it cannot—in my theory or in the theory on which Dryden's age operated—be called any kind of a successful version of Virgil.

Notes

1. My translation of Segrais, in the preface to his version of the *Aeneid*. All quotations of Dryden are from James Kinsley's edition (Oxford, 1958).

2. *The English Georgic* (Baltimore, 1969), p. 8.

3. See the ninth (unnumbered) page of the Life of Virgil by Chetwood which prefaces Dryden's 1967 edition of Virgil's *Works*.

4. William J. Cameron, "John Dryden's Jacobitism," *Restoration Literature: Critical Approaches*, ed. Harold Love (London, 1972), p. 277; George Watson, "Dryden and the Jacobites," *Times Literary Supplement* 72 (1973), p. 302, col. 2.

5. *A History of English Poetry*, III (London, 1903), 521.

6. In his life of Pope in *Lives of the Poets: a Selection*, ed. J. P. Hardy (Oxford, 1971), p. 224.

7. See Rudolf Pfeiffer, *History of Classical Scholarship* (Oxford, 1968), p. 27.

8. See Maurice Johnson, "A Literary Chestnut: Dryden's 'Cousin Swift,'" *PMLA* 67 (1952), 1024-34.

9. *Dryden: The Critical Heritage*, ed. James Kinsley and Helen Kinsley (London and New York, 1971), p. 324.

10. Luke Milbourne, *Notes on Dryden's Virgil* (1698; rpt. New York and London, 1971), pp. 32, 80, 136.

11. Joseph Spence, *Polymetis* (1747; rpt. New York and London, 1976), p. 310.

12. George R. Noyes, ed., *The Poetical Works of John Dryden*, 2nd ed. (Boston, 1950), in his note to line 492.

13. Spence, p. 314.

14. *The English Epic and Its Background* (New York, 1954), p. 480.

15. L. Proudfoot, *Dryden's Aeneid and Its Seventeenth-Century Predecessors* (Manchester, Eng., 1960), p. 209.

16. Proudfoot, p. 183.

RESOURCES

Chronology of Vergil's Life and Times_____

70 B.C.E.	First consulship of Pompey and Crassus. Publius Vergilius Maro is born at Andes, near Mantua, Italy, on October 15; his father is either a potter or a day laborer, and thus a plebeian, married to Magia Pollia, his employer's daughter.
63	Conspiracy of Catiline during the consulship of Cicero.
60	First Triumvirate.
59	Julius Caesar assumes governorship of Cisalpine Gaul, thus making Vergil a Roman citizen.
c. 55-c. 49	Vergil receives his early education at Cremona and Mediolanum (Milan).
55	Second consulship of Pompey and Crassus.
52	Third consulship of Pompey.
49-45	Great Roman Civil War.
c. 48-c. 44	Vergil studies rhetoric and philosophy in Rome.
44	Julius Caesar is assassinated.
43	Second Triumvirate. Vergil returns to Mantua and begins writing the *Eclogues*, a series of ten pastoral poems.
41	Land confiscations begin, and Vergil's family's farm is seized.
c. 40	Octavian (later Augustus) restores the farm to Vergil's family.
c. 40-37	Vergil moves to Rome; he lives there and in Campania.
38-35	Octavian conducts war against Pompey.
37	The *Eclogues* is published. Vergil meets Maecenas, who becomes the poet's patron.

32	Marc Antony divorces Octavia, daughter of Octavius; his war with Octavian begins.
31	Octavian defeats Antony at Actium.
30	Fourth consulship of Octavian. Deaths of Antony and Cleopatra. The *Georgics*, Vergil's poem on the farmer's year modeled on Hesiod's *Works and Days*, is published. He begins writing the *Aeneid*.
27	Octavian assumes the name Augustus.
25	Marcus Agrippa completes the Pantheon at Rome.
23	Vergil reads sections of the *Aeneid* to Augustus. Augustus creates the role of *imperator* and thereby takes to himself extensive political, military, and priestly powers. Death of Marcellus, who appears in the procession of unborn heroes in *Aeneid* 6.
19	Vergil begins a trip to Greece and Asia Minor. He returns from Athens with Augustus and dies at Brundisium (Brindisi) on September 21; he is buried at Neapolis (Naples). The *Aeneid* is preserved by order of Augustus; the work is edited by Varius and Tucca by commission of Augustus.

Works by Vergil

Poetry

Eclogues, 43-37 B.C.E. (also known as *Bucolics*; English translation, 1575)

Georgics, c. 37-29 B.C.E. (English translation, 1589)

Aeneid, c. 29-19 B.C.E. (English translation, 1553)

Bibliography

Anderson, Theodore M. *Early Epic Scenery: Homer, Virgil, and the Medieval Legacy.* Ithaca, NY: Cornell University Press, 1976. Begins with a discussion of Homeric and Vergilian description and traces a discontinuity in the development of epic from Homer to the medieval romance.

Anderson, W. S. "Vergil's Second Iliad." *Transactions of the American Philological Association* 88 (1957): 17-30. Discusses Vergil's narrative on the fall of Troy and addresses the work's sources and originality.

Beye, Charles Rowan. *Ancient Epic Poetry: Homer, Apollonius, Virgil.* Ithaca, NY: Cornell University Press, 1993. Examines the influence of Homer and Apollonius of Rhodes on the *Aeneid.* Critics frequently credit Apollonius's portrait of Medea as Vergil's inspiration for the complex character of Dido.

Commager, Steele, ed. *Virgil: A Collection of Critical Essays.* Englewood Cliffs, NJ: Prentice-Hall, 1966. Uniformly excellent collection of essays includes C. M. Bowra's "Some Characteristics of Literary Epic," C. S. Lewis's "Virgil and the Subject of Secondary Epic," Theodore Haecker's "Odysseus and Aeneas," Brooks Otis's "The Odyssean and Iliadic *Aeneid,*" Adam Parry's "The Two Voices of Virgil's *Aeneid,*" and Bernard Knox's "The Serpent and the Flame: The Imagery of the Second Book of the *Aeneid.*"

Comparetti, Domenico. *Vergil in the Middle Ages.* Trans. E. F. M. Benecke. 1895. London: George Allen & Unwin, 1966. Despite the age of the original edition, this remains a standard work for those concerned with Vergilian influence. Offers an excellent examination of how the *Aeneid* and the so-called messianic eclogue acquired the mystical and prophetic associations they did during the Middle Ages and how these associations became attached to Vergil.

Conte, G. B. *The Rhetoric of Imitation Genre and Poetic Memory in Virgil and Other Latin Poets.* Trans. Charles Segal et al. Ithaca, NY: Cornell University Press, 1986. Considers the ways in which the *Aeneid* presents Homeric elements even as it introduces a Roman emphasis on the story of Troy's fall and its aftermath.

DiCesare, Mario A. *The Altar and the City: A Reading of Vergil's "Aeneid."* New York: Columbia University Press, 1974. Considers the combined roles of destiny, war, and religion in Vergil's poem. Presents an excellent examination of the implications of *pius Aeneas.*

Duff, J. Wight. "Virgil." *A Literary History of Rome from the Origins to the Close of the Golden Age.* 3d ed. Ed. A. M. Duff. New York: Barnes & Noble, 1960. 316-52. Excellent study of the poet's life as well as an overview of the *Eclogues, Georgics,* and *Aeneid.* The volume's subsequent chapter examines the minor poems attributed to Vergil.

Highet, Gilbert. *The Speeches in Vergil's "Aeneid."* Princeton, NJ: Princeton University Press, 1972. Argues that it is the speeches rather than descriptions of appearance or behavior that most vividly characterize the men, women, and deities of the *Aeneid*. Provides analysis of all the speeches of the poem and uses statistical as well as more traditional critical arguments to reach conclusions. Shows that Vergil's rhetorical models were poets rather than orators.

Horsfall, Nicholas, ed. *A Companion to the Study of Virgil*. 2d rev. ed. Leiden, Netherlands: Brill, 2001. Chapters 4, 5, and 6, by Horsfall himself, on the *Aeneid* as myth and history; on Vergilian style, language, and meter; and on the nonliterary evidence for Vergil's impact on imperial Rome are especially interesting and are suitable for both general readers and scholars.

Johnson, W. R. *Darkness Visible: A Study of Vergil's "Aeneid."* Berkeley: University of California Press, 1976. Considers the *Aeneid* as allegory, emphasizing the social, political, and psychological resonance the *Aeneid* and its cyclical view of Roman history would have had for the imperial reader.

Kallendorf, Craig. *In Praise of Aeneas: Virgil and Epideictic Rhetoric in the Early Italian Renaissance*. Hanover, NH: University Press of New England, 1989. Begins with the differing ways the *Aeneid* was read from antiquity to the Renaissance, and then considers the work's influence on Petrarch, Giovanni Boccaccio, Coluccio Salutati, Maffeo Vegio, and Cristoforo Landino. Each of these poets in differing ways attempted to refine, emend, or complete Vergilian poetry with elaborate and highly ornamented language, Maffeo going so far as to write a thirteenth book to the *Aeneid* in order to complete its narrative.

Knauer, Georg. "Vergil's *Aeneid* and Homer." *Greek, Roman, and Byzantine Studies* 5 (1964): 61-84. Offers a suitable distillation in English of Knauer's major study *Die Aeneis und Homer* (Göttingen, Germany: Vandenhoeck & Ruprecht, 1964). Examines every line of the *Aeneid* and offers what Knauer believes is a Homeric parallel. The danger for some readers is to imagine that the *Aeneid* entirely lacked originality. Despite the exceptional nature of Knauer's study, one could reasonably argue that some of his correspondences are superficial. In any event, the ways in which Vergil redirected the Homeric elements in his poem furnishes their originality.

Knight, W. F. Jackson. *Roman Vergil*. 1944. Harmondsworth, England: Penguin, 1966. Intriguing anthropological study of the effect that publication of the *Aeneid* had on the Roman world. Includes observations on Vergil's use of language and his style.

_____. *Vergil: Epic and Anthropology*. London: George Allen & Unwin, 1967. Presents an excellent synthesis of Knight's works on the relationship of the second and sixth books of the *Aeneid* bearing the titles *Vergil's Troy* and *Cumaean Gates*, originally published as separate essays in 1932 and 1936 and reprinted here as parts 1 and 2 of the volume. Part 3 deals with the notion of the holy city as envisioned by the Babylonians and reimagined by the Greeks and Romans.

Otis, Brooks. *Virgil: A Study in Civilized Poetry*. Oxford: Clarendon Press, 1964.

Indispensible study of all of Vergil's poems, suitable for the general reader as well as the scholar, presents just about everything one might say about their structure and method of composition. Argues that the *Aeneid* particularly focuses on the process of "civilizing," or the process of becoming aware of the requirements and norms of community. To some degree, this theme emerges in all of Vergil's poetry.

Pöschl, Viktor. *The Art of Vergil: Image and Symbol in the "Aeneid."* Trans. Gerda Seligson. Ann Arbor: University of Michigan Press, 1962. Landmark study of the *Aeneid* focuses on the exponential effects of recurring motifs: *amor* (love), *labor* (work), *dolor* (sorrow, grief, suffering), *pietas* (humility, religiosity), and the overriding motif of *fatum* (Fate, destiny).

The Vergil Project: Resources for Students, Teachers, and Readers of Vergil. http://vergil.classics.upenn.edu. Online resource includes the *Aeneid* translation of John Dryden, the early-twentieth-century translation of Theodore C. Williams, and a literal English translation, as well as the exhaustive Vergil commentary in English by John Conington and Henry Nettleship, and the ancient commentary of Servius.

Werner, Shirley. *A Bibliographic Guide to Vergil's "Aeneid."* http://www.vroma.org/~bmcmanus/werner_vergil.html. Impressive undertaking includes a biography of the poet as well as information on ancient scholarship, a long bibliography, various essays on style, a Latin text, and an English translation.

CRITICAL
INSIGHTS

About the Editor _____

Robert J. Forman is Professor of English and Classics and Director of the University Honors Program at St. John's University, New York. He attended New York University and has done postdoctoral work at Yale University, the University of Minnesota, and the American Academy in Rome. He has written a commentary on *Aeneid* 10 (NYU Dissertations, 1973); a book titled *Augustine and the Making of a Christian Literature* (1995), on Vergil's influence upon Saint Augustine; and a book-length annotated bibliographic study of classical drama for Salem Press (1989). He is a native New Yorker with an abiding amateur's interest in New York City history.

About *The Paris Review* _____

The Paris Review is America's preeminent literary quarterly, dedicated to discovering and publishing the best new voices in fiction, nonfiction, and poetry. The magazine was founded in Paris in 1953 by the young American writers Peter Matthiessen and Doc Humes, and edited there and in New York for its first fifty years by George Plimpton. Over the decades, the *Review* has introduced readers to the earliest writings of Jack Kerouac, Philip Roth, T. C. Boyle, V. S. Naipaul, Ha Jin, Ann Patchett, Jay McInerney, Mona Simpson, and Edward P. Jones, and published numerous now-classic works, including Roth's *Goodbye, Columbus*, Donald Barthelme's *Alice*, Jim Carroll's *Basketball Diaries*, and selections from Samuel Beckett's *Molloy* (his first publication in English). The first chapter of Jeffrey Eugenides's *The Virgin Suicides* appeared in the *Review*'s pages, as have stories by Rick Moody, David Foster Wallace, Denis Johnson, Jim Crace, Lorrie Moore, and Jeanette Winterson.

The Paris Review's renowned Writers at Work series of interviews, whose early installments include legendary conversations with E. M. Forster, William Faulkner, and Ernest Hemingway, is one of the landmarks of world literature. The interviews received a George Polk Award and were nominated for a Pulitzer Prize. Among the more than three hundred interviewees are Robert Frost, Marianne Moore, W. H. Auden, Elizabeth Bishop, Susan Sontag, and Toni Morrison. Recent issues feature conversations with Jonathan Franzen, Norman Rush, Louise Erdrich, Joan Didion, Norman Mailer, R. Crumb, Michel Houellebecq, Marilynne Robinson, David Mitchell, Annie Proulx, and Gay Talese. In November 2009, Picador published the final volume of a four-volume series of anthologies of *Paris Review* interviews. The *New York Times* called the Writers at Work series "the most remarkable and extensive interviewing project we possess."

The Paris Review is edited by Lorin Stein, who was named to the post in 2010. The editorial team has published fiction by Lydia Davis, André Aciman, Sam Lipsyte, Damon Galgut, Mohsin Hamid, Uzodinma Iweala, James Lasdun, Padgett Powell,

---

Richard Price, and Sam Shepard. Recent poetry selections include work by Frederick Seidel, Carol Muske-Dukes, John Ashbery, Kay Ryan, Mary Jo Bang, Sharon Olds, Charles Wright, and Mary Karr. Writing published in the magazine has been anthologized in *Best American Short Stories* (2006, 2007, and 2008), *Best American Poetry*, *Best Creative Non-Fiction*, the Pushcart Prize anthology, and *O. Henry Prize Stories*.

The magazine presents three annual awards. The Hadada Award for lifelong contribution to literature has recently been given to Joan Didion, Norman Mailer, Peter Matthiessen, John Ashbery, and, in 2010, Philip Roth. The Plimpton Prize for Fiction, awarded to a debut or emerging writer brought to national attention in the pages of *The Paris Review*, was presented in 2007 to Benjamin Percy, to Jesse Ball in 2008, and to Alistair Morgan in 2009. In 2011, the magazine inaugurated the Terry Southern Prize for Humor.

The Paris Review was a finalist for the 2008 and 2009 National Magazine Awards in fiction and won the 2007 National Magazine Award in photojournalism. The *Los Angeles Times* recently called *The Paris Review* "an American treasure with true international reach," and the *New York Times* designated it "a thing of sober beauty."

Since 1999 *The Paris Review* has been published by The Paris Review Foundation, Inc., a not-for-profit 501(c)(3) organization.

The Paris Review is available in digital form to libraries worldwide in selected academic databases exclusively from EBSCO Publishing. Libraries can contact EBSCO at 1-800-653-2726 for details. For more information on *The Paris Review* or to subscribe, please visit: www.theparisreview.org.

Contributors

Robert J. Forman is Professor of English and Classics and Director of the University Honors Program at St. John's University, New York. He attended New York University and has done postdoctoral work at Yale University, the University of Minnesota, and the American Academy in Rome. He has written a commentary on *Aeneid* 10 (NYU Dissertations, 1973), a book titled *Augustine and the Making of a Christian Literature* (1995), on Vergil's influence upon Saint Augustine, and a book-length annotated bibliographic study of classical drama for Salem Press (1989). He is a native New Yorker with an abiding amateur's interest in New York City history.

Walter Petrovitz is Associate Professor of Classics and Linguistics at St. John's University in New York City. He received his doctoral degree in linguistics from the Graduate Center of the City University of New York. His publications include works on the relationship between syntax and semantics, grammatical pedagogy, and the use of linguistic models for the analysis of literature. With regard to Vergil, his research has focused on the classification of literary allusions according to their grammatical components.

Patrick Loughran is a writer and editor based in London. His work has appeared in *The Times of London*, the *Irish News*, and *Al Majalla*, and on the *Paris Review* Daily. He is from Belfast.

Bernard J. Cassidy earned his Ph.D. in classics from Fordham University. He is Professor Emeritus of Classical Studies in the Department of Languages and Literatures at St. John's University, New York, where he taught Latin, classical Greek, and classical studies (particularly Roman law) for forty-two years. He currently edits a Web page called the Law Room at VRoma.org. During his tenure at St. John's, he also served the university briefly in administrative posts, including Associate Dean of the College of Liberal Arts and Dean of the School of Education.

Fiorentina Russo is Assistant Professor of Italian Language and Literature at St. John's University in New York. She completed her Ph.D in Italian studies at New York University in 2007 with a dissertation on Dante titled "The Presence of Saturn and the *aetas aurea* in Three Figures of Dante's *Comedy*: The Medusa, the Siren and Matelda," which she is currently revising for publication. Her research interests include Dante studies, medieval Italian studies, Italian dialect poetry, and translation.

Kathleen Marks is Associate Professor of English in the College of Professional Studies at St. John's University in Queens, New York, where she teaches world literature and other courses. She received her Ph.D. from the University of Dallas in Texas. Her book *Toni Morrison's "Beloved" and the Apotropaic Imagination* (2002) analyzes Greek influences on the postmodern writer's most significant novel. She lives with her husband and daughter in New York City.

Viktor Pöschl was, at the time of his death in 1976, Professor of Classics at the University of Heidelberg. He joined the faculty there in 1939. He also served as docent in Munich, Prague, and, after the war, Graz. His principal work, *Die Dichtkunst Virgils: Bild und Symbol in der Äneis* (The poetic art of Virgil: picture and symbol in the *Aeneid*), which appeared in English translation under the title *The Art of Virgil*, was first published in 1950.

Francis A. Sullivan, S.J., was born in Boston in 1922. He attended Boston College, Fordham University, Weston College, and the Pontifical Gregorian University in Rome. A Jesuit priest with primary interest in church history, he taught at the Gregorian University from 1964 to 1970. His essay in this volume considers the perennial question of human suffering as one of the primary themes of Vergil's poem.

Robin Mitchell-Boyask received her bachelor's degree in classics from the University of Chicago and her doctorate in comparative literature from Brown University. She is Professor of Classics and Chair of the Department of Greek and Roman Classics at Temple University and a Visiting Professor at Bryn Mawr College. Though her research interests are concentrated in Greek drama, she has written widely in many areas of classical studies.

Clifford Weber is Professor Emeritus of Classics at Kenyon College in Gambier, Ohio, where he spent his entire academic career. Until his retirement in 2003, he was the department's Latinist and accordingly taught most of the Latin courses offered by the department. Occasionally he taught intermediate Greek (Homer, Plato), and for lay audiences he offered courses in linguistics and in the history and literature of the Augustan age, where his interests as a scholar lie. Most of his publications have to do with Roman poets of the first century B.C.E., among whom Vergil has perennially been a primary interest.

Richard F. Moorton received his Ph.D. at the University of Texas, Austin, and joined the faculty of Connecticut College in 1983. In addition to classical epic, his interests lie in the ancient roots of modern culture. He has written also on Aristophanes as well as on Eugene O'Neill.

J. H. Waszink, the eminent Dutch scholar, is best known for his edition and English translation of Tertullian's treatise against Hermogenes, originally published in 1956. He also published a text and German translation of Tertullian's treatise *De anima* (on the soul), also against Hermogenes. His primary area of interest is early Christian literature.

Mary Randall Stark taught for many years at the historic Girls' Latin School in Boston, now known as the Boston Latin Academy. She graduated from Smith College in 1931 and served as an officer of the Classical Association of New England (CANE) until her death in 1964. Her writings are pedagogical and consider the obstacles classical literature can present for contemporary students and teachers.

Michael C. J. Putnam joined the Brown University faculty in 1960. His primary interest is in Latin literature and its influence, with a specialty in the poetry of Republican and Augustan Rome. His books include *The Poetry of the "Aeneid"* (1965), *Vir-*

gil's Pastoral Art: Studies in the "Eclogues" (1970), *Virgil's Poem of the Earth* (1979), *Essays on Latin Lyric, Elegy, and Epic* (1982), *Virgil's "Aeneid": Interpretation and Influence* (1995), and *Virgil's Epic Designs: Ekphrasis in the "Aeneid"* (1998).

George E. Duckworth was, until his death in 1972, Professor of Classics at Princeton University. He was a prolific writer whose official bibliography lists seven books and fifty-one articles, as well as numerous articles for four encyclopedias. His primary fields in Latin literature were comedy and epic, and he is especially celebrated for two major studies: *The Nature of Roman Comedy* (1952) and *Structural Patterns and Proportions in Vergil's "Aeneid"* (1962). Both of these remain standards among works of criticism. His essay reprinted in this volume immediately preceded his book-length study of mathematical proportions and structural symmetry in Vergil.

William Frost was born in New York City and attended Bowdoin College and Yale University. Until his death in 1988, he taught in the English Department of the University of California, Santa Barbara. His interests ranged widely, from Latin poetry and Jane Austen to Geoffrey Chaucer and John Dryden. He coedited three volumes of the highly respected California Edition of Dryden's works.

Acknowledgments

"The *Paris Review* Perspective" by Patrick Loughran. Copyright © 2012 by Patrick Loughran. Special appreciation goes to Christopher Cox, Nathaniel Rich, and David Wallace-Wells, editors at *The Paris Review*.

"The Poetic Achievement of Virgil" by Viktor Pöschl. From *The Classical Journal* 56.7 (April 1961): 290-299. Copyright ©1961 by the Classical Association of the Middle West and South, Inc. Reprinted with permission of the Classical Association of the Middle West and South, Inc.

"Virgil and the Mystery of Suffering" by Francis A. Sullivan. From *The American Journal of Philology* 90.2 (April 1969): 161-177. Copyright © 1969 by The Johns Hopkins University Press. Reprinted with permission of The Johns Hopkins University Press.

"*Sine Fine*: Vergil's Masterplot" by Robin N. Mitchell-Boyask. From *The American Journal of Philology* 117.2 (Summer 1996): 289-307. Copyright © 1996 by The Johns Hopkins University Press. Reprinted with permission of The Johns Hopkins University Press.

"The Dionysus in Aeneas" by Clifford Weber. From *Classical Philology* 97.4 (October 2002): 322-343. Copyright © by The University of Chicago Press. Reprinted with permission of The University of Chicago Press.

"The Innocence of Italy in Vergil's *Aeneid*" by Richard F. Moorton. From *The American Journal of Philology* 110.1 (Spring 1989): 105-130. Copyright © 1989 by The Johns Hopkins University Press. Reprinted with permission of The Johns Hopkins University Press.

"Vergil and the Sibyl of Cumae" by J. H. Waszink. From *Mnemosyne*, Fourth Series, vol. 1, fasc. 1 (1948): 43-58. Copyright © 1948 by Brill Academic Publishers. Reprinted with permission of Brill Academic Publishers.

"The Golden Bough for the Student of Vergil" by Mary Randall Stark. From *The Classical Journal* 26.4 (January 1931): 259-265. Copyright ©1931 by the Classical Association of the Middle West and South, Inc. Reprinted with permission of the Classical Association of the Middle West and South, Inc.

"Daedalus, Virgil, and the End of Art" by Michael C. J. Putnam. From *The American Journal of Philology* 108.2 (Summer 1987): 173-198. Copyright © 1987 by The Johns Hopkins University Press. Reprinted with permission of The Johns Hopkins University Press.

"Mathematical Symmetry in Vergil's *Aeneid*" by George E. Duckworth. From *Transactions and Proceedings of the American Philological Association* 91 (1960): 184-220. Copyright © 1960 by the American Philological Assocation. Reprinted with permission of The Johns Hopkins University Press.

"Dryden's Virgil" by William Frost. From *Comparative Literature* 36.3 (Summer 1984): 193-208. Copyright © 1984 by Duke University Press. All rights reserved. Reprinted with permission of Duke University Press.

Imagery; flames, 8-9, 35, 37, 39, 114, 181, 221, 245, 259; serpents, 10, 35, 37, 39, 109, 312, 321

Jacoff, Rachel, 65
Johnson, W. R., 142, 261
Justice, 70, 107, 162, 183, 203, 267

Kallendorf, Craig, 84
Kerényi, Carl, 159, 166
Knight, W. F. Jackson, vii, 218, 300

Labor, 34, 111, 113, 127-128, 238, 247, 262
Law, Roman, 49
Leo, Friedrich, 209
Lewis, C. S., 54
Livius Andronicus, 55, 92
Loughran, Patrick, 341
Love. See *Amor*
Lyric poetry, 53, 74, 101

Maass, Ernst, 209, 213
Maecenas, 19, 52, 241
Marks, Kathleen, 341
Marx, Leo, 178
Metamorphoses (Ovid), 146, 150, 152, 155
Metrical patterns, 35, 149-150, 188, 266, 300; hexameter, 56, 225, 293; Saturnian, 56-57
Milton, John, 54, 79
Mitchell-Boyask, Robin, 342
Moorton, Richard F., 342
Motifs. *See* Themes and motifs

Naevius, Gnaeus, 32, 52, 56, 91, 216
Nethercut, W. R., 177, 192
Norden, Eduard, 208, 218

Octavian. *See* Augustus
Odyssey (Homer), 3, 5, 32-36, 45, 133, 137, 226, 254, 257; ending, 252; translation by Livius Andronicus, 55
Oral poetry, 31, 54, 92
Otis, Brooks, 144, 182, 186
Otto, Walter F., 160, 166

Page, T. E., 146
Paradise Lost (Milton), 54, 79
Parry, Adam, 161, 177, 189, 192, 204
Paschalis, Michael, 144, 151
Pax Romana, ix, 7, 19, 22, 44, 71, 73
Pease, Arthur, 146, 153, 155
Penates, 10, 49, 192
Petrovitz, Walter, 341
Pietas, 34, 43, 117, 180, 185, 241, 256
Pity, 118, 239, 242, 246-247
Platonic ideas, 92
Punic Wars, 11, 31, 45, 56, 130
Putnam, Michael C. J., 133, 135, 187, 192, 206, 342
Pöschl, Viktor, 111, 171, 182, 185, 256, 262, 341

Quint, David, 125

Rage. See *Furor*
Reckford, K. J., 192
Religious rituals, 10-11, 40-41, 147
Rome, founding of, 36, 45-46, 58
Rosivach, V. J., 177, 195
Russo, Fiorentina, 341

Segal, Charles Paul, 256
Serpents, 10, 35, 37, 39, 109, 312, 321
Servius, vii, 17, 58, 76, 89, 107, 201, 204, 295
Snakes. *See* Serpents
Sorrow. See *Dolor*
Stark, Mary Randall, 342
Statius, 68, 80, 155, 251, 253; in *The Divine Comedy*, 62, 66-68

Storms, 20, 32, 39, 52, 108, 127, 170
Sullivan, Francis A., 342

Thebaid (Statius), 68, 251, 253
Themes and motifs; *amor*, 34, 38, 120,
    245; *dolor*, 34, 39, 133, 135, 138,
    240, 242, 249-250, 255, 263-264;
    fathers and sons, 9, 14, 91, 199, 237,
    239; *fatum*, 8-9, 14-15, 34, 39, 75,
    94, 109, 111, 119, 122; *furor*, 38, 114,
    120, 182, 241, 250; Golden Bough,
    22, 36, 40, 64, 232, 247; hunting, 39,
    144, 156-159, 171, 187, 189, 287;
    justice, 70, 107, 162, 183, 203, 267;
    labor, 34, 111, 113, 127-128, 238,
    247, 262; *pietas*, 34, 43, 117, 180,
    185, 241, 256; predestination of
    Roman Empire, 107; religious rituals,
    10-11, 40-41, 147; storms, 20, 32, 39,
    52, 108, 127, 170
Theocritus, 18, 53, 74, 92, 226
Trojan War, 7, 26, 32, 37, 46
Trojan horse, 38, 243
Turnus (*Aeneid*), 206; comparison with
    Achilles, 90; as beast of prey, 185;

death, 15, 43, 110, 135, 137, 241,
    249, 268; killing of Pallas, 15, 43,
    118; moral position, 182

Vance, E., 199
Vergil; and Augustus, vii, 9, 19, 21, 24,
    44, 52, 68, 73-74; biographical
    information, 17; death, 21, 74; in *The
    Divine Comedy* (Dante), 59-72, 78;
    education, 17; influence on Western
    poetry, 97; and Maecenas, 19, 52,
    241; spelling of name, 22

Waswo, Richard, 84
Waszink, J. H., 342
Weber, Clifford, 342
Whitfield, J. H., 79
Whitman, Cedric H., 107, 110, 267
Williams, R. D., 80
Wordsworth, William, 80, 323
Work. See *Labor*
Works and Days (Hesiod), 19, 74, 226

Ziolkowski, Theodore, 81